RED LAND, RED POWER

||||||||||||||||||||||||||||||||||||||||||||||||||||||||||||||||||||||||||||||||||||||||

NEW AMERICANISTS

A SERIES EDITED BY DONALD E. PEASE

RED LAND, RED POWER

GROUNDING KNOWLEDGE

IN THE AMERICAN INDIAN NOVEL

Sean Kicummah Teuton

DUKE UNIVERSITY PRESS *Durham and London* 2008

© 2008 Duke University Press

All rights reserved

Printed in the United States of America

on acid-free paper ∞

Designed by Amy Ruth Buchanan

Typeset in Scala by Tseng Information Systems, Inc.

Library of Congress Cataloging-in-Publication

Data appear on the last printed page of this book.

|||||||||||||||||||||||||||||||||||||||||||||||||||||||||||||||||||||||||

For Artemis-Diana Nanyehi Yandell-Teuton
born 9 December 2005

This America
has been a burden
of steel and mad
death,
but, look now,
there are flowers
and new grass
and a spring wind
rising
from Sand Creek.

—**Simon J. Ortiz**, *From Sand Creek*

CONTENTS

||||||||||||||||||||||||||||||||||||||||||||||||||||||||||||||||||||||||||||

ACKNOWLEDGMENTS

||||||||||||||||||||||||||||||||||||||||||||||||||||||||||||||||||||||||||

I have had the fortune of many friends, colleagues, and mentors who shared their time and thoughts for the writing of this book. Of that long list, space allows me to mention only a few. For their tireless insights, I wish to thank Robert Warrior, Satya Mohanty, Craig Werner, and Paula Moya. Whether on the telephone or on a ride through Osage lands, Robert was always there to help me work through ideas and dare me to make bold claims. Satya gave me a way to talk about what we can know and was ever available for a walk in the woods. Over strong coffee, Craig helped me unearth the narrative to shape this book. Paula was a model of intellectual courage in her reading and in my writing. Michael Hames-García, John Su, Craig Womack, Arnold Krupat, and my brother Chris Teuton also read parts of this manuscript at various stages and offered their candid and meticulous advice.

At the University of Wisconsin, Madison, I found in the Department of English lasting support for this project, and several of my colleagues there read and commented on some or all of the manuscript. My thanks go out to Anne McClintock, Jeff Steele, Lynn Keller, Teju Olaniyan, Tom Schaub, Susan Friedman, and Roberta Hill. In the American Indian Studies Program, I am grateful to Paul Nadasdy and Larry Nesper, who shared their ideas on American Indian identity, and to Ada Deer, for her memories of Red Power. In the Minority Studies Reading Group, charged responses from graduate students to a book chapter fueled my research, especially those of Julia Doggart, John Riofrio, Samaa Abdurriqib, Lauren Vidal, and Matt Hooley.

A few organizations have been extremely generous and, in a profound way, gave a social and intellectual place for this book to grow. I thank the Future of Minority Studies Research Project and all of those who selflessly built it and continue to nurture it. In gratitude, I thank the Indigenous

Professors Association, where scholars like Michael Yellow Bird show great support for emerging Indian scholars. For their generous support to complete the writing of this book, I thank the School of American Research and the Woodrow Wilson Foundation.

I would like to show appreciation to the citizens of the Cherokee Nation for listening and sharing, especially Principal Chief Chad Smith, Hastings Shade, Richard Allen, Pat Moss, Stacy Leeds, Tom Holm, Ellen Cushman, and Daniel Justice. For their strength, I thank all of the members of the Echota Grounds. I thank my parents, who raised five brothers. Finally, I thank Kay Yandell for her mind—and, most of all, her heart.

PREFACE

||||||||||||||||||||||||||||||||||||||||||||||||||||||||||||||||||||||||||

In the shadow of ships, where riveters hammer and welders rain down showers of sparks, Dan McGhee sweeps wood and paint chips, steel shavings and cigarette butts, into a neat pile, when the whistle screams. On 21 September 1943, he tears open a Lucky Strike, sprinkles tobacco on the waves, torches another, turns his collar up, and shuffles out of the Oakland shipyard, heading home to his woman and supper. He plods through the Eastern garden, up the walkway to the strange, low porch steps of the rented home with Japanese architecture. A toe fumbles on the step, slips, and McGhee crashes to the ground, his head a confusion of love, loss, and home. Days later his wife, Oba, opens her grieving fingers and lets fall a train ticket in the conductor's palm. She smooths her dress, and then sits down to endure the rattled ride back to Oklahoma, her man's body awaiting only cars away. She swears never to ride the train again.

Like many other Native people of their generation, my great grandparents, unable to pay the taxes on their federal "allotment," had lost their land, and sold on the hope of what came to be called Indian "relocation." They left Oklahoma and headed to Oakland, California, for work during World War II. Born in 1877, Stooeastah, or Dan McGhee, experienced massive changes in the Cherokee Nation. In 1838, his own grandparents settled on Honey Creek, after their displacement west, in what came to be called the Trail of Tears. After 1898, McGhee witnessed the hegemony of the Curtis Act to allot communally owned Cherokee territory into individual parcels, a plan designed to conclude Cherokee tribalism by transforming the people into yeoman farmers, and, conveniently, selling off the so-called surplus land to European American settlers. McGhee watched the insidious railroads tear through his homeland, and he saw the final and desperate erasure of the Cherokee Nation when the promised Indian

Territory became the state of Oklahoma in 1907. Having been reared in a Cherokee school, having spoken Cherokee as his primary language, and having sworn off his painful "white man shoes," I imagine that McGhee foresaw the end of his life when he finally headed west to the "darkening land," the traditional destination of Cherokee souls. From his place in Cherokee history, one might see the life of McGhee as the clear-cut story of an Indian suffering a white man's world. But lives intersect.

In the same year Dan McGhee died, Dillon Myer, working as the director of war relocation under Harry Truman, engineered the evacuation of Japanese Americans from their homes to concentration camps and even to Indian reservations. In so doing, their property, businesses, and homes were now conveniently available to other Americans. But this was hardly the first case of this form of injustice. In this pattern, groups of people have been demonized, dehumanized, criminalized, torn from their land, and sent into exile, thus making their property available for others to take. Indeed, in 1838 the Cherokees suffered a similar exile when seven thousand federal troops, under the command of General Winfield Scott, felled trees and built roads into isolated Cherokee mountain towns to strip, literally hand by hand, the people who kneeled there hugging their trees. So in 1943, Myer merely refined this program, albeit with utmost efficiency, when Japanese Americans were later "compensated" for their loss, though Cherokees have never been fully compensated for theirs. Later, as commissioner of Indian Affairs (1950–52), Myer designed the relocation program to move American Indians off their lands and into urban areas, thereby once again securing tribal mineral resources for the production of Cold War weapons and preparing Native peoples for the "termination" of their legal relationships as tribes with the U.S. government.

How strange, then, must have been that evening when my great-grandfather hit his head on the porch of the confiscated Japanese American home. Though separated by people and history, such histories often violently collide to reveal a shared stake in the future not only of subjugated groups but of all of us in the United States. Were Dan McGhee and Japanese Americans to know their shared part in this narrative of domination and were they to organize against it, what social justice might have blossomed in the United States? And, were all Americans to discern this entrenched pattern of demonization and exile, betrayal and theft in our colonial history, what ethnic cleansing might have been averted?

Beginning with such narratives, this book seeks to ground studies of American Indian life and art in a material past and present. For only in linking and testing our theoretical claims in the real world will any of us ever really understand how over half of all Native people today reside in urban areas, or, despite this displacement, why Indian people so defiantly defend a distinct cultural identity. Indeed, in situating Indigenous literature within narrative histories that intersect, scholars expand and empower Native studies. For in so doing, we are asked to deal more honestly with unpleasant truths often expurgated from our histories, such as the lottery winners in Georgia who rushed to their stolen Cherokee homes or my great-grandparents who availed on the low rent of a confiscated Japanese American home. But while I seek to discover the historicizing narratives that, across cultural and social differences, often join us, I also attempt to claim different ground on particular histories that define us. Were we not to dare articulate those real events that shape discrete cultural identities, we risk undermining the very differences that enrich a diverse society.

Looking down the hill from Oakland, Dan McGhee would have seen Alcatraz Island, where Indians had been imprisoned since the 1870s. He never would have dreamed, however, that in a mere thirty years his grandchildren's generation would in 1969 occupy that worthless island for months in the name of Indian rights, thus setting off the Red Power movement of Native consciousness-raising and American Indian writing—the era and subjects of this book. Again, the ironies of Indian displacement pervade. Native people like my great-grandfather had been displaced to cities only to bolster a savvy population of Indigenous organizers. From my own experience, I was a child of that Red Power era, and, like a child, I lived on some of the innocent hope of the movement. During the 1970s, with my father often away, I saw my mother, Judith Fox, become beautiful. On afternoons, we five brothers would await her return from her waitress job, then rub her feet as she silently planned our escape with food stamps and a new husband. It was a time when she, like many inspired by Red Power, began to grow proud of her Indianness. As a first-generation college graduate and a professor of English, I recall those Indians of other eras and am made aware of the privileged ground on which I now stand, where such a life was not possible for Dan McGhee or Judith Fox. From such a view, I hope to look out on a new Indian Country where social transformation is for many of us now more than ever within our grasp. But, as I argue and demonstrate in this book, it is a transformation that must be theoretically grounded in the past and the land, in identity and experience, concepts I develop in the pages ahead.

To do so, I have sought to organize a new approach to Native studies. I begin by engaging a widespread theoretical assumption in the field, often growing out of poststructuralism, which I characterize as a rejection of our human capacity to make normative claims to knowledge. Denied this capacity, however, Indian scholars are unable to justify how Native cultures can change and still be authentic, or moreover, how Indigenous people can experience legitimate cultural or political growth in relation to community and land. I thus foreground the epistemological claims of this position to disclose its limitations in decolonizing Native America. My concern, however, about the usefulness of theory in American Indian studies should be understood as a forward-looking critical examination of what is thought to be a progressive position in the field.

With these practical goals for Native culture and literature in mind, I explore an alternative theoretical position drawn from Indigenous oral philosophy, which I call tribal realism. I link this view with other minority scholars, who develop a similar "postpositivist realist" view, which allows for genuine debate and exchange across cultures, while still respecting how social location may grant special access to knowledge. Though all of us may share a world, that world is also different for tribal peoples, especially as long as colonialism exists. Indeed, in recognizing these social facts of colonial control, tribal realism develops more secure knowledge about American Indian culture and literature. From this more grounded perspective, our theoretical attachments to history or culture are less obstacles to block objective knowledge than they are tools to serve it. Notwithstanding the humane goals of skeptical theories of knowledge, the U.S. government implicitly employs this position to disable Natives' relationship to land, people, and self. For this reason, I argue that Indian people can and should engage such relations as a serious philosophical issue. Properly theorized, identity, for example, can produce reliable knowledge about a colonized world. From a realist perspective, such concepts are certainly mediated—but also relational. Identities are theories we develop in order to explain our pasts, our lands, our daily lives. Through identity we may intellectually evaluate our experiences, and new accounts of our experiences may demand a change in self-conception. In so doing we achieve a homeland and a culture and a politics.

I have set out to compose a more objective view to Native knowledge because without a workable understanding of how we know the world—in relation to our own selves, our personal and collective tribal pasts, our homelands, and our colonized present—we cannot adequately plan an

Indian future. Such an understanding must enable us to imagine and realize a decolonized Indian Country, first in terms of lands (as I show in part 1 of this volume) and then, growing from that ground, in terms of politics (part 2). In each chapter, these central cultural and philosophical issues facing Native peoples guide my readings of the Red Power novel, particularly as it represents the political and moral transformation of Native people responding to various forms of repression. Red Power provided the social vision for this kind of novel to emerge. This was a time when American Indian activists, scholars, and artists, across myriad differences, joined hands and raised their voices to claim a forgotten history and a stolen land. So began a political awakening that made available alternative narratives of tribal lives: new knowledge for a new Indian future.

How often it is that scholars, when meeting me, ask where I am from. As a Cherokee citizen with light skin, I imagine I invite curiosity when some seek to place me. But as I hope this book will show, our own worlds have a lot to do with what we come to know, and we come to know other worlds by examining and sharing our own. Trusting that truth, I offer much of myself in this book to be clear about from where and for whom I speak. As Dan McGhee's reluctant trail west would attest, to be "from" the land of one's ancestors is a right, ironically, denied many Indigenous people. Here, I work to show Indians like McGhee another way home, at least intellectually, where they may justify the recovery of land and culture. This book is my own best attempt to honor those lives.

INTRODUCTION

||||||||||||||||||||||||||||||||||||||||||||||||||||||||||||||||||||

IMAGINING AN AMERICAN INDIAN CENTER

For the sake of our children, for the sake of the spiritual and material well-being of our total community we must be able to demonstrate competence to ourselves. For the sake of our psychic stability as well as our physical well-being we must be free men and exercise free choices. We must make decisions about our own destinies. We must be able to learn and profit by our own mistakes. Only then can we become competent and prosperous communities. We must be free in the most literal sense of the word.
—**Clyde Warrior,** February 1967

Do you see what happens when the imagination is superimposed upon the historical event? It becomes a story. The whole piece becomes more deeply invested with meaning. The terrified Kiowas, when they had regained possession of themselves, did indeed imagine that the falling stars were symbolic of their being and their destiny. They accounted for themselves with reference to that awful memory. They appropriated it, recreated it, fashioned it into an image of themselves—imagined it.
—**N. Scott Momaday,** March 1970

On 9 November 1969, a young American Indian student dove from a borrowed sailboat into the frigid waters of San Francisco Bay and swam 250 yards against swift currents to reclaim Alcatraz Island as Indian land. Richard Oakes, a Mohawk man from the St. Regis reservation in upstate New York, had migrated to San Francisco to join a community of Indigenous people "relocated" to urban areas during the 1950s era of federal tribal termination.¹ By the 1960s, generations of Indian people in the Bay Area had grown restless about their displacement and poverty, and young people responded by organizing across tribal groups and raising their voices in public protest.² While attending San Francisco State College, Oakes worked to organize members of the Indian student group who shared a similar vision of renewal for American Indians. The San Francisco State College group soon reached out to bring its dream of change to Indian student organizations at the University of California at Berkeley and at Los Angeles. Among Native students, the Red Power Indian movement had begun.³

This book concerns the writing that began around 1969 and grew into an inspiring decade for American Indian people. During the era of Red Power, Native writers imagined a new narrative for Indian Country, and they did so neither by longing for an impossibly timeless past nor by disconnecting Indians' stories from the political realities of their lives. Instead, writers of the era struggled to better interpret a colonized world and then offered this new knowledge to empower the people. In this introductory chapter, I begin to chart the development of that liberating theoretical vision in the literature of Red Power.

Oakes's courageous leap into dangerous waters remains a fitting image of political change in Indian Country. Initially a defensive rampart during the Civil War, Alcatraz Island later became a prison for American Indian military leaders during the so-called Indian Wars of the nineteenth century. Reclaiming Alcatraz, the Red Power leaders believed, would lay bare one of the most glaring ironies of colonialism: Indigenous people imprisoned in their own lands.⁴ Oakes's plunge heralded a new form of Indian activism, shaped by those who had grown tired of the slow machinery of the federal government and who were deeply suspicious of the Bureau of Indian Affairs (BIA). Red Power was as much physical as intellectual; Indian organizers drove the movement with the bodily momentum of drumming, singing, dancing, marching, and even swimming. Though the federal policies of termination and relocation unraveled entire communities, urban Indians were especially prepared to contend with the particular racial oppression they encountered in cities. In urban centers such as Minneapolis, Denver, and San Francisco, young Indian people came together to imagine a collective future free of U.S. government control. Urban displacement thus helped to create a startlingly new form of political activity in Indian Country: Red Power was young, urban, intertribal, and ready to confront an imperialist world with a full range of spiritual, physical, and intellectual weapons. Red Power protesters were angry, but their anger was justified in the countless public disclosures of their colonial experiences in Native America. In this way, the movement grew not out of romantic claims to a pure Indian past and culture, as often characterized in the mainstream, but rather through an ongoing encounter with the world as members sought to produce more enabling accounts of American Indian lives. As Ponca activist Clyde Warrior describes it, Natives were prepared to "learn and profit" from their mistakes.

Aware of the unpredictable shifts in American attitudes, American Indian scholars and activists living in the midst of Red Power took advantage of an upsurge of interest in Indians to publish the crucial texts defining Red Power. In 1969, the young Sioux legal scholar Vine Deloria Jr. composed his "Indian manifesto" under the provocative title *Custer Died for Your Sins*. He chided U.S. culture for its fickle relationship to American Indians: "Indians laugh themselves sick when they hear these statements [that the United States must remain in Vietnam to keep its promises]. America has yet to keep one Indian treaty or agreement despite the fact that the United States government signed over four hundred such treaties and agreements with Indian tribes" (1988, 28). For many, the most exciting aspect of Deloria's book was its vision of a liberated Indigenous future. His final chapter, "A Redefinition of Indian Affairs," reads at times like the Ghost Dance prophecy of the nineteenth-century Paiute visionary Wovoka, in which industrialized America recedes, the bison repopulate the Plains, and Native people return to their ancestral homelands: "The eventual movement among American Indians will be the 'recolonization' of the unsettled areas of the nation by groups of Indian colonists" (263). Deloria recognizes the connection between Red Power and the African American freedom movement, but cautions that specific cultural groups must pursue specific goals: "Civil Rights is a function of man's desire for self-respect, not of his desire for equality. The dilemma is not one of tolerance or intolerance but one of respect or contempt. The tragedy of the early days of the Civil Rights movement is that many people, black, white, red, and yellow, were sold a bill of goods which said that equality was the eventual goal of the movement. But no one had considered the implications of so simple a slogan. Equality became sameness. Nobody noticed it, but everyone was trained to expect it. When equality did not come, black power did come and everybody began to climb the walls in despair" (179). In 1969, Deloria was alerting Indian leaders that Red Power militancy risked attracting the same government-sponsored assassinations perpetrated by the FBI's COINTELPRO against the Black Power movement.[5] Recognizing Black Power's tendencies toward romantic posturing, Deloria stressed the need for self-criticism that would allow the diversity within Indian Country to fuel but not burn out Red Power.

Ironically, the FBI would ultimately crush the militancy of Red Power only to see it reemerge in the form of a powerful revival of traditional spirituality in Indian communities. In his 1973 book *God Is Red*, Deloria summarized the surprising outcome of the year's occupations: "[A] result of the Indian activist movement was the tremendous surge of interest in traditional religions and customs. At the BIA occupation and again during the Wounded Knee confrontation, medicine men had been prominent in performing ceremonies for the activists" (1994, 23). Added to these cultural strides were material developments; the movement drove the passing in 1978 of new legislation such as the Indian Child Welfare Act and the American Indian Religious Freedom Act to protect Indigenous lives and customs. The revived interest in the recovery of Indian cultural identity and homelands, which consumes contemporary Native culture, derives directly from the intellectual and political vision of Red Power. Though it raises questions that I address below, the very presence of Native scholars in U.S. universities attests to the success of the movement and thus gives credence to Deloria's vision of a reflowering Indian America. Even more promising is that Indian communities may be carrying out the recolonization that Deloria hoped for decades ago. A front-page article in the *New York Times* in 2001 announced that for the first time in a century Natives comprised the fastest-growing population in North Dakota.[6]

Today, Indian scholars of Red Power build on the foundation laid by Deloria with research that traces the creative origins of Native cultural revival and that confronts some of the internal tensions within the Indian movement. Robert Warrior returns to the era: "By the late 1960s and early 1970s the diversity of the viewpoints among North American Natives had become so pronounced that no group was able to unify all the various elements" (1995, 34). Reservation Natives went west to add their voices to those of the protestors, though the struggles faced in rural places differed significantly from the problems faced by Bay Area Indian urbanites. Protestors disagreed on whether similar Indian rights struggles or different tribal beliefs, for example, should form the basis of the movement. Various tribal beliefs themselves differed significantly, ultimately underscoring the multiculturalism of twentieth-century Indian Country. Regretfully, activists often allowed their different experiences to divide them and thus undermine Red Power philosophically. Because many of today's Indigenous scholars and activists consider the location of a shared experience a major goal of Red Power, they seek to balance tribal unity and tribal autonomy. For the new Native scholars, then, one central challenge is to reconsider the theoretical grounds for experience as in American Indian tribalism. To serve this need, I develop a more expansive concept of Native experience to better support an Indian liberation movement.

In fact, the search for common ground involving tribes with specific experiences has been a central political issue for centuries. Before Europeans arrived, tribal peoples began organizing across cultural and geographical boundaries in such powerful confederacies as the League of the Iroquois, which was formed at least as early as the sixteenth century. In 1763, the Ottawa leader Pontiac organized his so-called rebellion across Ottawa, Potawatomi, Ojibwe, Huron, and several other tribal groups. In 1806, the Shawnee leader Tecumseh gathered in solidarity the Shawnee, Kickapoo, Winnebago, Menominee, Ottawa, Wyandot, and dozens of other tribal nations to halt the further encroachment of the United States into American Indian homelands.[7] Aware of this history of pan-tribal alliances, Red Power activists developed a new, more sophisticated form of resistance to American imperialism. Boldly intellectual, they were better trained than their forebears to translate their culture-specific tribal values to European Americans.

Upon reclaiming Alcatraz for Native people, the Indians of All Tribes read their proclamation to the press. With bitter irony, they announced their discovery of a new uninhabited land and declared their right to remain by a treaty delineating a fair purchase of the tiny, worthless island: "We, the native Americans, re-claim the land known as Alcatraz Island in the name of all American Indians by right of discovery" (Josephy, Nagel, and Johnson 1999, 40). The protest statement exuded a new intellectual rigor that would characterize the Red Power movement. Red Power Indians presented a darkly humorous inversion of the deplorable state of Indian Country to encourage white Americans to view Native life more as Native people did. Movement organizers began by interpreting their experiences of colonialism on reservations, which they represented as thinly disguised prison camps designed to confine and control Indigenous people. As they looked around their world, they began to see their poverty not as the fitting consequence of their hapless lives, but as political subjugation enforced by an occupying power. In their proclamation, the Indians of All Tribes made explicit their formerly vague feelings of hopelessness — their "imprisonment" — by audaciously declaring Alcatraz prison an appropriate site for a future Indian reservation:

> We feel that this so-called Alcatraz Island is more than suitable for an Indian Reservation, as determined by the white man's own standards. By this we mean that this place resembles most Indian reservations, in that:
>
> 1. It is isolated from modern facilities, and without adequate means of transportation.
> 2. It has no fresh running water.
> 3. It has inadequate sanitation facilities.
> 4. There are no oil or mineral rights.
> 5. There is no industry so unemployment is great.
> 6. There are no health care facilities.
> 7. The soil is rocky and non-productive; and the land does not support game.
> 8. There are no educational facilities.
> 9. The population has always exceeded the land base.
> 10. The population has always been held as prisoners and kept dependent upon others.
>
> Further, it would be fitting and symbolic that ships from all over the world, entering the Golden Gate, would first see Indian land, and thus be reminded of the true history of this nation. This tiny island would be a symbol of the great lands once ruled by free and noble Indians. (41)

The document was a watershed for American Indians. With humor and irony, it expressed a clear analysis of colonialism. The colonizer comes to control tribal nations methodically so that, after the initial military conquest, the slow destruction of an entire culture is hardly noticed. Nations are brutally conquered, but the domination of a people occurs within the person, in a slow erosion of one's sense of self-worth.

Following the occupation of Alcatraz in 1969, a decade-long flurry of events would define the time of Red Power. The era is now proudly remembered among seasoned organizers and continues to inspire a growing number of Indigenous scholars. Driven by Red Power, American Indian intellectuals recall the great moments of the Indian movement for Native liberation: the 1972 march on Washington for the Trail of Broken Treaties; the 1973 takeover of Wounded Knee; the 1975 intervention of the American Indian Movement on the Pine Ridge reservation; the 1978 Longest Walk on Washington to reenact the displacement of Indian peoples from their homelands. Between these touchstone events, elders, faith keepers, students, scholars, and activists organized dozens of occupations of stolen American Indian territories, staged takeovers of corrupt BIA offices, and filed multiple legal claims demanding the return of stolen lands and property, as well as compensation for centuries of cultural destruction.[8]

During Red Power, Indigenous writers such as Kiowa intellectual N. Scott Momaday began to explore in the Native novel this process of political awakening as a moment of insight to understand oneself in relation to a dominant nation. Contrary to many current conceptions of culture, which assume that identity is largely externally imposed and therefore restrictive, Momaday and others harnessed Indian identity to serve their artistic vision and cultural renewal. Cultural identity during Red Power became a rich form of inquiry into one's past and cultural world. As a founding Indian voice at the rise of Red Power, Momaday declares his identity to be an inroad to a massive resource of tribal knowledge. In a well-known statement from a 1971 lecture, he explains how an encounter with his ancestral history granted him greater access to a more nuanced, more encompassing Native self-conception: "I think of myself as an Indian because at one time in my life I suddenly realized that my father had grown up speaking a language that I didn't grow up speaking, that my forebears on his side had made a migration from Canada . . . along with Athapaskan peoples that I knew nothing about, and so I determined to find out something about these things and in the process I acquired an identity" (quoted in Schubnell 1985, 141). Momaday does not present American Indian identity as self-contained or unchanging but rather embraces the complexity of tribal knowledge in which tribal identity is flexible and developing. He achieves identity through insight and hard work, in an interpretive process engaged with his own self-conception and a tribal world.

Like Momaday, we require a reasonable means of evaluating different kinds of tribal and self-knowledge. This book studies a process similar to that which Momaday describes in his journey to Kiowa personhood. Momaday trained himself in his own cultural knowledge in a project of social and historical inquiry, through which he discerned a fuller account of his social and cultural situation. His new understanding of himself as a Kiowa man with a specific tribal history better explains his cultural background and present world: why his father spoke Kiowa but he himself did not, for instance. The author discovered his present Indian life to be hardly accidental but in part the product of a colonial history that systematically silenced Indigenous languages. From this realization, Momaday was led further to theorize his Native self, in what we might consider a moment of political awakening. What I will call the Red Power novel often presents a similar empirical process of decolonization, in which the interaction between the concepts of identity and experience drives a dynamic of political awakening and cultural recovery. To articulate this process, I engage identity not as a self-evident fact of birth but as a philosophical issue that can support and be supported by a more defensible and useful epistemological position. Ultimately, I target concepts such as identity and experience in order to investigate and build a strong position on Indigenous knowledge. Native cultural identities and tribal experiences can help us to understand how domination shapes the Indian world today. In turn, these new understandings transform American Indian identity. Momaday's corrected vision of a tribal past, land, and self, however, calls for a supple means of evaluating categories of culturally produced knowledge. For not all theoretical claims are equally justified. That is, we need to be able to deliberate among claims to knowledge not only in Indian America but also across national borders, where Indian-U.S. colonial relations frequently present competing histories. To illustrate, let me provide an anecdote from Red Power in which such contentious claims to identity and history likely precipitated a hate crime.

On 20 February 1972, the Yellow Thunder family found Raymond beaten to death in his pickup truck in Gordon, Nebraska, a small border town whose economy relied, in part, on the sale of liquor to the Oglala people of Pine Ridge, the neighboring Sioux reservation. Raymond Yellow Thunder was a middle-aged ranch hand who sought off-reservation work but returned home regularly. When he did not arrive one weekend, his family knew that something was wrong. An investigation revealed that four white men had grabbed Yellow Thunder while he was standing in front of a bar. They stripped him, beat him, and put him in the trunk of their car, then drove around for a while. Eventually, they took him to the American Legion hall, where a dance was underway. There, the abductors forced Yellow Thunder to dance for the crowd, and later beat him again. He escaped to his truck, there only to die. In response to this case of sadistic brutality came the emergence of the American Indian Movement (AIM), which arrived in Gordon to demand redress. Comanche intellectual Paul Chaat Smith and Robert Warrior introduce the incident: "It was a tremendous and unexpected response to the death of a rather ordinary man. Raymond Yellow Thunder's story reached out to every Indian person who could see in him not just another Indian drunk, but a brother, a father, an uncle, or a cousin" (1996, 117). For many Indigenous people, Yellow Thunder's death served as an emblem of colonial oppression. In an era of growing Native consciousness, that beating emboldened American Indians to recover alternative histories and make evaluative claims against the dominant narratives that reproduced their subjugation.

Many citizens of Gordon, however, responded differently to Yellow Thunder's death. Suspiciously, local police and courts refused to allow the Yellow Thunder family to view the body. We can imagine the underlying racism that reproduces cultural and historical distortions to justify such a crime. A local rancher might have understood Yellow Thunder's presence, and that of other Natives from the nearby reservation, as an invasion of his town by an inferior people rather than as the result of his own country's treaty breaking and land theft. On hearing his claim, though, a historically informed person would likely conclude as erroneous the rancher's account of how European Americans came to possess Sioux territories. The rancher might even declare an inherent right to confiscate American Indian homelands based on a colonialist assumption that Indians comprise an inferior and thus doomed race that should make way for his civilization. On this manifest destiny, he would be obligated to colonize Indian lands and force Native people to surrender their "savage" ways. Like Indigenous peoples' own claim to history, this rancher's cultural narrative is clearly socially constructed, but to a large U.S. population a colonialist history and a white supremacist identity would seem flawed because such notions inaccurately account for our colonial past and attempt to justify the denial of human worth. They do not describe the world that all of us, white or Indian, know. I argue that, whether culturally inherited or politically chosen, our claims to knowledge can—indeed, must—be evaluated. We need a way to distinguish between cultural narratives that provide assessments of colonialism or protect human worth and narratives that condone imperialism or allow racist domination. To make these distinctions, we can engage concepts such as experience and identity as theoretical tools to produce knowledge of our shared world. Simply put, it is unacceptable to say that all knowledge is constructed and to leave it at that. How people explain themselves in the world entails real political consequences for which all of us must be accountable.

During Red Power, Indians offered public reevaluations of competing histories. In reclaiming Alcatraz Island for Native people, they reclaimed and revalued the lives of American Indians like Raymond Yellow Thunder. They began to recover the "true history of this nation" in the suppressed history of American lands "once ruled by free and noble Indians." The growth of Red Power thus describes what I find to be a practical implementation of an alternative, historically grounded theory. I read Red Power as a materialist, political, and artistic vision that informs today's Native writers and scholars. In the midst of the Indian movement, vaguely felt experiences of colonialism were made explicit and were evaluated for accuracy in explaining Indigenous lives and their relationship with the United States. Red Power leaders gleaned new social knowledge through their political work, knowledge that was verified or revised as the movement grew: "If Oklahoma Indians realized the repressive conditions under which they lived, many simply accepted that Indians' fortunes were supposed to be harder than whites because Indians were stupid. However, most of the Oklahoma tribes maintained their own societies and ceremonies belying the myth of inferiority that kept them in social and economic bondage" (V. Deloria 1994, 7). With the inspiration of Red Power, American Indians began to ask why mainstream stories of Indian degradation contradicted their own experiences of a rich cultural life. In declaring and sharing their right and capacity to express themselves culturally, many Natives began to recover their tribal knowledge and to strengthen their identities as they elaborated new, more enabling accounts of Indian domination and resistance.

While they practiced their new theoretical vision of justice for Indian peoples, Oakes and other American Indian students were refining this vision in American universities. Native students brought their identities and experiences to college campuses, creating "Native American studies." Pressuring universities to accept a more diverse student body, American Indian students and professors demanded a place in the university for the production of Native ideas in a body of knowledge produced by and for American Indian people. Crow Creek Sioux scholar Elizabeth Cook-Lynn recalls participating in this exciting moment for Indigenous people: "For four days in March 1970, American Indian scholars met at the First Convocation of American Indian Scholars at Princeton University. . . . This milestone event set the agenda for strategy discussions that would bring about a change in the way Native life in America was studied. The main aim of these discussions was to assert that Indians were not just the inheritors of trauma but were also the heirs to vast legacies of knowledge about this continent and the universe that had been ignored in the larger picture of European invasion and education" (1997, 9). Departing from the ingrained anthropological approach to studying Native peoples, American Indian scholars announced that the study of a people is likely to improve when the people themselves contribute to it. Most importantly, notice the scholars' imaginative shift in self-conception: Natives are not helpless victims of colonial devastation, but instead the shrewd protectors of Indigenous thought. Like the Red Power activists on Alcatraz, like the Indians of Oklahoma, these Native intellectuals underwent a moment of creative realization. For decades, mainstream academics had said that Native people were spiraling in decline: depressed by their cultural loss they continued to lose their culture. But this assumption failed to explain why Native people were still dancing and still practicing the old ways, as well as continually inventing new ones—on Alcatraz, on reservations, in cities, in universities. If American Indians were hopelessly conquered, how could they be sharing tribal knowledge at Princeton? At the close of the decade, Native scholars and organizers had built from the ground up a process-oriented view of Indigenous knowledge and a vision of cultural renewal to inform the criticism, politics, and art of American Indians. I now introduce these interrelated theoretical issues as they inform the Red Power movement, the growth of Native studies, and the organization of this book.

American Indian Studies Today

Into the 1980s, the production of American Indian cultural knowledge as a discipline remained a site for imagining a Native emergence. Yet, despite Red Power's historicist beginnings, Native scholars such as Paula Gunn Allen, Ward Churchill, and Annette Jaimes began to espouse what many today might call essentialist conceptions of American Indian life.[9] In their stance on Indigenous nationhood, such scholars and organizers often did not consider more complex accounts of the diverse and changing tribal consciousness in North America. In forceful, exhortative tones, such intellectuals frequently drew on a collection of idealist notions about Indian history, culture, and identity. In advancing such a critical discourse, they hoped to establish a clearly defined infrastructure from which to resist the intellectual and material invasions of the U.S. mainstream. Of the many issues they addressed, the concept of identity was the most contentious. To build an anticolonial movement, these scholars argued, Natives must have a clear understanding of the contemporary tribal self. American Indian scholars composed an often essentialist program not only to benefit Indigenous people but also to edify those who had been defining—indeed, naming—tribal peoples for centuries.

Of course, the essentialist formulation preserves but also limits Native knowledge. From this approach to Indigenous inquiry, Native people become restricted in their capacity to know the world. Each tribal person, on this view, possesses an unchanging, self-evident tribal understanding. In *The Sacred Hoop*, Laguna and Sioux scholar Paula Gunn Allen famously describes this perspective as "a solid, impregnable, and ineradicable orientation toward a spirit-formed view of the universe, which provides an internal structure to both our consciousness and our art, . . . [and is] shared by all members of tribal psychic reality" (1992, 165). Note the rigid language of Allen's declaration: a single worldview held by "all" Native people is provided intact, in advance, and cannot be revoked, for it is an "internal" and "ineradicable" essence. In this restrictive view of tribal awareness, Native people have little room to develop. Allen's essentialism might have led the Lakota people to refuse the entrance of the horse, which was to become central to their culture. In Indian Country, tribal people looking to their own cultural histories might question Allen's generalization. Like the leaders of Red Power, they might also seek cultural improvement, an achievement that her essentialist views often disallow. Beyond Indian Country, in the universities where many American Indian intellectuals work, one comes to understand the charge of essentialism that Allen's declaration invites. The category of Indian is, in fact, not homogeneous across space and time but rather responds to the contingencies of history. Accepting this fact in the scholarly work of Native studies, Muskogee scholar Craig Womack writes: "To be sure, there is no one pure or authoritative act that constitutes Native literary criticism" (1999, 5). When struggling, however, to support our claims regarding tribal origins, homelands, nationhood, and spirituality, some Native scholars today unnecessarily rely on various forms of essentialism. Such claims do require defense, but they need not be essentialist. To serve this need, in this study I introduce the concept of an Indigenous "center" of Native thought to develop a theory of Indian identity, tribal experience, and social transformation. Employing Indigenous and Western philosophical notions of evaluation and knowledge, thereby avoiding essentialism, I propose an epistemological view of communally conferred objectivity, which I call *tribal realism*. I define and elaborate this position in the pages ahead.

Today, most Indian scholars, in some way, respond to the above question of change in tribal knowledge, and so their work might be loosely characterized in relation to three intellectual attitudes toward essentialism: some scholars defend essentialism as a necessary political strategy; others reject it by exposing its fixed claims to knowledge; still others resolve it by historicizing their ideas. Of course, these theoretical views often converge, diverge, or entangle, sometimes within a single scholar's argument. Native intellectuals who take the second path often turn to various forms of poststructuralism in order to liberate static views of knowledge regarding American Indian history, experience, and identity.[10] In the 1990s, American Indian scholars such as Kimberly Blaeser, Louis Owens, and Gerald Vizenor began this dismantling of such supposed cultural foundations. Building on Anishinaabe theorist Vizenor's notions of "trickster discourse" and "mixedblood" or "crossblood" identity,[11] such scholars have sought to correct the essentialist insistence that Native culture remains immutable despite external social and historical influences. Anishinaabe critic Kimberly Blaeser discusses Vizenor's introduction of the oral traditional trickster conception of identity to American Indian studies: "In Vizenor's writing the trickster figure becomes nearly synonymous with and a metaphor for the tribal mixedblood, whose symbolic role is to subvert the artificial distinctions of society. Like the trickster, whose very identity reflects all duality and contradiction, the mixedblood is a marginal character, one who exists on the border of two worlds, two cultures, the white and the Indian. In fact, the existence of the mixedblood resists even that definitiveness" (1996, 155). While an era might be behind us, some Native scholars and most non-Native scholars still accept Vizenor's view of tribal knowledge, perhaps because, as Blaeser describes, the trickster either promises to liberate Indigenous identity, or, more modestly, helps to challenge colonialist stereotypes. Yet perhaps most attractively, the trickster provides a model to survive a capitalist world at war with tribalism. I imagine that this hope underlies the late Choctaw-Cherokee scholar Louis Owens's interest in this position on Indian selfhood and, more deeply, on knowledge. Indeed, Owens appears to choose a mixedblood trickster identity as the only perceived alternative to essentialism: "For those of us who, like most of the authors we recognize as Native American, are mixedbloods, the hybridized, polyglot, transcultural frontier is quite clearly internalized. For all of us, however, territory remains a constant threat, an essential fiction of the colonial mind" (1998, 27). Beneath such claims seems a view of knowledge as necessarily unstable, yet purportedly liberating in its very instability: "Frontier, I would suggest, is the zone of the trickster, a shimmering, always changing zone of multifaceted contact within which every utterance is challenged and interrogated, all referents put into question" (26).

For Owens, Indigenous people, since the arrival of Europeans, are now immersed in at least two cultures. Now, albeit culturally, mixedbloods all, Indians inhabit the interstitial space between the American colonies and the Indian territories, without being fully determined by either. Convinced that all identity categories rely on an unacceptable essence, such trickster critics have traded these supposedly failed categories for indeterminacy. This position, however, has led to a few theoretical limitations. First, no Native person would deny that American Indians bear the influence of European Americans, but so do European Americans of American Indians, as do other groups of other groups. Indeed, if all of us, red, white, black, or otherwise, display this influence of other cultures in our lives, this trickster theory works less to appreciate than to undermine cultural difference. In this trickster space, where race and colonialism continue to operate but have been rendered invisible, scholars, in the end, cannot explain crucial differences in social and political power, nor lay claim to a distinct tribal history and hold it up to the world. As tricksters, moreover, Native scholars have cast the focus of their studies away from the production of ideas to serve Indigenous lives into the margins of cultural interaction, where things Indian are often valued only insofar as they are indebted to U.S. culture.[12]

Finally, self-identified mixedblood critics, writing in this zone of the trickster, have been left with little theoretical recourse but subversion. Indeed, they can deconstruct the Western image of the Indian, but, to remain epistemologically consistent, they cannot justify their own normative claims to American Indian identity or history. This trickster position thus has promised to liberate Native people from essentialist definitions of Indians, but, disconnected from a distinct culture and land, it ultimately cannot support a coherent Native identity nor protect actual Native territories. I argue, however, that theoretical categories, foremost identity, need not rely on essentialism. As sound scientific theories rely not on eternal truths but empirical evidence, good social concepts rely not on absolutes but coherent explanations of the self in society. Identities enable us to read the world, and can be revised better to do so. The trickster critique notwithstanding, as long as tribal people are colonized, concepts such as identity and nation will be indispensable tools of political resistance, and even on decolonization, such open-ended constructs will remain valuable modes of interpretation. Responsible Indian scholars should recognize that views of knowledge underlie social concepts such as identity or experience. In neglecting to consider the implications of our theories—theories with real-world political consequences—Native scholars undermine the very claims on which American Indians make their best appeals for justice.

More recently, Indigenous intellectuals such as Elizabeth Cook-Lynn, Robert Warrior, and Jace Weaver have shifted the focus of the critical conversation to the real lives of Indian people,[13] and in effecting this shift, they have returned the field to the process-driven mode of social transformation that defined Red Power. Such scholars have begun to root our studies in land, community, and the past. In so doing, they are empowered to make evaluative claims to normative knowledge, which, in turn, better support the philosophical and actual recovery of Indian lands, histories, and identities. Their call to rematriate the discourse, however, is hardly a new development in the American Indian history of ideas, but rather responds to a longstanding commitment to critical accountability in Native history and society. Such Native intellectuals continue to produce work that neither relies on reductive essentialism nor resorts to trickster indeterminacy. Instead, such Indian scholars compose convincing accounts of American Indian life by consistently training a critical eye on history. Here, I write of history as an epistemological challenge: the claim of the material world on ideas, and the claim of intellectuals to history. Like these scholars, I am committed to historicism as a methodological approach dedicated to refining our ideas in the world, as they refer to a social context to ground the crucial political contentions of our times.

With the 1995 publication of *Tribal Secrets*, Robert Warrior took Indigenous studies by surprise, though his assertion of "intellectual sovereignty" amounts to nothing more audacious than a reasonable request to recognize a colonized intellectual history: "A guiding principle of my work . . . has been to produce a book that explores [how,] after more than two centuries of impressive literary and cultural production, critical interpretation of those writings can proceed primarily from Indian sources. . . . [For in practicing intellectual sovereignty], we stand on firmer ground in our interlocutorial role with Eurocentric scholarly theories and categories, whose methodologies and disciplinary traditions too often become monoliths to be either copied uncritically or made into bugbears that are engaged in an endless dance of criticism and dependence" (1995, xvi, 2). If we are to seek justice, we must begin by recognizing this history of repressive colonial relations. European imperialism has silenced resistant voices—voices without which we are denied a full account of American Indian life. Understood in this light, the plea for scholarly self-determination to end critical "dependence" is not only ethically just but also intellectually necessary. Indian scholars using Warrior's approach are extending intellectual traditions with deep roots in North American history. Such work is "counterhistoricist" for it not only exposes but also corrects inaccurate constructions of American Indian culture neither by appealing to essentialism nor by resorting to deconstruction, but by presenting alternative knowledge built on accounts that adhere to the social facts of Native life.

Native intellectuals developing this historicist approach write of Indian Country as comprised of certain social facts that define American Indian existence. A study shows that Native people today are far more likely to be subject to a violent crime committed by European Americans than are any other racial group in the United States (Southern Poverty Law Center 1990, 3). Of course, the researchers' work with the data, as well as our explanations of "the facts of life" in Native America, will certainly be socially mediated. But if, judging by the facts, our material account of American Indian life is convincing, then that explanation is, from a theoretical perspective, normative. No doubt such facts are imperative to decision making, though our interpretations of social facts may change as we grow and our world changes. In recognizing the necessity of historical ground for a theoretical construct like Indian Country, these intellectuals proffer a world that is constructed yet nonetheless "real" because that world exists independent of our theories. It is through our theories, however, that we can gain access to it. Implementing what I describe as an emergent tribal realist theoretical framework, Indigenous scholars place concepts such as knowledge, experience, and identity at the center of their arguments for national liberation and social justice.

In spite of the fundamental importance of identity to Indigenous social struggles, the humanities field in the United States continues to question the necessity of the concept. American Indian scholars who thus pursue a philosophically grounded politics of identity must contend with the concerns that critique raises. Some theorists conclude that, because the concept of identity requires some level of intellectual violence to be maintained, it is theoretically untenable, even harmful. Other concerned critics, indeed, declare identity to be politically dangerous in a world fractured by nationalism and racial tension. In turn, the concept of experience has weathered less critique; if human experience is unavoidably mediated, theorists argue, it cannot be known or owned. Whether a tribe works to retain a collective understanding as a distinct people from a specific place with a unique history, or whether a Native woman struggles to protect her personal self-understanding as a tribal person, it is through identity that Indian people, defying this critique at play in books, schools, and the media, continue to develop their cultures.

Whenever I must present my "CDIB" identification card from the Department of the Interior in order to authorize my identity biologically in terms of racial purity—my "certified degree of Indian blood"—I am reminded that the United States polices my Native identity. So despite the warnings from within and beyond Indigenous studies, in this book I attempt to reclaim American Indian identity in an utmost urgent response to the ongoing colonial relations between Native nations and the United States. For if we simply abandon this theoretical issue, U.S. institutions will continue to restrict Indigenous identity. As we well know, the North American history of empire building underwrites the destruction of Indian cultural identity with its policies moored to manifest destiny— policies which insist that Indians relinquish their identification with their cultures and especially with their resource-rich ancestral homelands. To resist U.S. imperialism invested in erasing the Native presence, identity is quite probably *the* central site for the preservation of tribal culture, history, and nationhood.

For a theory of identity to serve either cause, we require a means to determine which conceptions of identity best guide this process of decolonization and cultural renewal. What is more, colonial relations yearn for an understanding of the unique histories and legal entitlements of Indigenous peoples, an assessment that requires an account of Native identities different from those of North American settlers. To meet these practical demands, we must be able to distinguish among identities and evaluate them. From a practical view of American Indian identity, we value a claim on its ability to explain one's world. On this basis of epistemic reliability, Native identity may be reconceived to better produce cultural knowledge. In so doing, we transform politically, mobilizing the Fourth World.[14] Looking back on the past two decades in Native studies, I find that neither position on cultural identity—the essentialist retreat or the trickster dislocation—provides a philosophical discourse to adjudicate our various claims. During the Indian movement, organizers, scholars, and writers engaged the very process described above. The theoretical alternative that I offer is drawn from and redraws the political awakening and cultural growth experienced by characters in the Red Power novel.

In working to ground American Indian discourses, Native scholars participate in a tradition of tribal intellectualism that considers American Indian art and thought as a response to the experience of being Native in the world. Although Indigenous intellectuals such as William Apess, Charles Eastman, and Ella Deloria wrote within quite different historical, social, and political climates, whether during eras of colonial invasion, removal, allotment, termination, or relocation, they share a concern with locating American Indian ideas in Native experience and tribal history. For the moment, we might consider such Indian figures as models for a historicist mode in Native critical thought, which I seek to theorize in this work. Organizing this legacy, Robert Warrior reshapes Native canons in terms not of great works but of "great ideas" to better discern the continuity in tribal intellectual consciousness: "When we take that tradition seriously, . . . we empower our work. . . . We see that, far from engaging in some new and novel practice that belongs necessarily to the process of assimilating and enculturating non-Native values, we are doing something that Natives have done for hundreds of years—something that can be and has been an important part of resistance to assimilation and survival" (1995, 2). Warrior is able to establish our intellectual tradition through his process of "cross reading," in which Indian scholars put Native texts in conversation with those beyond Native America, to develop a "cultural criticism that is grounded in American Indian experiences but which can draw on the insights and experiences of others who have faced similar struggles" (xxiii). He holds Indian self-understanding and tribal history as primary concepts through which to pursue Native independence, cultural recovery, and artistic flourishing.

This materialist intellectual tradition in English reaches back to the colonial period when American Indians struggled against invasion, the dissipation of alcohol, the cessation of tribalism, and the assimilation into Christian and capitalist culture. Immersed in this struggle throughout his work, the Pequot minister William Apess pursues the social facts of his existence, thereby relentlessly linking his Native identity to his experience of the world. Born in 1798, a survivor of outrageous attacks on his community, Apess writes in testimonial fervor to reconcile the historical memory of these acts of genocide with his commitment to Christianity, both derived from European culture: "Can you charge the Indians with robbing a nation almost of their whole continent, and murdering their women and children, and then depriving the remainder of their lawful rights, that nature and God require them to have?" (1992 [1829], 13). In his brazen reversal, Apess preempts any charge of Indian moral degradation. His historical claim to high crimes of conquest and genocide, though, is more than a rhetorical indictment of hypocritical Christians—it is also a disclosure of colonial experience. Apess exhorts Indigenous people, on the one hand, to draw on this experience to reclaim and resist attacks on their moral lives, and charges European Americans, on the other, to account for their colonial history as invaders. Cherokee scholar Jace Weaver explains that Apess works within a tradition of community-based intellectualism, in which Natives write to preserve American Indian well-being, recover culture, and promote tribal autonomy: "[Apess] uses Christianity to break through his alienation. He employs it to claim the full humanity of Indians and his own Indianness in particular. In his writings he increasingly reaches for an Indian Christian nationalism that aims at separatism" (1997, 59).

In placing Native studies within a tradition of expanding Indigenous selfhood and tribal experience, we discover a shared critical concern in the writings of early-twentieth-century American Indian intellectuals such as the Sioux writer Charles Eastman, who, though criticized for his assimilationist views, firmly grounds us in Indian land and history, and even lashes out against white hypocrisy. Eastman can speak with a sharp tongue on the historical responsibility of U.S. citizens. Consider his recollection of one morning in 1887 during a stroll with his European American benefactor, Mr. Moody. Stopping at a marker, Moody declares: "Eastman, this stone is a reminder of the cruelty of your countrymen two centuries ago. Here they murdered an innocent Christian." Eastman calmly replies, "Mr. Moody, it might have been better if they had killed them all. Then you would not have had to work so hard to save the souls of their descendants" (1977 [1916], 74). The subtle ambiguity in pronouns tempts Western readers to designate "they" the Christians and "them" the Indians, whom Eastman, in his own purported self-hatred, wishes destroyed. Semantically, however, Eastman empowers "they" as his Native countrymen, and indicts "them" as the European Christian conquerors, whose souls need saving for their brutal treatment of Eastman's people. Such textual moments in which identity, land, history, and language intersect call Indian scholars to locate and reclaim Native voices. So doing, readers might discover their interpretive error and come to view the world more as do American Indians.

In a final example of historicist writing, I turn to the Sioux scholar Ella Deloria. Born in 1889 and a protégé of Franz Boaz, she considers colonial change among her Dakota people. During a somewhat arid period for Native intellectuals, in 1944 Deloria published *Speaking of Indians*. Writing for a largely Christian audience, Deloria's account of her people's transformation is measured yet moving, because she lets her views of changing Native identity take shape in real-world experiences: "But they were a people used to accepting fate with fortitude and dignity. They still repeated their favorite adage, 'Since it must be so, it is so,' and they turned to the white man's way with remarkably little bitterness. Had they better understood what fundamentally must be done to make the change, they might have made better headway than they did. In retrospect we can see the mistakes, the stupidities, the indignities that made the going rough. At that they started out well enough, almost too well, with proverbial beginner's luck. The thoughtful and the objective were anxious for the future. The rank and file took each day as it came, preoccupied with the mere business of keeping alive under strange conditions" (1998 [1944], 84). Written over two decades before Red Power, Deloria's portrait of personal dignity and quiet negotiation in a conscious cultural transformation anticipates the literary craft of N. Scott Momaday, James Welch, and Leslie Marmon Silko: the "long outwaiting" of the Jemez people in *House Made of Dawn*; the test of Yellow Calf and his band in *Winter in the Blood*; the patient words of Josiah about precious water in *Ceremony*. Only through rooting her views in the lives of Dakota people, reflecting on their social meanings, is Deloria able to provide a convincing account of colonial depression and a vision of renewal. With striking perception, she performs the very process of creative self-reflection she illustrates, and even models for future American Indian intellectuals of Red Power and today a process of remembering and reimagining a more enriched Indian past for a more enabling Indian future. Despite or through their association with Christianity or capitalist culture, these writers maintain an Indigenous viewpoint because they speak from experience and to history. In rooting our ideas in a community of experience, contemporary Native critics place themselves in a tribal realist intellectual tradition. Thus proceeding, historically focused American Indian scholars follow the words of Womack, who declares: "I will seek a literary criticism that emphasizes

Native resistance movements against colonialism, confronts racism, discusses sovereignty and Native nationalism, seeks connections between literature and liberation struggles, and, finally, roots literature in land and culture" (1999, 11).

Because I feel the necessity of working within, and philosophically deepening, the American Indian critical tradition described above, in this book I plan to clarify some of the claims made lately among Native scholars who I find share elements of this tribal realist standpoint. I thus offer an alternative theoretical position to American Indian knowledge, identity, land, and experience. Native scholars implicitly use this approach when they say the world out there is real because it affects us in a very real way. For it would be dangerous for American Indians to enter ancestral places of worship while dismissing the historical fact that these stolen lands are now patrolled by the U.S. military. Because they must encounter and explain these social facts, those who implement tribal realism are committed to evaluating and improving their interpretations of a shared world. Such interpretations are certainly socially mediated, but, unlike those critics influenced by trickster discourse, tribal realist intellectuals deal with theoretical dependence as an opportunity to modify their views as they compose more normative social knowledge.

The discussion above thus evokes the sensitive issues of social power in our interpretation of Indigenous literature and culture. Of course, identity plays a significant part in any cross-cultural literary and social analysis. Add to this interpretive challenge the ideological workings of colonial modernity, and we only further distort, through our identities, our knowledge of another world. The United States boasts of being the wealthiest nation in the world, yet many of its citizens remain drastically impoverished and are denied their rights to meaningful work, affordable housing, and health care. Reared in extreme colonial circumstances and within institutions that reproduce colonialist values regarding non-Western peoples, it is not surprising that scholars often inherit a view of the world informed by this imperialist cultural narrative. To correct this vision, scholars can interrogate the legacy of U.S. domination and its often-sublimated involvement in research on Native literature.

To do so, we can begin developing a more workable view of social mediation. Though our theoretical attachments cannot be avoided, some might be more useful than others, some hindering us to appreciate tribal cultures, others actually preparing us to read Indian texts. Scholars of Native texts might adapt an approach similar to that of today's progressive social analysts. This new vision of cultural interpretation, one that moves beyond the objectivist dream of disinterested observation, informs the work of the acclaimed anthropologist Renato Rosaldo. He was challenged to explain death and mourning among the Ilongot people until his wife's untimely passing: "The ethnographer, as a positioned subject, grasps certain human phenomena better than others. He or she occupies a position or structural location and observes with a particular angle of vision. Consider, for example, how age, gender, being an outsider, and association with a neocolonial regime influence what the ethnographer learns. The notion of position also refers to how life experiences both enable and inhibit particular kinds of insight. In the case at hand, nothing in my own experience equipped me even to imagine the anger possible in bereavement until after Michelle Rosaldo's death in 1981. Only then was I in a position to grasp the force of what Ilongots had repeatedly told me about grief, rage, and headhunting" (1989, 19). As Rosaldo carefully explains, one's social location of reading need not be always restrictive; some theoretical mediation might grant insight to Native life and art. With this view in mind, I propose a literary anthropology fundamentally committed to interrogating and benefiting from the role of identity in the practice of Indigenous criticism. If the goal of our research is to produce more conclusive scholarship on Native literature and culture, then I suggest we begin to question and produce helpful background knowledge, examining how personal location influences (impedes or assists) cultural and literary analysis. In what I introduce as a "normativist" reading methodology, inquiry is not a search for disinterested knowledge but a process of refining one's theoretical perspective by becoming self-critical.[15] Such an interpretive approach thus accepts and benefits from the constructivist critique, for, on this alternative view, one can read through one's location to correct and construct a more comprehensive account of an Indian world, because that new account now better explains the surrounding social facts that make up that world. In the following pages, I test and elaborate this approach by focusing on several concepts central to American Indian social transformation and national liberation: homelands, in chapter 1; identity, in chapter 2; experience, in chapter 3; praxis, in chapter 4; and social interaction, in my concluding chapter.

As an emergent Indigenous scholar, I feel a responsibility to present some challenging claims, but I strongly believe such claims must be substantiated in our texts. Liberating ideas rely on liberating readings of liberating literature. To demonstrate my alternative approach, I focus on three widely read novels written by American Indians during the Red Power movement of the 1960s and 1970s: N. Scott Momaday's *House Made of Dawn* (1968), James Welch's *Winter in the Blood* (1974), and Leslie Marmon Silko's *Ceremony* (1977).[16] I use these works to explain how tribal realism might better account for changes in Native life brought about through political awakening and the characters' and the community's engagement with their tribal land, oral traditions, culture, and history growing from and fueling the consciousness of the period. I consciously select three works that Native and mainstream scholars and readers know well, and I read them critically to show that they present indispensably valuable ideas to serve Native intellects. Then, in my concluding chapter, I explore how a number of today's Indian writers further develop the claims of Red Power by attending to its legacy in the lives of Native people today. In the spirit of Alcatraz, I propose that we consider our identification with tribal lands (part 1: Red Land) as the umbilicus of American Indian studies and as the epistemological grounds prepared for the growth of Native identity and Native political consciousness (part 2: Red Power). For I believe that Indian scholars today face a decisive moment in the field, in which we are challenged to test and defend our ideas not only in our literatures but also in the world—where, few would disagree, our ideas refer to actual political realities.

Normativity and the Oral Tradition

"Objectivity," the production of reliable knowledge, is the underlying pivotal point on which a growing number of scholars in and beyond Native studies disagree. Indian scholars influenced by trickster theory tend to define objectivity in positivist terms, as the achievement of pure knowledge absolutely free of theoretical mediation. This book, however, redefines the pursuit of objectivity as a mediated process that recognizes and corrects error in the search for more accurate accounts of the world. I call this goal of inquiry "normativity," in tribal realist terms. Though analytic philosophers today have moved beyond positivism, critics in Indigenous studies employing the trickster still assume that all claims to knowledge necessarily involve this Enlightenment-era model of objectivity, in which knowledge must be achieved free of theoretical attachments to history, society, or culture. Of course, the subjective nature of all inquiry precludes ultimate certainty in our observations of the world. Scholars nonetheless continue to set their terms of inquiry to attain a positivist "view from nowhere."[17] Convinced that "knowledge" must assume a reliance on these unmediated foundations—what the literary profession associates with essentialism—Native cultural critics supporting tricksterism have thus often ruled out the possibility of achieving any reliable knowledge at all. Faced with the undesirable situation in which inquiry is an unavoidably tainted process and value-free objectivity is impossible to achieve, scholars relying on this position tend to turn away from the production of knowledge. Instead, scholars continue to investigate this problem. In their most progressive mode, such American Indian critics pursue further critiques of knowledge as an irreversible tangle of ideology.

In an alternative to such Western positivist views of knowledge, I turn to an epistemological understanding held among tribal peoples of North America, articulated and negotiated in Indigenous oral philosophy.[18] With an impressive reserve of research, Native philosophers, linguistic anthropologists, and folklore experts study how people of oral cultures manage their knowledge by collaborating on an intellectual body of stories wholly adequate to their moral lives and social world. Contrary to the popular view that American Indian cultures remain in an unchanging past, Native cultures survive and indeed flourish through this ongoing production of knowledge maintained in the oral tradition. To serve tribal change, Indian storytelling must remain a dynamic, continuous site of theoretical investigation, evaluation, and revision.

As an ever-changing body of tribal philosophy, the oral tradition thus accepts and negotiates challenges to tradition. Even the old ways and values vital to a Native community at times require reflection and revision to ensure that tribal people adapt and thrive in a rapidly changing world. To practice this open-ended philosophical evaluation, tribal members must hold a view of knowledge and experience that overcomes the Western tendency to demand a verifiable reality in mutually exclusive categories, such as either authentic or inauthentic, either oral or written, either dream or reality. In this regard, written forms of American Indian tellings, whether modifications of traditional stories or adaptations of foreign genres, can be oral yet written, new yet authentic. Tribal people can transform the novel into a unique Indigenous literary form. Choctaw scholar Michael Wilson explains this different conception of knowledge in a reading of Leslie Marmon Silko: "In contrast to the scientific methods of Tedlock and others, Leslie Marmon Silko, Laguna Pueblo novelist and essayist, challenges the distinctions crucial to the sciences: pure/impure, past/present, orality/ writing. Instead, Silko suggests a much different approach to representing the oral tradition, conceiving of it not as an artifact for study, but . . . as a living tradition whose value and power expand and continue to have relevance for the present. Consequently (and ironically), the oral tradition itself has, as Silko demonstrates, a fundamentally different way of conceptualizing itself than do the scientists who seek to represent it" (1997, 133). I hope to deepen our understanding of this "fundamentally different way" by reframing this distinction in epistemological terms. Wilson suggests that European American researchers cannot explain a tribal view of oral knowledge within a traditionally Western model of inquiry. To clarify this difference, we might organize these divergent cultural views of knowledge in terms of objectivity. For Wilson, Western epistemologies tend to hold a positivist conception of knowledge as absolute certainty that cannot be obtained, while tribal philosophies tend to view knowledge in more normative terms. To Indians, what one knows of the world may be altered but steadily endures: "The ancient Pueblo people sought a communal truth, not an absolute," writes Silko (1996b, 269).

For this reason, "new" knowledge may enter a tribal community to be incorporated within an Indigenous worldview. In an influential essay, "Toward a National Indian Literature," Acoma writer Simon Ortiz explains that this adaptive process is not simply artistic but indeed political. Indian people consciously shape their bodies of knowledge with new practices, values, and even languages to resist domination and build nations: "This is the crucial item that has to be understood, that it is entirely possible for a people to retain and maintain their lives through the use of any language. There is no question of authenticity here; rather it is the way Indian people have creatively responded to forced colonization. And this response has been one of resistance; there is no clearer word for it than resistance" (1981b, 10). Because Native community members maintain a more flexible model of knowledge, they can assimilate new values, practices, and views into tribal consciousness. American Indians become not mixedbloods caught between two worlds but simply Indians, refining their cultures through time. Wilson continues his discussion of the Pueblo epistemology: "Thus, a Pueblo perspective suggests that literature is a normative process—continually re-creating meaning in the present, seeking a 'communal truth' that is a changing but stable center of value. Furthermore, a storytelling culture constantly moves toward integrating its individual elements—points of view, old and new stories—into a complex, changing community. It does so not only in spite of conflicting points of view but also *because* of these different points of view, for they provide valuable correction and supplemental information" (1997, 135). Notice that the Pueblo people understand knowledge as the practice of meaning gathering: not as the final identification of an unmediated truth, but as an ongoing process in which community members offer multiple perspectives. In a social process that employs the localizing force of language, tribal members are drawn into a culturally regulated center of knowledge.

In a tribal model of normativity, knowledge is challenged and maintained through a sophisticated understanding of error. Rather than seek merely to eliminate error, as do positivists, people of storytelling cultures tend to value error as fundamental to inquiry. An inaccurate claim to knowledge presents an opportunity for participants to locate such an error, to seek out the views or values that might have led to this incomplete understanding of a tribal world. In this manner, the oral tradition describes a dialectic in which error interacts with objectivity as tribal theorists move toward a more complete picture of Indigenous life. Wilson explains the role of error in Native inquiry: "In this conception of the oral tradition, and of the creation of meaning in general, conflict is not inherently negative and in fact can be seen as having positive influences if it is conceived within the context of a dialogic philosophy that accepts truth as provisional rather than absolute" (1997, 135). We might now see the theoretical implications of a tribal view of normative knowledge and fallibility. Because theory dependence is not shunned but indeed embraced, intellectuals eagerly contribute to the production of knowledge as an energetic process. This is why Indigenous philosophy is deeply creative. Writing on the function of "myths" in tribal life, Christopher Vecsey suggests that the performative context of community encourages an oral philosopher to produce collective knowledge without diminishing his or her own unique aesthetic: "The most central motifs are present in all versions of the same story. Thus a single story exists, but with no absolutely fixed text from which others vary. On the contrary, all variants are equally valid, each a new performance reflecting the storyteller's style, talent, and interest" (1991, 21). Contributors to the body of knowledge that constitutes the oral tradition present new narratives that may contradict or modify it, so the limits of what we can know are always being challenged and reaffirmed, tested and extended. Cree philosopher Neal McLeod discusses the political implications of this view of tribal knowledge that can imagine and accommodate new patterns of life: "It seems that open-endedness with discursive space and action of a community is desirable and necessary to maintain a vital life-world, with the provision that it does not threaten the destruction of a community. . . . If Indian women get more political power, Indian communities will remain intact. And if some Pueblo Indians are atheists, the whole community is not going to collapse" (1998, 66–67).

Because these alternative accounts must be consciously created, the oral tradition is predicated on a specifically tribal conception of the imagination. Among many Native peoples, to imagine is not to see an illusion; it is to manifest that which once did not exist, to order the world in the way Momaday describes in the epigraph to this introduction. This Indigenous understanding of the imagination thus might be distinguished from narrower, Western notions of imagining. Karl Kroeber describes this difference:

> I find that most useful definitions of imagination are those in common usage, in which "to imagine" ordinarily means two different but related processes linked by a conception of "fantasy." When someone says, "Ah, you're just imagining that," you are accused of "fantasizing" in its most usual sense: inventing mentally what has never existed and presumably never can, or willfully ignoring physical actualities for psychically engendered "unrealities." When, however, you are urged to "use your imagination, stupid," there is a positive appeal to fantasy: a demand that you employ your psychic capacities to reach beyond what is immediately present here and now and beyond routinized rational patterns toward some novel possibility. The injunction to "use your imagination" urges you to allow your mind to move toward something not yet realized but realizable. Imagination in this sense underlies every kind of planning, every purposeful human accomplishment; it is in fact the primary power that *constitutes* culture. (1998, 64)

Kroeber beseeches mainstream students of American Indian oral literature to consider this difference in definitions of the imagination.[19] Paul Tidwell suggests that he and other European Americans may negotiate their cultural distance from Native literature and even develop morally by engaging a tribal model of the imagination: "If imagination functions within stories to remind us of the tragicomic aspects of experience . . . , then stories—those we hear about others and those we remember—can act as agents of change" (1997, 626). When a tribal people tell their story of their collective emergence, they are not unconsciously rehearsing a concretized narrative. To the contrary, they willfully reinvent their world in a profound act of the imagination. Through this oral enactment, Natives confirm and expand their relationships with each other, with other creatures, and with the land. Kroeber and other oral literature specialists explain this Native practice as "world renewal": "American Indian ideas of 'renewal' as restoration of traditional ways are misunderstood if regarded as mere exercises in repetition. Indian imaginings that revitalize their culture and its relation to the environment never exclude the possibility (even the desirability) of transformation through reassessment of tradition" (1998, 66). Though not assuming a seamless oral tradition leading up to Red Power, this book places Indian oral philosophies of normative knowledge production at the center of plans for world renewal during Red Power and in its writings.

Trade Languages and the Realist Theory

To travel in the colonial Southeast was to master "trade languages." At one time, any European or Indian trader had to know at least one such language to travel beyond the boundaries of his nation, engage in diplomacy, or exchange trade items and knowledge. Then or now, were I to refer to myself as one of "Ani Yunwiya" or as a "Tsalagi" person, many probably would not understand that I am a member of an Indigenous group of the Smoky Mountains. But were I to say that I am from the Cherokee Nation, they would probably understand. The term "Cherokee," however, is actually derived from a Choctaw word to describe those people of the cave country, a name applied to my people through the Choctaw Indigenous trade language of the Native Southeast. As an Indian scholar, I still rely on trade languages. Like the currency attending wampum or treaties, trade languages enable us to communicate across cultural differences and to trade in intellectual capital, without diminishing our cultural autonomy or "authenticity." The English language has become a trade language, adapted by a vast number of people who wish to trade items and ideas—with no concomitant reduction in their cultural viability. In this book, I draw on a theoretical trade language called "realist theory" in order to exchange ideas with other scholars. My adaptation of this alternative theoretical position, however, does not weaken my tribal viewpoint; in fact, realism might even help expand my intellectual views to strengthen Native critical practice.

In the late 1980s, women, minority, and Third World scholars began to consider the importance of producing knowledge to benefit not only suppressed groups but also a world all of us inhabit. Though members of the dominant culture were asked to form a distant appreciation of the knowledge produced within a subjugated group, minority scholars were finding that such cultural relativism ultimately confined their knowledge to the local. For on that position, rarely did mainstream scholars take minority struggles earnestly enough to be changed by them. In a 1989 essay, "Us and Them: On the Philosophical Bases of Political Criticism," Satya Mohanty made explicit this gathering sense among minority scholars, when he explained that relativism as an interpretive position or political practice is strikingly limited: merely to appreciate difference "leads . . . to a sentimental charity, for there is nothing in its logic that necessitates our attention to the other" (1989, 23). Instead, Mohanty argued, our expansion of human knowledge requires not only the local but also the global, a recognition of the most basic capacity as humans, despite differences, to evaluate moral action and make decisions. Questioning the relativization of cultural knowledge, Mohanty called for a more universal basis for analysis across cultures, in a view of human agency as "not merely the capacity to act purposefully but also to *evaluate* actions and purposes in terms of larger ideas we might hold about, say, our political and moral world" (1989, 22). This necessarily broad category of *universal moral agency* was found better to serve the collective production of knowledge as well as anticolonial struggles. Movements for national liberation and human emancipation, after all, have often relied on similar, broad-based Kantian claims to the intrinsic worth and rights of humanity: "If I see someone in danger of drowning I will not need to satisfy myself about his moral character before going to his aid. I owe assistance to any man in such circumstances, not merely good men," writes Gregory Vlastos in his famous civil-rights-era essay "Justice and Equality" (1962, 47).

In the 1990s, feminist philosophers such as Linda Martín Alcoff began to confront "the problem of speaking for others" as a serious theoretical issue of power closely tied to a person's *objective social location*, the register of social factors that constitute a person's daily life: "There is a growing recognition that where one speaks from affects the meaning and truth of what one says, and thus one cannot assume an ability to transcend one's location. . . . Thus, the work of privileged authors who speak on behalf of the oppressed is coming more and more under criticism from members of those oppressed groups themselves" (1991, 7). From this concern for the affirmation of universal moral agency, on the one hand, and the recognition of objective social location, on the other, minority scholars began to seek a view of identity and culture that not only attributed special knowledge or *epistemic privilege* to persons experiencing the world through oppressed social locations, but also made this knowledge incumbent on a general society.

With these challenges to cultural relativism, minority intellectuals were now able to assert the importance of including suppressed voices, not to repair disadvantaged groups, but to produce more objective knowledge. Scholars in women's studies began formulating an approach to knowledge that resisted the essentialist impulse, yet also avoided the total destabilization of concepts fundamental to subjugated groups, such as "women's lives." Scholars began to confront the problem of essentializing the category of woman as part of a deeper issue regarding the very production of objective knowledge, as in the sciences. In a 1991 book, *Whose Science? Whose Knowledge? Thinking from Women's Lives*, feminist philosopher Sandra Harding began with the now-familiar critique of power in society and, in her study, the sciences, asserting that "science is politics by other means" (10). Like many other scholars, Harding is critical of the way our views of the world are situated, and shares with these scholars the conclusion that inquiry is always socially and historically mediated. She argues, in fact, that this disclosure often comes from those who do not benefit from but are dominated by the production and application of power-driven knowledge: "For those who have suffered from what seem to be the consequences of the sciences, their technologies, and their forms of rationality, it appears absurd to regard science as the value-free, disinterested, impartial, Archimedean *arbiter* of conflicting agendas, as conventional mythology holds" (10).

Yet Harding was able to reach beyond the oppositional critiques of masculinist discourses and technology led by, for example, Judith Butler or Donna Haraway.[20] The critical framework for her "feminist standpoint epistemology" does not attempt to overcome the social location of women's lives. Rather, Harding accepts and values that very situation as productive of a different yet broadly binding form of knowledge, what she calls "strong objectivity": "A feminist standpoint epistemology requires strengthened standards of objectivity. . . . They call for the acknowledgement that all human beliefs—including our best scientific beliefs—are socially situated, but they also require a critical evaluation to determine which social situations tend to generate the most objective knowledge claims. They require, as judgmental relativism does not, a scientific account of the relationships between historically located belief and maximally objective belief. So they demand what I shall call *strong objectivity* in contrast to the weak objectivity of objectivism and its mirror-like twin, judgmental relativism" (142). Feminist standpoint theorists such as Harding then shared with others this view of knowledge as a process engaged with historical location, experience, and error as we move toward a "maximally objective belief." In his 1997 *Literary Theory and the Claims of History*, Mohanty thus employed this revised model of objectivity. Presenting a cultural materialist approach influenced by Marxism,[21] in that book he foregrounds the *social facts* that comprise one's world to develop a more thorough account of identity in the pursuit of social justice, a theory of knowledge Mohanty introduces as "postpositivist realism."

By the end of the decade, dissatisfied with the theoretical positions available to understand minority literatures and serve political action, and inspired by these progressive theorists, some forward-looking minority intellectuals began to flesh out the realist approach to knowledge, identity, and experience. Drawing on the philosophy of science and the works of Charles Sanders Peirce, W. V. O. Quine, Hilary Putnam, and Donald Davidson, realism acknowledges that identities, for example, are socially constructed, but also claims that we can nonetheless evaluate various identity constructions according to their comparative ability to interpret our experiences, thereby producing reliable knowledge of the world. Many scholars and community organizers became drawn to realism as a theoretical position because it values experience and identity as legitimate social and philosophical issues at home and in anticolonial studies of culture and literature. In 2000, an interdisciplinary group of scholars produced a collection of essays entitled *Reclaiming Identity: Realist Theory and the Predicament of Postmodernism* (edited by Paula Moya and Michael Hames-García) where they elaborate the realist approach to identity and experience in readings of minority and postcolonial literatures and cultures.

In *Reclaiming Identity*, scholars working within a realist framework offer a richly detailed view of knowledge because they redefine objectivity not as an absolute from which inquiry must depart, but rather as an ideal toward which it attempts to move. Recognizing the constructivist claim that our views of literature or the world are unavoidably mediated, realists counteract positivism so that mediation itself undergoes scrutiny as scholars work to evaluate and identify harmful ideology, while acknowledging useful forms of mediation. Realist theorists thus argue that the situatedness of inquiry not only cannot be avoided but also *should* not be avoided—some theoretical dependence might even serve our inquiries.

Michael Hames-García presents this realist notion of *fallibility* in seeking knowledge: "In contrast to the foundationalist approach, postpositivist realism puts us in the world with nothing but our theories to make sense of things. There is thus an element of contingency and uncertainty in a postpositivist realist approach. However, unlike the conceptual-scheme relativism that characterizes some other reactions to positivism, postpositivist realism considers a theory-independent reality to exist and assumes that our theories of the (social) world can help us to understand it and are, to some extent, dependent on it" (2000, 108). A realist theory of knowledge thus holds that social identities, for example, function like theories, processing data as they appear, and, like theories, they are capable of producing normative knowledge of the world. Built on our experiences, our identities are clearly constructed, but the fact that they are theory mediated is not peculiar to identities; in fact, all inquiry—scientific and otherwise—proceeds with inherent historical and social attachments. In this study, then, the theoretical position I draw on relies on this more attainable notion of *theory-mediated objectivity*, in which a value-free social location or a pure subject is no longer a theoretical goal. We now know of its impossibility. Instead, as these realists show, a more reasonable form of objectivity can be pursued by revising the binary of certainty versus uncertainty. Realists account for error—for we do make mistakes and learn from them—by building error into our dialectical inquiries: error converses with objectivity as we move closer to a better understanding of the world.

Realists provide a theoretical trade language for a genuine anticolonial criticism that scholars in American Indian studies might be seeking, especially because this position asserts that international diplomacy and social justice are not goals for which only the colonized or oppressed must work. In her 2002 study, *Learning from Experience*, Paula Moya explains this realist implication that political awareness supports our collective knowledge production: "Realists contend humans' subjective and evaluative judgments are neither fundamentally 'arbitrary' nor merely 'conventional.' Rather, they are based on structures of belief that can be justified (or not) with reference to their own and others' well-being. These judgments and beliefs, thus, have the potential to contribute to objective knowledge about the world" (2002, 16). In American Indian studies, the theoretical availability of either essentialist or trickster conceptions of Native knowledge has kept Indigenous scholars working within a binary leading to cultural ossification or political apathy. Until recently, there have been few convincing philosophical alternatives to these two opposed theoretical positions. As a practical approach to philosophical issues regarding knowledge, culture, identity, and experience, realism holds that such concepts can be constructed but nonetheless capable of producing stable accounts of the world. Identities can be politically and epistemically significant and still not essentialist. The realist model of objectivity thus might provide us with an opportunity to explain in Western philosophical terms the process of knowledge gathering practiced among North American Indigenous peoples. In other words, I find realism a helpful means of articulating and sharing a tribal epistemology. Elaborating this theory to accommodate Indian experience, I develop tribal realism in the following chapters.

The Red Power Novel

Such a theoretical position might help to explain the political emergence of a new tribal national consciousness in Red Power. Writing during this period, N. Scott Momaday, James Welch, and Leslie Marmon Silko adopt what I see as a tribal realist approach to identity, experience, and politics in their novels: the protagonists cannot recover their lands, their pasts, and their lives until they reconnect with the elders, healers, and other members of their communities. In so doing, they undergo a process of remembering and reinterpreting experiences of colonialism and related feelings of self-hatred. Upon achieving a more enabling picture of themselves in the Indian world, they are transformed. American Indians writing during the Indian movement, and those influenced by it, understand the crucial place of tribal knowledge, identity, and experience in the decolonization of Indigenous peoples. Such authors respect the role of identity in explaining the rich realities of Native life—both the everyday stress of colonialist subjugation and the affirmation of Indian stories that engender cultural growth. Red Power writers situate American Indian identity as a concept central to forging knowledge of ancestral lifeways and homelands. In recognizing that the recovery of Native knowledge entails a complex process of interpretation, these authors elucidate just how American Indian people can awaken politically, reclaim a history, and build a community.

This book studies the outpouring of fiction produced during and inspired by Red Power. A full year prior to the 1969 occupation of Alcatraz, Momaday prophetically anticipated this era with *House Made of Dawn*, in which Indians gather under the stars on a mountain above Los Angeles to drum and sing and imagine a new life. From the spray paintings on the walls of Alcatraz to the revolution-inciting folk music of Buffy Saint-Marie, American Indians sought through art a vision of cultural renewal. With its narrative scope and character development, the novel was especially equipped to support this emerging consciousness in Native America. The young and nameless narrator of Welch's *Winter in the Blood*, for example, comes home to heal his wounded knee, a reference to the 1973 defense of the Wounded Knee battleground of the Great Sioux Nation. To express their political and cultural hopes, Indigenous writers opened the European novel, breathed into it an Indian voice, and created not a literary form caught between cultures, but the Red Power novel.

Some critics of Native literature are often curious about the great attraction of American Indian writers to the novel as the chosen form for their creative work, while others have come to question how these writers can implement a nontribal form to represent an authentic Native voice. Of course, this concern regarding the question of authenticity reveals a general desire within the dominant European American culture that Native peoples remain unchanged. I am thus grateful to those theorists who, in studies of the postcolonial novel, have quelled the demand for purity in Indigenous cultures.[22] Critics often study the Native novel as a type of bildungsroman. According to M. H. Abrams, "the subject of these [bildungsroman] novels is the development of the protagonist's mind and character, as he passes from childhood through varied experiences—and usually through a spiritual crisis—into maturity and the recognition of his identity and role in the world" (1971, 113). Any reader of the Red Power novel will recognize in these "novels of formation" that protagonists do invariably face some sort of challenge and experience a spiritual crisis, and, upon its resolution, they better understand themselves and the world. In *Winter in the Blood*, a young and nameless Blackfeet man wanders home, where he investigates his familial and tribal history and discovers his own place in these. Noticing the resemblance of these Red Power narratives to the European "novel of education," critics like Alan Velie and Shamoon Zamir declare that they have discovered the origin of the Native novel, when they overlay European forms on American Indian narratives to show how Indigenous writers imitate the genre.

We might, however, be wary of Eurocentric premises concerning the source of non-Western cultural practices.[23] We must ask why critics assume that American Indians are incapable of inventing and preserving their own literary genres or that their art must be made more sophisticated by borrowing from the colonial culture. I offer a different explanation for the rise of the Red Power novel: in times of crisis, Indigenous people draw on traditional tribal narratives of quest, feat, return, and regeneration. Such Culture Hero stories are ushered out when flood, famine, or war threaten to destroy the people's ways of life. Cherokee people possess story cycles of a young person who, instructed by elders to wander from his troubled community, quests to retrieve new knowledge to solve the crisis and thus remake the world. Susan Scarsberry-García explains how Momaday's novel draws on such life-giving narratives: "Navajo story patterns reveal a hero or heroes (or occasionally heroines as in Mountainway or Beautyway), often 'outsiders' from birth, forced by circumstances to leave home and combat numerous terrifying obstacles that confront them for reasons unknown. After undergoing a symbolic death experience and being reborn through the aid of the Holy People or spirit helpers, the heroes return home to their people to teach the healing ceremonial that remade them" (1990, 8–19). We might better understand the Red Power novel by recognizing that the era's writers explored these Indigenous stories of trial and renewal not only in the novel but also in poetry. Writing during this period, Simon Ortiz tells of his personal, as well as collective, journey to knowledge and rebirth in *Going for the Rain* (1992 [1976]). During desperate times of drought, a person from the pueblo is sent to bring back the rain. Ortiz sees his people facing a similar crisis, only now it is a cultural drought, enforced by a colonialist nation, that threatens to dry up the Indian way of life. Ortiz begins with an old Acoma song:

Let us go again, brother; let us go for the shiwana.
Let us make our prayer songs.
We will go now. Now we are going.
We will bring back the shiwana.
They are coming now. Now, they are coming.
It is flowing. The plants are growing.
Let us go again, brother; let us go for the shiwana. (37)

In at least two significant ways, the Red Power novel tends to differ from the American novel; both ways concern the implementation of Indigenous storytelling practices. First, while the American novel tends to celebrate leaving home to develop one's character, the Native novel often relies on the opposite movement. In the Red Power novel, American Indians have already left home, and their stories begin on their return, a return that marks the actual growth and the collective moment of cultural regeneration. William Bevis even argues that underlying the American novel is a U.S. tradition of escaping family and "lighting out for the territories," an ethic he claims is fueled by the frontier myth of manifest destiny and westward expansion.[24] Whether it is *Huckleberry Finn* or *The Great Gatsby*, the American novel is a special kind of bildungsroman that often bolsters the building of empire, claims Bevis. He explains this distinction: "The Bildungsroman, or story of a young man's personal growth, became in America, especially, the story of a young man or woman leaving home for better opportunities in a newer land" (1987, 581). Most novels written during Red Power, however, exude a yearning to return to the homeland from which protagonists have become estranged. All three central Native novels in this study present young American Indians coming home to their communities after battling with the imperialist world beyond. Their recovery and healing can take place only at home, through a process of self-reflection and reinterpretation of their past and present relationships, among trustworthy members of the tribal community. In fact, according to Bevis, "homing" in the Native novel demonstrates an Indigenous moral value: "In Native American novels, coming home, staying put, contracting, even what we call 'regressing' to a place, a past where one has been before, is not only the primary story, it is a primary mode of knowledge and a primary good" (582).

When American Indians return with their discoveries, they must present this new knowledge to members of the tribal community. Novels responding to Red Power also tend to differ from the American novel in this important respect. As Native storytelling is an intrinsically collective practice, so are the travels of the protagonists interpreted collectively, in the presence of elders, healers, and other listeners. According to Lawrence Evers, tribal peoples practice storytelling to reintegrate the individual with the community and the people with the land: "Through the emergence journey, a collective imaginative endeavor, the Navajos determined who and what they were in relation to the land" (1985a, 212). So many travelers in American novels set out to fulfill an expressly individual quest; their experiences and insights are rarely shared. In the Indian novel, however, those who return from their journeys must offer their new knowledge of a strange world to those who have remained. These travelers are then cleansed and reintegrated. In *Ceremony*, Tayo must tell the medicine person Ku'oosh all he has learned so that Ku'oosh can protect not only Tayo but also the entire community.

Among American Indian people, personal growth is closely tied to the growth of one's tribal community. For this reason, the confused Tayo must reintegrate with his tribal community if he and his community are to awaken politically and decolonize. Returning to the community and continuing to reinterpret his experiences, this wounded and isolated individual ridden with personal guilt is transformed into a moral leader of his people. The community, in turn, devises new ways of contending with colonial loss by reinterpreting its experiences of oppression. In *Ceremony*, as in other Red Power writing, healing and strengthening Indigenous cultural knowledge involves building a community for its production through ongoing emotional and cognitive work. The Red Power novel thus explores how we can decolonize our nations by growing politically and culturally in a process that values the continuity of identity and experience in the production of normative knowledge.

To some extent, the terms we use as scholars cannot help but affect the reception of our ideas, especially over time. While the term "Indian" is an arbitrary term recklessly applied to hundreds of distinct Indigenous peoples when errant Europeans invaded North America, the history of the term "American" is even more interesting. In later accounts of European invasions of the New World, explorers came to call the original inhabitants of the "Americas" "Americans." Inventing the myth of the Vanishing American destined to disappear in the march to civilization, while dispossessing tribal people of lands and resources, by the close of the nineteenth century Europeans finally came to be called the Americans. Today, if we refer to Indigenous people as "First Americans" or "Native Americans," Native peoples appear to be not Indigenous but an immigrated group. In this work, then, I identify a specific tribal people whenever possible, using the name they publicly call themselves, in order not to generalize across often extreme differences.[25] Of course, tribal people do share a land and a history, and certainly a history of conquest. Long before Europeans arrived, Native peoples were traveling the continent, trading goods as well as ideas. For this reason, I also use the terms "Indigenous," "Native," "American Indian," "Indian," and "tribal" interchangeably. With the same caution, I use the terms "European American," "North American," "white American" and "Western" interchangeably. Finally, to abbreviate the United States of America, I use the term "United States" to account for our shared place in this American hemisphere.

This study begins with land, in part 1: "Red Land." In chapter 1, I consider various views of the Indian relationship to homelands. I then provide an alternative approach to "embodying lands," through what I call "somatic place," in a reading of N. Scott Momaday's *House Made of Dawn* (1968). The title of this novel refers to a Navajo healing ceremony meant to reintegrate tribal members as dwellers in the land. Momaday's protagonist, Abel, home from World War II and distanced from his land, cannot recover his tie to homeland until he comes to terms with his own bodily sense of self. Through a process that accommodates the recovery of physical, social, and cultural wellness, Abel reattaches himself to his Native land and puts to rest his inchoate experiences of colonialism.

The second chapter extends this theory of American Indian cultural growth from the individual to the Native community, moving from a consideration of the land to a discussion of tribal historical identifications with land. I begin with an examination in American Indian studies of theories of selfhood, which I find impoverished to account for the ongoing decolonization of Native communities. In a reading of James Welch's *Winter in the Blood* (1974), I present an alternative view of Indigenous "historical identity" to explore how a young Blackfeet man experiences a political awakening and, by "placing the ancestors," recovers his masculinity and cultural identity. Through a process of remembering and reinterpreting colonial experiences of displacement and cultural destruction, Welch's narrator finally grows closer to a land and history from which he has been painfully distanced.

From the ground of part 1, in part 2: "Red Power" I engage the political struggles that grow from and protect Native lands. Chapter 3 opens with a critical assessment of skeptical strains in Native theory, which often undervalue Indian experience. In a discussion of the variety of tribal experiences, I show how American Indian experience, though mediated, can be nonetheless reliable. I explore how a clearly theory-dependent form of personal experience, the emotions, not only can provide knowledge of the tribal social world, but indeed is fundamental to the political awakening and cultural growth that drive anticolonial efforts. In a reading of Leslie Marmon Silko's *Ceremony* (1977), I illustrate how insights gleaned from personal as well as religious experience can produce knowledge of the world that all of us can use, in a process that aids human consciousness.

In "learning to feel," the protagonist Tayo recovers from a war that has damaged his ability to experience the world as a spiritually gifted Laguna man.

The fourth chapter addresses a growing awareness that American Indian cultural and literary theory should be accountable to material social concerns and movements for anticolonial resistance. The chapter begins with a critical analysis of the tradition of historically grounded Native political thought that led to the Red Power movement. So doing, I ask scholars to respond to the political urgency in Native studies by historicizing their work, by "hearing the callout" of subjugated Indians such as Native prisoners. In an analysis of written statements made by the imprisoned Indigenous men I worked with at Auburn prison in western New York, I theorize the place of the oral tradition in political resistance to show how the interaction between prison work and scholarship can be a form of intervention, in an explanation of praxis in Indian studies.

My concluding chapter extends some of the tribal realist claims of the preceding chapters to offer a social vision of Indian Country in the years ahead. In response to the increased cultural interaction in urban and off-reservation communities, contemporary tribal writers have begun to explore in the novel a more expansive account of the social world in Indian Country. In a cluster of readings from more recent Native literature— Sherman Alexie's *Reservation Blues* (1995); Betty Louise Bell's *Faces in the Moon* (1994); Robert Conley's *War Woman* (1997); Janet Campbell Hale's *Jailing of Cecelia Capture* (1985); Irvin Morris's *From the Glittering World* (2000); Greg Sarris's *Watermelon Nights* (1998); Leslie Marmon Silko's *Almanac of the Dead* (1991); Gerald Vizenor's *Bearheart* (1978); James Welch's *Heartsong of Charging Elk* (2000); Craig Womack's *Drowning in Fire* (2001); and Ray Young Bear's *Remnants of the First Earth* (1996)—I consider how the social categories of class, gender, and sexuality complicate and enrich our vision of Indian lives. This final chapter argues for a more comprehensive account of tribal social experience as a goal of normative cultural knowledge.

The title of this book came to me while sitting for hours in the mid-summer sun of Oklahoma. From our clan arbor, I looked out on the ceremonial grounds and suddenly realized that tribal knowledge grows from the land and the people, and the people meet to renew this relationship. In the dances, the songs, the fire, the medicine, tribal knowledge changes yet endures. I approach the history, culture, and writing of the Indian movement with the above issues and inspirations in mind. I believe literature can represent reality, and, so doing, gives us a place in which to imagine what kind of social vision it would take for Indian Country to flourish. Though I offer here my own best attempt to organize a Native view of knowledge to support that vision, such work must be not an individual but rather a collective process. So I ask other scholars, students, and community organizers in Native America and beyond to challenge each other and work together to build from the ground up a theory of intellectual and national liberation. From this exploration of the Red Power novel, I hope to craft and share a few practical tools to serve and defend American Indian life and art.

PART I. RED LAND

1

||||||||||||||||||||||||||||||||||||||||||||||||||||||||||||||||||||||||||

EMBODYING LANDS: SOMATIC PLACE IN

N. SCOTT MOMADAY'S *HOUSE MADE OF DAWN*

By making Alcatraz an experimental Indian center operated and planned by Indian people, we would be given a chance to see what we could do toward developing answers to modern social problems. Ancient tribalism can be incorporated with modern technology in an urban setting. Perhaps we would not succeed in the effort, but the Government is spending billions every year and still the situation is rapidly growing worse. It just seems to a lot of Indians that this continent was a lot better off when we were running it.

—**Vine Deloria Jr.,** March 1970

You can forget about everything up there. We could see all the lights down below, a million lights, I guess, and all the cars moving around, so small and slow and far away. We could see one whole side of the city, all the way to the water, but we couldn't hear anything down there. All we could hear was the drums and singing. There were some stars, and it was like we were way out in the desert someplace and there was a squaw dance or a sing going on, and everybody was getting good and drunk and happy.

—**Ben Benally,** in *House Made of Dawn*

This book grew out of my own experience of being displaced from my ancestral homeland. I am a Cherokee Indian from Appalachia, even though I was an adult when I first saw the old Cherokee lands east of the Mississippi. To say I am from a place where as a young person

I had never been might confuse some readers, and it might even invite criticism. Many Indigenous people, however, understand themselves and their attachment to land through tribal stories about the history of that land, contained in the oral tradition. Listeners come to understand such stories in the context of many other related stories; such narratives of self, nation, and homeland are the inspiration for this book. I grew up in a large, low-income family, and I was the first ever to attend college. When I left for the east to enter graduate school, I found myself on the exciting yet fearful edge of a transformation in myself as an intellectual and as an Indian. I departed from the only Cherokee community I knew—that of my relatives in Oklahoma—to return for the first time to our ancestral homeland in the Smoky Mountains, and finally to set eyes on the holy places that I knew only from stories. Wondrous supernatural beings and their exploits—which took place on the very ground beneath me—began to live for me. These stories had kept our culture alive even after we suffered "removal" from these lands on which we had lived for centuries. In 1838, the United States dispossessed Cherokees of their land in the Southeast and marched them to present-day Oklahoma. It was a bitter trek and it took at least a fourth of the lives of our tribe. Upon arrival, Cherokees began to form a relationship with this strange land and to rebuild their community of social relations through their oral tradition. By recounting the tribal histories and legends that occurred on the peaks of certain mountains and at the banks of well-known rivers, and by creating new narratives of new lands, Cherokee elders provided the people with a moral and spiritual education. This is how the oral tradition continues to bind Natives to landscapes they have inhabited for centuries.

When I first set foot in the Smokies, I was startled by my sudden sense of outrage at the injustice of being restricted from our ancestral home, for I realized that without our lands it becomes difficult to hold the body of knowledge we use to maintain our cultural identity. In an odd mixture of anger and joy, I discovered that we had truly been kept from our motherland, its verbal art, its narrative history. From this awakening to Indigenous exile, I sought to understand the connection between identity and geography, and to explain how political awareness aids in the recovery of this connection. In those Cherokee lands, I began a long process to recover a relationship with the very earth to which our oral tradition refers, because I was now better able to attach the stories to the land. In theoretical terms, my new understanding of place and self was neither a given always waiting for me to uncover (as essentialist scholars tend to hold) nor merely invented and thus arbitrary (as skeptical theorists often claim). Rather, in tribal realist terms I began to discover a deeper sense of myself by reinterpreting my experiences of American Indian displacement and subjugation in the new yet ancient story-laden land. In the following chapters, I examine this process of cultural identification with tribal lands and its attendant claims. Part 1 of this book thus begins with "Red Land" to consider a central social construction in Native thought: that Indigenous people, by definition, grow from the land, and that everything else—identity, history, culture—stems from that primary relationship with homelands. In this chapter, I consider how the interactive components of oral tradition and bodily wellness mediate an ethical relationship with American Indian lands in N. Scott Momaday's *House Made of Dawn*. In the next chapter, I extend this understanding of Native geography to explain the interpretive connection between Indian land and identity in the context of community and memory in James Welch's *Winter in the Blood*.

In 1969 N. Scott Momaday stood on the shores of Alcatraz Island. Though the author has always officially kept politics away from art, his novel *House Made of Dawn* gathers its greatest energy in portrayals such as that offered in the epigraph above, when Indians from various tribes drum, sing, and pray in the hills above Los Angeles. It is a scene surprisingly reminiscent of the Alcatraz occupation and the spirit of Red Power, in which Native people across Indian Country gathered to revalue their cultures and emerge politically. When *House Made of Dawn* won the Pulitzer Prize in 1969, some critics announced that American Indian literature had finally matured—that is, it finally reflected literary merits recognizable to U.S. mainstream culture. Winning this prize in 1969 (the same publication year of Vine Deloria's *Custer Died for Your Sins* and Alfonso Ortiz's *The Tewa World*), *House Made of Dawn* declares a beginning for the political awakening and cultural revival that was to characterize the era of Red Power. I thus begin this study by opening Momaday's fine novel, as a founding emblem of Red Power and the Red Power novel. In recent years, Momaday has been rebuked for his purported essentialism regarding Indigenous land and identity, but I show that Momaday's first work is demonstrably not essentialist. Instead, *House Made of Dawn* labors with the recovery of identity and culture, all through the struggle to know one's homeland. In its recognition of the need for a secure place in which to conduct this discovery of land and identity, the novel is consonant with the era, as well as with other voices of Red Power, such as Deloria's in the epigraph above. Considering this concern for essentialism in Momaday's work, I preface my reading of *House Made of Dawn* to discuss Indigenous peoples' cultural attachments to lands, which can find stable ground in the oral tradition.

Oral Traditional Homelands

In the preceding pages, I have been sharing my account of the loss of Cherokee cultural geography and the process for its recovery, which relies on the evaluation of experiences as they shape self-understanding. In that first visit to the Southeast, I soon discovered that to decolonize our lands we must first decolonize our identities. Since land, identity, and experience are inextricably linked sources of knowledge, the political struggle to decolonize Native America also bears close yet subtle ties to cultural identity: the deeper understanding of oneself as a colonized Indigenous person, dispossessed and displaced from ancestral lands, brings greater clarity to one's often vague experiences of oppression. In other words, the political is continuous with the epistemological. The recovery of ancestral places is thus, in part, a process of identification with lands. For this reason, the political defensibility of American Indians' relationship to the earth depends on the clarity of theories about individual and collective tribal selves. A clear understanding of Native identity thus explains the relationship to homelands, and, interactively, the land shapes American Indian self-understanding. Through this mutually constituting dynamic of land and identity, Indian people build what is often called a sense of place. Because Native cultural identity organizes experiences of homelands, dispossession, and exile, American Indian studies requires a thoroughgoing account of the constructed yet legitimate status of Native cultural geography. To support an Indian geopolitics, I propose a philosophically grounded approach to land and selfhood that I call geoidentity. Clearly, Native concepts of land, identity, and experience prove vital to Indian livelihood. In the next chapter, I focus on the concept of American Indian identity, and in chapter 3 I address tribal experience, but here I wish to introduce the interweaving of land, identity, and experience in the preservation of Indian culture.

Valuing such concepts, American Indian scholars are often reminded, and are thus well aware, of the problems with essentialist approaches to Native culture and lands. One obvious but rather prevalent use of essentialism has to do with genetics as a source of encoded tribal knowledge of homelands. One's blood, it is claimed, leads one back to one's land

and people.[1] To Indigenous scholars with essentialist leanings, biology not only determines whether one is a Native person but also how one develops socially, morally, and geographically. In Native studies, cultural critics such as Arnold Krupat and Elvira Pulitano object not only to the clearly racialist entanglements of such theories of biological essence,[2] metaphorical or otherwise, but likely also to the analysis of American Indian placemaking that these views preclude. From this view, the relationship to lands can neither be examined nor developed, for it is believed to be given in advance, timeless and unchanging, and hence cannot be questioned. Perhaps underlying this critique of the uncritical identification with homelands is the worry among theorists of the postcolonial[3] that strong attachments to lands contribute to a destructive form of nationalism, in which the idea of homeland relies on the absolute conception of territory as the destined extension of a people.[4]

In her essay in *The Remembered Earth*, Paula Gunn Allen appears to express an essentialist view of American Indian cultural geography. She begins by stating, "We are the land. To the best of my understanding, that is the fundamental idea embedded in Native American life and culture in the Southwest. More than remembered, the Earth is the mind of the people as we are the mind of the earth. The land is not really the place (separate from ourselves) where we act out the drama of our isolated destinies. It is not a means of survival, a setting for our affairs, a resource on which we draw in order to keep our own act functioning. It is not the ever-present 'Other' which supplies us with a sense of 'I.' It is rather a part of our being, dynamic, significant, real" (1979, 191). Allen explains the Native attachment to the land as an almost mathematical equivalence rather than a mere affinity. In these terms, tribal people and the land are interchangeable homogeneous components of an organic whole. The distinction of American Indians from the land is an illusion, because Native people, Allen explains, are inseparable from the land. Allen accounts for the relationship of American Indians to homelands in these mystified terms that cannot be questioned. We, in fact, must accept her claim on terms of religious belief. Like faith in a deity, a strictly spiritual explanation of Indigenousness can either be accepted as truth or dismissed as superstition, but it cannot be examined. For this reason, Westerners have largely departed from ontology in philosophy, leaving the study of religion to the theologians—though this schism has no doubt diminished the moral understanding of human existence. When offered such nonphysical, tribal accounts of American Indian lands, scholars working within a

European tradition that rejects metaphysical knowledge are likely to *toler-ate* but not to seriously consider these explanations. To demystify Allen's approach to Native homelands, we might remember that, while the bones of our families form the earth under our feet, it is the stories of their lives that inform the land.

Allen's statement poses a critical problem to Native scholars theoriz-ing place: How do we explain the Indigenous relationship with the land without appealing to spiritual concepts, which are often mystified yet fun-damental to that relationship? Later in her essay, she begins to explain Native geography in social terms, thus shifting her holistic view of land to the place of humans, where she considers how Native writers suffer the pain of dislocation and await the recovery of homelands. In so doing, Allen recognizes that Native identification with lands can be wounded and "lost," remembered and regained. And if it can be regained, it can be ex-plained. Of Navajo writer Larry Emerson's short story "Gallup" she claims: "The protagonist, lost on a Saturday in Gallup, alienated from himself, his people and his family, still can remember what was good about being, can wonder at its disappearance" (1979, 192). Allen thus migrates toward an admittedly underexamined, though finally nonessentialist, theory of American Indian dwelling as a conscious social practice. Jace Weaver understands this need to resist essentialist or romantic explanations of American Indians' connections to the natural world: "One strain of this stereotype of Natives as 'environmental perfectionists' holds that they did not *use* the land, existing on it as in some ecological stasis box and leaving no tracks or traces of their presence. This seemingly affirmative, if highly romantic, vision in reality contributes to the exploitation of Natives and their land. It denies Indian personhood and erases Natives from the landscape where they lived for countless generations before the advent of European invaders" (1996, 4). After all, since invasion, Europeans have justified on essentialist footing their very presence on Native lands, from the Puritans' idea of the preordained City on the Hill to the metaphysics of manifest destiny in the nineteenth century.[5] In their potential also to serve empire, essentialist explanations of the human place in North American land should be tempered with a more self-examining, and thus politi-cally enabling, theory of American Indian dwelling. On a realist theory of Indigenous place, American Indians critically construct, evaluate, and improve their relationship with the land through and for tribal identity. Linguistic anthropologist Keith Basso asserts that "place-making is . . . a form of cultural activity" (1996, 7). In this profoundly social sense, selfhood is continuous with homeland.

Of course, Native sense of place is also imbricated with other crucial cultural conceptions such as history and morality, and other practices to sustain cultural knowledge. As I have described, this vital relationship to the land is maintained in oral tradition through language, the medium by which tribal peoples recall and interpret significant events on the land to serve an ethical theory. In this way, Native sacred sites are such not only because ancient cultural events transpired on them, but also because stories of those places continue to guide moral behavior and sustain culture. The cultural construction that is sense of place demands work of the imagination to recall exactly how a tribal event took place and to interpret the story to answer today's ethical questions.[6] This is a process Basso calls "world-building" (1996, 5). But in creating a past mediated through earth, experience, and story, this oral dynamic should not be treated, as by Indian trickster critics, as a "fiction of the colonial mind" as Louis Owens describes it (1998, 27), or as nonterritorial "transmotion" in the words of Gerald Vizenor (1998, 182). Native relationships with the land are not illegitimately fabricated because geoidentity operates in reference to a reality composed of material facts. If this were not the case, senses of place would be insignificant and interchangeable; instead, the materiality of the land itself often determines the realm of possibilities for a homeland, as a community adheres to the distinct ecological character of a region over time. Indeed, the very fact of the land—its particular features and rhythms— shape a tribe over millennia into a specific people with a cultural tradition created in response to unique topography.[7] Basso describes this process thus: "For Indian men and women, the past lies embedded in features of the earth—in canyons and lakes, mountains and arroyos, rocks and vacant fields—which together endow their lands with multiple forms of significance that reach into their lives and shape the ways they think. Knowledge of places is therefore closely linked to knowledge of the self, to grasping one's position in the larger scheme of things, including one's own community, and to securing a confident sense of who one is as a person" (1996, 34).

Language, the vehicle for Native places, sustains and communicates ideas through oral tradition, a flexible collection of stories to explain one's relationship to the land. It is nothing less than the corpus of communal knowledge through which ideas are introduced and evaluated, accepted or rejected, and replaced or refined on their ability to order the world. In managing this open-ended hermeneutic, storytelling cultures offer new, revised accounts of events tied to places, and thus maintain a center of historical and moral value. Regulated through the normative lens of oral tradition, American Indian attachments to land are continually shaped yet stable. In "Through the Stories We Hear Who We Are," Leslie Marmon Silko explains how her Laguna people "depended upon collective memory through successive generations to maintain and transmit an entire culture, a worldview complete with proven strategies for survival. The oral narrative, or story, became the medium through which the complex of Pueblo knowledge and belief was maintained. Whatever the event or the subject, the ancient people perceived the world and themselves within that world as part of an ancient, continuous story composed of innumerable bundles of other stories. . . . The myth, the web of memories and ideas that create an identity, is part of oneself. This sense of identity was intimately linked with the surrounding terrain, to the landscape that has often played a significant role in a story or in the outcome of a conflict" (1996a, 30–31, 43). Because oral tradition acts as a communal tool for the democratic interpretation of tribal knowledge, its function is highly social in maintaining a people's collective attachment to a place.

Through this reciprocal relationship with the earth, one knows one's homeland by recalling some of the countless stories that took place on that land's specific topographical features: on the peaks, in the hollows, at the banks of streams, within the whirlpools. Indigenous people maintain their social world by pointing to significant places and recalling (often word for word) the legendary and historical events held secure in the tribal imagination. Storytellers are the elected keepers of a group's oral tradition, for they are especially adept at reconstructing a narrative world where stories reduce the distance between the individual and the community, and between the community of today and that of ancient times.[8] Barry Lopez explains this function as the creation of an "interior landscape": the imagined response to the story-laden landscape, the internalized place world of the mind (1984, 51). The storyteller fulfills her or his responsibility by realigning tribal members' interior landscapes with the geography on which they daily interact. Most important, Indian people value story to convey and sustain a moral universe and to preserve a cultural identity. For this critical reason, tribal peoples must dwell within the edifying features of their ancestral geography. Denied their homelands, they risk disintegration. To displace Native people to unknown lands is thus an attempt to destroy them—to "obliterate all aspects of their moral relationship with the land," as Basso puts it (1996, 67). Because American Indian placemaking practices are socially constructed, however, they can be reconstructed, regained in the wake of colonial displacement, through the very process described in *House Made of Dawn*.

Bodily Homelands in *House Made of Dawn*

Momaday counters essentialist land views by chronicling the process through which American Indians can recover their relationship to their homelands. The hero in *House Made of Dawn*, Abel, does not innately "sense" a spiritual connection to lands he barely remembers.[9] He makes no romantic return to the lands of his ancestors, and he is not mystically held there by the spiritual power of the land upon his Indian biology. Instead, the protagonist struggles with the excruciating problem of being a stranger in his own land. Abel works very hard to relearn a lost attachment to his place of origin, the Pueblo community of Walatowa. In the final paragraph of this cyclic narrative, we return to Abel trying to know his homeland. He is running on the land with the dawn, but only with a great deal of physical, emotional, and spiritual effort, precariously "reeling on the edge of the void" (104): "He was running and his body cracked open with pain, and he was running on. . . . He was running and a cold sweat broke out upon him and his breath heaved with the pain of running. His legs buckled and he fell in the snow. The rain fell around him in the snow and he saw his broken hands, how the rain made streaks upon them and dripped soot upon the snow. And he got up and ran on. He was alone and running on" (211–12). *House Made of Dawn* opens and closes with Abel running the ceremonial race over tribal lands at dawn, on the morning of the death of his grandfather Francisco. His participation in this event marks in him the ancestral descent of Pueblo traditional knowledge. Finally accepting this challenge, Abel strips to the waist, smears his chest with ash, and attempts to move with the land. Like the land itself, Abel "cracks open" and is "running" as the rain runs down his broken hands, streaking and dripping the ashes of his landmarked body into the very earth, reintegrating him with the universe, as he regains what I call his "somatic place." Abel's fall and will to rise, to continue the race, suggest that he holds a commitment to begin the onerous yet indispensable task of coming to know the land and his role in it. He will sometimes fail, but in locating and evaluating his errors in theorizing place, he will develop a more complete and thus more normative way of knowing the land, in tribal realist terms. He will recover his place in the Walatowa homeland.

Through Abel's less than noble behavior, Momaday subverts the reader's desire to romanticize American Indians as noble savages now vanishing. Most critics refuse to recognize that the protagonist, although he suffers the brutality of a conquering nation, is not altogether a likeable character.[10] Abel returns from World War II, a war to defend his own enemies, but does not undergo the ritual cleansing of warriors used in Pueblo tradition to deactivate the power to kill. Abel spends several years in the dehumanizing U.S. prison system; Abel is an alcoholic. For these reasons he is socially ill, and so mistreats even those who care for him. In Los Angeles, his Navajo friend Ben Benally notices that Abel is cruel and sexist regarding his social worker Milly: "I felt kind of funny when she was dressed like that, and, you know, he would make jokes and say things about her sometimes, and I laughed all right, but I didn't like it much, because I thought a lot of her and she was good to us" (163). And later, regarding Abel's experience with a lover, Angela, Ben objects to Abel's show of disrespect: "I was kind of mad because he was going on like that, bragging and joking about some white woman" (177).

As a perhaps unwilling representative of Indigenous culture, Momaday has the courage to create a very human though less than sympathetic character whose actions risk reinforcing the disapproving stereotype in the colonialist dichotomy, that of the ignoble savage (Berkhofer 1979, 23–24). Ultimately, Abel's complex development refutes both popular assumptions of savage nobility or ignobility and so helps compose a text given to literary realism. Larry Landrum notes how such realistic tendencies in *House Made of Dawn* work as a "cultural strategy" to undermine both romantic and modernist forms: "The fragmentary doubling of Indian cultural material on modernist discourses and imagery tends to break down Romantic irony and problematize the conceit of mythic universality and timelessness underlying modernist consciousness" (1996, 777). Disagreeing with Elizabeth Cook-Lynn and her portrayal of the novel's anticolonial force, Alan Velie finds the work "highly romantic for a novel," because of its "lyrical" and "idyllic" portrait of reservation living (1997, 176). But Cook-Lynn heralds the novel as a nonromantic text because of its potential to enable political awakening through a nonessentialist representation of Native life: "It is considered a classic because it is a work that explores traditional values, revealing truth and falsity about those values from a framework of *tribal realism*. It is diametrically opposed to fantasy, which often evades or suppresses moral issues" (1996b, 72). In its ability to subvert Western discourses in both form and content, *House Made of Dawn* encourages a reading that engages philosophically American Indian attachments to homelands.

In this story of dwelling, Abel and other American Indians struggle to know a land from which they have been physically and psychically removed. Abel as well as others "theorize" ways of relating to Indigenous lands; Abel fails again and again until eventually, through social engagement and social practice, through the instruction of his grandfather and others, he learns the way to his land. "The way" to Walatowa is a process similar to that offered in Momaday's subsequent work, *The Way to Rainy Mountain*. The narrator recovers a homeland through accessing a variety of sources: anthropology, tribal oral tradition, familial stories. Like the author himself, as well as his parodic embodiment Tosamah, Abel seeks instruction in finding a way home and a method for recovering his sense of place from not only his tribal elders but also other Indigenous people who share a similar desire. Even well-meaning but ineffective non-Native people, Father Olguin and Milly the social worker, try to help Abel "adjust." Though many attempt to show Abel how to return, ultimately it is he who must begin the physical, bodily act of discovering his way home— in running the race at dawn. Through a complex process of returning both in memory and in reality to tribal landmarks—stories of himself and his people that take place in significant places in his homeland— Abel reconceives his place in the land and reconstructs a relationship with his homelands that is more suitable, not because Indians belong on "the reservation" in any essentialist way, but because his new knowledge of the land better informs his own experiences and his place in his tribe. Abel thus heals his attachment to home not by satisfying the essential spiritual demands of his own Indianness but by following a discernable process to compose a more substantive view of himself in relation to his ancestral place.

The power of language to create a world mediates between American Indians and the land. Momaday makes this point throughout his essays and interviews and clearly holds imagination and language as central tools to sustain and recover Indigenous cultures. *House Made of Dawn* demonstrates the irreplaceable role of language in the lives of American Indians. Abel labors to regain his voice, without which he cannot explain himself in relation to his land; Abel is not "dumb" but "inarticulate," for within the Native ability to speak is the ability to reflect, to evaluate one's past and actions, and then to act purposefully according to the knowledge this reflection creates. Language grants rational agency.[11] Without this ability to possess a history, Abel cannot grow. Abel's illness is not, however, merely one of social adjustment but rather it is existential—for if he cannot reclaim his tie to his homeland, he fails to exist fully as an Indian. The central problem of language in *House Made of Dawn*, then, has drawn critics such as Marilyn Nelson Waniek to explain Abel's predicament as a linguistic sickness (1980, 23). Momaday structures his novel to present the absence of Abel's voice; each of the four parts of the modernist text gives utterance to those who know the protagonist while Abel scarcely speaks. Shifting between places and events, he merely relates his often random and confused thoughts.

Because of the problematic place of language in *House Made of Dawn*, critics of the novel are divided on the question of whether Abel ever speaks, recovers his language, and articulates his place in his homeland. Robert Nelson (1993) holds that because Abel never sings aloud, he is still without language and hence still ill. As Momaday writes at the novel's conclusion: "He was running, and under his breath he began to sing. There was no sound, and he had no voice; he had only the words of a song. And he went running on the rise of the song. *House made of pollen, house made of dawn. Qtsedaba*" (212). According to Nelson, Abel has not been healed; he has not grown (89). Karl Kroeber seems to understand Abel's silence as the inescapable aphasia of an uprooted Kiowa author, himself seeking a tribal voice: "Momaday's personal displacements thus echo those of his people, and one is tempted to read the protagonist of his novel as echoing Momaday's own difficulties in establishing his Indian identity" (1993, 17). On the other hand, Lawrence Evers affirms the work of linguistic anthropologists who recognize the generative quality of language among tribal peoples to restore order and bring harmony to a person or people. Evers explains the linkages between "the native American's relations to land and his regard for language" to argue that Abel recovers his voice, his tie to the land, and is thus restored to order: "Here at last he has a voice, words and a song. In beauty he has begun" (1985a, 212, 227).

In its sophisticated view of tribal relationships to the North American earth, *House Made of Dawn* asks readers to struggle, as Native characters struggle, with the "distance" between language and land.[12] Though Abel recalls an oral tradition, he is still unable to announce the stories of his people's origin, an act that would reground him in Walatowa. Many critics

of this difficult novel underread the psychic severity of Abel's physical dislocation from his homeland: displacement is suffered and healed—mediated—through the body in its motion with the land. Abel's challenge is
to reembody his Native voice. John Big Bluff Tosamah and Ben Benally,
the other displaced American Indians in Los Angeles, are able to speak
of home, verbosely so. Tosamah retells the origin and migration story of
the Kiowa people, and Ben sings his Navajo prayers to the land in near
silence, sharing them with Abel. Yet both remain unfulfilled, misled, and
somehow out of place. For such reasons they deride or admire Abel for
his woeful bodily belonging to homelands. Momaday's novel is in part a
comparative study of belonging to lands, a study that clearly foregrounds
Abel as a tribal person bearing a profound physical as well as linguistic
desire to reconnect with the land. Abel's illness strikes at a level deeper
than language: only when his body is in tune with the land can he sing and
thus be home.

This is not a numinous explanation of Indigenous geography, though
it demands a belief in the creative force of embodied language: one must
imagine the deep connection between the self and the land. American
Indian somatic place is maintained in a social practice that perpetually reintegrates bodies with the world through ceremonial movement attuned
to the rhythms of the tribal universe. Momaday describes the centrality
of the novel's ritual race at dawn: "I see [it] as a circle. It ends where it
begins and it's informed with a kind of thread that runs through it and
holds everything together. The book itself is a race. It focuses upon the
race, that is the thing that does hold it all together" (1973, 33). Structured
by the ritual physical act of running, in a race with no beginning or end,[13]
House Made of Dawn describes a ceremony: a process of recovery in which
Natives, through running, dancing, and singing, retune their bodies and
voices to their tribal lands, and in so doing regain their sense of place.
Few critics, however, have recognized the structural and substantive importance of ceremonial bodily movement to the novel. To my knowledge,
only Paula Gunn Allen has confronted the importance of motion in the
novel; Abel's violence is an act of "stopped movement," his healing a restoring of "balanced motion with what moves" (1992, 149). Allen, however, is unclear about Abel's recovery of sense of place, appealing to essentialist claims regarding temporality. I find Abel heals not because he
has achieved "achronicity" in motion to stave off colonial time, as Allen
argues, but rather because he has recovered a more tribally normative way

to relate to his homeland. In the end, Abel heals because he has resitu-
ated his body as an interactive component with the sentient land, now an
ordered part of the Jemez earth.

To dramatize this process, *House Made of Dawn* celebrates the dignity
of the living world and its concomitant personhood.[14] Abel's grandfather,
Francisco, grounds the novel with his traditional insight. He is a true
"longhair" of the section bearing this name, of the pueblo whose steadfast
ways resist the colonialist erosion of Walatowa culture. As he, feeble yet
graceful, ambles through the town, he remembers the function of ceremony to reaffirm the interrelatedness of all life: "And the old man had
an ethnic, planter's love of harvests and of rain. And just there on the
obsidian sky, extending out and across the eastern slope of the plain, was
a sheer and perfect arc of brilliant colors. It made him glad to be in the
midst of talk and celebration, to savor the rich relief of the coming rain
upon the rows of beans and chilies and corn, to see the return of weather,
of trade and reunion upon the town. He tossed his head in greeting to the
shy Navajo children who hid among the camps and peered, afraid of his
age and affliction. For they, too, were a harvest, in some intractable sense
the regeneration of his own bone and blood. The Dine, of all people, knew
how to be beautiful" (76). Francisco has an emotional relationship with
the soil because he recognizes its intrinsic personhood. The renowned social geographer Yi-Fu Tuan calls this deeply felt attachment to place "geopiety" (1976, 12). Abel's elder pauses on the day of the Feast of Santiago,
when the pueblo invites their former enemies, the Navajo people, to come
and eat from their homes. In the context of this day to commemorate the
peace that ended the historical raids of food stores, Francisco reaffirms
his love and respect for the land and the radiant interrelatedness of life,
the exchange of gifts, and the balance restored in their giving. Perhaps the
rain comes upon the horizon to ensure the coming harvest. In this passage Francisco describes the beauty of reciprocity, in his visual movement
from the sky to the plain, and then to the people of Walatowa, the human
social context in a far broader scheme of relationship. The sound of the
celebrants' talk mingles with the coming patter of rain, and the colors of
corn, chilies, and clay streets. Weather, trade, and reunion return upon the
town in a cycle of equal exchange; old and young, Pueblo and Dine, share
laughter and trust in the coming food. And then, at the completion of the
old man's arc of creative vision, the bounty of the land mingles with that
of the people, when Francisco declares a reverence for the "regeneration"

of not only human but all life, here embodied in children: "For they, too, were a harvest."

From his angle of vision, Francisco "the longhair" shows that an enriched account of the relationship of humans to the land must begin with respect, an openness to learning from—rather than foisting one's views upon—the land. The etymology of the word "respect"—"to look back"—contains the concept of self-reflection; our critical thinking requires respect in order to consider how our own unexamined ideas about the world might be inaccurate and in need of reevaluation or further development. In an attempt to "see" the land for what it is—more normatively, that is—American Indians practice respect for and reflection on the land's meaning.[15] The novel portrays this problem of seeing oneself clearly in relation to place. Father Olguin is blind in one eye and is always an outsider in Walatowa, while Abel has trouble seeing upon his return from the war. Abel finally heals, and then correctly sees himself in the land: "Pure exhaustion laid hold of his mind, and he could see without having to think" (212).

House Made of Dawn demonstrates how Indigenous people maintain a relationship with the land through the ritual movement within it. In addition to rearticulating the oral tradition to reinvent the world through the human voice, the body must move upon the land in synchrony with its rhythms: ceremonial dances and ritual athletic games are ways of achieving the "perfect" state of motion in accordance with the earth's dynamics. Francisco recalls such a moment, one of his life's glories: "*And the moment came in mid-motion, and he crossed the stick to the heated drum and the heavy heated drum was in his hand and the old man turned—and nothing was lost, nothing; there had been nothing of time lost, no miss in the motion or the mind, only the certain strange fall of the pitch, the deeper swell of the sound on the warm taut head of the drum. It was perfect*" (208). Francisco achieves a moment of immediacy when his mind and body exist in absolute time with the other dancers, the rhythms of the seasons, and the ceremonial calendar. The young drummer achieves a "moment," much like that of the moment in the space-time continuum of quantum physics in which position is a locus of multiple realities. Francisco and the people of Walatowa find "perfection" at the intersection of the land, the living, the dead, and the seasons in synchronized rhythm with each other. "Nothing was lost" in this moment, for all has been understood, accounted for, and incorporated into the whole. The alliterative phrase "no miss in the motion or the mind" clarifies the aesthetic at work in the ceremony, in which beauty is a matter of proper motion in accordance with the earth. Francisco remembers the mystery inherent in the "strange" change in sound, recalling the unexplained and holy regenerative power in the dance, understood in the fertility image of the maternal fullness of the womblike stretched drumhead skin: "the deeper swell of the sound on the warm taut head of the drum."

The dancers perform proper "perfect" motion for the other tribal members, and thus present a model for an aesthetic and moral theory of bodies in place. Various characters in *House Made of Dawn* theorize place in terms of this model, as they evaluate their repeated attempts to live morally as well as beautifully. The Anglos of Walatowa are awkward in this Indigenous place in part because they have not learned the correct theory of motion and, worse, they are unwilling to attend to the land's instruction. Upon her arrival at the pueblo, Angela's world is upside down: "The sky is so blue. It was like water, very still and deep, when I drove through the canyon a while ago" (28). Father Olguin races through town, almost hitting a child, in a cacophony against the harmony of the town: "He felt the whip of momentum pass through him, the enormous weight of motion that fell upon the engine and drove it down on the coils. Then in the ebbing pitch and rock that followed, as the cloud of dust and laughter drew down upon him, he saw the cradle board fixed to the wagon" (73). But the recently returned Abel, though a tribal member, also feels a failure to attune himself to the rhythm of the people and land. In fact, his inability to harmonize physically peaks during the *corre de gaio*, the rooster pull competition, an event that drives him to kill the albino man Juan Reyes Fragua: "When it came Abel's turn, he made a poor showing, full of caution and gesture" (42). Movement on the land, then, is a central social practice that integrates American Indian people morally and aesthetically in homelands, a practice that can be theorized and evaluated, recovered or improved, among tribal peoples. Margaret Astrov explains that motion and movement are so central to Navajo life that the tribal language protects these as spiritual values. Unlike English, which depends largely on the noun, "Navajo is a language of the verb" (1950, 45). An entire volume in Father Berard's *Learning Navaho* is dedicated to words of motion. Astrov also explains the role of motion in the Navajo universe as an element of right action. Dine traditional stories of origins as well as proper codes of social behavior are evaluated in terms of proper movement: "The concept of motion as the organizing theme of Navaho ideology is conspicuous in most of the recorded myths and ceremonies of these people. On motion life depends. The patient is restored by way of ritually directed movement, and the enemy is ceremonially slain by having 'motion' taken away from him" (52).

"Where are you going?" say Jemez people in the traditional greeting. In his essay "The Morality of Indian Hating," Momaday explains the significance of this age-old expression. Like the Navajo people, the Jemez people derive a moral theory from the relationship between language and movement on the earth. The Jemez greeting keeps the people "of a good mind" because words have the power to alter the physical universe (Porter 1992, 18–19). Daily they must go out in the world as healthy bodies moving well on the land. Significantly, more than the dancing and singing of ceremonies, the race at dawn strengthens this ancient linkage among language, motion, morality: "It is a long race, and it is neither won nor lost. It is an expression of the soul in the ancient terms of sheer physical exertion. To watch those runners is to know that they draw with every step some elemental power which resides at the core of the earth and which, for all our civilized ways, is lost upon us who have lost the art of going with the flow of things. In the tempo of that race there is time to ponder morality and demoralization, hungry wolves and falling stars. And there is time to puzzle over that curious and fortuitous question with which the people of Jemez greet each other" (Momaday 1997, 74–75). Having been home for a week, Abel wakes, approaches the canyon, and realizes that he has lost his hold on his people's language; he cannot utter a prayer: "Had he been able to say it, anything of his own language—even the commonplace formula of greeting 'Where are you going'—which had no being beyond sound, no visible substance, would once again have shown him whole to himself" (58). Abel recognizes the mysterious yet real ability of language, with "no visible substance," to bring self-knowledge. He cannot announce the morally locating Jemez greeting. Abel is thus trapped in a linguistic paradox: he lacks both language and location, he is both silenced and displaced; the possession of either speech or place would allow the recovery of the other. But Momaday shows above that the very act of movement, the race at dawn, is also an act of the imagination, one that provides Jemez people a way out of this cyclical paradox. Running on, in accordance with the rhythms of ceremony tied to the land, immersed in the flow of life, one becomes open to new ways of conceiving the moral self in relation to tribe, land, and language.

Abel begins his re-placement in his homeland by remembering a

former, more whole self in relation to family and place. At the first dawn
of his return, he arises sick from drink and climbs a hill to look out over
the land. He recalls seven (a ritual number) moments in his life, each
occurring in significant places laden with cultural meaning. These memories each function as an independent "story" of Abel's development, and
he tries to retell and resituate them through the traditional oral process.
Here, while Abel recounts the stories of his life, the narratives that make
up who he is, he struggles to accommodate the recent tales of leaving
home for a foreign war: "This—everything in advance of his going—he
could remember whole and in detail. It was the recent past, the intervention of days and years without meaning, of awful calm and collision, time
always immediate and confused, that he could not put together in his
mind" (22). On the dawn of his homecoming Abel "wakes" to the problem
of deriving meaning from his experiences on his homeland. Like the land
itself, he remains indolent and indistinct, reluctant to enter the centering
dynamic of memory, place, and knowledge: "In the early morning the
land lay huge and sluggish, discernible only as a whole, with nothing in
relief except its own sheer, brilliant margin as far away as the eye could
see, and beyond that the nothingness of the sky" (10). Abel is linked to
the land here; views of self and land are interdependent in this morning
vista. Abel endeavors to recover knowledge of both himself and the earth,
and thus he begins a process of remembering and relearning to produce
a fuller picture of himself and the homeland, neither "huge and sluggish" nor "discernible as a whole," but a view of himself in the land that
is more meaningful to self and tribe, unlike the nihilistic "nothingness,"
or what the military physicians would call his shellshock. To discern a
fuller understanding of the relation of self to land, Abel meditates on his
childhood with his brother Vidal and with his mother; his encounter with
the witch Nicolas *teah-whau*; the death of Vidal; his young adulthood when
he hunted with Francisco; attending the Buffalo Dance; an early sexual
encounter; and his association with the Eagle Watchers Society. Each of
these seven memory fragments marks a significant stage in the development of Abel as a male tribal member, and each suggests that Abel, like
Francisco, has successfully undergone a ceremonial training that anchors
him to the ancestral land.

In these memories, one notices two repeating and related images that
bring to light the confused process of gathering knowledge for Abel to
re-place himself: the land's mysterious nature and the necessity of right
motion. In each memory fragment, Abel knows the land well but never

completely. Abel trusts the land to cohere and mesh with his view of him-self and his people in their proper movement with their homeland. His clear view of the land ruptures when either the land thwarts meaning or life gets out of tune. At these moments in his past, Abel shrinks from the relation to land he has achieved through tribal ceremony. His early response to the land's propensity to mystify and its potential for arrhyth-mic motion begins an unhealthy relationship to his self and the land, which eventually threatens his destruction. Though Abel struggles at this moment with such ill-boding memories, he still is unable to locate an alternative theory of dwelling that would better accommodate the land's mystery and motion. He will continue to suffer for about seven years, bodily and spiritually, until, broken on the beach in Los Angeles, he finally theorizes a more enabling view of himself in the Walatowa earth.

At the age of five, Abel plays comfortably on the land with his brother Vidal and others until, one spring morning during work in the fields, he and Vidal wander off to the canyon: "Vidal took him to the face of the red mesa and into a narrow box canyon which he had never seen before. The bright red walls were deep, deeper than he could have imagined, and they seemed to close over him. When they came to the end, it was dark and cool as a cave. Once he looked up at the crooked line of the sky and saw that a cloud was passing and its motion seemed to be that of the great leaning walls themselves, and he was afraid and cried" (11). Abel "knew already the motion of the sun and the seasons," but here his understanding of the land fails (and by extension his understanding of himself), for he fears rather than accepts the sublime mystery and power of the land. The land soon overwhelms his imagination when the "crooked line" is eclipsed by an obscure motion that destabilizes his sense of proportion. Abel loses his mother soon after—an event that likely adds to his fear of the inscru-tability of life's movements. Later, Abel associates his encounter with a witch called Nicolas *teah-whau* with a mysterious hole in the earth. The witch "screamed at him some unintelligible curse" (12), and the snake-killer dog barks into this place that seems to hold the mysteries of evil: "Slowly it backed away and crouched, not looking at him, not looking at anything, but listening. Then he heard it, the thing itself. He knew then that it was only the wind, but it was a stranger sound than any he had ever known. And at the same time he saw the hole in the rock where the wind dipped, struck, and rose. It was larger than a rabbit hole and partly concealed by the chokecherry which grew beside it. The moan of the wind grew loud, and it filled him with dread. For the rest of his life it would

be for him the particular sound of anguish" (12). Many tribal groups believe the land's power is so great that it must finally remain a mystery to
humans' limited understanding. Abel cannot live correctly in the land because he fears its finally unknowable power. Abel's "dread" and "anguish"
of the land's inscrutable force haunt him, anticipating his later experience
of the war-torn landscape, where wet leaves and dirt become meaningless
objects: "He reached for something, but he had no notion of what it was;
his hand closed upon earth and the cold, wet leaves" (24). Abel comes to
resent the land's denial of complete meaning, and it is for this reason that
he kills the embodiment of meaningless inertia—the "white man," Juan
Reyes Fragua.

The narrative of *House Made of Dawn* functions to balance opposites,
as Charles Larson notes (1978, 86). Abel's memories of terror in the land
are stabilized with those of moments in places crystalline with beauty
and meaning. Abel remembers when, as a youth one morning in Valle
Grande, he happened upon a male eagle and a female eagle playing catch
with a rattlesnake as they soared high above the canyon: "He had seen a
strange thing, an eagle overhead with its talons closed upon a snake. It
was an awful, holy sight, full of magic and meaning" (14–15). Because the
eagles dance in perfect rhythm with the snake, coasting in midair, they
represent to the young "eagle watcher" proper motion and meaning, the
order of the earth laid bare. The poetic representation of this display of
beauty and perfect motion deserves full quotation here:

> They were golden eagles, a male and a female, in their mating flight.
> They were cavorting, spinning and spiraling on the cold, clear columns
> of air, and they were beautiful. They swooped and hovered, leaning
> on the air, and swung close together, feinting and screaming with de-
> light. The female was full-grown, and the span of her broad wings was
> greater than any man's height. There was a fine flourish to her motion;
> she was deceptively, incredibly fast, and her pivots and wheels were
> wide and full blown. But her great weight was streamlined and per-
> fectly controlled. She carried a rattlesnake; it hung shining from her
> feet, limp and curving out in the trail of her flight. Suddenly her wings
> and tail fanned, catching full on the wind, and for an instant she was
> still, widespread and spectral in the blue, while her mate flared past
> and away, turning around in the distance to look for her. Then she
> began to beat upward at an angle from the rim until she was small in
> the sky, and she let go of the snake. It fell slowly, writhing and rolling,

floating out like a bit of silver thread against the wide backdrop of the land. She held still above, buoyed up on the cold current, her crop and hackles gleaming like copper in the sun. The male swerved and sailed. He was younger than she and a little more than half as large. He was quicker, tighter in his moves. He let the carrion drift by; then suddenly he gathered himself and stooped, sliding down in a blur of motion to the strike. He hit the snake in the head, with not the slightest deflection of his course of speed, cracking its long body like a whip. Then he rolled and swung upward in a great pendulum arc, riding out his momentum. At the top of his glide he let go of the snake in turn, but the female did not go for it. Instead she soared out over the plain, nearly out of sight, like a mote receding into the haze of the far mountain. The male followed, and Abel watched them go, straining to see, saw them veer once, dip and disappear. (17–18)

The role of eagles in American Indian spirituality is well known. Generally speaking, tribal peoples revere these high-flying birds for their ability to transcend to the sky world and to see the living world from the vantage point of the Creator: "The eagle ranges far and wide over the land, farther than any other creature, and all things there are related simply by having existence in the perfect vision of a bird" (57). The eagles play in synchronized motion with time and location, high above and deep below the rim of the canyon, thus suspended in midair yet at direct eye level with Abel's vision. The holy sight marks a locus of different axes in time and space, as if life were moving in concentric spheres set to music. Because Abel descends from the Bahkyush people,[16] who comprise the Eagle Watchers Society, his experience carries great spiritual weight. He interprets it privately for days. Finally, he relates his ecstatic vision to the old Patiestewa of the Society, then says: "I think you had better let me go" (19).

Because of the significance of his vision, Abel is allowed to go with the Society into Valle Grande to honor the eagle. On their journey they stop to camp at story-laden holy places, where they pray and make offerings to the great birds. In this way, the Society moves over the land like the eagles and other nonhuman persons. In prescribed ceremonial motion, they migrate as a community of watchers, in time with the movement of the sun, moon, and stars as they mark the land known for generations among the members of the pueblo.[17] The Eagle Watchers greet a captured eagle, for it too is a person who moves and makes the world: "They gathered around the old eagle and spoke to it, bidding it return with their good will and sorrow to the eagles of the crags" (22). Abel confirms his eagle vision when he successfully captures a beautiful female—but still he moves wrongly in the land when he kills the eagle in secrecy later that evening: "That night, while the others ate by the fire, he stole away to look at the great bird. He drew the sack open; the bird shivered, he thought, and drew itself up. Bound and helpless, his eagle seemed drab and shapeless in the moonlight, too large and ungainly for flight. The sight of it filled him with shame and disgust. He took hold of its throat in the darkness and cut off its breath" (22). Critics of *House Made of Dawn* often write without knowledge of the specifics of ceremonial traditions, and Momaday also deliberately conceals the meaning of ritual practices in order to preserve tribal secrecy. For this reason, writers on the novel are often confused about obscure events enshrouded in witchcraft and the supernatural. Michael Raymond claims that Abel's killing of the eagle displays the protagonist's early antisocial behavior: "He experiences the twentieth-century sense of alienation before ever leaving the pueblo. . . . As an adolescent, Abel unexplainably strangles an eagle he captures during a ceremonial Eagle Watchers Society hunt" (1983, 62). Floyd Watkins claims that "Abel's choking of the eagle is not merely the result of his shame and disgust. It is also ritualistic" (1977, 138). Elsie Clews Parsons, an ethnographer of Pueblo culture and on whose work Momaday draws, confirms the sacrificial role of eagles: "Hopi eagles are killed on a set ceremonial day, offerings of miniature bows, arrows, and 'dolls,' and of food are made to them and they are buried or cast away in a special place, an eagle cemetery" (1939, 187). That Abel kills the eagle alone, away from the fire and the guidance of the Society, suggests that he has broken from the communal involvement in this time-honored practice. It seems Abel believes the bound body of the eagle to be a violation of the eagle's former perfect motion, which he experienced in his vision. Unable to move, the eagle is now meaningless in Abel's eyes, and thus it represents a wrongful transgression of the land's order. In killing the eagle Abel commits the sole yet grave crime of flouting the consent of the Society.

Abel next remembers his grandfather's words: "You ought to have done this and that" (22). In many ways, Francisco is to Abel the voice of tradition, the living embodiment of the ancestors who trust the present generation to ensure the continued flourishing of the people of Walatowa. For Pueblo peoples the tradition of the past is an unavoidable context for the reckoning of present actions: "The people of the town have little need. They do not hanker after progress and have never changed their essential way of life. Their invaders were a long time in conquering them; and now, after four centuries of Christianity, they still pray in Tanoan to the old deities of the earth and sky and make their living from the things that are and have always been within their reach; while in the discrimination of pride they acquire from their conquerors only the luxury of example. They have assumed the names and gestures of their enemies, but have held on to their own, secret souls; and in this there is a resistance and an overcoming, a long outwaiting" (58). Indigenous resistance to colonialism is a subtle and painstaking position through which members of the community have for centuries "assumed" aspects of the dominant culture in order to survive, though all the while the core of culture remains intact—"the essential way of life" maintained through social practice. This portrait of Native resistance discredits mainstream accounts of the colonial relations. Granting its own ultimate penetrability, empire underestimates the tenacity of Indigenous people by assuming that the dominated will eventually tire, submit, and assimilate. In the quotation above, the Pueblo people have gracefully incorporated the ways of their conquerors into their own worldview so that European values and religion must answer to the Walatowa world.[18] On these relations in *House Made of Dawn*, Bernard Selinger concludes that the entire novel is "infected by hybridity" (1999, 57). Like all cultures, Native cultures have never been pure. Selinger, however, sets a separate standard for Natives to insist that cultural change indicates cultural infection. Such critics, in the end, rely on an undisclosed desire for an Indian essence. Rather than becoming "confused" by their contact with other cultures, American Indians, like other groups, incorporate what they find useful to maintain a normative notion of identity and belief.

Abel peaks in his disruption when he slays Juan Reyes Fragua, "the albino." On the Feast of Santiago, a day the town celebrates the tale of a rooster whose sacrifice brought forth food for all the Pueblo people, Abel agrees to compete in the "rooster pull" with Fragua, in which horseback riders pull from the ground a rooster buried to the neck. Fragua beats Abel to the rooster, snatches it up, and with it flails Abel before the onlooking crowd. In this act Fragua is ungraceful and rude, as if he does not possess the ability of correct motion: "The white man leaned and struck, back and forth, with only the mute malice of the act itself, careless, undetermined, almost composed in some final, preeminent sense" (44). Fragua violates custom by humiliating his opponent in a self-aggrandizing display of "careless" motion. In the midst of his struggle to recover proper movement, Abel finds Fragua's behavior intolerable.

Days later, the drunk men face off in a bar and talk surreptitiously: "The two spoke low to each other, carefully, as if the meaning of what they said was strange and infallible" (81). Abel is thwarted again in his desire for meaning; here, Fragua embodies a void between language and the land. They then leave in the rain to fight in the sand dunes across the highway, where Abel kills Fragua. The cloudy event unfolds in Christian imagery that some critics consider to be sexual:[19] "The white man raised his arms, as if to embrace him, and came forward. But Abel had already taken hold of the knife, and he drew it. He leaned inside the white man's arms and drove the blade up under the bones of the breast and across. The white man's hands lay on Abel's shoulders, and for a moment the white man stood very still. . . . The white hands still lay upon him as if in benediction, and the awful gaze of the head, still fixed upon something beyond and behind him" (82–83). Abel's bizarre killing of Fragua concerns many critics because it is perhaps the least comprehensible event in *House Made of Dawn*, but is usually read as a colonial allegory of Native and white interaction.[20] Indeed, one cannot resist the implications of a "white man" locking Abel in a deadly Christian embrace. Evers notices an allusion to the white whale of *Moby Dick*: "As the whiteness of the whale does to Ishmael, it suggests an emptiness in the universe, a total void of meaning" (1985a, 220). The mystical ambiguity of Juan Reyes Fragua, who is a member of the pueblo yet also is estranged for his physical strangeness (albino people are prevalent at Jemez and are said to be regarded with suspicion), clearly codes him as a potentially evil presence. Father Olguin, Benally, and Tosamah are convinced Fragua is a witch—a *sawah*, in the fading words of Francisco. But in his halting movements described above, foretold in his speech of "strange meaning" in the bar, "the albino" is likely evil because he also bears the threat of chaotic motion, stopped rhythm in a land predicated literally on synchrony. Like the haunting hole and the shaming bound eagle of Abel's youth, Fragua dishonors right motion in the Pueblo world. Abel's deliberate motion contrasts with the jerking, diffuse groping of Fragua. And so Abel kills the man because he finds in him the aberration of meaningless motion, language, and land.

The murder often bewilders and even frustrates readers because it cannot be understood without some knowledge of the supernatural in Pueblo culture. In his arcane representation of the killing, Momaday leads mainstream readers to confront Indian culture on its own terms. Remembering his trial, Abel recalls his reason for murdering Fragua: "For he would know what the white man was, and he would kill him if he could.

A man kills such an enemy if he can" (102–3). Abel believes he has found evil in the "white man" and so decides to destroy this malevolent force. Like his killing of the eagle, however, this is also a crime of individuality: again, Abel acts without the consent of the community. In this regard the albino has succeeded in his witchcraft, for he has made Abel transgress the moral code of his culture. In his evil "benediction" the "white man" has evoked the "whiteness" in Abel so that he, like the albino, acts unethically. Abel's acontextual movements also prove meaningless. Evers notes that the murder takes place in the midst of the celebration of Porcingula, the patroness of Walatowa, an event through which the townspeople ritually expel various forms of oppression; Abel could have confronted the community with his fears of witchery at this time, but "separated from that community, he acts individually against evil and kills the white man" (1985a, 221). In the years before his return, Abel suffers without an answer to the moral question of how to maintain a meaningful relationship between himself and the land. He comes to learn that he should not attempt to destroy individualistically that which denies meaning, but should instead confront negative forces within the interpretive context of the tribal community.

Abel at first cannot practice this traditional Pueblo philosophy because he has drifted from the cultural center of life and value in Walatowa. Abel's grandfather Francisco still moves gracefully, aware of his place in the world, as he works the corn and contemplates the problem of interpreting the past and his place in tradition: "All day his mind had wandered over the past, habitually, beyond control and even the least notion of control, but his thoughts had been by some slight strand of attention anchored to his work" (65). In the pueblo, thought and action, motion and meaning, interact and function as a balanced way of being. Tradition holds that even evil, though it must be carefully managed, has its place. Francisco hoes the corn and feels the presence of this negative force: "He was too old to be afraid. His acknowledgement of the unknown was nothing more than a dull, intrinsic sadness, a vague desire to weep, for evil had long since found him out and knew who he was. He set a blessing upon the corn and took up his hoe. He shuffled out between the rows, toward the dim light at the edge of the cornfield" (68). Knowledge in the Pueblo world is never complete. Instead, Francisco has been taught to accept a measure of mystery, which he senses here in his old age. He contends with the unknown as he does with the ordered beauty of the land—emotionally, with a "planter's love" or with a "dull, intrinsic sadness." A cosmos greater than humans "knows" Francisco and has "long since found him out," but he does not hope to destroy it; Francisco (and the pueblo) instead incorporate evil, this void of meaning, into the tribal epistemology. He restores harmony: he blesses the land and backs away.

In part 2, "The Priest of the Sun," Abel wakes on the beach after a beating by the corrupt police officer, Martinez. He is removed from his homeland, like a fish out of water, "among the most helpless creatures on the face of the earth" (89). More than six years in prison have further damaged his understanding of his body in relation to place: "The walls of his cell were white, or perhaps they were gray or green; he could not remember. After a while he could not imagine anything beyond the walls except the yard outside, the lavatory and the dining hall—or even the walls, really" (104). The dislocating chaos of the war and prison have distorted Abel's notion of belonging to the land, so that he has little outside these "abstractions beyond the reach of his understanding" (104). His imagination severely blunted, Abel again struggles to regain his former knowledge of himself in relation to place. In faltering consciousness, his hands badly broken, Abel reconsiders what it means to dwell.

Into this modernist collection of memory fragments steps the Reverend John Big Bluff Tosamah, "orator, physician, Priest of the Sun, son of Hummingbird" (109). Tosamah is likely a previously "relocated" Kiowa man. Like Abel, Benally, and others, he has been encouraged by the American government to leave his homeland and move to an urban location in order to enter mainstream North American living. The federal policies of termination and relocation for American Indians can be viewed as a Cold War plot to displace Indigenous people from their lands, so that tribal nations could be dissolved and mineral-rich lands be made available for the production of U.S. military weapons. As part of this relocation, Tosamah contends with removal by leading a congregation of displaced urban Indians in Los Angeles in the peyotist Native American Church. Although critics such as Carole Oleson and Bernard Hirsch find Tosamah cruel, Momaday and some other readers find him also humorous, a comic relief in a serious novel. Either way, he is eloquent in his storytelling of the migrations of his people and their tenure in the land.

In *The Way to Rainy Mountain*, Momaday retells nearly verbatim the story of the Kiowa people's slow migration to their homeland, a spiritually guided movement through which this group of travelers began to conceive of themselves as a distinct people in relation to their land. As they moved over the land their collective identity consciously changed in response to it, in their interpretations of their experiences of new places. Through the centuries, the Kiowa people began to know themselves and the land more richly as they refined the oral tradition that sustains their community and sense of place. Tosamah celebrates his people's emergence as a people in relation to the earth—in the basement of an office building, ironically, where he, "big, lithe as a cat, narrow-eyed," booms with "the voice of a great dog" before the congregation: "It was a journey toward the dawn, and it led to a golden age. Along the way Kiowas were befriended by the Crows, who gave them the culture and religion of the plains. They acquired horses, and their ancient nomadic spirit was suddenly free of the ground. They acquired Tai-me, the sacred sun dance doll, from that moment the chief object and symbol of their worship, and so shared in the divinity of the sun. Not least, they acquired the sense of destiny, therefore courage and pride. When they entered upon the Southern Plains, they had been transformed. No longer were they slaves to the simple necessity of survival; they were a lordly and dangerous society of fighters and thieves, hunters and priests of the sun" (129). Momaday offers an alternative theory of American Indian culture that allows for the ongoing development of an Indigenous people. The Kiowas are not the keepers of a static collection of values and practices, indelibly adhered to a single essential geography. Much to the contrary, the Kiowa people attained their "golden age" by evaluating and incorporating new knowledge into their views of themselves, the land, and the world. They "acquired" the Sun Dance, their spiritual identity, from the Crow people, and from this religion they developed a better understanding of the land. They developed a moral theory of dwelling founded in agency and reciprocity and care for the living world. In this regard, the Kiowa culture changes but is also "authentic" in that it maintains their peoplehood.

Tosamah emphasizes one main cultural development for his people the Kiowa: their "sense of destiny." Though they once merely "survived"— that is, sought shelter and food, simply existed—they began to question how they *should* live: they evolved an ethics. This "idea" of themselves as a distinct people with a unique tradition—their tribal identity—was predicated on a normative conception of who the Kiowa people should endeavor to be. Their ethics of habitation shaped and continues to shape the way they live on the land. For this reason, almost inseparably, Rainy Mountain stands for the Kiowa people. In an earlier sermon, Tosamah insightfully explains the normativity maintained in Tai-me: "It represents the oldest and best idea that man has of himself" (96–97).

As a tribal people, the Kiowas maintain this knowledge in their oral tradition. On their ancient migration to the southern Plains, they lived for a time near a fabulous feature in the land, a site in present-day Wyoming that North Americans call Devil's Tower. Still today, in their tribal narrative Kiowa people retell their story of dealing with this mystifying landmark, where Rock Tree is both a spiritual and a real place. Tosamah describes the Kiowas' response to this unexplained mark on the land: "There are things in nature which engender an awful quiet in the heart of man; Devil's Tower is one of them. Man must account for it. He must never fail to explain such a thing to himself, or else he is estranged forever from the universe. Two centuries ago, because they could not do otherwise, the Kiowas made a legend at the base of the rock" (131). They say that a long time ago eight children, seven sisters and a brother, were at play. The boy suddenly turned into a bear and began to chase after his terrified sisters. A huge tree appeared and told the girls to climb up, and then that tree began to grow up into the sky. Angered, the bear boy clawed and marked the tree in his attempt to catch his sisters. But the seven sisters soon reached the sky and became the stars of the Big Dipper. Tosamah's ancestors tell this story to "account" for the land—to bring meaning to the earth. The Rock Tree is now part of their world, for language has brought order to the land, where a narrative makes sense of places, telling of the tribe's stopping place in their long journey to geoidentity. "The Kiowa journey, like that recounted in emergence narratives of other tribes, may be seen as a movement from chaos to order, from discord to harmony," writes Evers (1985a, 212). This tribal world requires that people and the land share a similar narrative, for all share inseparable agency in the process of life. So the Kiowa people were compelled to know the Rock Tree, or they would cease to be; otherwise, they, like the land, would not be meaningful.

Tosamah's sermon, booming off the basement walls, resonates with the congregation. The relocated Natives understand the attachment to distant homelands, the wound that this separation leaves, and the struggle to maintain—in memory and story—a relationship with the land. This portion of *House Made of Dawn* representing the Indian community in Los Angeles can be read as a social study of the various experiences of and strategies to overcome Native displacement. Tosamah shares with others his oral traditional ties to the Kiowa places, and, through this communal process, helps listeners to participate in a practice of reaffirming Indigenous belonging to lands. Perhaps most significant, though, Tosamah (in the indirect speech of tribal elders) reminds other American Indians of their shared intellectual tradition that links thought and land. In these terms, the Priest of the Sun attempts to inculcate in displaced tribal people the intellectual skills to survive and overturn their disinheritance. In thought and action, these gatherings, then, resemble a pan-Indigenous practice of re-creating a sense of place—even in the city—through the bracing bonds of kinship. Benally brings to this urban group his strongly grounded Navajo spirituality; his Dine Nightway prayer song functions specifically to locate tribal members in the land.[21] On a hill overlooking the city, amid the sound of drums, Ben prays for Abel the night before his friend is to return home:

> May it be beautiful before me,
> May it be beautiful behind me,
> May it be beautiful below me,
> May it be beautiful above me,
> May it be beautiful all around me.
> In beauty it is finished. (147)

Of course, the community also bears all the marks of social dysfunction; alcoholism and depression, alienation and self-hatred, can make daily living unbearable without the support of other survivors. It is startling, however, how few of the novel's critics recognize U.S. colonialism as the primary force in the erosion of the characters' urban tribal social world.

Similar to the geographical emergence of the Kiowa, these Indians arrive in a strange land and, across tribal origin and tradition, form a collective geoidentity. The members of this urban community, though, are perhaps more likely than mainstream U.S. citizens to create a sense of place because, as Tosamah dramatizes, they possess a socially sustaining body of knowledge designed to navigate through such social and spatial ruptures. To truly relocate, tribal members must be able to evaluate and order their experiences of various lands in terms of their symbolic resonance. On this view, Cherokee lands in the west no doubt speak of home but hardly bear the mythological richness of the ancestral home, the Old Place, the Smoky Mountains. Such an understanding of place as a comparative, evaluative process frustrates critics who wish to posit facile separations between Indian Country and "modern America." Perhaps for this reason, the Los Angeles section of the novel draws much critical attention. It is surprising how many scholars of *House Made of Dawn* insist that the city is somehow a symbol for white culture—market driven, spiritually empty, alienated from "nature" and socially alienating—and that while

Indigenous people desire to belong, in the end cannot survive there. S. K. Aithal provides a sentimental reading of Abel's life in Los Angeles: "Abel probably realizes that even those like Angela who love him do not wish to see him become a part of white society, which has been his secret dream" (1985, 163–64). Such readers pine over American Indians, pleading that they remain pure, authentic, or "uncontaminated," as a natural or spiritual reservoir for a nostalgic America. If we recall the ancient cities of precontact North America, the Indian movement's urban beginnings, and the city Indians today, who comprise half the Native population, we cannot sustain the view that Native people are failing strangers to the city.[22] Few critics, however, recognize that more than any other feature of urban living, it is poverty and not contact with Western culture that damages the lives of American Indian people—a point I develop in my concluding chapter. Momaday, in fact, foregrounds the shared social reality of class as a deep source of misery in urban areas, when characters who are not Native, such as the sad Old Carlozini or the poor white dustbowler Milly, also suffer alienation, alcoholism, and unhealthy and crime-filled living conditions in the city.[23]

A more complex understanding of dwelling must account for the different ways that different people make their homes. While the category of class in *House Made of Dawn* helps explain why all poor people, not just Indians, endure placelessness in the city, economic status cannot entirely account for the ways that uprootedness affects cultural and personal lives differently, even among Native people. After all, Abel seems to suffer more from displacement than do Benally or Tosamah, as Michael Raymond states: "What also seems certain is that the others who suffer from the same sort of placelessness as Abel do not suffer as much as Abel. They seem to have either overcome the sense of not belonging or at least come to grips with it" (1983, 69). According to Raymond, Momaday uses "mythic pluralism" to free the essentialist boundaries between red and white cultures. He writes that Indigenous characters in the novel put down roots by embracing cultural plurality: "A character's acceptance of or adjustment to the many cultures around him marks that character's discovery of his sense of place" (69). To find one's own relation to land, argues Raymond, one must accept the culture of the other who also dwells on that land. For Abel, this means that finding his own relation to his ancestral homeland depends on "accepting" or "adjusting" to the dominant culture around him. Raymond overlooks that Pueblo communities have a much older and thus more complex sense of place than do other immigrated people. He instead presents a nonevaluative model of dwelling in which Native geoidentity depends on the presence of other cultural groups. In neglecting to evaluate the ethical implications of various claims to place, Raymond ultimately renders all senses of place interchangeable. With sleight of hand, the uniqueness and the comparative merit of different cultural geographies are erased.

An evaluative approach to culture might prove useful in critical discussions of dwelling such as these, which threaten to defuse Indigenous struggles to protect and recover homelands. Raymond concludes that "everyone has tenure in the land" (1983, 70). A tribal realist notion of dwelling, however, helps to specify how some forms of displacement might be more oppressive than others. Though an immigrated Italian Catholic woman and a displaced Navajo man might both experience subjugation in the city, the Navajo man is likely also to experience existential, epistemological, and moral alienation because he is displaced from the very land on which his culture's ethical theories rely. Corlozini contends with isolation, crime, and poverty. Benally endures these and more in his exile from land that sustains his moral universe: his is a cosmic dislocation. Such a view seeks more complex accounts to chart out differences in ecological location; why, for instance, Indians contend with the United States dumping nuclear waste on their reservations, while others often do not.[24] Our relationship to the land may be evaluated in terms that refer to these social facts of our dwelling. Momaday shows that Indian cultural identity is linked to social location, and in so doing he discredits Raymond—for even if all have "tenure in the land" our histories on and knowledge of the land can and must be comparatively evaluated. Thus we find that American Indian people are likely to possess an epistemic privilege, a more comprehensive view of dwelling, a greater "tenure" than those more recently arrived to North America. According to Momaday, "The other, latecoming things—the beasts of burden and of trade, the horse and the sheep, the dog and the cat—these have an alien and inferior aspect, a poverty of vision and instinct, by which they are estranged from the wild land, and made tentative" (57).

In "Self-Hatred and Spiritual Corruption in *House Made of Dawn*," Bernard Hirsch argues that Native people often disdain their "Indianness" because they need it. To Hirsch, even the dirty cop Martinez hates himself for betraying his culture and attempting to enter the mainstream, so he directs his rage at Abel: "His . . . beating of Abel . . . reveals the self-hatred that is the price of the Anglo authority he covets" (1983, 308). In reading the Native relocation experience we might certainly see self-hatred, but we also see self-love; it is a deep agape love of land and of people to help American Indians make sense of their lives in the city. It is noteworthy that Hirsch does briefly mention the inverse of this view of the urban Native self: "And as regards Tosamah and Benally, it is indeed painful to watch them disparage that which they most love and most need—their Indianness. . . . Like [other urban American Indians, Tosamah] both loves and fears his Indianness" (309, 310). Hirsch describes a key process in revitalization movements among oppressed peoples. Similar to the free-dom schools of the South, urban Indigenous communities collectively de-velop alternative narratives of social reality, which draw on affect as well as intellect to reinterpret experiences of racism and concomitant self-hatred. Alfonso Ortiz (1972) explains the importance of emotions to Pueblo life: "If worldview provides an *intellectually* satisfying picture of reality, reli-gion provides both an intellectually and *emotionally* satisfying picture of, and orientation toward, that reality" (136). In chapter 3, I develop a full theoretical account of the emotions; for our present purpose, we find that the emotions (here love) do not provide urban American Indians self-evident knowledge of an oppressive existence in the city. Instead, love of self and others makes available new accounts to be interpreted through the context of shared experience, which an urban Native community pro-vides. To refuse the opportunity to embrace this source of knowledge is not to remain unaffected in a neutral environment but rather is to risk the self-destruction that U.S. colonialism promotes.

In Ben Benally's friendship with Abel we see the place of the emo-tions to sustain an anticolonial urban Indian community. Though Benally maintains some illusions about the strengths of American culture, he loves himself as he loves others. He loves the land. In part 3, "The Night Chanter," Ben delivers his entire monologue from his tenement window-sill on the day of Abel's departure for home. Ben's first-person voice brings humanity and agency to a colonized world, a genuine sound to ground a novel otherwise dangerously silenced.[25] "Benally's sane, quiet voice ap-plies a leavening perspective to the book's turbid events," writes Baine Kerr (1978, 177). Benally draws his generous emotional strength from his rich spiritual training back home at Navajo: "He lives his religion on a level deeper than intellect, the level of spirit and emotion" (Oleson 1973, 73). Among Navajo people, the emotional commitment to their Creator shapes social relationships and finds its origin in traditions of kinship and the moral responsibilities to community that they entail. In *Navajo*

Kinship and Marriage, Gary Witherspoon describes the moral component of kinship: "The culturally related kin universe is a moral order because it is a statement of the proper order of that universe—that is, the ideal state of affairs or the way things ought to be. It refers to a condition in which everything has its proper place, fulfilling its proper role and following all the cultural rules. The rules which govern the kin universe are moral rules. They state unconditionally how kinsmen behave toward each other and how groups of kinsmen function. They are axiomatic, based on a priori moral premises" (1975, 12). Ben thus gives Abel his only coat: "He left today. It was raining, and I gave him my coat. You know, I hated to give it up; it was the only one I had" (139). Irony pervades Ben's long explanation of friendship: friends do not have to explain; Ben "hates" his loss but loves Abel. In the Navajo world Ben cares for Abel, for he must. Witherspoon's notion of kinship within a shared ancestral and geographical origin likely describes Ben's responsibility to care for his friend: "We were kind of alike, though, him and me. After a while he told me where he was from, and right away I knew we were going to be friends. We're related somehow, I think. The Navajos have a clan they call by the name of that place" (153). For centuries the Navajo and Pueblo people have exchanged traditions; members of the Coyote Pass People Clan of the Navajos are descended from Jemez people who joined the Navajos after Diego de Vargas, leading the Spanish reconquest of the Pueblos, burned Jemez on or after summer 1696. The friends share ties to the same landscape. Ben's biological relation to Abel, though, is only a basis for kinship; kinship is meaningful only when maintained through moral practice: "In Navajo culture, kinship means intense, diffuse, and enduring solidarity, and this solidarity is realized in actions and behavior befitting the cultural definitions of kinship solidarity" (Witherspoon 1975, 21).

In his generosity and love, Ben helps develop the kind of social solidarity that Navajo ideas of kinship demand.[26] In Los Angeles, though, the stakes are higher, for love must override hatred by proving to be a more enabling response to the oppressed conditions of the urban Native community. Indeed, internalized racism or self-hatred makes one believe that one's poverty is evidence of one's inferiority (Hirsch 1983, 309). Ben and others have likely established an anticolonial community that interrogates, through shared experience, the federal displacement from tribal homelands, as well as reaffirms the rich and viable heritage of Native cultures. No doubt part of this process is the simple sharing of care—for example, of food: "I had a sandwich, and I asked him if he wanted to split it with me, but he said he wasn't hungry. I ate about half of it and acted like I didn't want any more. I put the rest down on the plank between us and kept hoping he would change his mind and take it, but he didn't. Finally, I had to throw it away" (152). At the expense of hunger and waste, Ben allows Abel his dignity. Caring for self and others—loving—helps community members revalue their tribal cultures, their personal selves, and their bodies.

On the beach, Abel remembers his former body: "He had loved his body. It had been hard and quick and beautiful; it had been useful, quickly and surely responsive to his mind and will. He was thick in the chest and shoulders, not so powerful as his grandfather, but longer of reach and more agile. And his hands were slender and strong. His legs were lean and tapered, long-muscled, too thin for a white man's legs: the legs of an Indian. Once he could have run all day, really run, not jogging but moving fast over distances, without ruining his feet or burning himself out" (100). Abel regards his body and his mind as not separate but reciprocal parts of his whole existence, "surely responsive to his mind and will." While running, he and his body and the land moved together in beauty, holding agency with one another. Abel's deep regard for his physical self is thus tied to his intellectual and spiritual identities, each informing each. Now in crisis he seeks knowledge, through love of the body, to help him recover a self. Abel "loved" his body in the way one might honor a relationship with a loved one, with whom one shares a history of trust, care, and sustenance. In a final dimension of the body, Abel's body not only served his practical needs but also brought him aesthetic pleasure: it was "hard, quick, and beautiful." *House Made of Dawn* introduces a conception of the Indian body that reaches well beyond mere physical fitness, in which the notions of wellness or regard better explain the body in the land—a state I have been calling somatic place.

Abel was not born to know the land as part of himself but rather has been taught: his mind, body, and the land are interdependent. Francisco educates his grandchildren with traditional stories of their long-standing interaction with the land: a relationship of deep regard and respect through which knowledge is shared, maintained, and developed among members of the tribal community. In Walatowa, the people demonstrate through ceremony the life-giving power of language to remake the living world. Through the ritual movement of their bodies on the land of ancestors, they describe a moral relationship with the earth, which must be carried on as a social practice upheld through the bonds of kinship. For this reason, Abel has been taught to love inseparably his body and the land, and through this relationship he derives, like other Native people, a knowledge of the earth better suited for its care and survival. Francisco attaches Abel's body to the land through story when he explains to his grandsons the movements of ceremonial life that are inextricably bound to the solar calendar:

> They could see the black mesa looming on the first light, and he told them there was the house of the sun. They must learn the whole contour of the black mesa. They must know it as they knew the shape of their hands, always and by heart. The sun rose up on the black mesa at a different place each day. It began there, at a point on the central slope, standing still for solstice, and ranged all the days southward across the rise and fall of the long plateau, drawing closer by the measure of mornings and moons to the lee, and back again. They must know the long journey of the sun on the black mesa, how it rode in the seasons and the years, and they must live according to the sun appearing, for only then could they reckon where they were, where all things were, in time. (197)

Notice that Abel must know the land as he knows his own body, in terms of morally guided movement. Like Francisco, Abel must hold a love for the land not only to produce better knowledge but also because it is "good" to love this guiding force. Selinger, however, questions the place of power in Native cultures; the sun's authority is inherently abusive and thus should be "subverted": "The sun, the symbol of the patriarchal Kiowa culture, maintains its authority through a look of surveillance" (1999, 45). Selinger assumes that all authority is illegitimate. William Bevis, however, disagrees: "The source of respect for the past in Indian life and novels is respect for authority. . . . A culture believing that power corrupts, naturally encourages dissent" (1987, 589). In either case, the recognition of authority is a fundamental socially guided practice in many Native traditions. Accepting this authority, meaning in the land is never fully revealed; instead, a degree of mystery always remains and is accepted in the maintenance of normative knowledge: a hermeneutical caveat that Abel eventually learns to heed.

On the beach, at the transitional site between sea and earth, space and place, Abel finally comes to terms with his belonging to his homeland. His hands, the symbolic map for his knowledge of himself, his place in the land, and his movement upon it, have been badly broken by the abused authority of Martinez, an authority to which Abel refuses to bow:

"Martinez told him to hold out his hands, and he did, slowly, like maybe he wasn't going to at first, with palms up. I could see his hands in the light and they were open and almost steady" (174–75). Feeling the pain of his body he once loved, the awe in being pursued by the spirits of ancestors, the runners after evil, Abel recalls the race at dawn:

> The runners after evil ran as water runs, deep in the channel, in the way of least resistance, no resistance. His skin crawled with excite-ment; he was overcome with longing and loneliness, for suddenly he saw the crucial sense in their going, of old men in white leggings run-ning after evil in the night. They were whole and indispensable in what they did; everything in creation referred to them. Because of them, perspective, proportion, design in the universe. Meaning because of them. They ran with great dignity and calm, not in hope of anything, but hopelessly; neither in fear nor hatred nor despair of evil, but simply in recognition and with respect. Evil was. Evil was abroad in the night; they must venture out to the confrontation; they must reckon dues and divide the world. (103–4)

Ancestral tradition calls to Abel in this emotive, near-death moment, through which he grasps the insight to survive and recover knowledge of his homeland: a meaningful relationship with the land demands our moral work. The old men, who represent tradition, seek knowledge in a potentially meaningless universe, in spite of the night. They do so by at-tending to the rhythms of the earth, and moving over it with the sonorous pace of water, their bodies known as a necessary component of the land itself. Through their running, the people of Walatowa make sense of their place in the world: ecological order is not self-evident but is maintained through social practice. Abel learns how he should know the land. Like Francisco and the old runners, he learns that meaning is never complete nor wholly available. Instead, the people must accept the existence of evil, of meaninglessness, of disorder in the universe—they must even run out to meet it. Thus Abel awakens to an Indigenous principle of dwelling: one must endeavor to know a not entirely knowable land. Years before, he tried to destroy evil and it threatened to consume him. Now he rec-ognizes that, like the runners, he must go out to meet the unknown not with dread but with respect, as the people continue to make a good and a beautiful world.

2

||||||||||||||||||||||||||||||||||||||||||||||||||||||||||||||||||||||||||||

PLACING THE ANCESTORS: HISTORICAL IDENTITY

IN JAMES WELCH'S *WINTER IN THE BLOOD*

I sometimes think of what it means that in their heyday—in 1830, say—the Kiowas owned more horses *per capita* than any other tribe on the Great Plains, that the Plains Indian culture, the last culture to evolve in North America, is also known as "the horse culture" and "the centaur culture," that the Kiowas tell the story of a horse that died of shame after its owner committed an act of cowardice, that I am a Kiowa, that therefore there is in me, as there is in the Tartars, an old, sacred notion of the horse.
—**N. Scott Momaday,** *The Names*

Yet I had felt it then, that feeling of event. Perhaps it was the distance, those three new miles, that I felt, or perhaps I had felt something of that other distance; but the event of distance was as vivid to me as the cold canvas of First Raise's coat against my cheek. He must have known then what I had just discovered. Although he told me nothing of it up to the day he died, he had taken me that snowy day to see my grandfather.
—**The narrator,** in *Winter in the Blood*

I stand on Honey Creek as the light moves through the walnut trees to play on the golden water, and consider the events that took place on this very piece of land back in 1838, when my family arrived in exile from our original Cherokee homelands in the Southeast. We have returned to this land with carloads of relatives, and I recall the children playing in the creek while the older people talked about the site where our ancestors built some of the first log houses. Stepping past the Rose of

Sharon that grows through the bleached boards of a fallen shack, I pause to pick up a green walnut. I remove my boots, roll up my pants, and wade into the creek. I look to the water and to the trees, and I try to imagine our lands through the eyes of my ancestors. Through the years, I have come better to know Honey Creek and the stories about my family living there, and I have done so in a way that informs my world today and shapes how I think of myself as a Cherokee man. I have considered my relationship to this piece of land, in conversation with relatives and in scholarship, in hopes of understanding myself through the experiences of my forebears during those early hard times. As one of my familial ancestors recalls our displacement: "My mother was about twelve years old when they were forced to leave Georgia and I have heard her say that before they left their homes there that the white people come into their houses and look things over and when they found something that they liked, they would say, 'This is mine, I am going to have it'" (McGhee 1937, 2). Through a similar process, N. Scott Momaday shapes what I call historical identity, as he meditates on his relationship to ancestors and the inherited social values for which they fought and died. In Blackfeet and Gros Ventre writer James Welch's *Winter in the Blood*, the nameless narrator proceeds with the same wandering and evaluative speculation in his recovery of a more complete understanding of himself and his past. Such moments of historical imagining place *Winter in the Blood* in the midst of Red Power.

All through *Winter in the Blood*, the narrator searches for a way to put to rest his nagging sense of "distance"—a distance from himself, from his Blackfeet culture,[1] from his tribal homelands. He finally closes this distance and comes home—personally, culturally, and geographically. Among American Indians, the decolonization of communities as well as of individuals often involves such a process of recovery, a conscious act of reclaiming knowledge of a tribal self, knowledge that often has been distorted by centuries of European and American oppression. Like other colonized people, the Blackfeet narrator organizes his cultural recovery through the principle of identity. In the epigraph above, the young man draws his first sense of himself as a man from his father. He is the son of First Raise. He suddenly "discovers," however, that he is also the grandson of the heroic Yellow Calf. Now more deeply immersed in a family and tribal past, his identity grows historically. The new depth of this self-understanding as an Indian encourages the narrator not only to sustain his relationship to his people and lands but also to understand the workings of colonialism.

This narrative thus not only illustrates the maintenance of culture but also describes a procedure of political growth. New knowledge about colonial relations of power develops one's own relationship to a community and history as well as to a dominating culture. In *Winter in the Blood*, then, political awakening and the recovery of Blackfeet selfhood are intertwined, each informing the other. By reinterpreting a distant yet somehow familiar event, Welch's narrator regains knowledge of his tribal history, culture, and lands, all of which serve to enrich his self-understanding as a Blackfeet man. Because the real-world preservation of Indigenous culture and the protection of homelands similarly depend on this process of decolonization, Native studies might benefit from a more convincing account of the recovery of American Indian cultural identity. To serve that need, in this chapter I develop a tribal realist approach to Native identity to show that identities need not be based on a cultural or racial essence but instead can operate as revisable constructs to reconnect with tribal pasts, a process that produces new knowledge to inform our selves in the present world. On charting the theoretical debate on identity in American Indian studies, I offer a shorter, more speculative reading of *Winter in the Blood* in which I embrace the humor in the narrator's wandering masculinity.

Identity and Knowledge in Indian Studies

Of the many issues that Indigenous intellectuals engage, the concept of identity draws considerable critical attention in Native studies; for American Indian peoples to build an anticolonial movement, the understanding of the modern tribal self must be clear.[2] As early as 1984, Taino intellectual José Barreiro recognized the importance of identity in the process of Native cultural renewal when he declared that "there appears to be surfacing an agreement among informed observers of American Indian education that a strong identity—that is, the fullest possible knowledge of one's own language, culture, cosmology and history—is a necessary prerequisite for any successful venture into the non-Indian world" (1984, 4–5). American Indian scholars theorize cultural identity not only to benefit Native people but also to reform U.S. institutions, which have been defining and naming tribal peoples for centuries. With Native nations today under new pressure, however, I feel that scholarship on Indian identity might confront more than the issue of individual social acceptance in a tribal community or in mainstream American culture. In this chapter, I thus approach the question of American Indian identity from this very practical perspective: our identities affect our politics. Whether we disclose the role of our social identities in our lives, they continue to operate in our views of the world, in the values we come to hold. But since our identities are socially produced, they can be rethought and recast to empower Native lives. With this goal of collective tribal self-definition in mind, I would like to consider an alternative theory of Indigenous identity.

In American Indian studies, the concept of Native identity bears an opaque intellectual history that since the 1990s has been undergoing alteration among Indigenous trickster scholars. Such scholars have developed the trickster identity, perhaps in response to poststructuralist theories which have warned that the struggle to develop one's cultural identity is actually a search for foundations—namely, timeless essences in which American Indian cultures inhere impervious to external historical and social forces. As I outline in my introduction, in the 1980s Native scholars set forth an often essentialist view of American Indian identity by emphasizing a metaphysical attachment to the world. From my discussion of essentialism regarding Indian lands in the previous chapter, however, we might see that, even though this theoretical position reclaims intrinsic Native self-worth on its own terms, essentialism also mystifies beyond self-reflection and potential for change, and thus limits the possibility of the continued development of tribal persons and communities. As Robert Warrior explains: "Appeals to essentialized worldviews . . . always risk an ossifying of American Indian existence" (1995, xvii). In its preclusion of open national development, essentialism not only fails to promote sovereignty, ironically, but also offers no theoretical means of evaluating its own or other theoretical positions for their ability to politically mobilize Indian Country.

Perhaps in response to the insularity of the essentialist position, Native intellectuals have become drawn to trickster theories predicated on the oral traditional trickster who purportedly embraces contradictions and inhabits the borders of knowledge. In developing such theories, Indian scholars have been able to question the reliability of knowledge production in conditions of unequal colonial relations. Employing these trickster theories to critique power in a U.S. cultural and social context, scholars frequently have explored, for example, how imperialist discourses of inquiry distort representations of Indigenous cultures. To challenge the study of American Indian peoples, trickster intellectuals have interrogated the colonial legacies in fields such as anthropology to reveal how historical and cultural attachments at times shape observers' conclusions regarding Native lifeways. Native scholars implementing tricksterism have explained how the racial construction of the misnomer *Indian* is historically tainted with colonialist coercion in order to deconstruct this identifying category. "The use of the word 'Indian' is postmodern, a navigational conception, a colonial invention, a simulation in sound and transcription," writes Gerald Vizenor (1990, xxiii). Scholars in Native studies widely recognize these strides supported by the constructivist trickster critique. But the challenge to confront the use of delimiting categories of analysis such as "race" is also often a call to deconstruct other knowledge products such as cultural identity, because trickster theory, like all social theories, in the end maintains an undisclosed view of knowledge. With trickster knowledge avowedly indeterminate, scholars have been unable to justify normative claims to evaluate among identities. While trickster discourse promises to challenge dominating constructions of Native identity, as a principle this same logic could be used to dismantle *all* identities, those not only erroneously produced by dominant cultures but also those legitimately achieved by Indigenous cultures.

As a view of knowledge, the trickster theory of identity has relied on the critiques of the concepts of identity and experience. Even though trickster theorists have no intention of dismantling all Indian identities, we might still take seriously the full critique from which the trickster theory stems. Such critiques tend to expose how the constructs called identity cannot avoid the use of power to subdue internal differences to invent a stable "subjectivity." In this position on identity and knowledge, the individual is actually incoherent and fragmented, though she or he may sustain the illusion of coherence. From this view, scholars theorizing alterity often deconstruct the self to expose a matrix of power that necessarily influences the production of both the self and social knowledge. Such scholars often argue that, for example, the category of identity "Anishinaabe person," which must inevitably exclude in order to identify culturally, is constructed by the very oppressive forces it hopes to resist.[3] In this critique, identities are illegitimate ways of organizing one's view of the world because they are constructed from necessarily subjective personal experience. And experience, such scholars claim, cannot be an adequate source of knowledge for it is mediated by social and linguistic signification.[4]

Gerald Vizenor has led the trickster turn in American Indian studies with his fiction and criticism that embrace, explore, and advance this theoretical position. Though I would agree that Vizenor's fiction ultimately inhabits the more or less stable moral center represented in the behavior of one whom he himself calls "the compassionate tribal trickster . . . the one who cares to balance the world" (1981, xii), his criticism, which is my present concern, advocates a skeptical view of tribal knowledge that leads to a number of disabling theoretical problems for American Indian scholars and activists. In his benchmark article "The Ruins of Representation," Vizenor charges Charles Larson with employing an essentialist approach to experience in Native culture and literature: "Larson must search for racial purities in tribal literature because [he denies] crossblood identities and tribal survivance" (1993a, 15). In deconstructing "racial purities" and instead asserting a more freely defined model of American Indian identity predicated on marginality or hybridity, Vizenor attempts to liberate Native discourse from colonialist demands that American Indians be "authentic" and adhere to an ahistorical, static model of tribal living.[5] Because trickster theory helps challenge dominating constructions of Native people, it has been a popular theoretical position in Indigenous studies.

Native scholars, in their efforts to disrupt the foundations of Eurocentrism (which has produced, for example, the image of the Noble Savage), have supported the trickster formulation of American Indian identity. This identity also has often been explored in a trickster discourse called mixedblood or crossblood identity,[6] terms poised in uneasy relation to race and popularized by Vizenor. The trickster formulation promises to liberate concretized definitions of American Indian identity and culture, but the position might also have drawn critical support among Native scholars because it provides a model for being Native in a colonized world with challenging cultural interactions. For Vizenor asserts that American Indians are not bound by a fixed cultural category but rather inhabit the interstitial space between the colonies and the nations, the white and the Indian, and thus subvert the demands of each cultural register. The liberation of colonized identities is certainly a worthy goal in American Indian studies. But in exposing the always inaccurate ways that Western history and culture produce the Indian, Native scholars—if they are to be epistemologically consistent—must support a mode of inquiry that discounts *all* normative knowledge about Native peoples. If we deconstruct the Indian, how are we then able to present a reliable construction of tribal peoples either for U.S. society or for ourselves? Noticing these theoretical problems, some American Indian scholars find that by subverting tribal identities Native trickster positions actually undermine the ground on which Indian people recover culture and demand redress.

Native scholars implementing trickster theories have thus liberated at a cost. For if such scholars endeavor to subvert constructions of tribal identity, from a trickster view of knowledge, they are still unable to distinguish distorted colonialist constructions from more accurate constructions. In their deconstruction of tribal experience, moreover, trickster critics inadvertently delegitimate the status of experience altogether. In this view of identity and experience, with the progressive idea of difference itself subverted and identity uprooted from experience, Indian people are left with their own "ruins of representation," for in the end they are challenged to explain how tribal experiences might be different from mainstream or industrialized experiences. Most important, Indigenous scholars drawing on trickster discourse to theorize Native literature and culture—because they have been labored to provide the means to evaluate the relationship between experience and identity—are unable to account for the recovery of Native culture or to justify the growth and development of Native people through cultural practice. Though tricksterism and its binary opposite, essentialism, still find support within American Indian studies, neither view of knowledge is ultimately politically efficacious to answer the call for a First Nations intellectually based politics. This is the request that Elizabeth Cook-Lynn remembers as the organizing force for the fostering of American Indian studies in 1970, at the First Convocation of American Indian Scholars, at Princeton University, where Native scholars "called for the development by Indians of bodies of Indigenous knowledge" (1997, 9). To justify this development, scholars must be theoretically equipped to make normative claims.

From that historic moment, Native scholars in Indian studies have often sought in American Indian identity a basis for the above defense of Indigenous lands and values, though discerning the theoretical position for its grounding has been troublesome. During the past few years, however, a growing number of Native scholars committed to tribal development have led critics to question the reliability of trickster thought to serve political action. The discursive trickster subverts endlessly, but Native community organizers might seek a theory to help them discern exactly which structures of power should be subverted: Should Indigenous activists subvert treaty rights? Or if colonialism constructs the Indian, who remains after the Indian is deconstructed? Those American Indians who actually travel across and are often detained at colonial borders might not find this cross-blood cultural margin so liberating. A politics of pure subversion thus cannot avoid the difficult theoretical imperative of adjudicating between self-defeating and self-liberating acts of subversion. In resistance to U.S. imperialist attempts to erase Indigenous identity, many everyday Indian people claim their cultural identity as central to the preservation of tribal culture, history, and nationhood. As a philosophical construct to serve our everyday lives, identity can be explored, theorized, better understood, and even owned by Native peoples to serve Native peoples. American Indian scholars may avoid the loss of identity in their communities by sheer default in engaging Native cultural identity as a genuine theoretical issue.

In seeking a more grounded Indian cultural theory, such scholars remind us that Native self-understanding is immensely important in the preservation of tribal cultures. Indeed, the history of colonialism in the Americas is a history of eliminating the Indigenous presence—not only through the destruction of Native lives through warfare, but also through federal policy designed to erase the tribal identity of those who survive. The removal of Native nations from their ancestral lands; the taking of Indian children from their families to boarding schools, in part to silence the children's tribal languages; the outlawing of tribal religious practices; and the enforcement of tribal enrollment and "certified degrees of Indian blood" were and are colonial impositions to control the identities of Native peoples and to make the Indian into a capitalist, Christian citizen of the United States.[7] In valuing Native identity as a vital means of recovering from this history and reestablishing an Indian presence, such Indian scholars recognize that we need not deconstruct—but, in fact, reconstruct—Indian identity. Craig Womack finds in trickster criticism the "tendency to decenter everything, including the legitimacy of a Native perspective" (1999, 6). Reclaiming our history, he adds: "It is way too premature for Native scholars to deconstruct history when we haven't yet constructed it" (3). More specifically, in regard to trickster views of Native cultural identity, Cook-Lynn disapproves of the crossblood approach because "there is explicit . . . accommodation to the colonialism of the West. . . . an identity which focuses on individualism rather than First Nation ideology" of responsible community membership (1996b, 67).

Facing a similar challenge in their own fields, some minority and Third World scholars have been noticing the limitations of skeptical thought in anticolonial criticism: namely, the detachment of identity from social location. The philosophical challenge posed to such minority discourses, then, is to return to cultural identity its capacity to refer to the social facts that constitute social location. During the past decade, scholars dissatisfied with the theoretical positions available in understanding minority literatures and promoting social justice began to develop a realist approach to identity and culture. Even though realist theory acknowledges that identities are historically and socially produced, it maintains that we can nonetheless evaluate various identity constructions according to their ability to interpret our experiences.[8] Paula Moya presents a realist claim to identity because she recognizes that "a politics of discourse that does not provide for some sort of bodily or concrete action outside the realm of the academic text will forever be inadequate to change the difficult 'reality' of our lives" (1997, 135). In reconsidering the possibility of normative knowledge achieved through the referential link between cultural identity and social location, Moya and other scholars employing realism find identity a philosophically defensible basis for political resistance and the recovery of culture. In Native studies, decolonization often involves a similar process of social change, recovering a relationship to self and tribe that has been displaced by historically produced yet erroneous knowledge. Argued in these realist terms, the narrator of *Winter in the Blood* discovers a Montana Blackfeet cultural identity not by unearthing a ready-made history, but through this process of recovery. For this reason, the protagonist's closing of the distance and his discovery of himself, his community, and their past, represent not an essentialist romance, but an epistemically justified program of cultural renewal.

Scholars and community organizers are drawn to realism as a theoretical position because it does not dismantle but rather reclaims the concepts of experience and identity in anti-imperialist studies of culture and literature. Drawing on Moya's description of the realist theory of cultural identity (1997, 137–38), let me summarize its basic claims:

1. Different social facts are causally relevant to the experiences we will have. The "facts" of race, gender, class, or sexuality constitute an individual's social location in a cultural and historical registry. For this reason, a person racially categorized as American Indian will likely have experiences that are different from those of a European American.

2. Experiences influence but do not entirely determine the formation of an individual's cultural identity. Identity within any cultural group is nuanced because experiences are theoretically mediated.

3. Identities possess a cognitive component that allows for the possibility of accuracy and error in social inquiry. The theory-mediated

quality of experience allows us to interpret the same experience in better or worse ways and to revise our interpretations.

4. Some identities are more enriched than others because they can better account for the social facts that constitute social location. The cultural identity "Indigenous Exile" is likely to refer more accurately to an ancestral tie to homelands and a history of colonialist displacement than the identity "Native American," a racial marker associated with the U.S. Census Bureau.

In *Winter in the Blood*, Welch engages the theoretical place of identity in explaining the rich realities of Blackfeet life—both the everyday stress of colonialist oppression and the joy of stories that teach something new about an Indian self, past, and land—as cultural actors grow culturally and justifiably come home. Unlike theorists who have sought to deconstruct Native identity, Welch situates American Indian identity as a central concept in recovering knowledge of ancestral lifeways and homelands. Even though he recognizes that the recovery of Native knowledge through evolving identity represents a complex process of interpretation, Welch can still support this recovery because he understands the epistemological relationship between identity and experience. Avoiding both essentialist and trickster theories of American Indian identity, *Winter in the Blood* shows how the revitalization of Native cultural identity is neither a search for a pristine origin nor a wholly fabricated process. Instead, the novel reflects an approach to cultural recovery in which identity functions as a *cognitive* (as opposed to a purely affective or emotional) apparatus through which Indigenous people evaluate personal and tribal experiences to produce more accurate knowledge of their world. In this theory of Native identity, the Blackfeet narrator's homecoming—in all its aspects—is more complete not because the narrator discovers the essence of being American Indian, but because his new understanding of himself as a bearer of Blackfeet tradition in the social location of his homelands is historically more justified. Welch shows how Indian identities can be grounded in historical facts, not essentialized beyond understanding.

I now direct this discussion to Louis Owens, a theorist who implements tricksterism to understand the Native novel, and who writes on *Winter in the Blood*. Even though Owens begins with a skeptical account of identity to explain the condition of the nameless narrator, he ultimately seeks an alternative view of American Indian identity to understand what he values in the narrator as an "act of recovery." In hopes of deepening what Owens recognizes as a need for a more socially enabling explanation of identity recovery in the Native novel, I employ a view of Indian identity that explores the notion of a cultural center with which American Indians can measure personal and cultural growth. Later, in the final section of this chapter, I show how Welch's novel of a Blackfeet man returning to his tribal community and homelands represents a process of cultural recovery in which identity, experience, social location, and knowledge are connected. In my reading, I develop a more grounded conception of Native cultural identity by charting the narrator's recovery of his relationship to the land and the values this process generates.

Recovery and Normative Knowledge

Owens's ambivalent use of trickster discourse perhaps best illustrates how it has often been inadequate to Native literary analysis. Of course, *Winter in the Blood* at first might appear to be amenable to trickster theories of reading and knowledge. In such readings we might find that, although the narrative attempts to move chronologically, linear time defies coherence and is ruptured by painful flashbacks and surreal dreams. Most important, the narrator himself seems to embody the discursive problem of interpretation: his struggle for self-knowledge is thwarted by a disunified past, present, and future, a relentless destabilizing process that makes him unable to connect himself to a body of knowledge that might resemble a cultural and historical center and that thus denies the young Blackfeet man a coherent identity.[9]

But Owens also seems to recognize the limitations of trickster identifications. His struggle with trickster discourse peaks, it seems to me, when he attempts to explain how an extremely colonized Native person regains a place in her or his culture. On this issue he speaks directly to American Indians and must meet the ethical responsibility of preserving Native lives. Owens's reading of *Winter in the Blood* thus reveals a desire for a theory to make sense of the cultural development in the novel's Blackfeet narrator, beginning with the critical problem of the concept of recovery itself. Owens approaches this question of cultural renewal through the theoretical account produced by David Harvey (1989):

> We can no longer conceive of the individual as alienated in the classical Marxist sense, because to be alienated presupposes a coherent rather than a fragmented sense of self from which to be alienated. It is

only in terms of such a centred sense of personal identity that individuals can pursue projects over time, or think cogently about the production of a future significantly better than time present and time past. . . .
Postmodernism typically strips away that possibility by concentrating
upon the schizophrenic circumstances induced by fragmentation and
all those instabilities . . . that prevent us even picturing coherently, let
alone devizing strategies to produce, some radically different future.
(Quoted in Owens 1992, 131)

To Harvey, the discursive claim is most troubling because it threatens
to deny oppressed people hope for a better future; the described human
condition, according to Harvey, limits human agency by determining
human lives often without our knowledge. From this position—on which
the trickster theory ultimately relies—the alienated postcolonial self can
no longer even be considered as such, because the colonized subject cannot identify the cultural "center" from which it is alienated. This lack of
self-knowledge locates the problem of uncertainty not in the alienation
of the self from one's culture but in the very absence of a coherent self
to be alienated, or a coherent culture to be alienated from. On this view,
the individual—and certainly a colonized individual struggling under
the conflicting demands of tribal and assimilated senses of self—cannot
plan a future.[10] One cannot project or chart one's moral, historical, or cultural growth because one has no normative, central concept of identity by
which to measure one's development.

Here is Owens's response:

Welch's narrator, however, is neither a victim nor a celebrant of
this kind of postmodern fragmentation and transience; he is, in fact,
alienated precisely in the [Marxist] sense described here. For Welch's
narrator there is a "coherent . . . sense of self" and a "centred sense
of personal identity" that may indeed be recovered. It is a recovery
dependent upon a renewed sense of identity as Indian, as specifically
Blackfoot, and Welch's novel represents such a recovery project. Once
the narrator has made significant progress toward that rediscovery of a
coherent, culturally determined identity, he will be able to unify past,
present, and future and begin finally to project a future at least slightly,
if not radically, different from the present. (1992, 131)

Strikingly, Owens's support for the possibility of an individual's cultural
recovery as represented in Welch is initiated with a lengthy quotation that

describes its impossibility. In the end, however, he cannot help but reject this theory of identity. To follow his argument, Owens agrees with such skeptical theories up to a point: the state of knowledge, our condition, consists in ever-shifting forces that make the possibility of conceiving of a self born out of a coherent history a challenging affair. Owens rightly exposes the problem of knowing ourselves in terms of essential cultural truths, and he recognizes the fact that we inevitably construct a coherent narrative in order "to unify past, present, and future." Ultimately, though, to recover Indigenous identity Owens must reject "fragmentation and transience."[11]

Owens's use of such concepts as "progress" and "discovery," or "project[ing] a future . . . different from the present" demonstrates his ultimate dissent from the theory of identity that Harvey describes. After all, concepts of progress, discovery, and a better future require a more stable ground for knowledge than that afforded by such discursive theories. The Blackfeet narrator can reintegrate himself with his culture only by reconciliation of the self to a normative notion of what it means to be Blackfeet, and this process of self-discovery and cultural development is one for which a trickster theory of identity cannot account. Owens responds that the narrator not only can plan a future but can also come to understand himself more clearly by imagining himself a secure Blackfeet man, connected to his ancestral past, culture, and lands, "living to the best of his ability," as Yellow Calf, the blind elder, says. Of course, the act of projecting an improved relationship to the world is deeply evaluative; that is, to secure a better life, the narrator would also have to be able to identify how his life is better or worse today, or he might even have to evaluate which practices, whether individual or communal, are best for the community. Such decisions, of course, require a normative vision, a more or less objective idea of what it takes to become fully human in the Blackfeet world—the world against which the narrator can gauge the comparative moral worth of his actions as he develops.

Trickster thinking, however, often precludes this evaluative process. The version of postmodernism that Harvey describes and Owens rejects is based on a view of objectivity that demands absolute certainty and is thus intolerant of error. The trickster cannot, then, provide an account of a "different future" or cultural development, because this view of identity does not allow for a self to imagine who a young Blackfeet man or woman should become—a normative idea of who a "good" Blackfeet person is. A more productive theory of selfhood would require an epistemology that investigates how our value-laden presuppositions influence our moral decisions—but one that also accommodates a normative notion of how we should live. From such a view, we may imagine alternatives to the colonially constructed Native self.[12]

So Owens explains the Blackfeet narrator's act of recovery as an act of the imagination, a process through which the narrator restores a past, reassembling the fragmented pieces as one would a jumbled puzzle. In returning to painful events such as the death of his brother, the narrator learns to forgive himself; or, in remembering, he realizes that First Raise, his father, really did love him. As Owens shows, the narrator relearns his culture from Yellow Calf: "With the revitalizing rain in the offing, for the first time the narrator engages his imagination in an attempt to comprehend a relationship involving deep commitment between man and woman" (1992, 142). But Owens does not explain how we might know whether new interpretations of the narrator's past experiences are more conclusive than previous interpretations. How does the narrator come to realize he was wrong about his family history? No doubt the narrator has his own account of error as he comes better to know himself. But to understand this social phenomenon we require a more adequate means to describe this process of cultural and ethical growth in the recovery of a Blackfeet cultural identity. Because Owens has not prefaced an alternative view of knowledge to explain individual social development—how we come to live better—he is ultimately unable to describe this vital decolonizing project.

For the narrator to recover his identity, he must appeal to an idea of what it means to be Blackfeet. Like other tribal cultures, Blackfeet culture functions as a repository of knowledge that collects and tests ways of living in the world, and thus maintains the importance of such practices within cultural values or spiritual beliefs. Of course, the body of knowledge within any cultural community is always changing, adapting new ideas and values to serve a worldview, as members encounter a changing world. In this manner, Indigenous cultural knowledge is not drawn from a rigid collection of essential truths but rather is continually constructed by tribal members. The constructedness of Blackfeet culture, however, should not discount its ability to refer in degrees of accuracy to their world. Since an alternative theory of culture requires a new way of conceptualizing how we produce knowledge, we might consider the development of cultural knowledge as an evaluative yet largely stable process where knowledge cultivates in a normative collection of ideas about Native people. A more politically enabling theory of Native culture, then, recovers a cultural center by redefining objectivity in these normative terms.

In her study of Salish-Kootennai culture, Theresa O'Nell identifies the notion of a cultural center as a source of anxiety for some Indian people because the center, as it is now understood, does not exist. Instead, she claims, widespread depression in the Flathead community stems from a feeling of failure to be authentically Native: "This elaborate lament, which I call the rhetoric of the 'empty center,' argues that there are no more 'real Indians.' . . . The rhetoric of the empty center is a conscious construction about what it means to be Indian. [It] culminates in a message that contemporary Flathead Indian identity is, in essence, inauthentic" (1996, 55). Tewa-Apache psychologist Eduardo Duran and Opelousas-Coushatta scholar Bonnie Duran describe a similar felt emptiness among American Indians, which they term the "soul wound": "The notion of soul wound is one which is at the core of much of the suffering that Indigenous peoples have undergone for several centuries" (1995, 24). If, however, we resituate the concept of the center in the normative terms I introduce above, Flathead culture can now imagine a future less colonized and more culturally viable. Such a notion of a cultural center frees Native persons from demands that they become "real" or "authentic." Further, it allows them to strive simply to be stronger tribal members, based on the normative idea of the ways an Indian person should live, as represented in a flexible though centered and centering collection of values. A healthy self-conception is never an all or nothing affair in which an individual is either a fake or a real Indian, but instead requires the careful evaluation of a community committed to maintaining an idea of being American Indian. In O'Nell's model, both colonialism and Salish-Kootennai culture construct identity by imposing concentric standards of evaluation: "The idealized characteristics of those in the inner circle and those outside the outermost circle are used to assess and negotiate the relative positions of individuals within the intervening circles" (56). Though O'Nell identifies the above evaluative process as a detrimental "system of authority," it is not inherently so. In fact, Flathead members might wish to make their own evaluations as they work to achieve their Indianness among tribal members in the most equitable terms.

Michael Wilson outlines this alternative view of the cultural center in an Indigenous model of objectivity, the moral component of which is communicated through oral tradition: "Thus, the participants in the oral tradition receive the stories not as artifacts but rather as changing sources of knowledge and entertainment. Their conception of literature has little commerce with the distinctions most crucial to anthropological science: distance and determinate representations. Instead, I would argue, the oral tradition provides a theory of reading that sees stories as rooted in place, as having indeterminate origins, where 'authentic' reproduction of the stories occurs at continually re-created moments of reception, and yet as having a normative function that . . . constantly pulls people and stories inward toward a relatively stable arena of life and value" (1997, 134). Wilson identifies oral tradition as a vessel for the transmission of a nest of "provisional truths" to which members of a tribal community can turn in their ongoing evaluations of individual behavioral practices as they lead and undergo traditional moral education.[13] Wilson's model of an American Indian cultural center agrees with O'Nell's model in that both versions understand the actively constructed and dynamic quality of its knowledge production, but Wilson fills O'Nell's empty center with a degree of moral agency—and corresponding potential for cultural development—to serve individual community members.

Historical Identity in *Winter in the Blood*

I have been exploring how the Native oral tradition configures a tribal realist theoretical method for the philosophical evaluation of Indigenous moral and social practice. From this view, the knowledge gained from tribal experience can still approach objectivity even though it might be historically mediated. Recall that I make this claim by drawing on a normative definition of objectivity that sees value-free knowledge as neither a possibility nor a worthwhile goal, for in evaluating and promoting productive forms of theory mediation, we can actually better conduct our cultural inquiries. Welch's novel describes such an interpretive process. In *Winter in the Blood*, oral tradition provides Blackfeet people with theoretically mediated ancestral knowledge. This is knowledge that offers a moral component, as the experiences of their forebears explain how Blackfeet people might live. In this novel, then, personal experience is also an extension of a collective tribal experience because of the connection to ancestors through heritage. Such ancestral tribal experience, transmitted through kinship and stories,[14] informs individual moral and social practice, molding cultural identity. Since Indian selfhood is so shaped by this inextricable connection with a tribal past, in this chapter I develop that process as historical identity.[15]

Unlike Indigenous novels that represent a tragic view of contemporary Native life, Welch's spirited novel uses dark humor to communicate
the often farcical experience of being an Indian today "on a great earth
of stalking white men" (54). It does so in the story of a thirty-two-year-
old (the eighth stage of spiritual training) Blackfeet man's modern vision
quest for a cultural purpose—for a name (Ewers 1958, 162–63). Perhaps
because of this novel's comic treatment of a ritual search, various critics
have debated whether the narrator does indeed recover his culture and
sense of place (McFarland 1993, 319–20). Peter Wild doubts that the narrator experiences any kind of cultural growth: "By book's end, despite
the listless comings and goings, the circumstances of his life seem to
have changed little" (1983, 27). But while other critics do agree that "the
winter in his blood has thawed" (Ruoff 1978a, 121), that he has recovered
his Blackfeet identity,[16] we still have not been able to provide a theoretical
explanation of this cultural recovery. I find that if we take seriously the
connection among knowledge, experience, and identity, we may articulate
this process of cultural recovery as a form of social inquiry. Drawing on a
view of cultural identity that contends that experiences possess a cognitive
dimension, I would like to show how tribal people evaluate and regulate
what they can know. In my theoretical account, Welch's narrator becomes
truly Blackfeet by deriving knowledge from ongoing cultural practices.

Because *Winter in the Blood* relies heavily on the power of ancestral
story to re-place individuals within Blackfeet culture and homelands,
cultural recovery involves appealing to kinship bonds between both the
living and the dead. The unnamed narrator of *Winter in the Blood* recovers
a Blackfeet identity by achieving more convincing knowledge of his ancestors and their ties to the land. On discovering that he is the grandson
of the hunter Yellow Calf, the narrator is suddenly reconnected to a richer
form of mediated access to traditional Blackfeet culture and its attendant tribal knowledge. In this powerful sense, he recovers a tribal history
to deepen his identity as a moral agent in the community. As the story
comes to light, he uncovers the fact that his grandfather—in an act of
moral solidarity—decided to break from his band and hunt for a woman
that his people wrongly abandoned. This resonating history, to which the
narrator is suddenly deeply attached, demands a revision in the way he
understands himself. In order to account for this experience, the narrator
recovers a new Indigenous identity. He thus grows culturally, not because
he returns to a cultural or historical foundation but because he now sees
his world more for what it is. His relationship to his forebears and their

land offers a comparatively stable center through which to guide his own revisable self-understanding.

Winter in the Blood moves between various places and times—between rural Blackfeet country and more urban and white areas; and between earlier days, just before the encroachment of the U.S. cavalry, and the contemporary era of colonization for Blackfeet people. The novel is, however, centered in a significant event that occurred in a specific place: one brutal winter in a valley of cottonwoods where the narrator's ancestors fought to keep their lives and their dignity: "'Many people starved that winter. We had to travel light—we were running from the soldiers—so we had few provisions. I remember, the day we entered this valley it began to snow and blizzard. We tried to hunt but the game refused to move. All winter long we looked for deer sign. I think we killed one deer. It was rare that we even jumped a porcupine. We snared a few rabbits but not enough'" (152). The other events in the novel hearken back to this central time and place; the narrator is drawn to the site of his ancestors' famine, as well as to the elder Yellow Calf, who eventually tells him of an event that shaped his life more closely than the young man ever knew. In Welch's characteristic language that is at once "sparse" and "sincere," as William Bevis notes (1997, 36–37),[17] Yellow Calf "remembers" a time among his people when food and warmth were scarce, when soldiers pursued his band to destroy them or force them onto reservations so as to end their traditional lifeways. Other Native peoples share similar stories of a significant event that demanded their survival and in which their ideas of themselves as a people were put to test, such as that of my ancestors' surviving their forced march from the Smoky Mountains to Indian Territory. Through story, we give meaning to our struggle. The experiences of mass death dealt by genocidal campaigns against Native people, even though we remember them bitterly, may help us to explain ourselves as we attempt to understand the actions of our ancestors in desperate times.

So when Kathleen Mullen Sands points out that "the function of storytelling in Indian communities is to keep life going, to provide a continuum of the past into the present, to allow for the predication of the future" (1985, 105), she does not fully recognize the frustratingly ironic place of story in the novel. The narrator's alienation from Blackfeet oral tradition deprives him of the very culturally integrative process that story engenders; only a profound act of the imagination can break this colonialist cycle of cultural deprivation. In *Winter in the Blood*, the land—as tied to story—sparks this creative moment of cultural revelation. The geographical location of this winter camp in the tribal memory becomes literal moral ground to which the band's descendants may go for ancestral knowledge. It is to this "winter in the blood," this winter that is part of their history (even if it is not in their conscious memories), to which the blood relation of Yellow Calf may return to more fully understand himself in relation to his past, and thus to recover his Blackfeet identity. In this way, Yellow Calf's narrative functions as a moral landmark in a novel otherwise deliberately distanced from history and tradition.

In the opening pages, the nameless narrator's return to his ancestral home is ironically estranging. Alienated even at home, he labors under a vague, pervasive feeling of distance among his people, a distance that becomes the nagging problem that complicates his identity:

> Coming home to a mother and an old lady who was my grandmother. And the girl who was thought to be my wife. But she didn't really count. For that matter none of them counted; not one meant anything to me. And for no reason. I felt no hatred, no love, no guilt, no conscience, nothing but a distance that had grown through the years.
>
> It could have been the country, the burnt prairie beneath a blazing sun, the pale green of the Milk River valley, the milky waters of the river, the sagebrush and cottonwoods, the dry, cracked gumbo flats. The country had created a distance as deep as it was empty, and the people accepted and treated each other with distance.
>
> But the distance I felt came not from country or people; it came from within me. I was as distant from myself as a hawk from the moon. And that was why I had no particular feelings toward my mother and grandmother. Or the girl who had come to live with me. (2)

The narrator begins his story of coming home with a declaration of unbelonging to both people and land; the women to whom he is related, his mother and grandmother, do not "mean anything" to him. But his sense of estrangement is most severe if we consider the importance of clan membership through matrilineal descent, and how ancestral knowledge is passed on through this kinship. Welch attaches the narrator's alienation from his maternal line to his alienation from the land itself, land that is both "milky" and thus fertile yet somehow "burnt" and inert. The narrator blames the land itself for the distance among his people and within himself: a cruel and unforgiving land has formed the people in its image. He attempts to place this feeling of distance, as he seeks to know why he does not know himself. At first, he can find "no reason" for his sense of distance, but later he identifies the "burnt prairie" as the cause. Finally, he realizes: "It came from within me." And if we look ahead to the new knowledge he gains of his hereditary connection to Yellow Calf and the winter, we see that the narrator's internal distance is real. Yellow Calf is like the "hawk" of his distanced self, the grandfather he comes to know as he comes to know himself, thus closing his distance from his ancestors: "His back shook, the bony shoulders squared and hunched like the folded wings of a hawk" (159). When the narrator finally closes this distance during his discovery with Yellow Calf, he gains a reason for his early feelings and even recovers a meaningful connection to his mother and grandmother.

As the narrator recovers his relationship to the women in his world, so he recovers his connection to the men. We thus might consider this restored tribal masculinity and how his alienation from it had contributed to his sense of distance. Near the end of *Winter in the Blood*, the narrator still muses on this sense of gendered distance as he struggles to close it, when he keeps a cow from sinking in the slough, its calf still bawling: "Some people, I thought, will never know how pleasant it is to be distant in a clean rain, the driving rain of a summer storm. It's not like you'd expect, nothing like you'd expect" (172). Throughout the novel, Blackfeet manhood is pitted in a similar tug of war between the feminine, blamed unfairly for its supposed coldness, and the masculine, engaged in a wandering search to contend with white men, and for impossibly nurturing women. Men's lives in the novel are haunted by a surreal distance, as is the author's narrative itself. At first, Welch's narrator seems to roam the pages in search of a place or time that will reveal a lost secret, and so we wander with the nameless Blackfeet man from ranch to town, from woman to woman—from memory to memory—in hopes of stumbling elegantly on some essential tribal belief. But in this nonromantic narrative, unmediated truths are ultimately unavailable, and we thus cannot completely close the aching distance that wracks us and the men of *Winter in the Blood*. Here, truth is eroded in the inescapable lapses into dream time triggered by painful events, and belief is complicated by both the young narrator and old Yellow Calf, when the narrator responds to Yellow Calf's portrayal of the world, "It's not a question of belief. Don't you see? If I believe you, then the world is cockeyed" (69). Later, Yellow Calf explains that belief plays little role in desperate decisions, recalling the winter of his band's famine: "It wasn't just a question of belief, it was the way things were" (155).

In the absence of an essential truth and static belief, the young man grasps toward an unresolved narrative of identity and wholeness: memory is all he has, but in his memory is "this shared secret in the presence of ghosts" (159). And so the son of First Raise retreats to and survives in memory—memory that establishes its own albeit jumbled narrative that ensures the paradoxical "close distance" that he and other men, dead and living, need in order to survive in their postcolonial landscape. The narrator finds himself cut off from all feeling, from all women, and ultimately from himself: "I was as distant from myself as a hawk from the moon" (2). He reels at the imposing white world, which blandly insists that men dominate women; it is an empowering world, but one from which Native men are also excluded. So he scuffles at its boundaries, moving between ranch and town, movie theater and saloon, attempting both to close and to maintain his distance from women. *Winter in the Blood* is a novel thus structured, in part, around a Montana Blackfeet man's search for a Native masculinity rooted in family and tribal history. Indigenous male wandering at first frustrates, and then eventually serves, the construction of Indian manhood. Robert Dale Parker traces this pattern of Native male character in the writing of the Red Power era in what he calls "restless young Indian men," a figure he finds introduced at least as early as the 1930s with novels by John Joseph Mathews and D'Arcy McNickle: "Under the influence of *Sundown* and *The Surrounded*, and even more under that of the ideologies and histories they represent and resist, a good deal of later Native fiction continues to revisit the preoccupation with restless young men who have nothing to do, and to reimagine the epistemology of Indian doing in a wider world that so often sees Indians as done to, and not as doing" (2003, 20). The narrator wanders the bars and wanders his past, waiting for his moment of knowing who he is: not the grandson of a drifter but the descendant of the principled hunter, Yellow Calf. His ludicrous search for the Cree woman who stole his gun and razor perversely echoes the tribute his grandfather paid to his grandmother so many years ago. And so, reconnected to his past he never knew, and to a woman, his grandmother, in a way he never knew, the young Blackfeet man finds a revived strength in being rejoined to women. He gleans for a moment this indomitable union between men and women, and perhaps closes his distance in search of her powerful sustenance. He finds his lost half, heals his "wild eye," and is again able to feel a sense of wholeness.

Blackfeet men in *Winter in the Blood* struggle to know themselves as men apart from mainstream white men, and sometimes even hate themselves for imitating their treatment of women. Arnold Krupat is right to remind us that American Indian novels written during Red Power actually "warned against the violent expression of rage" among Native men, but he also recognizes the possibility that this barely suppressed and bubbling rage against white culture might be misdirected toward Indian women in the novels: "A good deal of anger against women is expressed by characters" (2002, 107, 140). In his alienation from the land and from women, the narrator dramatizes the destructive effects of colonialism on American Indian men. While Native men suffer differently from Native women, the image of the fallen warrior may reinforce a negative stereotype among members of the dominant culture, who often desire to associate Native men with the frontier past. "The psychological, if not physical, impairment of Indian men is seen as critical to the colonial scenario. Indian women are more easily discounted regardless of the state of their mental health," according to Judith Antell (1988, 214). The narrator has internalized the majority culture's tragic image, and so he often pities himself; Yellow Calf chides the young man for this. The narrator is uncertain about how the older Indigenous men in his life have dealt with the oppressive mainstream masculinity. He at once admires those who can work and joke with European American men and ridicules those who pretend to have their power. When the neighbor Lame Bull arrives he asks the son of First Raise, "'Ho, you are fishing, I see. Any good bites?'" (7), then walks inside to marry his mother. In his usual indifferent banter, the narrator now calls Lame Bull "the proprietor," as if Lame Bull were now a white man of landed gentry.

In a sense, Lame Bull has married money in the old European tradition, but it is within the tribal marriage through which not women but men often gain new property from the union. Even so, in mocking admiration the narrator agrees with a shrug to work the ranch with him, for Lame Bull is also industrious and forthright. The narrator knows how difficult it is for Indian men to forego their traditional labor and now do the agricultural work of European men: he stands clear of the capitalist grin, the crashing fist, and the spray of blood that ends the employment of the hired hand Raymond Long Knife. He jests that Lame Bull's disproportionate body seems to be made for a landowner on a tractor: "Although he was thick and squat, half a head shorter than either Teresa or I, he had a long torso; seated on the bull rake, which was mounted on a stripped-down car frame, he looked like a huge man, but he had to slide forward to reach the brake and clutch pedals" (24–25). Lame Bull at times embodies white male authority: he fills the doorway in another man's house, sleeps with the narrator's mother in a bedroom built by the narrator's dead father, First Raise. Yet, Lame Bull poses no threat: "He grinned a silent challenge, and the summer nights came alive in the bedroom off the kitchen. Teresa must have liked his music" (23). Perhaps the narrator respects a man who dares to overtake his ranch land and home, who can work hard and fight, or then again, maybe he just does not care. After all, the narrator calls his mother "Teresa" and finds her cold and unnurturing: "I never expected much from Teresa and I never got it" (21). It could be that his feelings of distance as a man will allow him neither to hate Native men's concessions to white men, nor to love Native women. With the resurgent trope of men's distance, *Winter in the Blood* suggests that American Indian manhood can be strained by a relentless social and economic emasculation in the European American world. Lame Bull is an Indian man who finds success and comparative autonomy, though he sometimes might have to yield to mainstream masculinity to find that success; he is the proprietor but is not necessarily respected for this office, and thus he presents an interesting model of modern Indigenous masculinity as compared to that offered in the more traditional, humble, yet just as wily Yellow Calf.

In *Winter in the Blood*, the memories of dead men speak louder than the voices of living men. These Native men die either directly or indirectly from encounters with white men. To the narrator, the memory of the men in his life is more tangible than the reality: his memory of First Raise remains with him on the ranch: "It was always 'they' who found him, yet I had a memory as timeless as the blowing snow" (19). His memory of his brother Mose sleeps with him in his childhood bedroom: "two childhoods, two brothers, one now dead, the other servant to a memory of death" (38). The living serve the dead, and so are in a way also dead—removed from the living world, distanced. Mose was blindsided by a white man's car, while First Raise died a slower death repairing white men's machines and making them laugh. While we are warned about engaging binaries between a so-called white world and a so-called Indian world—a modern, technological, urban area, and a timeless, natural reservation—in this novel, such clear distinctions are difficult to avoid. In town, the narrator regresses into immaturity, going "up the line" from bar to bar, often scampering after the European American establishment, only to return home to wash it all off among healthy animals and pleasing vistas. Indeed, Mose dies crossing the restrictive boundary between these spaces, when his horse falters and collides with the white man's machine on the

Western, technological pavement. As John Purdy describes this highway: "The Highline goes only two ways—'up' for those who will make sacrifices to it, and 'down' for the rest—but there are other paths through the tan land" (1990, 143).

Like Lame Bull, First Raise conceived his masculinity in part through typically Western labor. The narrator harbors a respect and honor for his father that he does not have for Lame Bull, however. The narrator's long days haying even seem to be a tribute to his father, for throughout the days he lives in his memory of First Raise, repeating his corny motto: "Twenty dollars to kick a baler awake—one dollar for the kick and nineteen for knowing where to kick" (6). To the narrator, First Raise had a secret knowledge apart from white men and so was able to fool the men who took his land, wanted his women, and controlled his children. The memory of his father accretes in the narrator's mind until First Raise becomes a legend for him alone: "The toolbox had held my father's tools and it was said in those days that he could fix anything made of iron. He overhauled machinery in the fall. It was said that when the leaves turned, First Raise's yard was full of iron; when they fell, the yard was full of leaves. He drank with the white men of Dodson. Not a quiet man, he told stories and made them laugh. . . . He made them laugh until the thirty-below morning ten years ago we found him sleeping in the borrow pit across from Earthboy's place" (6). In the narrator's repetition of "it was said," he creates a myth of a fatherhood that perhaps never was. Here, we see the artistry of Welch's language: words graft themselves onto recurring images that are repeated in association with powerful events. Death follows laughter. How did First Raise die? Did he laugh himself to death before the white men? The narrator sees the painful irony in a father who died entertaining men, for he no doubt holds this to be First Raise's power over oppressive European American male society. That the father dies in a pit from which ranchers literally borrowed Indigenous land, never to be returned, suggests simultaneously that First Raise sought to take back what was "borrowed" by white men from Indians, and that he ultimately died from and in the masculine void the white American men had left him. The narrator is not, however, committed to any single image of Blackfeet masculinity, but instead possesses the insight of Yellow Calf, the humanity of First Raise, and the humor of Lame Bull. But existing in this ambiguous male space has its own problems; Andrew Horton puts it this way: "He is neither a kind of minstrel-show Indian like his father (entertaining whites) nor a dedicated farming Indian like his step-father, Lame Bull" (1978, 132).

Those Indian men who survive a mainstream European American world have sacrificed to do so. Even in traditional ways of Blackfeet men, such as hunting, the men in the novel are allowed no place. In Teresa's house, the narrator browses the pages of *Sports Afield* and reads about a group of white hunters on safari in Africa: "'They tracked the lion's spoor until the fourth day, when they found out that he'd been tracking them all along. They were going in a giant four-day circle. It was very dangerous, said McLeod, a Pepsi dealer from Atlanta, Georgia. They killed the lion that night as he tried to rip a hole in their tent'" (12). Welch darkly satirizes the great white hunter who becomes the hunted, who can find his target only at his feet, who shoots himself in the ass. But the passage also communicates a deeper despair for the reading narrator: white hunters cannot hunt but continue to rule Native people who can. The narrator recalls First Raise's perennial failure to execute his hunt—"a private ritual," according to Louise Barnett: "Perhaps First Raise never undertook the hunt because the gap between the dream and reality would have been too glaring" (1978, 124–25). So it is with comic sarcasm that Welch introduces the white "airplane man": "He had on one of those khaki outfits that African hunters like to wear. I thought of McLeod and Henderson in the *Sports Afield*" (45). Though the episodes in town among European Americans grow more surreal as the novel progresses, the narrator continues to sort through the senseless bars and streets—and to spend time with the ridiculous white hunter. He grows naive in the city and in the company of white men; he is foolishly drawn to the airplane man's crass wealth and power over women: "'Well, you take me—do I look like the sort who would run out on a wife and two beautiful daughters? Hell, by your standards, I was a rich man!'" (45). After all, the airplane man can catch the fish that the narrator cannot, as it seems that every white person and no Indian can.

Fish are strangely associated with American Indian women in *Winter in the Blood*. Native men struggle with finding them and catching them, only to discover that their flesh is too soft and not fit to keep. Like the seer Fish, who warns the people of the coming soldiers, fish are also the stuff of prescient dreams. That the fish in the novel are nutritional and even instructive, yet elusive and even dangerous, perhaps stems from the uncertain relationship with fish shared by Blackfeet and Gros Ventres peoples alike. "The ambiguity of the fish in the novel seems to relate directly to a strange ambivalence that existed in the traditional Blackfeet/Gros Ventres attitude toward fish. While, on the one hand, both cultures regarded fish as unclean and, hence, unfit to eat, on the other hand, they regarded fish as a mystic representative of considerable significance, particularly for the young," reminds William Thackeray (1985, 45). As the narrator recalls from his fitful hangover dream: "Suddenly a girl loomed before my face, slit and gutted like a fat rainbow, and begged me to turn her loose, and I found my own guts spilling from my monstrous mouth. . . . The gutted rainbow turned into the barmaid of last night screaming under the hands of the leering white men. Teresa raged at me in several voices, her tongue clicking against the roof of her mouth. The men in suits were feeling her, commenting on the texture of her breasts and the width of her hips. . . . The wanted men fell on the gutted rainbow and second suit clicked pictures of a woman beside a reservoir in brown light" (52). This fantastic sequence of images evokes the paranoia and lust of Hieronymus Bosch: gutted animals cry out like humans; mothers are sexual objects and give birth to chicks; lascivious white men grope voyeuristically all the while. Perhaps the dream reveals the narrator's deadened feelings toward women; to be with women is to destroy them, which in turn is to destroy oneself. The narrator's mother is tangled up in his image of women; she is at once sexualized and violated by those who oppress him. In fact, white men have developed a special fish lure that "calls to fish in their own language" (12). In their technological planning and plotting, great white hunters are now even better able than Indian men to close their distance from Indian women.

The distance in Blackfeet men seems to either kill them or make them run from women and home. Throughout *Winter in the Blood*, Welch traces the ineffable tension between Native women and Native men, a tension between women and their pull toward family, and men and their empty search for male power and identity. Often disempowered and emasculated, some American Indian men cannot find masculinity in marriage and family. "'Why would he stay away so much?'" the son of First Raise asks, as if the narrator had asked this many times. Teresa answers: "'He didn't. He was around enough. When he was around he got things accomplished. . . . Who do you think built the extra bedroom on the house? . . . He was around enough—he was on his way home when they found him, too'" (19). The son inquires why he did not see more, know more of his father, and the mother denies the father's absence with material proof: he built things, as if one could know the dead man better by spending time with the prefab monuments he left behind. And then:

"He was a foolish man," she said.
"Is that why he stayed away?"
"Yes, I believe that was it." (19)

The dialogue makes us ask whether a fool would know enough and feel enough to stay away. Teresa tells her son, also a wanderer, that he is "too sensitive." In doing so, does Teresa mean that Indian men should be less sensitive to an emasculating society—that this will keep them home? Caught like a fish between remaining sensitive and becoming steeled to the world, the nameless narrator struggles as his father might have done.

Of course, men's wandering in *Winter in the Blood* works neatly with what the narrator perceives to be women's cold and unmothering behavior. The women Welch represents here are either unnurturing "wild-eyed-spinsters," thieving of masculinity, or, like the narrator and other men, wandering for men and yet unsure about what that might cost. To a great extent, though, the Indigenous women in the novel also struggle against "stalking white men," and have been doing so for at least a century. "The best way to see the narrator's growth is to realize that his Cree girlfriend is just as lost and ostracized and just as in need of help in the Montana towns as the grandmother was during the desperate winter of 1883," as Jim Charles and Richard Predmore contend (1996, 57). In reading this novel over the years, I remain uncomfortable with Welch's exclusively straight portrayal of Indian men and his questionable representation of Indian women, who are figured in a reckless cow with a wandering eye who selfishly leads calves to slaughter. The narrator blames the spinster for his brother's death, because she arrogantly led the other cattle across the highway where Mose followed and was hit by a car. We nonetheless must account for the spinster's "wild eye." The author intermingles male and female tragic faults within one flawed and burdened animal: she cannot go "straight" for she cannot see. The untrusting wild eye makes her always half able to descry danger and to care for her young.

However, men seem to be half wild too. The narrator stays home to tend the ranch and hay the fields, but soon itches to wander off to town in search of a woman whom he never loved, sleeping with "the barfly," Malvina, Marlene, and perhaps others. In town, he closes in on the Cree woman who stole his gun:

"I'm looking for your sister," I said.

"How come?"

"A personal matter."

"How come?" . . . "What are you going to do when you find her?"

"That's up to her, I guess."

"You going to beat her up?"

"I don't know, maybe . . ."

"What did she do to you?"

"She took things that don't exactly belong to her," I mumbled. (42)

In all likelihood, the narrator does not even know why he seeks this elusive woman, nor does he know what he will do when he finds her. But he searches all the same to take back his potency or pride. Or, as Yellow Calf will show, he attempts to stay with her because he must; it is not a question of belief. Like the old blind protector, the narrator hovers around the Cree woman out of a suppressed desire to serve her.

When he finally does find her—we learn that her name is Agnes—he is frozen in his steps, caught between a discomfort at his closeness to her and a longing desire to shrink his distance from his feelings: "I wanted to follow her, to forget about the airplane man and his crazy business, his daughter and the purple teddy bear. I wanted to buy her a drink and sit with her and talk about whatever we had talked about before she stole my gun and electric razor. I wanted to be with her, but I didn't move. I didn't know how to go to her. There were people counting on me to make her suffer, and I too felt that she should suffer a little. Afterwards, I could buy her a drink" (102). Refusing to follow the airplane man in his wacky scheme would be the beginning of the narrator's new conviction not to be like the other Native men who scrambled after mainstream men. He could go to the woman who perhaps needs him—though we doubt it—just to talk. But he then hears the male advice of his elders, such as the "fishing" secrets of Lame Bull: "'Boy, you're going to catch her this time, I feel it in my bone—I mean bones—catchum, holdum, shrinkum—you got to treat these women rough once in a while or else they forget'" (71). At this mock-fateful moment—mock because Yellow Calf chose to stay with his woman in far graver circumstances—he must decide whether to go with the white hunter for money or to go get Agnes. Judging by the narrator's affiliation with Yellow Calf, the narrator will refuse to make her suffer, as others had asked Yellow Calf to scapegoat his grandmother during a famine of those now distant winters. In a parallel history with its own contemporary sense of crisis, the narrator concludes: "If I went through with it, I would become somebody else and the girl would have no meaning for me. Seeing her in front of the Silver Dollar had sparked a warmth in me that surprised me, that I couldn't remember having felt in years. It seemed funny that it should happen now, since I had felt nothing for her when we were living together" (102). The narrator's modern epiphany is no less powerful than Yellow Calf's. A glimmer of feeling seeps through when the narrator realizes that he will stay to be near Agnes, as Yellow Calf did years ago. And now even though he begins to close the ubiquitous distance that haunts him, he can do so only at a safe remove; he also cannot feel when he is too close.

When he finds another woman whom he did not intend to find, he treats her in a "half wild" way, too. In the most bizarre episode of Welch's novel, the narrator sleeps with Marlene in a dingy hotel room where he both loves and abuses her. At first, it appears that he has found comfort in a woman's body: "I never left the softness of her body. The first light of dawn caught me draped over her belly, my chin in the hollow of her shoulder, my eyes staring at a coarse black hair on the white pillow" (121). But then he does something that reveals his half wild pain: "I pinched her nostrils together and a great rasp began in her throat" (121). His subtle mistreatment of her grows into brutality: "'Kiss my pussy,' she murmured, and I slapped her hard across the cheek" (123). The narrator's frustrated cruelty toward Marlene appears even more elusive coupled with his emergent pity for her: "I sat up and looked at her. A kind of pity rose within me. Her naked body seemed so vulnerable, so innocent, that I wanted to cover her with my own" (122). The narrator's own body, slick with sweat and the grunge of town, no longer carries the cleaner dirt of innocence he remembers washing off with Mose: "That was a different kind of dirt—dust from the roads, chaff from the hayfields—not the invisible kind that coats a man who has been to town" (132). Covering Marlene's body with his own, the narrator resentfully squelches the innocence he has lost yet ironically upholds in his immaturity at thirty-two: "Sometimes I had to tell myself" (71). So we discern here the depth of his troubled masculinity: he cannot get enough life even from life itself—"it was not enough, not good. I wanted her to be alive" (123). Too close or too far, the narrator's manhood cannot survive at either distance. To heal this distance from women and himself, the narrator, Welch hints, will discover a past that reconnects and revives his faith in loving commitments.

Of course, the narrator knew a version of Yellow Calf's winter tale as told by his grandmother, but she omitted key parts of the story to avoid a return to the tortured memories of a time when the United States government actively sought to destroy her people. While the old woman's story remains clear in the narrator's mind as he lies in bed, now a man remembering, it still leaves him with an air of the unexplained. His feeling of absence, of an incomplete story of his familial past, haunts him as he associates it with the other aching memories of his brother Mose. These memories could offer an explanation if he were prepared to return to them, as he seems to in this moment of his life: "A low rumble interrupted my thoughts. I sat up and looked about the dark room. When I was young I had shared it with Mose and his stamp collection and his jar full of coins. In one corner against the wall stood a tall cupboard with glass doors. Its shelves held mementos of a childhood, two childhoods, two brothers, one now dead, the other servant to a memory of death" (38). Our own individual acts of decolonization often involve our reexamining the personal experiences that have shaped our lives. But because this reinterpretive project is likely to demand a return to times of loss, we often choose silence, especially when it guarantees the cultural invisibility and ahistoricity that accompanies modern mainstream living. Or perhaps it is worse if we decide to speak, for then we often tell a kinder story in which the abusive events have been removed. To avoid the pain of memory, we sacrifice the call for justice that telling the real story entails. And so the freeing of our selves is blocked by our own fear of drawing near the events that threaten a comfortable yet empty distance from our pasts. In the passage above, the narrator is called back from his distant place by a thundering sound, the "low rumble" of his brother's memory, and is thus compelled to confront an experience that obstructs his self-knowledge. In his recovery of his Blackfeet identity, the narrator will have to assume the agonizing role of "servant to memory," a title that makes him relive his nightmares of death and estrangement. But it is also a title that, in the end, provides a means to reinterpret his experiences and thus better explain his past and himself.

The repeated word "distance" throughout *Winter in the Blood* thus undergoes a gradual change in meaning. In the beginning, the narrator desires to become closer to himself and his Blackfeet culture, but he irreverently resents the epistemological responsibility that the process entails. As the novel continues, the young narrator slowly closes this distance by learning more about himself, his past, his people, and their land.[18] His recovery of new knowledge comes in degrees through a careful process of reinterpreting the past events of his people, as heard through the stories of his mother, his grandmother, and Yellow Calf. Through the theory that is oral tradition, he evaluates their experiences — and, by natural extension, his own — for their comparative ability to make sense of his life. And at the thrilling moment of his discovered tie to Yellow Calf the hunter, he finds greater immediacy in a stable center of value composed of his ancestry and their stories. As the narrator approaches this center, he experiences the unification of past and present, and his alienation diminishes. This experience of recovering an American Indian identity should not be taken lightly, even though Welch mingles farce with its presentation. As an experience similar to a paradigm shift in scientific inquiry, the recovery of cultural identity often demands a top-down reassessment of one's known world. Choctaw historian Devon Mihesuah explains this empowering moment as the "encounter" phase of Native identity, when "such persons experience a shocking event which jolts them into considering that their frame of reference for forming their identity is inadequate" (1998, 196). Such identitarian revisions — and their new political visions — do not come easy: the decolonization of the self demands the kind of moral growth that can only be recognized by answering colonial memory, explained again and again through one's reenvisioned cultural identity.

It is not until near the end of *Winter in the Blood* that we discover the point of searching for a historical identity in this surprisingly process-oriented narrative. All the seemingly senseless wandering of the narrator grows meaningful; even his wandering mind has found a point for its meandering through the past. Recursively working through memories, the narrator discovers who he never thought he was: his seemingly pointless visits to Yellow Calf are perhaps motivated by a deep and unknown drive to know himself through an encounter with his heritage. The "old man" does not even have to tell him who he really is; it is as if he knew all along.[19] He has always been grandson to a man who believes in an enduring relationship with women. At first, Yellow Calf seems plagued by a distance shared by other men: "He wasn't listening. Instead, his eyes were wandering beyond the irrigation ditch to hills and the muscled clouds above them" (151). But his eyes see nothing because he is blind. The utter blindness suggests that Yellow Calf is all "wild eyed" or, instead, more complete and secure than other men. Observing the old man, the narrator notices: "Something about those eyes had prevented me from looking at him. It had seemed a violation of something personal and deep, as one feels when he comes upon a cow licking her newborn calf. But now, something else, his distance made it all right to study his face. . . . But it was his eyes, narrow beneath the loose skin of his lids, deep behind his cheekbones, that made one realize the old man's distance was permanent. It was behind those misty white eyes that gave off no light that he had lived, a world as clean as the rustling willows, the bark of a fox or the odor of musk during mating season" (151). The narrator finds that the blind old man, like the fabled Tiresias, sees and feels far more than the narrator thought. The unknown grandson encounters a nurturing side in Yellow Calf's white eyes, as suggested in his embarrassment in watching him as if he were a mothering cow. With each sharing his own version of blindness across the generations, the narrator discovers here that the world is not always as it seems, and that even at its nadir life preserves dignity in its irrevocable past.

Yellow Calf now closes his own distance to share with the narrator in this elating moment in *Winter in the Blood*: "Perhaps he was recalling things he did not want to or he felt that he had gone too far. He seemed to have lost his distance, but he went on" (156). Seated in the sun beside his horse, the narrator feels this insight come to light:

> I thought for a moment.
> Bird farted.
> And it came to me, as though it were riding one moment of the gusting wind, as though Bird had had it in him all the time and had passed it to me in that one instant of corruption.
> "Listen, old man," I said. "It was you—you were old enough to hunt!"
> (158)

Welch offers no romantic narrative of an American Indian being mysteriously bestowed with tribal wisdom and self-knowledge: Bird "farts" to underscore the unavoidable "corruption" inherent in the process of decolonization and cultural recovery. Because producing and regulating knowledge is a cultural practice unavoidably mediated by theories, recovering knowledge requires a great deal of interpretive work that must distinguish between and account for both the sacred and the profane. By offsetting an otherwise pristine moment of ancestral knowledge with the play of fart-wisdom, Welch comments on the nature of tribal inquiry. Ancestral insight may ride the wind, but it is "not like you'd expect, nothing like you'd expect" (172). Knowledge arrives not through a sentimental search for the pure origin of Native culture, but with the *"awk! awk!"* of magpies. In a similar bodily moment, the narrator recalls his childhood when First Raise took him to see Yellow Calf, and First Raise pissed the narrator's name in the snow, teaching the boy his name, promising an identity, yet through a crude but sincere and humorous act.[20] Such profane, bodily insight speaks especially to the irreverent narrator. Unlike the questing Fisher King at which Welch hints,[21] the narrator has fought to uphold a persona of comic indifference toward his people and land. "Such realistic humor grounds the narrative vision and illusion in honesty and awareness," says Kenneth Lincoln (1983, 162).

The narrator now reconnects with what has been: "I began to laugh, at first quietly, with neither bitterness nor humor. It was the laughter of one who understands a moment in his life, one who has been let in on the secret through luck and circumstance. . . . And so we shared this secret in the presence of ghosts, wind that called forth the muttering tepees, the blowing snow, the white air of the horses' nostrils. The cottonwoods behind us, their dead white branches angling to the threatened clouds, sheltered these ghosts as they had sheltered the camp that winter. But there were others, so many others" (158–59). So the narrator closes the distance between himself and his past. For a brief moment, he and his grandfather disclose a mystery as they remember and rejoice and grieve for what was. The old man stayed behind to hunt for the young widow not to oppose the band's moral decision but to live with his own. All those years he stayed near but not too close, keeping the careful distance that he so needed. Yellow Calf settled his Indigenous masculinity in remaining neither near nor far, in the sharing of food and cover between companions. So doing, he puts an end to his grandson's wandering, at least for the moment, a rest to his restiveness that rightly leads critics such as Krupat to "read that novel as a bit more tentative in its conclusion" (1996, 43).

Though Welch regrounds us for a moment in a seemingly immutable past, he might actually do so at the expense of the present. Next to Yellow Calf's heraldic story, the image of men and women seeking each other through the honky-tonks of town clearly tarnishes. The oppression of Native people is still acute, and American Indian men still react to it in often-lamentable ways. Threats to Indigenous masculinity stalk today. But perhaps more than any other Indian novel written during Red Power (although Vizenor's *Bearheart* might be comparable), *Winter in the Blood* renounces masculine tragedy by balancing pathos with humor. Unlike Abel of *House Made of Dawn* or, as we shall see, Tayo of *Ceremony*, this narrator survives his male displacement through the self-preserving distance of irony. Set between the bookends of the two novels noted above, *Winter in the Blood* in fact insists on humor during its most serious moments, and also perhaps unlike them it avoids the label of didacticism. As Alan Velie notes: "It never approaches the stridency and bitterness of a protest novel. Throughout most of the book and certainly in most of the key scenes, the tone is richly comic" (1978b, 146–47). Even so, *Winter in the Blood* confronts the modern challenge facing Native manhood and suggests, with the reunion of Blackfeet men of different generations who are brought together in a mutual call back to the shared center between partners, that an American Indian man's wholeness and closeness can be recovered in tradition, and not in wandering but at home.

But even if the narrator gains new knowledge of himself and his relationship to his people, as revealed in Yellow Calf's version of his band's terrible winter, how can the narrator be sure it is more convincing? Owens describes cultural recovery as a reassembling of the jumbled pieces of "the puzzle of identity," but how can we be sure we reassemble the puzzle correctly? What process guides our interpretation of experiences, old, new, and recovered, and our views of ancestral stories? No doubt, this process of reinterpretation is confounded by the very cultural distance that the narrator strives to overcome: "I tried to understand the thinking, the hatred of the women, the shame of the men. Starvation. I didn't know it. I couldn't understand the medicine, her beauty" (155–56). If we, however, understand identity as an idea of ourselves, both individual and collective, that explains our experiences—our own and tribal ancestral pasts—we can evaluate such an idea on the basis of *how well* it explains our experiences. The narrator's new identity as the grandson of Yellow Calf necessarily explains more comprehensively the narrator's world. It makes sense of his place in his Blackfeet family in a largely Gros Ventre community, and of why his father ritually led him as a child to visit the old man. But most important, the narrator's reinterpretation of his tie to his ancestry places him in a world of rich history and belief and fills a previous cultural void, thus making greater sense of his world. Indeed, he is led to this new identity in ways that test conventional knowledge: "The answer had come to me as if by instinct, sitting on the pump platform, watching his silent laughter, as though it was his blood in my veins that had told me" (160). The young Blackfeet man has thus grown culturally: he now understands that winter in his blood.

Evaluating Tribal Identity

The narrator's new, more elaborated view of himself and his world is founded in knowledge gained from a renewed connection to his Blackfeet ancestors and the moral world they continue to sustain. His ties to them, though they run through bloodlines in his connection to family relations, such as his grandmother and Yellow Calf, are shared—mediated and interpreted—and are kept alive through oral tradition. With his newly discovered connection to a significant event in the land and past, he has now deepened his tribal historical knowledge, and thus further affirms his Blackfeet historical identity. Reconnected to the vast repository of oral traditional knowledge, the narrator possesses a greater understanding of his masculinity, and he will likely continue to grow culturally because he is now reattached to an enriched cultural center of value communicated through tribal story. In a similar manner during Red Power, Indigenous people gained new cultural knowledge through the recovered stories of their ancestors, and they reinterpreted their identities in relation to these expanded tribal histories. In this chapter, I have shown how a tribal realist theory of knowledge offers an alternative to two often-limited views on cultural identity. I do so by amending the antifoundationalist position to explain how cultural identity, though mediated, can be a reliable means of gathering historical knowledge of a tribal world. Recalling the role of identity in the political awakening of anti-imperialist struggles to serve Red Power, I propose an expanded understanding of tribal experience to better enable a legitimate project for social justice, an issue I elaborate next, in part 2, in my focus on American Indian politics.

Clearly, our justification for a politics of identity is challenged when we begin to compare various identities; suddenly, the search is on for the "real Indian," a pursuit that can never meet the demands of the American colonial imagination, as scholars such as Robert Berkhofer (1979) and Roy Harvey Pearce (1977) have demonstrated. To address these desires for the "authentic" Indian, a revised approach to American Indian identity might explain that some identities can be more justified than others because of their capacity to make sense of one's experience as an Indian person—a capacity that has been historically controlled by imperialist regimes of power. I argue that constructions of Native identities can be justified according to how well they refer to one's world and the depth of social growth they provide. Following from this claim, then, is the contention that identities can be romantic if they are not fully realized. No doubt such evaluations casually occur in everyday conversation, as one comes to learn, through the sharing of family and tribal history, where an American Indian person is "coming from." In these engagements, an Indian person invariably points to the world to explain his or her place in that world.

As I have been showing, a theory of identity should be able to account for varying degrees of epistemic access to reality: Indian identities thus may be evaluated for their comparative reference to society. In this way, we can distinguish legitimate identities from spurious ones, based upon how well such identities explain one's objective social location. Of course, our act of evaluating the ability of a particular cultural identity to evaluate is a sensitive process—one that, in a serious way, involves an intrusion into private worlds. But such evaluations can also be enabling, as we, for example, expose the economic exploitation of Native culture spearheaded by followers of the New Age, who often market bogus American Indian identities. From this perspective, we may also come to learn how a person's Indian identity explains a tribal past. Let us recall how Momaday, in his familiar statement on his tribal identity, describes the formation of himself as an Indian: "I think of myself as an Indian because at one time in my life I suddenly realized that my father had grown up speaking a language that I didn't grow up speaking, that my forebears on his side had made a migration from Canada along with . . . Athapaskan peoples that I knew nothing about, and so I determined to find out something about these things and in the process I acquired an identity . . ." (quoted in Schubnell 1985, 141). In coming to know his ancestral history, Momaday develops a Kiowa identity in an ongoing process of moral and personal growth. He achieves his more enriched view of his past through language and through transforming himself and his voice, "to make that language accessible to an Indian discourse," as Owens says (1992, 13).

Cultural identities, though, can also neglect to refer, especially when they evoke romantic, essentialist qualities of Native peoples. Such identity claims do not ring true to most Indian people, because they do not connect with a world that most Native people know. While it is true that Western epistemologies are less able to explain nonphysical ways of knowing, such as visions or totems, many American Indians also are less understanding of Native identities that seem less to refer to the social reality of being Indian. In her essay "Who Can Speak as an Indian?" Cherokee writer Diane Glancy explains her cultural identity as a voice that tells her she is Indian: "I hear it among the other voices. Late at night when the dish of scraps is set out back. Under the heavy trees in the distance where we used to drive to Arkansas. Not many times, but enough. The Indian voice speaks with my hands. I guess it's my pencil that's Indian. And didn't my red school tablet say *Big Chief?*" (1997, 9). Although we might imagine that Glancy places an offering outside for the spirit world, her words cited above are not as convincing a theory of American Indian identity because they refer entirely to an internal, private "voice" neither heard by nor shared with others. Hence, we are less able to discuss and understand their epistemic reference. Nez Perce and Osage writer William Penn often makes the same references, some of them biological, although his identity seems to be more grounded in the teachings of his grandfather: "It came out of race, perhaps, but it was not racial. It was why, when finches flew across the street, I called out greetings to them, 'Good morning, Juncos! How are you being?'" (1995, 2). Colonized cultural identity often requires emotional and cognitive effort to remember and reconstruct— imagine—who one could be. Joseph Bruchac begins his book-length explanation of his Abenaki identity as follows: "Jesse Bowman raised me to manhood without ever admitting his heritage, yet today I am known as an American Indian storyteller and writer. People in many parts of the country and other countries read my words. Some even think of me as a teacher, of sorts. My own children have followed the path that I now walk; and they too, adults now, tell the traditional stories, sing the old songs in Abenaki, and know the American Indian view of the world as their own. It is a Native view of the world that their father only fully realized was his own when he became an adult. How did this happen?" (1997, 5). Bruchac begins an honest inquiry into a Native heritage suppressed by racism, an oppressive social structure that inhibited his grandfather from ever fully realizing who he could be. If his new Abenaki identity provides a more comprehensive account of, say, the colonized legacy of acculturated Native peoples in the American Northeast, then his identity is more realized. Of course, some Native identities may refer to the social world more accurately than others; Indigenous people who speak their tribal languages are probably more likely to have access to a worldview that would otherwise be unavailable. An American Indian identity that draws on a tribal language would not, though, be more real because it is more "authentic," but rather because it would be more able to refer to a vast tribal repository of cultural knowledge. Evaluating American Indian identity should not be a careless task, however. Understanding how we see each other as Native people requires subtle and ongoing inquiry into the tribal lives that sustain us.

PART II. RED POWER

3

||||||||||||||||||||||||||||||||||||||||||||||||||||||||||||||||||||||||||||||

LEARNING TO FEEL: TRIBAL EXPERIENCE IN

LESLIE MARMON SILKO'S *CEREMONY*

In the bars, I thought. That's what you mean, but it's not important anymore. Just a girl I picked up and brought home, a fish
for dinner, nothing more. Yet it surprised me, those nights alone,
when I saw her standing in the moon by the window and I saw
the moon on the tops of her breasts and the slight darkness
under each rib. The memory was more real than the experience.
—**The narrator,** in *Winter in the Blood*

He nodded at Robert, but was involved with other things: memories and shifting sounds heard in the night, diamond patterns,
black on white; the energy of the designs spiraled deep, then
protruded suddenly into three-dimensional summits, their depth
and height dizzy and shifting with the eye.
—*Ceremony*

At the old Cherokee Female Seminary in Tahlequah,
Cherokee Nation, I stroll the campus, sit under the massive oaks, look
up at the clock tower with the Cherokee numerals, and imagine attending this strange, Westernizing school; the plaintive thoughts of the young
women as they, in long skirts, step around mud puddles on a spring day.
Several years ago, I stayed the summer in a dormitory here, studying the
archive at the old Seminary. On late nights, I traced the halls and pathways
of the campus, where back in the 1880s some of my aunts had left home
to attend, only to quit, homesick for Dodge, their community only about
fifty miles north. Perhaps like other American Indian scholars, I find
myself seeking to reduce such gaps in experience that restrict complete

knowledge of the world. The uncanny closeness I felt to my aunts' lives during those nights is difficult to explain in Western views of human experience, which tend to disregard the metaphysical as a source of knowledge. Among tribal people, however, such mystical experiences are often indispensable to understanding oneself in the world. Gather together such experiences—not only of ceremonial life, or even colonial subjugation, but the everyday moments that fill a memory: a walk on ancestral lands, a talk with a grandparent, a supper with family, a day's work—and understand the complex formation of Indigenous cultural identity. As we interpret the events of our lives, transforming them into what we call experiences, we create ourselves. Of course, that development is a collective effort among tribal people, in which the informed voices of Indian witnesses share and shape our histories, a social process that defines the "tribal" in tribal experience. Indian people thus develop their histories, their cultures, their very sense of national identity through the ongoing interpretation of experience.

As I discussed in the introduction, Red Power placed Indigenous experience in the midst of public appeals for Native rights. Scholars, activists, religious leaders, and everyday tribal people gave testimony of their lands and lives, on reservations and in cities. In sharing these differing experiences, individual Indian identity was reborn. But only with a self-reflexive, expanded relationship to tribal experience were Native people truly able to build a collective social movement. In this chapter, I turn to Leslie Marmon Silko's *Ceremony* to explore a tribal realist view of experience, in which experiences are capable of yielding theory-mediated knowledge of the Indian world. During Red Power, that knowledge was often political in content, for it disclosed to Native people the workings of power in their everyday lives. Here, in "Part 2: Red Power," I begin with this chapter to pursue empowerment in the era's literature, and then in the next chapter I consider the need for a more historically grounded political criticism.

In the epigraphs to this chapter, the writers James Welch and Leslie Marmon Silko situate experience and its memory at the center of their work, though *Winter in the Blood* and *Ceremony* employ American Indian experience quite differently. As I show in the previous chapter, the nameless narrator of *Winter in the Blood* contends with the troubling experiences of his own past and that of his ancestors by suppressing their memory, only to have them reemerge in other forms such as surreal dreams. In the quotation from *Winter in the Blood*, the narrator prefers the memory to the actual experience, for in the memory he is able to suppress the unpleasant elements of the experience—Agnes's abandonment of him—and instead retain the image of her beauty and desire for him. At this early moment in the novel, the memory of the experience seems more real, but this false knowledge only inhibits further inquiry into the experience that may better address his past. The nameless narrator of *Winter in the Blood* does, in the end, gain fuller knowledge of his community's tribal history and a more enabling relation to their present world. Like the narrator, Tayo of *Ceremony* faces a similar challenge to reconcile memory and experience, and he also suppresses his painful, inherited experiences in a place where he is able to live in a moment of powerful perception, as described in the epigraph above.

In *Ceremony*, however, the protagonist struggles with experiences of a critically different kind. Unlike the narrator's experiences, Tayo's are often metaphysical: they cannot be empirically verified within dominant Western thought. Because Tayo has forgotten his cultural training to accept and understand these experiences, he begins to believe he has lost his purchase on reality, as the military physicians have already concluded. His powers of perception plague him, tearing him away from everyday moments in the real world, in ways that lead even his Uncle Robert to question his sanity. Tayo "learns to feel" by moving beyond his dangerous solipsism to corroborate his emotions, dreams, visions, memories—all experiences—in a reliable Native social context. In discovering a tribal social organization for his formally misunderstood experiences, he is finally able to validate his non-Western experiences and gain useful knowledge from them. In theoretical terms, he does not retreat to a romantic view of religious experience and assume that the meaning of these metaphysical phenomena arrives intact and self-evident, but rather accepts the fact of its ideological mediation. Indeed, like the narrator, Tayo actively pursues a more adequate form of social mediation, one through which better to interpret his experiences of personal loss, war trauma, and imminent global devastation.

Despite the large body of writing on *Ceremony*, critics have yet to deal closely with the novel's exploration of the metaphysical, which repeatedly challenges Western views of knowledge. In reading tribal experience in this novel, we might encourage scholars to take the concept seriously in American Indian life and art, a characteristic of literature traditionally reserved for the English metaphysical romance. "[Whereas literary] realism is profoundly psychological precisely in the sense that it is interested in the effects of experience on individuals[,] metaphysical romance is more seriously concerned with the nature of experience itself" according to Edwin Eigner (1978, 2–3). In previous chapters, I have argued that Native scholars need not retreat to essentialism regarding Indian experience; here, such a position may lead critics to market *Ceremony* as a cultural object valued only within a Laguna cultural logic. Instead, *Ceremony* urges scholars and readers to reconsider the limits of a strictly empiricist view of human experience, and to expand the capacity of experience to encompass more than narrow historical fact. In this chapter, I explore the variety of Indigenous experiences: everyday emotions, inherited trauma, mystical visions. For it is our understanding of tribal experience in all its complexity that is the theoretical key to understanding this important novel and the colonial struggle it depicts.

On Tribal Experience

In American Indian literature, experience organizes the narrative in a great number of texts—ranging from testimony and autobiography to essay and novel.[1] Again and again, Indigenous people seek to give voice to their experiences, as they share their own lives and interpret them through the act of writing.[2] To do so, some Native scholars have leaned toward essentialism on tribal experience. In the introduction to the volume *The State of Native America*, Annette Jaimes Guerrero contends that since most of the contributors to the collection are American Indians, they "speak with an Indian voice" (1992a, 10). Or consider a more recent anthology of Native political writings, *Native Voices*, in which the editors—Yuchi/Seminole scholar Richard Grounds, Osage/Cherokee religious scholar George Tinker, and Lumbee legal scholar David Wilkins—write that, "since all the contributors are Native American scholars writing about Native America, they have an 'insider's' perspective and keen experiential insight" (2003, ix). Although one would hope the editors find that in having "Indian voices" such scholars are *more likely* to possess "keen experiential insight" from an "'insider's' perspective," as anyone in Indian Country might know, that view from inside is incredibly diverse. Paula Gunn Allen often avoids recognizing the particular differences among tribal groups and even among tribal members, and instead tends to present an essentialist view of a single American Indian experience: "Experiences that are held to be the most meaningful . . . are celebrated in the songs and ceremonial life of the people" (1992, 74).[3] Questioning this position on Native experience, trickster theorist Gerald Vizenor challenges those who "assume [to] discover and understand the essential tribal experience" (1993a, 15). Perhaps the ·intensity of profound tribal experiences leads Indian people less to question their mediated meanings, especially those of a religious or spiritual nature, as they often fueled Red Power.[4]

Despite differing Native views, tribal experience proves vital to any American Indian literary analysis or social movement. This said, the indispensability of Indigenous experience is only matched by its disregard in the majority culture. In Western philosophy, the rise of Cartesianism enabled thinkers to isolate human experience, for they knew that with experience lay the point of inquiry into knowledge of the world. This isolation began with the eschewing of nonphysical forms of experience—those found to be extremely mediated and thus nonverifiable, such as dreams, visions, and revelations. In so doing, phenomenologists such as Edmund Husserl clarified the interpretation of human experience, but also restricted vital phenomena from our inquiries. Today, literary theory bears this legacy and still relies on this model of experiential foundationalism to reckon with experience; personal experience must be self-evident and unambiguous to engender reliable knowledge. For better or worse, dominant literary scholarship rarely even considers the nonphysical forms of experience in its critique of experience.[5]

So let me declare the obvious, that, to Western eyes, tribal forms of experience such as dreams, visions, and ceremonial, athletic, and certainly narcotic revelations cannot possibly produce reliable knowledge. Tribal professors are thus greatly challenged when, in a largely Western classroom, they ask students to accept the Ho-Chunk autobiographer Crashing Thunder's revelation of a miniature soldier sitting on the knee of the Peyote road man, or the Crow autobiographer Pretty Shield's experience of a mouse speaking to warn of an enemy attack. To contend with this assumed incommensurability of Western and tribal views of experience,[6] Indian scholars can easily "secularize" their studies. I have done so myself; I have taken the easy route to explain religious experience as a phenomenon meaningful to tribal peoples within their own cultural contexts. But as Native literary scholars know, such cultural relativism does not confront the rigorous questions regarding human experience and thus will never ask Western readers to take tribal cultures seriously enough to be changed by an encounter with them. In the conclusion to *The Metaphysics of Modern Existence*, Vine Deloria outlines not only the role of the mystical in a tribal view of experience, but also its potential contribution to West-

ern, indeed, human knowledge: "Today we seek to expand our knowledge
of the world, the signposts point to a reconciliation of the two approaches
to experience. Western science must now reintegrate human emotions
and institutions into its interpretation of phenomena; Eastern peoples
must confront the physical world and technology. . . . Our next immediate
task is the unification of human knowledge" (1979, 212–13). Deloria recognizes that Native people, too, can benefit from adapting Western knowledge within their own scientific communities—a view that is entirely in
keeping with American Indian thought.

As experiences do not contain prearranged meanings waiting to be revealed, they often undergo a series of interpretations when tribal members
weigh one view of an event with another over time. Indigenous philosophy
indeed relies on this very process of interpretation, in which multiple accounts of the universe interact and corroborate to explain the world as we
presently know it. As I have shown in previous chapters, traditional Native
worldviews assume and accept this theory-mediated quality of knowledge.
Black Elk's greatest challenge is to interpret his vision well, but only with
the help of his community. From an Indian view, then, social mediation
in experience is not an obstacle but a path to knowledge. Through mediation, a community member tests various accounts of an experience to
determine exactly which interpretation best explains an event and enables
the social world. With story, tribal people draw on these accounts to maintain what Michael Wilson calls "a stable arena of life and value" (1997,
134). In this regard, some forms of mediation can actually help to produce more objective knowledge, because they enable us to read the world
from a different and particularly useful perspective. On this tribal realist
definition of theory-mediated objectivity, American Indian people might
possess a privileged understanding of colonial relations in North America,
because they occupy a unique location in the world and thus have access
to experience, and the resulting knowledge, that others might not. In this
manner, Native people provide cultural mediation to knowledge of our
shared colonial world that we otherwise would not possess. From this
standpoint, such oppositional knowledge, gained through experience, is
vital to attaining more complete accounts of a world all of us inhabit.

In the task to expand the concept of experience, perhaps less controversial is that of the emotions. Theorizing the role of emotions in social transformation, Satya Mohanty argues that, even though personal experience is
socially constructed, it is through this very mediation that experience has
the ability to yield more objective knowledge. Projects of recovery, accord-

ing to Mohanty, in fact demand a form of actively employed theory me-diation. Drawing on the work of the feminist scholar Naomi Scheman, he explains that when a woman in a consciousness-raising group "discovers" a more accurate emotion through which to understand her oppressive ex-perience, she does not appeal to "a fully formed emotion that was waiting to be released" (1997, 206). Instead, Mohanty argues, "the reason why we say that Alice 'discovers' she has been angry is that the anger underlay her vague or confused feelings of depression and guilt; now it organizes these feelings, giving them coherence and clarity. And our judgment that the anger is deeper than the depression or guilt is derived from (and cor-roborated by) our understanding that is based in part on a 'theory'" (208). Mohanty recognizes that emotions are profoundly mediated, yet, few will doubt, indispensable for understanding ourselves and our places in the world. Their importance in social struggles is enormous; indeed, without drawing on the emotions, we would be incapable of claiming our painful pasts or transforming ourselves politically for our futures.

Since such political transformations involve awakening to the insidi-ous operation of power in colonized lives, they often begin with a vaguely felt emotional reaction to one's oppressed social circumstances. As we re-interpret the initially unclear feelings of, say, shame about one's poverty, most likely among others who feel the same, we often arrive at more accu-rate, empowering, and motivating emotions, such as anger at the institu-tions that promote poverty. We may evaluate our "new" emotion based on the explanation, or theory, it provides of the social facts around us. So, like other experiential data, emotions can be evaluated and refined to allow us to explain the world more fully. One who moves from disabling shame to motivating anger has achieved this real political progress, then, through a reinterpretation of the emotions. Of course, this interpretive process in the emotions is indispensable to American Indian political struggles.[7] To narrate how personal experience can yield reliable knowledge, many Native people need look only to their own lives. I offer an experience of my own to demonstrate.[8]

For many Native people, going home involves tangled feelings of secu-rity and anxiety, because many of our communities suffer extreme domes-tic problems. Though my own family has been torn by poverty, domestic violence, and alcoholism, I still return to feel surprisingly secure in a familiar place among those with whom I share a history, no matter how painful. Despite its troubles, family is often the community we trust for describing and interpreting our experiences. During graduate school, I went home to take my mother to a preparatory examination for her badly needed hip-replacement surgery. There was only one physician in the area who would accept her welfare medical insurance, and my dark-skinned mother was not entirely comfortable seeing a white male doctor. We were a little late for her appointment, and the nurses were especially rude to us. They abruptly ushered in my limping mother to see the doctor. This brusque treatment humiliated my mother, and, confused and afraid, she complained to the nurses about their coldness. Upon hearing this complaint from the nurses, the physician swiftly entered our room to inform my mother that he would not perform her surgery. I had to help my crying mother walk all the way out of that clinic, past those smirking nurses. We both felt so ashamed. That night, a lot of family members came over for supper at my mother's apartment. Shouldering the day's events, we felt a vague sense of failure to obtain her surgery. As we exchanged food and talked curiously about what had happened, we came to share how embarrassed we often feel in such situations. My mother said she just could not let the doctors "take her dignity." Even so, we both felt oddly ashamed for having complained, and for being rejected and asked to leave. As the talk circled the room, many of us confirmed the same feelings of shame, but others, like my aunt, explained how they were actually often angry for such treatment, and we considered this alternative reaction. We found that our anger better explained the turn of events; it was more justified than shame. The conversations went on into the evening, as we confirmed our shared experiences of such events, and our new feelings of anger about them.

In this experience my initial feelings of shame were not pulled from an essential core of American Indian values, but rather were the highly theory-mediated and socially constructed reactions to the social facts that are often part of economic and racial oppression. Like many Indigenous families, we spent the summers back home in our tribal community. But my mother, through her involvement with the local Indian Center, as well as through her formation of an extended family, was able to reassemble an approximation of that community. In this community, we can better trust to share our experiences with each other. My mother and I, with the family, reinterpreted our original feeling of shame and then produced an emotion, anger, that was more adequate to our experience; with this new emotion, we in turn were able to organize a more cogent description of my family and Indian subjugation in U.S. society. By these standards, we have grown not only emotionally but morally and politically, for we can now explain more comprehensively the political features of our social world. The community setting of our evening clearly presents a mediated environment for the process of collective interpretation; my aunt actually intervened to change our views with an explanation that otherwise would be wholly personal. But our new feelings of anger are more able to expose the social facts of economic and racial domination in ways that politically mobilize American Indians. For this reason, our emotion of anger is not only a more productive explanation of events, but also more socially enabling than that of shame. Audre Lorde justifies the expression of anger not because it is politically strategic, but because this emotion is often more likely to reveal something about the oppressive social situations of, as she writes, African American women: "Anger expressed and translated into action in the service of our vision and our future is a liberating and strengthening act of clarification, for it is in the painful process of this translation that we identify who are our allies with whom we have grave differences, and who are our genuine enemies" (1984, 127).

Native communities function in this same way: as safe environments in which to share and evaluate often-unorganized emotional responses to troubled circumstances and events. In such contexts, as in my mother's apartment, the discussion is clearly political—theory-mediated—as we collectively evaluate the social facts to revise our accounts of the world. But in this kind of social arrangement, an American Indian community often comes to know feelings of rage or despair that have been confused with internalized forms of colonialism. As we discuss our experiences, we often discern how they are tied to broader experiences of oppression that can be historically located in the conquest of Indigenous nations and peoples. And so, part of a family discussion is coming to know, through our emotions, something about the politics of being Indian. We have created the conditions for a kind of emancipating growth that is not likely to flourish elsewhere. As Scheman argues, the alternative to this environment, the world outside our communities, is not neutral or value-free but is instead dominated by hidden political systems that can work to devalue the lives of Native peoples, often in the subtlest of ways (1980, 186). Social facts often have to do with ongoing colonial relations, in addition to gender or class hierarchies, which work to degrade Native cultures. By collectively organizing and interpreting a world comprised of these social facts, we can maintain a theory that makes sense of American Indian lives. Without such a social theory as "Native lives," we would not be able to explain the significant features of Indian Country and U.S. society. In its exploration of various forms of Indian experience, *Ceremony* is perhaps the foremost Native text from which to consider such American Indian lives.

Experience and Knowledge in *Ceremony*

This novel assumes a collective vision of resistance and renewal in which we, along with Tayo, are asked to consider the challenges of the volatile yet promising era of Red Power. For Tayo to be healed he must finally make sense of his experiences; to do so he must expand his interpretive framework as it modifies in response to the Laguna community. Jace Weaver concludes: "Ultimately, Tayo is able to achieve wholeness only by re-membering himself in the community" (1997, 134). From the first pages, even readers alien to Laguna cosmology recognize universal mythic movements to transcend the historical: the gods above invent the world below and name it; an injured hero embarks on a healing quest to gain new power.[9] Drawing and even absorbing us into the Laguna mythic consciousness, *Ceremony* transforms its readers. Toward this process, Kathryn Shanley affirms American Indian storytelling as a powerful form of colonial resistance, for it reconnects the Western individual with the communal whole (1984, 116). Silko accomplishes this task with European Americans despite the novel's announcement that it was not Columbus who invented the Indian but Indians who invented the evil white man! The novel's power to subsume, I contend, is what heralds *Ceremony* as the most canonized American Indian text.[10]

Ceremony opens catalytically, when the story and the ceremony are "set in motion," calling readers to grow with the narrative like a story in the belly. With the announcement of "Sunrise," we move with the rising sun toward rain in the West, as the story germinates from a fragmented account of drought, loss, and regret, into a graceful narrative of flourishing, regeneration, and gratitude. When Tayo encounters Ts'eh, a human figure of Yellow Woman the rain deity, he recalls this song for the sunrise:

Sunrise!
We come at sunrise
to greet you.
We call you
at sunrise.

Father of the clouds
you are beautiful
at sunrise.
Sunrise! (182)

As with many Indigenous songs or stories, the language of this Laguna song does not merely celebrate an object but instead acts performatively to change the physical world; its utterance alters the universe. In *Pueblo Gods and Myths*, Hamilton Tyler describes this practice widely shared among the Pueblos: "Each day, as the Sun rises the Zunis stand before their doors and toss an offering of cornmeal to greet their 'father'" (1964, 137). Like other spiritual leaders at dawn, Tayo helps bring the sun up, "calling" the sun to come, beckoning: Sun, rise. This hopeful awakening promises the birth of a new day, the emergence of a new story from the belly, and thus carefully preempts any assumption that this will be a story of American Indian cultural decline. And the novel ends not with a sunset, but with another sunrise: "Sunrise, / accept this offering, / Sunrise" (262).

Our introduction to the protagonist of *Ceremony*, however, is hardly propitious, though Tayo wakes, at sunrise, in his own ancestral homeland.[11] Tayo meets the sunrise nearly banished to his family's ranch, in their land's seventh year of drought, haunted by dreams of war and childhood, of the melded deaths of Japanese soldiers and loved ones, to the droning mixture of his mother speaking Laguna, Japanese voices, and the jukebox. These dreams and voices are not to be dismissed, for Lagunas, like many Native peoples, take nonphysical impressions seriously, as a form of experience that matters to this world. Tayo's internal world reveals that he is critically out of balance and order; one memory blends with and within another, his past a shuffled collection of images and experiences with little coherence. His mind's drive to return to his sleeping memories and his body's fear of what these experiences will demand of him make both sleep and wakefulness—living—unbearable: "So Tayo had to sweat through those nights when thoughts became entangled; he had to sweat to think of something that wasn't unraveled or tied in knots to the past— something that existed by itself, standing alone like a deer" (7). In suffering these nightmares, Tayo finds, like Abel and the narrator, that coming home demands more than merely returning one's body to ancestral lands. For Tayo, a true homecoming, one that heals beyond war trauma, will require a deep change in the way he relates to his individual, tribal, and mystical experiences of the past and present. He will need to reinterpret his painful memories—many of which take place elsewhere or are only his by supernatural relationship—in terms of the rooted center that his Laguna community represents and sustains. In this narrative, Western and tribal readers alike must reconsider the veracity of Tayo's metaphysics, and, by novel's end, like Tayo they are encouraged to deepen their appreciation of a suppressed form of experience that nonetheless conveys and maintains the world.

On the battlefield, Tayo's beloved uncle Josiah appears to remind him that his tribal approach to experience explains a troubled world that now requires more than strictly empirical explanations. Josiah's ghostly presence warns Tayo that the Western "facts" and "logic," which his cousin Rocky so admires, will not help them here:

> "But, Tayo, we're *supposed* to be here. This is what we're supposed to do."
>
> Tayo nodded, slapped at the insects mechanically and staring straight ahead, past the smothering dampness of the green jungle leaves. He examined the facts and logic again and again, the way Rocky had explained it to him; the facts made what he had seen an impossibility. He felt the shivering then; it began at the tips of his fingers and pulsed into his arms. He shivered because all the facts, all the reasons made no difference any more; he could hear Rocky's words, and he could follow the logic of what Rocky said, but he could not feel anything except a swelling in his belly, a great swollen grief that was pushing into his throat. (8–9)

Though Rocky "had reasoned it out with him," Tayo resists his cousin's mathematical explanation of his inverted universe, of the brutal facts that form the contours of their experiences, because they fail to adequately explain not only why they are away from home fighting the enemy's war, but also the sheer insanity of the destruction of life—represented all around him in the bloody reality of trenches filled with bodies. He first reacts to this inscrutable display with horror, registered in a bodily refusal to interpret, for such anathema defies logic. In the tradition of opposed twins evoked so frequently in Native oral traditions, Silko introduces the relationship between Rocky and Tayo as a comparative framework through which to engage Western and Indigenous models of inquiry and ways of knowing.

Tayo recalls his early experiences of sharing a room with Rocky when his aunt Thelma reluctantly took him in. The boys are set in racial contrast: Rocky the born-and-raised Laguna "pure blood," and Tayo the street kid from Gallup and, with a Laguna mother and unknown father, the impure "corrupt blood." But Silko dislocates mainstream assumptions that race imparts cultural "purity" by inverting the expected depth of the boys' social and religious beliefs. Rocky is hostile to Laguna spirituality; he has nearly converted to secular Western science, and plans to enter the American mainstream. Home their first year from boarding school and influenced by his new Western education, Rocky begins to reject his religious traditions: "Old Grandma shook her head at him, but he called it superstition, and he opened his textbooks to show her" (51). Tayo recalls an evening, years later, before their enlistment, when Rocky sat at the kitchen table studying to prepare for "the places he would live, and the reservation wasn't one of them" (77). Josiah is planning to breed cattle, and, after reading a BIA book on scientific cattle ranching, he concludes that the government people are not in a position to understand the Indian cattle business: "'I guess we'll have to get along without these books.' . . . 'We'll have to do things our own way'" (75). But when Josiah asks Rocky for his impression, Rocky snaps, "'Those books are written by scientists. They know everything there is to know about beef cattle. That's the trouble with the way people around here have always done things—they never knew what they were doing.'" (76). Rocky relies instead on "books and scientific knowledge—those things that Rocky had learned to believe in" (76). Rocky is finally sadly duped in his strict reliance on Western explanations of experience—explanations learned in schools and BIA programs: "But, Tayo, we're *supposed* to be here." Michael Hobbs contends that, in fact, Rocky dies because he is unable to question the promise of American experience presented in Army recruitment pamphlets; he cannot "read" his experience critically: "Rocky's reading is orthodox because it is naive and unevasive, and his interaction with white textuality indirectly costs him his life" (1994, 304). But if Rocky has learned to disavow his traditional beliefs and to embrace Western science and American progress, we might consider why Tayo, who does not receive the same long-term exposure to Laguna traditions but has attended the same schools, is not similarly seduced.

Indeed, despite his early upbringing, Tayo displays all the promise of a young man destined for the Pueblo traditional priesthood. Like Rocky, he attends the government school, where Laguna and other Indian children are taught that their nonphysical belief systems are superstitious and that Western secular knowledge properly explains the world: "Like the first time in science class, when the teacher brought in a tubful of dead frogs, bloated with formaldehyde, and the Navajos all left the room; the teacher said those old beliefs were stupid" (194). Not only do the U.S. schools ridicule traditional ways of knowing, but they also insist on the utter primacy of Western science. Watching a spider, Tayo recalls a Laguna story about Spider Woman, then checks himself: "In school the science teacher had explained what superstition was, and then held the science textbook up for the class to see the true source of explanations. He had studied those books, and he had no reasons to believe the stories any more" (94). But in the face of this institution, Tayo easily recalls the vast body of Laguna traditional stories of Hummingbird and Fly, Kaupata, and Arrowboy, remembering them at key moments of moral and spiritual decision. Despite his clearly substantial training in the ways and values of his people, a number of critics insist that, even before the war, Tayo grows up extremely alienated from his Laguna culture, even "deracinated" (Tarter 2002, 100). Ellen Arnold claims that although Tayo lives at Laguna, he has no tie to homeland: "Returning from war, he experiences ultimate deterritorialization—he is homeless, adrift in space and time, invisible, and inarticulate" (1999, 72). Though other culturally grounded characters in the novel likely do not speak their Native language, Dennis Cutchins also finds Tayo inarticulate, "stripped of his native language [and thus] "handicapped[,] his inability to speak Keresan . . . severely limits his capacity to cope with the world" (1999, 80). Though Ceremony displays considerable evidence of Tayo's significant cultural connections, many mainstream scholars nonetheless insist that Tayo is in cultural decline.

One can only conclude that such critics repair to the most popularized U.S. cultural narrative through which to manage the Indian: the myth of the Vanishing American. In fact, at least as early as his arrival to his aunt's home, Tayo has the education of his uncle Josiah and old Grandma, who spent enough time training him in his culture for him to recall his uncle's words during life's trying moments. In the jungle rain: "It was there that Tayo began to understand what Josiah had said. Nothing was all good or all bad either; it all depended" (11). Considering the behavior of animals, Tayo again recalls Josiah's wise words on the complexity of human struggle: "Josiah said that only humans had to endure anything, because only humans resisted what they saw outside themselves" (27). Though fatherless, Tayo receives from his Indian uncle the moral training that Indian fathers, in many traditions, are not to provide. Josiah, along with old Grandma, teaches Tayo the Laguna oral traditional stories, which serve to guide Tayo morally throughout his life. When Tayo carelessly kills even a fly, Josiah tells him the story of Greenbottle Fly, who brought back the rain, and then gently cautions: "'Next time, just remember the story'" (102). Tayo challenges the Western scientific explanations from school by recalling the teachings of old Grandma: "'Back in time immemorial, things were different, the animals could talk to human beings and many magical things still happened.' He never lost the feeling he had in his chest when she spoke those words, as she did each time she told them stories; and he still felt it was true, despite all they had taught him in school . . ." (95). Throughout his early spiritual education, Tayo is taught to "feel" the stories in his body, a sensory reaction to tribal experience that prepares him for his spiritual calling years later.

Moments such as these demonstrate that Tayo is far more culturally Laguna than many critics recognize. Indeed, he likely possesses more comprehensive cultural and geographical training than many European Americans whom we generally do not assume to be deracinated. And despite Tayo's supposed deterritorialization, he is clearly grounded in his homeland and retains his geoidentity upon his return from the war. Tayo recalls Josiah teaching him about the Laguna's very place of emergence, the Paguate Spring:

> "You see," Josiah had said, with the sound of the water trickling out of the hose into the empty wooden barrel, "there are some things worth more than money." He pointed his chin at the springs and around at the narrow canyon. "This is where we come from, see. This sand, this stone, these trees, the vines, all the wildflowers. This earth keeps us going." He took off his hat and wiped his forehead on his shirt. "These dry years you hear some people complaining, you know, about the dust and the wind, and how dry it is. But the wind and the dust, they are part of life too, like the sun and the sky. You don't swear at them. It's people, see. They're the ones. The old people used to say that droughts happen when people forget, when people misbehave." (46)

In this instructive moment, Tayo learns not only his people's ancient place of mythic origin, but also valuable lessons in how to care for the land against the temptations of Western capital, a memory that impacts him with all the more anguish since he has cursed the rain and contributed to the people's drought. Reminding Tayo that the land must be actively nurtured by humans, Josiah cautions him not to forget, suggesting the story of when the people became distracted with the ck'o'yo magic. Removing his hat in silent prayer, Josiah might have been presciently preparing Tayo to manage spiritual power and witchery: "'Remember that / next time / some ck'o'yo magician / comes to town.'" (256).

Josiah has taught Tayo about his people's ancestral places, their associated stories and their social meanings—where he is from and how to live—and these are quite enough to get him along in the world as Laguna. Tayo does not possess the holy songs and rituals, but even within the community only certain individuals are privy to the ceremonial knowledge maintained within the medicine societies. Pueblo knowledge about the Kachinas, the supernatural beings who bring rain and fertility, is held secret by the Kachina society: "Rio Grande Pueblo Indians are very secretive about the cult and masked rites and may deny that they exist. Katcina ceremonies are closely guarded; only those Pueblo Indians who know and revere the Katcina may see them," according to Santa Clara Pueblo anthropologist Edward Dozier (1970, 154).

So when Tayo returns to Paguate Spring after the war, and he does not know all the words to the prayers, readers should not assume outright that he is culturally adrift. He is an everyday Laguna with some, not all, spiritual knowledge: "He wished then they had taught him more about the clouds and the sky, about the way the priests called the storm clouds to bring the rain" (49). Tayo likely knows some, but regrets not knowing more, of the esoteric ways of the holy men. In a memory-within-memory, Tayo recalls honoring the spring before his departure for the war:

He knew the holy men had their ways during the dry spells. . . . Josiah never told him much about praying, except that it should be something he felt inside himself . . . These springs came from deep within the earth, and the people relied upon them even when the sky was barren and the winds were hot and dusty . . . The spider came out first. She drank from the edge of the pool, careful to keep the delicate eggs sacs on her abdomen out of the water . . . He remembered stories about her. . . . Dragonflies came and hovered over the pool. . . . There were stories about dragonflies too. He turned. Everywhere he looked, he saw a world made of stories. . . . It was a world alive, always changing and moving; and if you knew where to look, you could see it, sometimes almost imperceptible, like the motion of the stars across the sky. (93–95)

In nearly the same words, Tayo recalls the teachings of Josiah, who advises him to respond to his spiritual feelings in a sensory impulse to promote religious experience. Viewing a spider, the young man connects her with her mythic counterpart Spider Woman, the weaver of weblike narratives to organize the world and to affirm his maternal relation as a child of the earth before he leaves for war. Tayo has not entirely lost his Laguna language, because he dreams his mother's words (6), and in his "childish" grasp of Laguna, he works to understand the old dialect of the Laguna doctor Ku'oosh (34). Tayo thus regrets his limited religious training not because he is without his culture, but in fact because he desires greater spiritual knowledge within his culture. I even suggest that Tayo possesses a special gift for receiving Laguna spiritual knowledge, as shown by his multiple supernatural experiences, which he better understands as he matures.

Though he does not fire a gun, Tayo is among the soldiers who execute their Japanese prisoners, and he sees the face of Josiah in one as he falls: "he *knew* it was Josiah" (8). Rocky and the others reject the knowledge of Tayo's experience: "They called it battle fatigue, and they said hallucinations were common with malarial fever" (8). Such wartime visions and sounds—the relived experience of Rocky's death, the "screaming and the sound of bone crushing" replay in Tayo a waking sensory nightmare (28). He is further disturbed by occult experience, when he "hears the moaning voices of the dark whirling winds" of witches (233). Experiencing this other world every day, Tayo considers accepting the Army's diagnosis of his psychosis: "It was easier to feel and to believe the rumors. Crazy. Crazy Indian. Seeing things. Imagining things" (242). From these doctors, Tayo learns only that Western views of experience will not help him understand, but will only dismiss, his experiential world. To heal, Tayo must reevaluate his often-mystical experiences in relation to the facts that surround him—but in more encompassing, Laguna terms. Recognizing that his own and his community's health depends on the reliable interpretation of his known world, Tayo comes to accept, by degrees, this human task of revaluing tribal experience. "It took a great deal of energy to be a human being, and the more the wind blew and the sun moved southwest, the less energy Tayo had" (25). Until he reconsiders his supposed hallucinations in Laguna terms, as informative religious experiences, Tayo struggles against the forces that encourage him to grow and to become part of a dynamism that not only reveals the inherent balance of the living world, but also weaves humans into the web of relations that sustains it. In the Pueblo worldview, becoming human is an achievement. It is a process that requires forming a notion of how we should live to allow the world to remain balanced and alive. Through this theory of human growth, we, like Tayo or Yellow Calf, "lean into the wind to stand up straight"—that is, strengthen our ways of interpreting the human experience in the world.

The Navajo medicine man Betonie advises Tayo: "You've been doing something all along. All this time, and now you are at an important place in the story" (124). Western readers might be uncomfortable with this suggestion that we are mere actors in the great pattern of the universe, and our momentary decisions are nothing more than a passage in an ancient story largely beyond our understanding. But Silko takes great risks to introduce us to a tribal view of time and cultural development, in which the ceremonial calendar guides life's daily movements, and "getting ahead" might, in the Laguna world, mean improving one's "ear for the story and the eye for the pattern" (255). Alfonso Ortiz explains the annual Tewa religious practices, the "cycle of works": "The intent of each work is to harmonize man's relations with the spirits, and to insure the desired cyclical changes will continue to come about in nature" (1969, 98). Like Tayo, readers enter this cycle to experience tribal time, when, for example, Tayo sings to the sunrise. He describes his sentiments as "feeling they were right, feeling the instant of the dawn was an event which in a single moment gathered all things together—the last stars, the mountaintops, the clouds, and the winds—celebrating this coming" (182). Like Abel's eagle vision, this convergence of time and space, in which all things register within Tayo, haunts the protagonist until he is able to discover a means to interpret his insightful experiences. As readers, we too are drawn into this universal convergence, figured in the most creative terms. Robert Bell describes Silko's use of Navajo cyclical hero rituals in Tayo's medicinal treatment: "When the patient re-enacts the hero's adventure, identification is complete: time is stilled, this world yields to that of myth and legend, the natural and the supernatural meld; and the present moment, which joins past and future, becomes a centering process, a locus of consciousness and being forever becoming" (1979, 49). This converging process draws a counterpoint within *Ceremony*, however—it is a diverging formula plotted in the destructive pattern of a nuclear detonation.

We are taken to the Jackpile Mine where we are to complete this cycle, and where Tayo is to witness the self-destructive immolation of witches. The narrator then announces that, from this horrific moment, all of us share a responsibility for a world on the verge of destruction. It is both a metaphysical and an ecological alarm:

> There was no end to it; it knew no boundaries; and he had arrived at the point of convergence where the fate of all living things, and even the earth, had been laid. From the jungles of his dreaming he recognized why the Japanese voices had merged with Laguna voices, with Josiah's voice and Rocky's voice; the lines of cultures and worlds were drawn in flat dark lines of fine light sand, converging in the middle of witchery's final ceremonial sand painting. From that time on, human beings were one clan again, united by the fate the destroyers planned for all of them, for all living things; united by a circle of death that devoured people in cities twelve thousand miles away, victims who had never known these mesas, who had never seen the delicate colors of the rocks which boiled up their slaughter. (246)

This final scene describes a very different kind of convergence. Here, the destructive power of witchery plots our forced coalescence, as we, Indians and non-Indians alike, meet at the center of a terrible web where, despite our cultural differences, we are made to suffer needlessly. These two opposite images of convergence and divergence, however, do not represent a contradiction in the Pueblo worldview but in fact operate in a balanced dualism between creation and destruction, often in the figure of twins, such as the "twin mountain lions"—the shrine now dominated by Los Alamos (246).

Tayo, however, senses no such equilibrium. Like Yellow Calf, who says the deer tell him "this earth is cockeyed," he too perceives a world out of balance. As Betonie explains, Indigenous people created the "white skin people / like the belly of a fish / covered with hair," the destructive witches who now entrance all people, and use atomic energy to "boil up" a negative ceremony to plan the final divergence, the "fate of all living things, and even the earth." Yet so often in *Ceremony* it is the images not carefully considered that can be recklessly simplified to solve an apparent contradiction. If one employs the dualism of Keresan thinking, however, images must be understood in their particular contexts, as Josiah wisely advises: "Nothing was all good or all bad either; it all depended" (11). From this view, the above theme of dissolved boundaries—or of exposing their artificial existence—might be understood in their unique moments in the text. Whereas Tayo prays for "a single moment" so that the universe "gathered all things together," the destroyers "knew no boundaries," not to promote world harmony, but rather to release wholesale destruction, in the image of bodies piled in trenches in the Philippine jungles or vaporized against walls in Hiroshima, "in cities twelve thousand miles away."

Some critics thus assume that, in this image of boundary destroying, Silko advocates the dismantling of all theoretical and actual borders. Scholars calling for a general dissolution of cultural borders likely draw on recent theoretical claims about the dangers of categories and boundaries, producing readings such as that of Robert O'Brien Hokanson: "In cutting through Floyd Lee's fence, Tayo not only opens a way to regain his family's cattle but also aligns himself with the inexorable process of change that works against fixed boundaries and distinctions (1997, 123). Hokanson forgets that the white rancher has "transcended boundaries" to steal Indian property—in this case, cattle. Tayo here "works against fixed boundaries" only to *reinstate* those boundaries fairly, as he takes his stolen property back to his own clearly bounded lands. With Indigenous property of all sorts still under siege, however, the actual destruction of cultural and territorial borders is nothing less than disastrous for Native people. Borders are absolutely vital for the survival of colonized people. Such scholars seem not to grasp the complexity of Silko's text and political vision.[12] Other critics, however, have recently begun to do so: "Silko refigures Indian survival as dependent on the maintenance of cultural boundaries that must both separate—protect against the encroachments of the dominant culture—and connect—join with the dominant culture in recognition that mutual survival is interdependent and dependent on the stories, both old and new, tribal and Western, that can map that survival," writes Ellen Arnold (1999, 82). At least in this colonial circumstance, boundaries are indispensable to protect remaining Laguna lands, to organize Pueblo cultural identity, and to keep Tayo's mind from drifting into oblivion. Arnold challenges us to evaluate the place of boundaries in a given context—for example, one in which relations of power are unequal. Made to face such evaluative complexity, *Ceremony* asks us to consider and revise our very definitions of knowledge and reality, our experiences of this fifth Laguna world.

In the narrator's words cited above, we notice that because of the threat to the planet all of us now share, "humans are one clan again." Keresan cosmology tells of a time when a twinlike pair of sisters, Naotsete and Uretsete, shared a creative origin, but separated. Uretsete, "mother of Whites," departed with a separate technology to the east (Tyler 1964, 119–20). Silko perhaps draws on the traditional story to design her own myth of evil whiteness, for this story is Silko's own creation, what she calls "that awful story I made up" (Evers and Carr 1976, 32). In clever inversion, Silko crafts a story for the creation of an entire people by a coven of nonwhite witches from different parts of the world: "Some had slanty eyes / others had black skin . . . witches from all the Pueblos / and all the tribes." (133). But one assumes it was an American Indian witch who created the white-skin people, for, according to Betonie, "it was Indian witchery that made white people in the first place" (132). Though scarce criticism seriously engages the novel's ostensible racism about white people,[13] I have been troubled by this image in *Ceremony*, and I am tempted to emphasize Betonie's earlier caution for Tayo: "'Nothing is that simple,' he said, 'you don't write off all the white people, just like you don't trust all the Indians'" (128). The seeming contradiction is, however, actually clarified in the novel: Silko's "whiteness" is ultimately not a race but a destructive yet manageable *force* within all of us.

Ceremony communicates that this witchery cannot be undone: "It's already turned loose. / It's already coming. / It can't be called back." As with *House Made of Dawn*, in *Ceremony* destruction should instead be maintained and poised in balance with creative flourishing. The tendency to "grow away from the earth" and to believe that "the world is a dead thing" must be watched and kept at bay, as the Arrowboy poem reminds us: "'Ck'o'yo magic won't work if someone is watching us.'" (247). In the final scene of witchery, then, Tayo merely watches, holding back his desire to pierce Emo's skull with a screwdriver where "the GI haircut exposed thin bone at the temples, bone that would flex slightly before it gave way under the thrust of the steel edge" (252). Tayo suppresses the destructive whiteness within himself. The novel thus resolves the contradiction between innate race and learned social value. Betonie explains that Indians invented a destructive whiteness, and he even suggests that they did so to balance the world; the objectifying separatism of whiteness is a companion to the animating interconnectedness of Indianness. For only this account explains, after Tayo laments, "'They took almost everything, didn't they?'" Betonie's shocking disclosure: "'It was planned that way. For all the anger and frustration. And for the guilt too'" (127). This novel, then, shares a new logic of race. Silko reimagines the categories "white" and "Indian" to reject their racial attributions and to argue that the "whiteness" that leads "whites" to destroy life is a deeply socialized cultural value, rather than an inborn trait. Whiteness thus acts in the novel as an exploitative Western urge that anyone, of any racialized color, can accept or reject. By this same logic, humans can nurture their "Indianness" from within, as does Tayo, or even achieve, through moral action, a more tribal relation to humans and the land—an "Indianness." In a world where all of us, white or Indian, are restricted or privileged by race, we, however, should be vigilant for this reality, but in *Ceremony*'s world of ideas, "Indians" can become "white" and "whites" can become "Indian."

Notably, a number of environmentalist critics interpret this "final pattern" in *Ceremony* as an allegorical call to practice vigilance for destructive ecological actions,[14] while other scholars view the scene as a human rights watch for nuclear weapons in the service of aggressive wars and global capitalism,[15] and still others see the moment as a confrontation with a feminist Earth Mother.[16] Simon Ortiz celebrates in *Ceremony* a clarion call to recover Indigenous culture and defend tribal nations, "a special and most complete example of this affirmation and what it means in terms of Indian resistance, its use as literary theme, and its significance in the development of a national Indian literature" (1981b, 11). I believe Silko invites all of these allegories, testifying to the supreme ability of her narrative to serve particular cultural and social interests, yet simultaneously to call on our broader experience in human mythologies. Within this embracing artistry, her narrative melding of mythic and material also conforms to tribal views of experience. Folklorists and anthropologists have long documented the ability of an American Indian people to create a narrative that both recognizes a nonhistorical universe and grounds events in historical fact. According to Andrew Wiget: "In the progress of narrative time, the principal figures are a series of mediators who incarnate supernatural power and values in the present moment, thus communicating prototypical realities to each succeeding new world. In this way cultural institutions come to be understood as both created, historical realities and yet images of eternal verities" (1985, 3). With his language Wiget is careful not to claim that tribal peoples maintain "myth" and "fact" simultaneously; to impose a Western standard of historical fact on Native people would be to preclude understanding the operation of such a view of experience. At this point in our discussion, we can see the difficulty in applying European concepts such as "myth" to Native texts. Western thought reserves knowledge and experience for the empirically verifiable, and so forms of experience that cannot be measured and categorized in a material way are often relegated to the supernatural and the paranormal, the mystical and the mythic. Interpreting tribal experience with any of these terms risks reducing the value of nonphysical experience to superstition. To obviate this tendency, Silko carefully inserts tribal experience so that mainstream readers must rely on these supernatural experiences to understand the text and to value their universal appeal to overturn destructive worldviews. It is this very particular-in-the-universal quality of *Ceremony* that attracts Western readers to reconsider and even expand their concept of human experience.

In the Western rejection of the metaphysical, philosophers cite the problematic role of mediation between the dreamer and the dream. Yet even in the scientific community, intuition certainly mediates interpretation. But here many scientists such as Thomas Kuhn agree that it is a productive form of mediation, in the same way we found that certain emotions, such as anger rather than shame, in certain contexts might better enable the interpretation of an event. Whether scientists encourage the play of intuition at MIT, or women revalue a collective emotion in a battered women's group, a community has collectively identified, valued, and promoted a particular form of mediation for its ability to aid interpretation. From this view, I see no philosophical reason why metaphysical experience cannot be similarly valued. Intuition, emotion, and spiritual insight all share types of theory mediation that can be externalized and evaluated, employed and normalized, in social contexts. For the danger of extreme mystification associated with religious dogma, for example, stems not from their nonempirical knowledge per se, but rather from the assumption that religious experience constitutes an unquestioned fact. Unwilling to recognize the process of mediation even in spiritual revelations, we retreat from the evaluation of mediated experience altogether.

In traditional communities, however, the interpretation of experience does not occur in individualist environments of isolated observation. Indeed, whether in international laboratories or reading groups, such experimental social contexts promote alternative forms of mediation, which, in turn, enable new interpretations to emerge. In this Marxist idea, humans create the conditions in which better to interpret social or scientific phenomena. From this context, we might consider tribal societies to function like laboratories, where nonphysical mediation plays a role in our collective understanding of a person's mystical experience, as tribal thinkers consider and test various interpretations to arrive at a reasonable though provisional conclusion. In his article on tribal historiography, Arnold Krupat makes a similar point when he suggests that tribal history, though not necessarily factual in the Western sense, confers its own collective truth value in a tribal social context: "For the Lakota, tales of long, long ago (myth) and tales of more recent times (history) are equivalently *true*: they conform to what is publicly and culturally agreed upon as knowledge about what happened in the past, and it is that agreement rather than their factuality (or possible lack of factuality) that confirms their truth" (2002, 50). Krupat carefully organizes the stark differences between Western and tribal views of experience and history, and recognizes the West's fetishization of historical fact. Of course, one might object that entire communities can be wrong, and can descend into a broad mystification. But we should remember that healthy communities intersect, and invite critique and corrective from beyond, safeguarding us from orthodoxy (an idea I elaborate in my concluding chapter). Extending Krupat's critique, readers thus might not only work to understand tribal experience but also to accept Deloria's challenge, stated above, to develop a view of human experience that is shared across cultures. To return to our analysis, Silko also encourages Western readers to expand their view of experience to accommodate and thus benefit from tribal experience.

Any critic is challenged to offer a comprehensive reading of *Ceremony*, considering the awesome, discursive scope of this novel: the orchestrated interplay among myth, history, and land; the intimately detailed landscape and its careful melding with daily Laguna life; the subtle movement across space and time, often triggered by a brief memory or sensory experience; and, last, but probably most important, the growing global proportions of a godless, destructive human interaction with land, other nations, and matter itself. In the context of these stunning movements, it is puzzling to encounter widespread critical interest centered not on the issues above, but largely on the representation of Tayo's so-called mixed-blood condition. To enact its absorptive epic structure, this novel must have a special protagonist, and Silko brilliantly creates in Tayo a person who bears the physical features of opposed white and Indian races. In so doing, the author complicates the original embodiment of witchery in the white race. Readers who take Indian and white as racial, rather than cultural, categories in *Ceremony* are forced to relegate Tayo to the margins between races and cultures, where he can supposedly be revalued as a "hybrid." Hybridity remains a popular theoretical option because it purports to solve the perceived problem of borders by embracing racial and cultural indeterminacy. Among colonized people, however, some borders are necessary to assert cultural autonomy and interpret the world: "Boundaries are not our enemies; they are necessary for making meanings, but this does not make them innocent. Boundaries have real ma-

terial consequences," writes Karen Barad (1996, 187). The very term hybridity invokes an unstated nineteenth-century theory of race, in which
humans are categorized by physical features into races that deliver de-
finitive values and behaviors. Critics supporting hybridity theories celebrate Tayo as a model of hybrid "vigor": the best of both white and Indian
races and the values assumed to be associated with those racial features.
Analogies between Tayo and Josiah's spotted breed of cattle often form the
central discussion points of critics concerned with Tayo's racial status and
its larger implications for the maintenance of American Indian culture.
Such critics focus on the color of Tayo's eyes or hair, or the unknown race
of his biological father, usually declaring his father is European American,
though the text suggests he could be African American—for, as Thelma
disdainfully states, Laura "was running around with colored men" (34).
Hokanson wonders whether Tayo is "perhaps part Mexican" (1997, 115),
while Kristen Herzog is sure that he is indeed "fathered by a Mexican"
(1985, 28).[17]

Scholars employing hybridity explore the figure of the mixedblood to
consider this racialized category as a promising emblem of cultural adaptation. Louis Owens presents this "thesis in direct opposition to the more
common image of the suffering halfblood caught between two worlds"
(1992, 183). Though Owens seeks to overcome the restrictions of race,
he nonetheless relies on race to present his mixedblood model of Native
identity. For Owens, biological features often define the mixedblood. Like
Josiah's cattle, claims Owens, Tayo's syncretic physical features guarantee
a "new breed" better suited for the world. I, however, remain unconvinced
by scholarly attempts to reformat as hybrid the reviled nineteenth-century
image of the halfbreed, an image of racial contamination and resultant social devolution.[18] Despite their assertions that a theory of hybridity transforms the hated halfbreed into the liberated mixedblood, scholars still
tend to claim that Tayo is "caught between cultures" (Cutchins 1999, 81)
because of his "in-between condition" (Hobbs 1994, 306). The racial and
genetic underpinnings of hybridity theory are exposed in Naomi Rand's
assumption that Tayo identifies ideologically with a white father he has
never even met, through an apparently determinant genetic link: "Yet
Tayo is half-white. He . . . [seeks] . . . to be a Native American . . . while
attempting to obliterate his [white racial descent]" (1995, 28). There is no
doubt that Tayo is racialized, and for this reason at times he is mistrusted
by Lagunas such as Thelma, as well as by European Americans. But to use
the term mixed*blood* to assume that Tayo's perceived mixed biology indi-

cates mixed culture, is simply to reinscribe Thelma's racism. We might take to heart Night Swan's advice to Tayo that racism is often a distraction from personal accountability: "'They are fools. They blame us, the ones who look different. That way they don't have to think about what has happened inside themselves'" (100).

On *Ceremony*'s opening, Tayo vaguely understands his tribal experiences. Although his already disordered world has been damaged further by his involvement in a war to defend his former American enemies, we come to learn, as does he, that his spiritual disharmony and closely related colonial depression run deeper than his present shell-shocked condition.[19] As Tayo explains to the U.S. Army doctor: "It's more than that. I can feel it. It's been going on for a long time" (53). At first, we might take Tayo's statement to mean that his war trauma overlays the social traumata of homelessness, abandonment, and racism. But as the phrase "a long time" later bears out, Tayo's troubled mind has become a register for greater cosmic disharmony: "Maybe there would always be those shadows over his shoulder and out of the corner of each eye; and in the night the dreams and voices" (106). Even before the war, Tayo had already come into contact with persons who seemed to embody mythical forces, such as Night Swan, whose pervasive blue imagery invokes the Laguna rain deity, who "did not look old or young . . . ; she was like the rain and the wind; age had no relation to her," and with whom Tayo notices "the years, the centuries, were lost" (98). After they have sex and before he leaves, Night Swan cryptically foretells Tayo's challenge: "'Remember this day. You will recognize it later. You are part of it now'" (100). Shaped by these earlier mystical experiences and a heightened sense of a threatened world, Tayo is overcome by the sensory overload of a devastating world war that causes experiences to tangle in his skull without pattern, "the tension of little threads being pulled . . . things tied together, and as he tried to pull them apart and rewind them into their places, they snagged and tangled even more" (7).[20] Recalling the opening poem of Thought-Woman, spider, who weaves story and order into the world from random threads of thought, Tayo suffers not only from battle fatigue but also a deeper psychic disorder, and he seems to be called by figures such as Josiah and Night Swan to repair Laguna and even the broader world. For this reason, healers such as Ku'oosh attend less to the other veterans, Harley, Emo, and Leroy, than to Tayo, and repeat to Tayo the mysterious query, "There is something they have sent me to ask you" (36). As *Ceremony* proceeds, Tayo discovers a weblike interrelation of personal and collective experience of a cultural and colonial past. His at first disjointed individual narrative becomes intertwined and reorganized with traditional Pueblo stories of transgression, healing, and renewal. Through this reintegration process of revaluing, remembering, and interpreting tribal experience, which is at once a ceremony and a story, a mythology and a history, Tayo and readers alike are moved from the incoherent margins to an enriched center of human experience.[21]

Both Tayo and the community struggle with the problem of colonial influence and the challenge it poses to modern Pueblo lives. Thelma and others shame Tayo for being born of a drunk mother and an unknown father, for the color of his eyes, and for invading the family; Thelma reminds the townspeople that Tayo is not her son. His shame is further complicated by the deadening guilt he feels for breaking his promise to bring his cousin Rocky home safely from the war. Worst of all, though, Tayo silently bears terrible guilt for praying away the rain.[22] If Tayo is to become fully Laguna—that is, if he is to achieve a rich cultural identity—he must surrender his individualistic, colonized feelings of guilt and adopt instead a collective tribal feeling for the survival of his people; if the Laguna people are to thrive, they must undergo a similar change in their understandings of colonialism and the external cultural influences that they believe to be embodied by people of multiple heritage. *Ceremony* is thus built philosophically around a crucial moral debate among Lagunas: whether cultural change will cause either the destruction or the flourishing of the people. Though change has always been a part of Indigenous living, here the colonial stakes are most critical—they must clarify a theory of cultural development to evaluate and determine exactly which changes to accept.

In this novel, it is through Tayo that members of the pueblo must reconsider their assumptions regarding who a Laguna person is. This challenge thus refers outward to the broader community and its own self-definitions, as a tribal people coming to terms with colonial invasions of various degrees and kinds. One question they must ask is what changes have to take place in order to provide proper healing of the people—for example, of the young men infected by a global war. In short, the oppressed group in *Ceremony* must reimagine itself as an anticolonial community. Central to this transformation is a willingness to evaluate changes in the pueblo, notably by deciding whether new practices or behaviors are good or bad for the well being of Laguna people. Without this theory of growth, neither Tayo nor his people will be able to guide their destinies—they will not be able to decolonize. They secure freedom in their community by expanding their moral capacities through their discourse on cultural adaptation. Toward this visionary community, they must begin to imagine what Laguna Pueblo might have been had Europeans never invaded. While no Indian nation has ever been beyond external cultural influence, this sharing of a utopian vision of the day before conquest creates the stirring of historical and cultural agency. It begins a claim to a freed self. Like other Native groups, the Lagunas in the novel draw on their oral tradition as a source of embedded knowledge. With their ancient origins, such tribal narratives defy the demands of history, and in so doing they function as a deep repository of tribal information.[23] In representing a flexible center of normative truths that are continually being built upon, challenged, and revised, the Laguna oral tradition provides the community with a comparatively stable worldview that may be consulted during these times of colonial crisis. One fundamental purpose of Native story is to reestablish tribal harmony by gathering those who, for whatever reason, have drifted outside of the circle of relations. The storyteller must be trusted with this crucial task of realigning the minds of her listeners by retelling, for instance, the story of a nation's collective origins, migrations, and triumphs over various threats to their survival.

In Tayo's illness some tribal members reduce their challenge, lowering their eyes on the scapegoat. But in racializing and marginalizing Tayo, the community is delayed and impeded in administering the minimal treatment that he, as well as the community, deserves, to organize his material experiences of colonial depression and war hysteria. Fearing their judgment, Thelma refuses to claim Tayo as a real Laguna, and mutters, "You know how they are. You know what people will say if we ask for a medicine man to help him. Someone will say it's not right. They'll say, 'Don't do it. He's not full blood anyway'" (33). Finally, the people do decide that, despite Tayo's blood, he is indeed Laguna and must be helped, for the spiritual crisis of even one member jeopardizes the whole community. As the healer Ku'oosh tells Tayo:

"But you know, grandson, this world is fragile."
The word he chose to express "fragile" was filled with the intricacies of a continuing process, and with a strength inherent in spider webs woven across paths through sand hills where early in the morning the sun becomes entangled in each filament of web. It took a long time to explain the fragility and intricacy because no word exists alone, and the reason for choosing each word had to be explained with a story about

why it must be said this certain way. That was the responsibility that went with being human, old Ku'oosh said, the story behind each word must be told so there could be no mistake in the meaning of what had been said; and this demanded great patience and love. More than an hour went by before Ku'oosh asked him. . . . "You understand, don't you? It is important to all of us. Not only for your sake, but for this fragile world." (35–36)

Like the story-weaving Thought-Woman, Ku'oosh painstakingly reproduces the web of relations to explain the necessity of all participants in the Laguna world, and works to understand how Tayo and all his experiences can be woven cautiously and meaningfully into their network. Like Ku'oosh, both Tayo and the community work to incorporate alien experiences into their world by dissolving barriers to growth, realizing that their collective health depends on the reintegration of the individual into the whole. But the healer proceeds patiently, waiting for the young man to explain his sickness through a symbolic airing of "bad" stories, Ku'oosh quietly helping Tayo to reinterpret the events, the healer and patient together slowly gaining knowledge about what it takes to repair unprecedented illnesses, or worse, a world out of balance. In this healing process, the Indian doctor considers briefly the realities of race: "'Maybe you don't know some of these things,' [said Ku'oosh,] vaguely acknowledging the distant circumstances of an absent white father" (35). But both patient and healer work to understand the affliction holistically, in terms of experience rather than blood.

At first, Tayo is defiantly unwilling to share his secret world because he dreads the confirmation of his worst fear—that he has cursed the land: "He didn't know how to explain what had happened. He did not know how to tell him that he had not killed any enemy or that he did not think that he had. But that he had done things far worse, and the effects were everywhere in the cloudless sky, on the dry brown hills, shrinking skin and hide taut over the sharp bone. The old man was waiting for him to answer" (36). The association of "dry brown hills" with "shrinking skin" and "hide" speaks to the interconnectedness of Ku'oosh's world; the land, humans, and animals all share mutual stakes and responsibility in preserving life. Here, the shrinking skin of drought recalls the soldiers' bodies that lined the Bataan Death March, where the loss of human life—whether Japanese, Indian, or white—exacted the same price: "He saw the skin of the corpses again and again, in ditches on either side of the long muddy road—skin that was stretched shiny and dark over bloated hands; even white men were darker after death" (7). Tayo is thus sickened not so much by war than by what it ignites within him: tribal visions of global devastation, which cannot be understood within a Western experiential paradigm. To begin, he will have to expand his knowledge of his experiences as more than a Laguna man. Like Tayo, readers must expand their histories to engage colonial relations, as Silko directs us to grow through an encounter with our troubled pasts. But such processes of remembering depend on the reliable interpretation of an expanded experience. Indeed, personal healing may begin with an inquiry into the experiences in one's own life, but soon it must broaden as one begins to encounter the self in the greater context of the nation, land, and past. The success of this inquiry depends on the social conditions, or the comparative presence of various barriers that inhibit or promote one's ability to safely remember and reorganize tribal experience.

Seeking only to suppress these objectionable experiences, the military psychiatrists treat Tayo with drugs that, like the alcohol that calms his memory on return from war,[24] also deaden his recall and interpretation and thus block the healing process that depends on his return to experience: "The smoke had been dense; visions and memories of the past did not penetrate there, and he had drifted in colors of smoke, where there was no pain, only pale, pale gray of the north wall by his bed. Their medicine drained memory out of his thin arms and replaced it with a twilight cloud behind his eyes. It was not possible to cry on the remote and foggy mountain" (15). In Western worlds, such nonphysical experiences tend to be dismissed as "hallucinations"; indeed, Western physicians would likely categorize Tayo's alternative reality as schizophrenic. Critics working within Western views of experience thus hesitate to accept these experiences as knowledge and cannot even find the terms for them: "memory/hallucination" (Couser 1996, 112).

At the request of Ku'oosh, the Navajo healer Betonie agrees to see Tayo. As Tayo's eyes adjust to the interior of the hogan, he labors to absorb the many artifacts collected from all over the land over the years: boxes of roots, bundles of newspapers and phonebooks, bags of medicines hanging from the ceiling, Coke bottles — all an apparently random mix of old and new, modern and traditional, Indian and white. Then Tayo begins to discern a pattern: "He wanted to dismiss all of it as an old man's rubbish, debris that had fallen out of the years, but the boxes and trunks, the bundles and stacks were plainly part of the pattern: they followed the concentric shadows of the room" (120). From this moment, Betonie and Tayo appear to share a similar world in which they collect and manage multiple experiences, often the "fallout" of other's discarded material or memory, "We've been gathering these things for a long time," says Betonie (120). Yet despite the massiveness of this collection, Betonie organizes these elements and historical moments in a pattern that Tayo recognizes and comes to value in interpreting the world. Betonie makes his home in the foothills above Gallup, where Tayo and his mother used to live, and stays, he says, because his family had lived there long before the exploitative trading post called Gallup came to be. In this shrewd inversion of colonial presence, Silko suggests that Indigenous people can decolonize their minds by reasserting their first presence as early caretakers of this land and not homeless Indians in the riverbed: "'It strikes me funny,' the medicine man said, shaking his head, 'people wondering why I live so close to this filthy town. But see, this hogan was here first. Built long before the white people ever came. It is that town down there which is out of place. Not this old medicine man'" (118). Oddly enough, the impoverished colonial trade center that is Gallup is also the dance grounds of local Native people, where more recent mining and economic exploitation intersects with the power of longstanding ceremony.

Betonie begins in Tayo a process of remembering and of reevaluating his past experiences, some of which become "new" as Betonie questions and helps organize Tayo's experiential world, with Tayo growing spiritually through an albeit painful reclaimed experience: "Tayo felt the old nausea rising up in his stomach, along with a vague feeling that he knew something which he could not remember" (117). But unlike the veteran's hospital or the unwelcome kitchen of his aunt, here in Betonie's hogan the trusting social conditions promote new interpretations in a tribal context that accepts and understands mystical experience.[25] Tayo begins to feel the barriers to knowledge dissipate in this new environment, as Betonie assures him that he must trust if he is to begin to reexamine his world: "'If you don't trust me, you better get going before dark. You can't be too careful these days,' Betonie said, gesturing toward the footlocker where he kept the hairs. 'Anyway, I couldn't help anyone who was afraid of me.' He started humming softly to himself, a song that Tayo could hear only faintly, but that reminded him of butterflies darting from flower to flower" (123). Tayo's vision moves from an Army footlocker, which he associates with war and witchery, to a faintly familiar song and butterflies, the shape of the brand on his uncle's cattle. Moving through unpleasant into affirming memories, Tayo begins to trust. An important part of Betonie's treatment is to help Tayo externalize and specify the buried and confused emotions used to order not only his personal experiences, but also his relationship to past, culture, and land, all aspects of Tayo's world, which Tayo reevaluates through his knowledge of himself as a spiritually reaffirmed tribal person.[26]

Through this method of naturalizing Tayo's apparently "irrational" views of himself and his experiences, Betonie, by degrees, helps the sick man to adjudicate the knowledge gleaned from his experiences in normative Laguna terms:

> What Tayo could feel was powerful, but there was no way to be sure what it was.
>
> "My Uncle Josiah was there that day, Yet I know he couldn't have been there. He was thousands of miles away, at home in Laguna. We were in the Philippine jungles. I understand that. I know he couldn't have been there. But I've got this feeling and it won't go away even though I know he wasn't there. I feel like he was there. I feel like he was there with those Japanese soldiers who died." Tayo's voice was shaking; he could feel the tears pushing into his eyes. Suddenly the feeling was there, as strong as it had been that day in the jungle. "He loved me. He loved me, and I didn't do anything to save him." (124)

From my earlier discussion of the emotions, we see that they become vital for Tayo to explain an event so horrible as participating in the killing of one's own uncle. Though the emotions are considered an unreliable source of knowledge, without them Tayo would not be able to begin to make sense of the above calamity. His "feeling" is "powerful," yet he is unsure of its meaning. Because Betonie is more trained in tribal experience, and more aware of the effects of colonialism on Indigenous identity, he is able to help Tayo evaluate his guilt for its ability to accurately explain the social facts of his experience. In terms of Tayo's vision of Josiah in the jungle, Betonie is not interested in proving empirically whether Tayo has really seen him. To dismiss Tayo's vision as a hallucination would be to disregard information vital to the survival of all. Instead, in a Native view of experience what matters is that the sight of Josiah invokes greater concerns for the safety of the people and the land—indeed, all of humanity—as the vision strongly suggests. In this more encompassing context to protect the planet's future, the vision grows more meaningful. Betonie thus provides Tayo with an alternative medium through which to interpret his experience, and this new account makes better sense in Tayo's Laguna world. According to Thomas Couser: "By the end of the narrative, his 'dreams' no longer haunt him because they have been understood—as *memories*—within the proper cultural context of traditional myths, stories, and rituals" (1996, 112). In revaluing his former hallucinations as visions, Tayo not only reclaims his sanity, but now better understands what he has been feeling all along: "This has been going on for a long time," says Betonie, repeating the words of Night Swan. He also gains medicine to help him negotiate among different forms of experience: "He could feel the ceremony like the rawhide thongs of the medicine pouch, straining to hold back the voices, the dreams, faces in the jungle in the L.A. depot, the smoky silence of solid white walls" (152). In terms of Tayo's emotional response, Betonie has Tayo consider whether guilt is most adequate to explain what Tayo is experiencing; and if not, Betonie must help Tayo locate an alternative emotion through which to resolve the horror he has felt, so that he can heal emotionally and integrate socially into his tribal community. Thus reaffirmed in his sense of the world, Tayo is prepared to further develop his insights.

Betonie thus sparks in Tayo this process of spiritual development, and he does so not by handing him a single, static explanation for his past experiences but instead by explaining that Tayo has been growing all along, albeit without a coherent idea of or trajectory for himself: "'You've been doing something all along. All this time, and now you are at an important place in this story'" (124). Betonie thus gives Tayo a pattern to complete, to seek out and join the experiences that have confounded his life: stars, spotted cattle, a mountain, a woman. His task will be to organize his experiences in a way that makes sense of his world, a process that often involves experimenting with different responses to experiences, testing out each among other tribal members for its comparative ability to accurately portray social reality. As Tayo grows he will no doubt commit errors, but, as Betonie intimates, it is mystification, as much as insight, that is part of "the story" in one's self-correcting path to becoming a human being.[27] Over time, Tayo will probably revise his accounts to explain his experiences and his place in a collective culture, and these theories constitute his constructed yet reliable tribal understanding of the world. Betonie does not direct Tayo to a self-evident meaning for future religious experience; rather, he gives him a ceremony, one that requires Tayo's foresight and preparation to see its fulfillment. And in his enactment of this ceremony, in his pursuit of new ways of knowing the Laguna world, Tayo grows.

Betonie also must help to reintegrate Tayo into the Laguna community by showing him that other American Indians, too, often feel an irrational form of personal guilt for not doing more to shield others from the damaging effects of U.S. empire. Other tribal people blame themselves for the lives lost, with the ancestors, like Josiah, asking to be remembered and accounted for. Then how should we grieve? Silko seems to ask. By sheer synecdoche, Tayo again stands for the whole community in a Native worldview that has little notion of the unified Western individual. Says Tayo:

> "They took almost everything, didn't they?"
> The old man looked up from the fire. He shook his head slowly while he turned the meat with a forked stick. "We always come back to that, don't we? It was planned that way. For all the anger and the frustration. And for the guilt too. Indians wake up every morning of their lives to see the land which was stolen, still there, within reach, its theft being flaunted. And the desire is strong to make things right, to take back what was stolen and to stop them from destroying what they have taken. But you see, Tayo, we have done as much fighting as we can with the destroyers and the thieves: as much as we could do and still survive." (127–28)

Ceremony approaches its epiphany when Betonie, both individually and, through Tayo, collectively, draws out and calls into question the painful emotion of guilt. Although we bear the burden of knowing great loss, is guilt the best way to make sense of our colonial pasts? Or is there a more productive means of interpreting our lives to empower Indian people? To answer these questions, Silko now returns to a problem that has been building throughout the novel: the negotiation of cultural change. To illustrate, Betonie describes how he has had to change the ceremonies to better treat the new and more wicked forms of environmental and social destruction, but, as he reminds, this evaluative practice is not new: "You see, in many ways, the ceremonies have always been changing" (126). So, although the "desire is strong to make things right," there is no clear-cut way to decide how Native cultures should change to resist cultural invasion or to further decolonize.

Instead, healing and strengthening Indigenous identity often involves building a community that will nurture that identity, an ongoing process that often involves emotional and cognitive work. And, we might add, this effort requires a more empowering response to the world than that of guilt. Betonie recommends, rather, that we and Tayo reinterpret colonial relations in terms of responsibility. If we take Silko's suggestion that, like ceremony, cultural identity brings meaning to an otherwise incoherent world, then identity is most vital when it is open-ended, forged in a continual process of organizing the events of American Indians' lives: "The people mistrust this greatly, but only this growth keeps the ceremonies strong" (126). Because our moral growth often depends on remembering, as Tayo has, we face the danger of forgetting or misrepresenting, for example, our ancestors and the cultural values for which they stood and fought. We however cannot help but be historically fallible. This legitimate sense of loss is often part of Native literature and culture. But our greatest loss would be not to proceed for fear of error, thus losing the opportunity to encounter tradition as well as new ways of being human: "He pointed in the direction the boy had gone. 'Accidents happen, and there's little we can do. But don't be so quick to call something good or bad. There are balances and harmonies always shifting, always necessary to maintain. It is very peaceful with the bears; the people say that's the reason human beings seldom return. It is a matter of transitions, you see; the changing, the becoming must be cared for closely. You would do as much for the seedlings as they become plants in the field.'" (130).

A crucial aspect of this healing often requires that tribal members confront their own suppressed experiences of hegemony and thus decolonize their minds internally, as Tayo does upon finding his uncle's stolen cattle on a white rancher's land:

> [Tayo] was thinking about the cattle and how they ended up on Floyd Lee's land. If he had seen the cattle on land-grant land or in some Acoma's corral, he wouldn't have hesitated to say "stolen." But something inside him made him hesitate to say now that the cattle were on a white man's ranch. He had a crazy desire to believe that there had been some mistake, that Floyd Lee had gotten them innocently, maybe buying them from real thieves. Why did he hesitate to accuse a white man of stealing but not a Mexican or an Indian? . . . He knew that he had learned the lie by heart—the lie which they had wanted him to learn: only brown-skinned people were thieves; white people didn't steal, because they always had money to buy whatever they wanted. The lie. He cut into the wire as if cutting away at the lie inside himself. The liars had fooled everyone, white people and Indians alike; as long as people believed the lies, they would never be able to see what had been done to them or what they were doing to each other. (191)

"The lie" of Indian degeneration and white ascendancy sustains colonial domination by becoming internalized in Native self-conceptions.[28] Holding the lie nearly without hesitation, Tayo and other Lagunas consume and reproduce erroneous knowledge of their culture in subtle spaces; schools, churches, and media—largely organized by Western ideologies as institutions and economies in which American Indians are forced to participate—work to sustain American power and diminish Native cultures, through an often hidden political agenda. For this reason, Tayo's bitter realization marks a stunningly imaginative moment for a colonized person, and thus begins a process of revaluing the self through the ongoing engagement with experience as Tayo, like other Lagunas, exposes the colonial lies and unlearns the internalized lessons of oppression.

Over the years, few critics of *Ceremony* have recognized not only Tayo's but, by extension, the pueblo's profound moment of awakening to cultural and racial oppression, represented in Tayo's act of cutting the ranchers' barbed wire fences that guard stolen land and cattle, impose non-Laguna values on the people, and restrict free movement on Laguna lands. Many scholars, in fact, interpret this moment as a point of reconciliation between Western and Indigenous worlds, in which the boundaries between categories deconstruct to enable the free play of cultural exchange. It is also quite possible that Tayo, having recovered the drifting cattle, on his return might have passed through this gap in the fence and then mended it, as Yuki critic William Oandasan suggests: "After he re-crosses the fence, he mends it like a good neighbor, displaying now a respectful, though self-serving practice, as well as social maturity" (1997, 243). More than a mere act of courtesy, this cutting and mending might well represent in *Ceremony* a central thesis on the boundaries of human experience: in becoming a better human being, we must venture out to understand distant realms of experience, but should be cautious to adjudicate among them. On his entry into the mythic landscape of Yellow Woman–Rain Woman–Ts'eh Montaña and her husband Mountain Lion–Winter, Tayo leaves Western empirical experience behind. If readers are to take seriously that magical sequence, they will have to reconsider the adequacy of conventional understandings of experience to *Ceremony*. Indeed, Tayo learns not to assume that tribal and Western experiential worlds always gracefully coexist. Just after passing through to this mystical realm, Tayo's head collides with the material earth and the political reality of brutal ranchers, who consider him a trespasser despite his ancient claim to Laguna lands. At this moment, he discovers the necessity of maintaining boundaries among historical, mythic, and political experiential worlds: "He knew that if he left his skull unguarded, if he let himself sleep, it would happen: the resistance would leak out and take with it all barriers, all boundaries" (201–2).

In this intense stage of his spiritual development, Tayo sets out to reclaim Josiah's lost cattle, where at the crest of North Top, a centuries-old hunting land for the Lagunas, he discovers a place where "there was no sign the white people had ever come" (184). Now open to this precontact, mythic space, Tayo is able fully to enter the former world of his dreams, and is actually discovered by a woman who unmistakably embodies Yellow Woman: "She was wearing a man's shirt tucked into a yellow skirt that hung below her knees. Pale buckskin moccasins reached the edge of her skirt. The silver buttons up the side of each moccasin had rainbirds carved on them. She wasn't much older than he was, but she wore her hair long, like the old women did, pinned back in a knot" (177). In this other world, Ts'eh's husband, the embodiment of Mountain Lion the Hunter,[29] welcomes Tayo into their home, as they act out this ancient Laguna oral tale. When Tayo and Yellow Woman make love, Tayo seems to sink into the earth itself—recovering his nurturing relationship to it. In the process he becomes better able to negotiate among different forms of experiences: "But he did not get lost, and he smiled at her as she held his hips and pulled him closer" (181). Like Tayo, we readers are sent into this mythic space where events challenge our own sense of reality. When Tayo communes with a mountain lion, many readers balk at what they perceive as popular religion: "When the mountain lion stopped in front of him, it was not hesitation, but a chance for the moonlight to catch up with him. Tayo got to his knees slowly and held out his hand. 'Mountain lion,' he whispered, 'mountain lion, becoming what you are with each breath, your substance changing with the earth and the sky.' The mountain lion blinked his eyes; there was no fear" (196). Such moments in Indigenous literature have been incorrectly called "magical realism," a term that suggests such events never occur in the real world. But, as I have shown, tribal experience encompasses moments such as the above—though certainly unique—in a more comprehensive view of human reality. In Native thought, then, the moment above is simply "real," and, by distinction, the ability to induce metaphysical change in the world, magic.

As advised, Tayo recovers the cattle, remains vigilant for witchery, and thus returns rain to the land. Having completed these tasks, he is now prepared to enter the kiva—the Pueblo place of worship, an enclosed circular structure within the earth—and to share more expansively his insights with other spiritual leaders, who are trained to help interpret his supernatural experiences: "It took a long time to tell the story; they stopped him frequently with questions about the location and the time of day; they asked about the direction she had come from and the color of her eyes" (257). The old men have elected to embrace and absorb Tayo into the Laguna center, in the same way they adopted into their place of worship "a folding steel chair with 'St. Joseph Mission' stenciled in white paint on the back" (256). Owens insists that this kiva represents a "transcultural space" in which Tayo can now be truly hybrid (1998, 35).[30] By ending in the kiva, however, the very center of Pueblo religious belief, *Ceremony* instead strongly suggests that Indians and cattle can and do return. Like the spotted cattle, which though a desert breed intuit the direction of their homeland and pursue it across the bordering fences, Tayo, despite his appearance, by tribal experience is led home.

4

||||||||||||||||||||||||||||||||||||||||||||||||||||||||||||||||||||||||||||||

HEARING THE CALLOUT:

AMERICAN INDIAN POLITICAL CRITICISM

For a long time he had been white smoke. He did not realize that until he left the hospital, because white smoke had no consciousness of itself. It faded into the white world of their bed sheets and walls; it was sucked away by the words of doctors who tried to talk to the invisible scattered smoke. He had seen outlines of gray steel tables, outlines of the food they pushed into his mouth, which was only an outline too, like all the outlines he saw. They saw an outline but they did not realize it was hollow inside. He walked down floors that smelled of old wax and disinfectant, watching the outlines of his feet; as he walked, the days and seasons disappeared into a twilight at the corner of his eyes, a twilight he could catch only with a sudden motion, jerking his head to one side for a glimpse of green leaves pressed against the bars on the window.
— *Ceremony*

The walls of his cell were white, or perhaps they were gray or green; he could not remember. After a while he could not imagine anything beyond the walls except the yard outside, the lavatory and the dining hall — or even the walls, really. They were abstractions beyond the reach of his understanding, not in themselves confinement but symbols of confinement. The essential character of the walls consisted not in their substance but in their appearance, the bare one-dimensional surface that was white, perhaps, or gray, or green.
— *House Made of Dawn*

There are so many strifes within our people. Between nations, tribes, and clans that they have weakened our sacred hoop! Inside this iron house, we've put those differences, those strifes aside. To become *one* as our Great Spirit Grandfather wants us to be! If we on the inside can do this, why, we ask, cannot our brothers and sisters do this out there? Recently a brother and sister have come into our circle; at first not all of us could be sure of their hearts. But now we know and feel they are *one* with us. For them, some of my brothers are writing, drawing, painting to share with you out there! You see, I for myself, wish to make your faith stronger, your hoop larger. By bringing you into our circle in this iron house, we make all our peoples' sacred hoop that much stronger and beautiful.

— **Matthew**, Lakota prisoner, Auburn prison, January 1998

The guards above glare down from their towers as I approach. On the roof, a life-size statue of the Department of Corrections logo stands at attention: "Copper John," a Revolutionary War soldier, with bayonet at his side. Remember, I think to myself, these places were always colonial war prisons.[1] After teaching Indian men at Auburn Correctional Facility, in the heart of Iroquoia, almost every Friday night for five years,[2] I still feel a yawning dread when I pass through these walls. The correctional officers seem to look right through me, determining my true allegiances. In an irrational moment, I fear they have discovered that I am not just a volunteer and they plan to confine me. Established in 1816, Auburn prison is one of the oldest prisons in the state of New York. It was the first prison in the world to experiment with the isolation of single-occupancy cells, and it was also the first ever to use the electric chair, when in 1890 William Kemmler had to be electrocuted twice before being successfully executed. In 1929, prisoners rose up and destroyed the chair.[3] Auburn is a maximum security prison. Built on the former site of an Indian town called Wasco, the nineteenth-century Gothic architecture of Auburn prison imitates the medieval stone castles of Europe, complete with defensive parapets. Fifty-foot walls segmented by gun turrets provide surveillance of both those within and those beyond the prison: but these walls do not separate and replicate society inside, where a Constitutional law supposedly serves and protects its citizens. In prison, the rules to control might as well be arbitrary; instead, a shifting economy of force preserves order. For this reason, some prisoners possess greater power than some guards.

When I am even a minute late for the security screening, the guards will refuse my entry. I am often the only "volunteer" at the prison who is not a missionary to save fallen souls. The Christians wait and chat, their Bibles in hand, but they no longer speak to me nor hand me their *Watchtower* with the crying Indian on the cover. In the lobby, on the wall behind the counter, hang prints of products the prisoners are paid to produce at fewer than two dollars an hour, among which are cotton straightjackets.[4] Tonight's guards are newly employed young men, but stern and dressed in gray uniforms, even they appear hardened. Signed in and searched, I am escorted through a series of barred doors, when I finally enter the night air of the central yard. Not a tree stands on this huge square of asphalt, though some of the older men recall when the last lone tree was cut down in the early seventies. When blackbirds fly over the yard, Native prisoners collect their fallen feathers to make tribal shields. On each side of the yard ascend cell blocks seven stories high, sealed with one massive paned glass wall. The bodies behind the glass and bars surrounding the yard hoot, holler, and curse us.[5] The sound and smell of iron and sweat emanate into the yard.

I hear the group members arrive long before I see them; there is a great echo in prison. I feel relieved for the moment, knowing that most of the men have avoided the additional punishment of isolation, "the box," and have received the reward of "callout"—when the guards slide back the iron bars and call a waiting man to step from his cell. I am happy to suddenly hear the men's own callout, as they shout hello to me from down the hall. They bound through the door dressed in green work pants, ragged white thermal shirts, and boots. I am always shocked to look upon their broken bodies. In the prison, men receive appalling nutrition and health care.[6] They smile, though they look like prisoners of war. We greet each other the way men do in prison. We shake hands and lean our shoulders in to meet while patting each other's back with the left hand. Most all of the men have the signature four-inch knife scar on the right side of the neck, which I assume to be a mark of initiation. In prison, knives are easy to make and, I have been told, are often hidden within one's reach. In this first moment of the evening, I try to spend time greeting each group member, but some of the more animated men take more of my time and this makes the quieter men feel neglected. Whitehorse, a Lakota man, insists on showing me this week's drawings, while Ricky, who is Mohawk, stands in the corner, hands in pockets, wide-eyed and watching. Small and defenseless, and literally trembling, Ricky has reason to cower. The Tuscarora group leader Richard is quiet and serious, and he shakes my hand calmly. Rocko, who is Seneca, and Sweets, an Onondaga man, get out their snacks they bought at the commissary to share. For the opening prayer, we take hands, right palm up, left palm down. After reporting on who got put in the box and why, who is up for parole and the legalities of their cases, we settle in to share and discuss an arranged topic for the evening. Sometimes the men pair off to braid each other's hair. Later we drum, sing, and dance.

After years of working with Native prisoners, I still find it difficult to communicate, let alone theorize, the realities of American Indian imprisonment.[7] How should an Indian scholar represent to the U.S. public the private trauma of Indigenous men imprisoned in their own ancestral lands?[8] Perhaps seeking a medium for this experience, Native prisoners, activists, and intellectuals often rely on narratives—sketches, journals, and novels—when writing about prisons. Native prisoners founded the Auburn Group in 1973, the year of the Wounded Knee takeover, at the height of Red Power and just after and before, respectively, the publications of *House Made of Dawn* and *Ceremony*.[9] In the epigraphs above, American Indians struggle to comprehend and resist their institutionalization, whether in hospitals or prisons. In so doing, they hope to take back their bodies and replace them in homelands. In *Ceremony*, Tayo becomes a voiceless, shadowy body owned by the state—first through the military and then through the mental hospitals that often serve the military in managing the damaged bodies and minds of soldiers. More directly than *Ceremony*, *House Made of Dawn* engages Indian imprisonment during Red Power, though the novel has received little critical attention on the topic of Abel's incarceration. In both novels, there is a sense that the Native prisoner has been reduced to a cell number and thus becomes a mere body, an "outline" or an "abstraction" to be managed by the prison as one would the cleaning and disinfectant detail, the painting of the two-dimensional walls. I began working in prisons to reverse that erasing process among imprisoned Indian men and to facilitate an imaginative return of Native men to tribal places. Each time I enter the classroom, one of the men usually approaches me with his writing. In Matthew's statement in the epigraph above, for example, he beseeches his fellow prisoners to recognize their achievement of intertribal unity and to widen their circle to include me beyond the prison walls. In resisting his confinement by

engaging those outside his world, Matthew expands his Native consciousness to grow intellectually as well as politically. Writing in prison Matthew
composes inherently political work, but writing across the walls, he defies
his confinement—and the legitimacy of the prison.

I begin with this narrative of work with Native prisoners to invoke the
centrality of political writing to the liberation of Native America but, more
importantly, to consider the influence of political intervention on scholarship. As an Indian scholar in graduate school, my visits to Auburn prison
lay bare our colonial relations as well as relentlessly grounded my ideas
about American Indian culture, literature, and our collective struggle for
decolonization. In my intervention with American Indian prisoners, I was
finally able to discern the operation of U.S. imperial power, which is made
more transparent in prison. There, I discovered the hidden risks that one
takes to write about domination. Most of all, I found in Native prisoners
a model for true intellectual and political development. Like Matthew, I
had to encounter another world were I ever to challenge my own. To go
beyond the walls that divide by class and education is perhaps the most
empowering activity an Indigenous intellectual can pursue. This chapter traces a similar political transformation in Indigenous literary tradition, when Native intellectuals through the generations harnessed their
experiences of colonial subjugation to inform their ideas, thereby uniting
theory and practice. I thus argue, perhaps simply, that an ethical American Indian theory must enter the world to change and be changed by the
world. To do so, I turn to our intellectual tradition of historically engaged
political writing to introduce a theory of Native praxis; then, in closing, I
return to the classroom—in the writing of Indigenous prisoners—to demonstrate this theory. What drives Indian intellectuals to political action?
In moments such as that described above, when we are overwhelmed by
the experience of Native criminalization—and, more broadly, other observations of anti-Indianism[10]—American Indian scholars awaken politically
and begin putting their ideas to work. I term that demand for justice "the
callout."

The Callout in Native Critical Traditions

On a stormy September day in 1772 in New Haven, before a crowd of
Europeans, Africans, and Indians, Samson Occom, an ordained Christian
minister, delivered "A Sermon, Preached at the Execution of Moses Paul,
an Indian":

My poor kindred,

You see the woful consequences of sin, by freeing this our poor miserable country-man now before us, who is to die this day for his sins and great wickedness. And it was the sin of drunkenness that has brought this destruction and untimely death upon him. There is a dreadful ire denounced from the Almighty against drunkards; and it is this sin, this abominable, this beastly and accursed sin of drunkenness, that has stript us of every desirable comfort in this life; by this we are poor, miserable and wretched; by this sin we have no name of credit in the world among polite nations; for this sin we are despised in the world, and it is all right and just, for we despise ourselves more; and if we don't regard ourselves, who will regard us? (1987 [1772], 478)

Both Occom and Paul were Mohegan. In spite of colonial attacks on his people, Paul made a life for himself in an altered world: he served in the colonial militia, worked as a sailor, and had even converted to Christianity. But Paul began to drink heavily and, while drunk, killed a wealthy white man. For this offense he was sentenced to be hanged, and he asked Occom to preach at his execution. Years later, Occom's plan to found Dartmouth College to educate American Indians was betrayed by the famed missionary Eleazor Wheelock. This event took a toll on him and he, like Paul, began drinking and later died.[11] How strange and sad that day in New Haven must have been: two men of the same tribal homeland standing in the rain divided by a gallows; divided by European education and occupation; divided before a crowd who saw perhaps only the law-abiding and lawless, the God fearing and the Godless. We might attribute to mere coincidence the opposed yet parallel lives of Moses Paul and Samson Occom were it not for the same colonial fate that both men ultimately met. For a time, Occom escapes Paul's criminality by luck of a Western education, only to die from the very alcoholism he preached against. Working closely with American Indian prisoners often encourages meditations, as that offered above, on Indigenous "immediacy"—a term I propose to describe this shared colonial experience among Indians in otherwise different social and economic locations that unites our intellectual work in American Indian studies. Such shared experiences often unite Indian people across the distinction of privilege in Indian Country, even today. An opportunity to succeed presents itself through the fortune of social conditions, a safe and secure home, or the denial of these. On this socially leveling fact of modern Native existence, American Indian intellectuals base their deepest commitments to making ideas defend the real lives of those around us.[12]

As a plea to Indigenous people to refuse the weapons of their destruction—the colonizer's liquor—so that American Indians may recover their lives and revitalize their communities, Occom's call finds its place in a tradition of Indian intellectual discourse concerned with empowering tribal members. Indeed, the minister dares even to rebuke those who attempt to corrupt young Native people: "And here I cannot but observe, we find in sacred writ, a wo against men who put their bottles to their neighbours mouths to make them drunk, that they may see their nakedness: and no doubt there are such devilish men now in our days, as there were in the days of old" (1987 [1772], 480). Occom does not censure only Indians: he calls on all for a humanistic, anti-imperialist resistance to the insidious entry of whiskey traders and their unfamiliar drug into American Indian communities. Then, turning to Native people, he objects to using alcohol because it feeds the cycle of racial self-hatred begun by colonial invasion: "For this sin we are despised in the world, and it is all right and just, for we despise ourselves more" (478). Occom's message speaks to American Indian communities even today. In the end, he asserts that our recovery must begin within ourselves: "If we don't regard ourselves, who will regard us?" (478). Native wellness of both body and mind must begin with a love of self, a regard to resist and overthrow those who endeavor to harm us. Occom's sermon is thought to be the first publication in English by an American Indian. It is most significant, though, that this first work is a piece of political criticism. We may draw from this early moment of tribal immediacy a context through which to trace the origins and objectives of a publicly accountable American Indian political criticism.

Steeped in a discourse of demotic politics, it is not surprising that American Indians in the nineteenth century began to adapt European political writing to defend the sovereign status of their nations. While I will not provide here an extensive Native intellectual history, let me present a few figures whose work is intensely political as well as intellectual,[13] thus conveying the sense of immediacy I have been describing. Though less critically known than William Apess, the Cherokee statesman Elias Boudinot appeared with the Pequot minister to lecture publicly against the impending 1830 Removal Act to force Indians west of the Mississippi. Boudinot is credited with founding in 1828 the first Native newspaper, the *Cherokee Phoenix*. His commitment to the public discussion of politics is best represented in his famous "An Address to the Whites," a speech he delivered in the First Presbyterian Church in Philadelphia in 1826 to raise money for a school in the Cherokee Republic. Boudinot masterfully negotiates between opposing political forces: the U.S. government coveting Indigenous lands, the Christian Board of Missions demanding the destruction of traditional Cherokee culture, the plantation-owning Cherokees seeking a capitalist economy, and the traditional Overhill Cherokees resisting the intrusion of Western ways. Serving his people in a public forum before a Christian congregation, Boudinot's "An Address to the Whites" recalls the political grace of Occom's "Sermon": "I now stand before you delegated by my native country to seek her interest, to labour for her respectability, and by my public efforts to assist in raising her to an equal standing with other nations of the earth" (1983 [1826], 69).[14]

This immediacy of American Indian political criticism is probably most painfully felt in the writings of Charles Eastman, who fled with his people from the U.S. military to Canada, and then returned as a young man to become a physician and a major voice in the Society of American Indians. Like Occom, Apess, and Boudinot, Eastman delivered public lectures that could be politically charged. Though Eastman had become a part of European society, having married into a prominent white family, and having been accepted in Eastern circles, his distance from the severe colonial issues facing a branch of his own people, the Dakota Sioux, was suddenly truncated when he became the doctor at the Pine Ridge agency. On 28 December 1890, Eastman witnessed the aftermath of the Wounded Knee Massacre, when five hundred soldiers opened fire on the men, women, and children of Big Foot's encampment. Like Occom, Eastman found himself in an uncanny moment of immediacy:

A majority of the thirty or more Indian wounded were women and children, including babies in arms. As there were not tents enough for all, Mr. Cook offered us the mission chapel, in which the Christmas tree still stood, for a temporary hospital. We tore out the pews and covered the floor with hay and quilts. There we laid the poor creatures side by side in rows, and the night was devoted to caring for them as best we could. Many were frightfully torn by pieces of shells, and the suffering was terrible. General Brooke placed me in charge and I had to do nearly all the work, for although army surgeons were more than ready to help as soon as their own men had been cared for, the tortured Indians would scarcely allow a man in uniform to touch them. (1977 [1916], 110)

As a Native intellectual experiencing firsthand the brutal force of U.S. empire building, Eastman was challenged to either face or turn away from this cataclysmic event. Perhaps to escape the closeness of this colonial reality, Eastman participated in the Society's near-collective denial of Indian hating in the United States. Today, Indian scholars wonder about this response to material reality. In a sentence, Robert Warrior explains the bleak social context in which turn-of-the-century Native scholars struggled for an attainable politics: "This generation was the integrationist legacy of post-Wounded Knee existence" (1995, 7). In the face of such deplorable U.S. treatment of Indian nations, Eastman nonetheless incorporates his testimony of Wounded Knee into *From the Deep Woods to Civilization* (1977 [1916]), which at the time attracted a large U.S. audience for whom this murderous event would be difficult to ignore. As the simple story of an Indian becoming an American, his autobiography will contradict and confuse. For against that narrative, Eastman ultimately indicts the United States for "the savagery of civilization."

On another front of the nineteenth-century Indian Wars, the United States had coerced Native nations to allot their collective lands to individual tribal members and to surrender to the United States the "surplus" land to sell to European homesteaders. White settlers, railroaders, oilmen, and miners flooded into formerly Native national lands. The General Allotment Act,[15] later called the Dawes Act of 1887, devastated Native economies, ecologies, and societies: individual property eroded communal moral consciousness. Unable to pay their newly imposed property taxes, American Indians by the thousands were again dispossessed of their lands. The craven Dawes Act precipitated the loss of twenty-six million acres of Indian land (Wilkinson 1987, 20). The dream of a Native state to be called "Sequoyah" dissipated when Indian Territory was forced into Oklahoma statehood in 1907, and white settlers headed for yet another land rush of Indian lands in the former Cherokee Outlet. Facing these desperate times, early- and mid-twentieth-century Native letters is thus marked by a reduction in overt political writing for a mass market. Its major writers began to disengage politically and remained cautious about raising their anti-colonial voices. Perhaps with the exception of Luther Standing Bear (1978 [1933]), political writing went underground or became more indirect— regrouping from colonial defiance to community preservation, from address to novel. Writing during this time of daunting social upheaval for American Indians, Native intellectuals such as Gertrude Bonnin (1985

[1921]), D'Arcy McNickle (1978 [1936], 1988 [1978], and Fey and McNickle 1970 [1959]), and John Joseph Mathews (1981a [1945], 1981b [1932], 1988 [1934]) were concerned with protecting tribal lands and cultural practices by supporting the 1934 Indian Reorganization Act to restore tribal self-governance, which was developed by John Collier, Franklin Roosevelt's commissioner of Indian affairs. So, even though McNickle and Mathews pursued social and political projects to benefit their tribal communities and American Indian–European American relations in general, they concurrently wrote novels such as *The Surrounded* (1936) and *Sundown* (1934), respectively, which were surprisingly tentative about the survival of tribal cultures. They often represented the colonial conflicts between Native nations and the United States as nihilistic and culturally incommensurable collisions between radically different peoples, as in McNickle's *Wind from an Enemy Sky* (posthumously, 1978). Like Eastman, their colonial experiences and political demands appear somewhat restrained in their fiction.

McNickle was Cree Métis but enrolled in the Confederated Salish Kootenai Tribes on the Flathead reservation in Montana where he was born. Though he never stayed long in his community after leaving for Oxford in 1925, McNickle worked closely with John Collier on his "Indian New Deal" and helped found the National Congress of American Indians. In contrast to the despairing tone of his fiction, McNickle's books on tribal histories and political theory present more affirmative views of American Indians in the twentieth century. In *Indians and Other Americans: Two Ways of Life Meet* (1959), coauthored with Harold Fey, McNickle writes a statement of Native diplomacy and attempts to explain the troubled history of Indian policy in terms of differing philosophical and political views to a broad U.S. American audience, including members of the United States Congress.

Unlike McNickle, Mathews pursued his politics more locally by helping to organize and build his Osage community. In his commitment to explain abroad the history and lifeways of his social world at home, Mathews carried on the political work of Sioux anthropologist Ella Deloria (1998 [1944]) and of Creek journalist Alexander Posey (1993), both of whom wrote about their tribal histories and the contemporary political challenges facing their home places in such works as *Speaking of Indians* (1944) and the Fus Fixico letters, respectively. Mathews grounds his writing in the needs of the lives of those from his home place in an era fraught with doubt. Jace Weaver (1997) calls this tribal persistence to defend American Indian communities "communitism": "In their efforts, one can see the continuing communitist struggle for Natives as Natives that was the predominant theme during the period, in literature as in politics" (88). To this political purpose, Mathews worked in Osage government and even established the Osage Tribal Museum in 1938. These real world practices no doubt informed his critical writing, but not as forcefully as one would expect. He wrote a history of the Osage people, *Wah'Kon-Tah* (1932), which became a selection in the Book-of-the-Month Club. In *Talking to the Moon* (1945), Mathews meditates on the relationship of Osages to the earth and its rhythms, in an ecological memoir of his home deep in the Osage Blackjacks region, where he daily walked through the lands, imagining the human place in the living world and the consequences of the destructive oil business on life's delicate balance.

The years following World War II, in which we see a relative scarcity of American Indian intellectual writing,[16] might be understood as a time of cultural germination and of political planning for the social and literary outpouring of the 1960s and 1970s. Since I have already reviewed in my introduction this vigorous period in Native intellectual history, let me merely emphasize here the fundamental role of history in grounding American Indian political struggles.[17] The enormous success of the Indian movement grew from scholars and activists initiating the social transformation enabled through the assertions of personal experience and tribal histories, as Red Power organizers described for the popular media their own lives and the poverty in tribal territories. What became a popular form of testimony at political demonstrations relentlessly linked theoretically American Indian identity and tribal experience. For this reason, Native scholars and activists of this period held social location as a primary means of calling attention to the deplorable material colonial relations between the United States and Native nations.

When in 1969 Alfonso Ortiz published the controversial study *The Tewa World*, he drew on both his experience as a tribal member of the San Juan Pueblo and his Western scientific knowledge of cultural systems of meaning. Ortiz also authored numerous articles on Native lifeways that presented the personal, emotional, and intellectual lives of American Indians.[18] Significantly, the literature of the Indian movement departs from earlier forms, influenced by modernism and its use of the dialogic narrative. Though Red Power authors are said to implement modernist structures, characterized by the fractured narrative and the privileging of characters' psychological internality, their works remain rooted in and concerned with the meaning of tribal experience. In *House Made of Dawn*, Momaday infuses his narrative with historical and anthropological fact as well as with oral tradition. Other Native writers such as Simon Ortiz, Leslie Marmon Silko, and James Welch compose works grounded in Native communities—novels in which actual tribally significant events and places are named and described. American Indian intellectuals of the Red Power period realize their commitment to tribal communities by creating art and writing criticism attendant to the facts of everyday Native existence in the real world. As we recall, Native intellectuals of the Indian movement did not seek to escape the demands of history, for they viewed it as hardly a trap; instead, they harnessed the force of experience to fortify a progressive politics.

Even this historical sketch of American Indian political criticism displays a tradition of Indigenous cultures developing theoretical paradigms to serve practical actions in the midst of ongoing U.S. forays into Native homelands. Responding to the immediacy of direct and startling experiences of colonialism within their communities, Native intellectuals have been driven to defend their people not with war but with ideas, as American Indian scholar-activists meet and debate, often publicly, the cultural issues often masked by racist assumptions of superiority and a manifest destiny to control Native nations. When Native scholars recall experiences of domination or privation within their own communities or families, they discover the necessity of theories relevant to the real lives of their people—those whom their scholarship can serve. This exhortation to us by our tribal constituents is often characterized as "heeding the voices of our ancestors," in the words of Mohawk scholar Taiaiake Alfred (1995, 73). It is the calling of a history that lays claim to our tribal selves.

As this intellectual tradition shows, a practical criticism in American Indian studies should thus recognize that what we call "theory" must refer closely to our real worlds: the social, economic, and ecological conditions in which we live. As an empirically tested process, theoretical inquiry continually attempts better to explain and challenge the political subjugation of Indian Country. This concern for the unification of theory and practice is exemplified in the work of Antonio Gramsci, who, like many American Indian prisoners in colonial history, was imprisoned for his threatening ideas. Like other members of oppressed groups, Gramsci derived his "philosophy of praxis" from his own experiences of political subjugation. He was a peasant of rural Italy who through circumstance achieved a formal education and, as such, embodies both of the social groups Marx requires for revolution: the "traditional" intellectuals and the "organic" intellectuals. Gramsci's attachment to his rural culture profoundly influenced his formal intellectual training. His community of origin, for example, maintained a deep spiritual relationship with the land, in which the forces of the universe required prayer to maintain their balance and order. This mystical upbringing, coupled with his secular formal education, might have thrown Gramsci into ideological contradiction were he not able to reconcile his organic intellectual self with his newly forming traditional university-trained intellectual self. To stabilize a cultural, intellectual, and spiritual life otherwise "caught between two worlds," he thus decreed: "All men are intellectuals, one could therefore say, but not all men have in society the function of intellectuals" (9).

According to Gramsci, though traditional professional intellectuals of the literary and scientific fields maintain positions that may transcend class groups, they nonetheless derive their intellectual power from overseeing a historical class structure. Organic intellectuals, however, evolve from *within* a particular social group; they are organic because they grow out of the everyday work environment particular to their class. In his regard for the intellectual capacity of all workers, Gramsci shares Lenin's stinging critique of the Left, in which Lenin declares that "all distinctions as between workers and intellectuals . . . must be obliterated." Subverting the elitist tendencies of the bourgeoisie to control the proletariat, who are thought incapable of creating legitimate social theories, Gramsci asserts that workers indeed can develop their own theories from within their own social world. Because organic intellectuals are, by virtue of experience, more able to interpret the lives of their social class, Gramsci suggests that they are better prepared to serve the political aims of their struggle. So not only does Gramsci hold that organic intellectuals can acquire the skills of traditional intellectuals, but, more controversially, he insists that the organic intellectual can best serve the broader class struggle because the traditional intellectual, by definition, is not equipped to achieve the experiential knowledge of the organic intellectual.

While we should be careful in drawing on Marxist theory to serve not class but anticolonial struggles, Gramsci offers a compelling framework through which to develop a strong praxis in American Indian studies as well as to approach the writings of Native prisoners. Any oppositional movement, at the very least, demands experiential communication between the theoretical and the empirical.[19] Like many scholars today writing for American Indian nations in crisis—scholars who are concerned with the political salience of unifying theory and practice — Gramsci finds that

> the identification of theory and practice is a critical act, through which practice is demonstrated rational and necessary, and theory realistic and rational. This is why the problem of the identity of theory and practice is raised especially in the so-called transitional moments of history, that is, those moments in which the movement of transformation is at its most rapid. For it is then that the practical forces unleashed really demand justification in order to become more efficient and expansive; and that theoretical programmes multiply in number, and demand in their turn to be realistically justified, to the extent that they prove themselves assimilable into practical movements, thereby making the latter yet more practical and real. (1971, 365)

American Indian nations are undergoing their own "movement of transformation" as tribal members consider reinstating traditional governments and recover cultural knowledge and ancestral lands. In this political context of reinvigorated Indigenous nationhood, the dialectical relationship of theory to practice, as Gramsci explains, proves indispensable in developing and testing the "right" ideas to serve the actual needs of Native communities beset with colonialist intrusions. To serve this process, Gramsci might argue that our readings of culture and books should be "realistically justified"; that is, they should provide cogent explanations that aggressively seek accurately to engage American Indian lives and those whom literary texts represent. Concomitantly, the practical demands of oppressive economic and social conditions on reservations may be a call to action for Native scholars.

Those American Indian scholars who remain close to the daily life of their tribal communities are often best prepared to pursue this kind of political scholarship. Readers might bear with this controversial idea, for I wish to support it theoretically. My earlier claims about the theoretical basis of cultural identity and the epistemic status of experience may explain the ethical callout of Native organic intellectuals. As I discussed, the inherited and lived colonial realities of political subjugation and cultural destruction, the incontrovertible facts of social location, shape but do not entirely determine the experiences that American Indians are likely to have. Such experiences inform cultural identity, and identity, in turn, serves to interpret these experiences. On this understanding of tribal social location, experience, and identity, Indian people reserve the possession of advanced knowledge of a Native world that others are not likely to have. When we lay claim to those experiences to fortify our tribal selves, we forge a political identity. Worthy political identities are thus made from the very same experiences that the dominated undergo, but are consciously created through self-reflection on and disclosure of that domination. From this view, it also stands that Indigenous political identities can be born from interpretations of a formerly unknown, dominated world that we seek to encounter. In coming closer to our own and others' colonial experiences, we can also *choose*—that is, self-consciously construct—our political identities. When we experience a political awakening to anticolonial resistance, we often do so through this increased access to actual material conditions facing our tribal constituents. So doing, such scholars deepen their knowledge—and their political investment—in the liberation struggle for Indian people.[20]

If American Indian intellectuals have long held the discussion of politics as a cultural value inseparable from the body of Native understanding, we might ask why some Native intellectuals and writers of the recent decade have not been more politically engaged. Surely the caution cannot be attributed to an aggressive colonial circumstance similar to that of the early twentieth century. The 1990s nonetheless at times marked the obscuring of political issues facing the real lives of American Indians in their communities, a change in intellectual and artistic focus that began after the slowing of the civil rights movement. Some American Indian scholars started to seek a more sophisticated theoretical framework through which to challenge the myth of the Vanishing American and other tragic views of Native cultures and literatures. In employing trickster theories, Native intellectuals such as Betty Louise Bell (1992), Kimberly Blaeser (1996), Laura Donaldson (1995), Louis Owens (1998), Kathryn Shanley (1999), and Gerald Vizenor (2000) have sought to deconstruct harmful representations of American Indian identity and lifeways.

Cherokee scholar Betty Louise Bell has advocated replacing the colonized identity "halfbreed" with the indeterminate subject position of "crossblood," from which hybrid Native writers would negotiate power in the space between colonizer and colonized: "The Native American 'I' has, from colonization, been a hybrid identity, composed and mediated by the settler's language, experience, and imagination. . . . For the crossblood, . . . the stories of tribal lives before and after conquest survive in coexistent individualized narratives, neither succumbing to the other, neither being colonized by the language or history of the other, but creating a space where memory and imagination actively interact with the world" (184, 185). The crossblood position has attempted to account for a colonial past that, in this view, has often taken the ability to write one's own history. Crossblood intellectuals have tended to consider external social and material forces, such as the imposition of colonial languages and the displacement of tribal peoples from their lands, to erode one's ability to write with Indigenous agency. Accepting that colonized Indians are on some level always constructed, even to themselves, by their colonizers, crossblood scholars have thus sought the small freedom promised in ideological and cultural indeterminacy. Such trickster criticism has often claimed that Native people today live hybrid lives that liberate by remaining permanently dislocated: "Vizenor locates agency in the tricksters' capacity for transgression and metamorphosis. Tricksters exist on the borders of splintered lives and divided opposing cultures, speaking and healing in a divided crossblood space" writes Bell (185). Like other crossblood theorists of Native culture and literature, Bell has been drawn to Vizenor's ahistorical trickster fiction perhaps because it evades, and thus must not defend, a history that American Indians are forced to forget.

In Vizenor's novel *Bearheart* (1990 [1978]), Belladonna Darwin-Winter Catcher is often confused about her Indianness. Her name suggests multiple interactive cultural determinants: the Christian worshiper of a "Beautiful Lady" or the Virgin Mary, the rational evolutionary, and the tribal historian. She encounters "the hunter," a trickster who is of little help in discerning how she should behave or define herself. He says: "Indians are an invention. . . . You tell me that the invention is different than the rest of the world when it was the rest of the world that invented the Indian . . . An Indian is an Indian because he speaks and thinks and believes he is an Indian, but an Indian is nothing more than an invention" (195). The hunter insists that Indian identity is a pervasive colonial construction beyond which Native people cannot conceive a genuine tribal identity. While we should not assume that the hunter represents the author's views on identity, *Bearheart* nonetheless provides little guidance on how to construct one's own Native selfhood. American Indian critics celebrating this hunter have inadvertently subverted the goal of Native oral tradition to morally ground individuals within the tribe by making the trickster into an indiscriminate subverter of all claims to self-knowledge. In *Bearheart*, Vizenor suggests that the cultural specificity of tribal values constitutes a "terminal creed." The white hunter corners Belladonna and states: "'My father said the same things about the hunt that you said is tribal . . . Are you telling me that [what you identify as a tribal value] is exclusive to your mixedblood race?' 'Yes!' snapped Belladonna. 'I am different than a whiteman because of my values and my blood is different'" (194). Because Belladonna asserts her cultural difference but cannot name essential tribal values that no white man shares, the hunters execute her with a poison cookie, announcing that she "is a terminal believer and a victim of her own narcissism" (145). In holding that claims to knowledge can only be terminal, the trickster position on Native culture and identity has been thus oddly reliant on essentialism.

Whether as Coyote, Rabbit, Raven, or Nanabozho, the trickster in traditional tribal narrative, however, most often serves as a negative example to remind tribal people to regulate social values. In *American Indian Thought* (Waters 2004), the first collection of Native philosophical essays ever produced, Indian philosophers find trickster behavior to diverge from, and thus underscore, normative moral behavior: "The idea is simply that the universe is moral. Facts, truth, meaning, even our existence are normative. In this way, there is no difference between what is true and what is right. On this account, then, all investigation is moral investigation. The guiding question for the entire philosophical enterprise is, then: what is the right road for humans to walk?" writes contributing Cherokee philosopher Brian Yazzie Burkhart (2004, 17). This Ojibwe story, for example, teaches by showing how Naanabozho often acts impulsively on his unexamined appetite, and so thwarts his own interests. He finally attains his goal only after he learns to deliberate before he acts: "While walking along the river he saw some berries in the water. He dived down for them, but was stunned when he unexpectedly struck the bottom. There he lay for quite a while, and when he recovered consciousness and looked up, he saw the berries hanging on a tree just above him" (quoted in Thompson 2000, 54). That oral traditional trickster reminds us through his hasty and unself-aware behavior that we should reflect before diving in for our desires, for what we truly need might be right in front of us. Within traditional stories, the trickster restores Vizenor's supposedly terminal creeds of "balance" and "harmony" as normative principles self-critically valued within the community. To balance the world, for example, the trickster must invoke a moral theory through which to evaluate which tribal values might be helpful or harmful in achieving balance. It is this process of evaluation that tricksterism has often precluded, for while Native critics agree that tricksters work to challenge colonial definitions, on this position they cannot evaluate among definitions. To do so, from this view,

would be to support a terminal creed. In the service of cultural indeterminacy, moreover, ahistorical narratives such as *Bearheart* might not be the
most politically enabling genre at this time. For liberation is not won by
escaping the colonial context but instead by creating the social conditions
for tribal cultures to flourish.[21]

Nonetheless, by the early 1990s this strain of Native criticism had
begun to move the focus of American Indian studies away from the material conditions of Native cultures and toward the realm of the imagined,
which is often maintained in oral trickster narratives. Vizenor has been
instrumental in liberating Native discourse from the dominant scholarship on American Indians in books such as *Narrative Chance: Postmodern
Discourse on Native American Indian Literatures*: "Native American Indian
literatures are unstudied landscapes, wild and comic rather than tragic
and representational, storied with narrative wisps and tribal discourse.
Social science theories constrain tribal landscapes to institutional values,
representationalism and the politics of academic determination. The narrow teleologies deduced from social science monologues and the ideologies that arise from structuralism have reduced tribal literatures to an
'objective' collection of consumable cultural artifacts. Postmodernism liberates imagination and widens the audience for tribal literatures; this new
criticism rouses a comic world view, narrative discourse and language
games on the past" (1993b, 5–6). Vizenor rightly objects to Western ways
of reading American Indian literatures, because these approaches are
often historically linked to colonialism. Though the Enlightenment arose
from a desire to liberate thought from superstition, contemporary theory
reminds us that it became too sure of itself: European intellectuals began
to assume that, unlike the "superstitious" cultures they were presently
colonizing, their own ability to produce objective knowledge was free of
historical and social bias. "Ruthlessly, in despite of itself, the Enlightenment has extinguished any trace of its own self-consciousness," according
to Max Horkheimer and Theodor Adorno (1972 [1944], 4). It is perhaps
no coincidence that the world's most aggressive period of imperialism
corresponds with the Age of Reason. Bearing the ideological baggage of
the founding period of science, anthropology and the social sciences ap-
proached the problem of interpreting other cultures and literatures by
assuming the primacy of their own as rational and uniquely equipped to
uncover universally applicable laws of human nature in all inquiries. Because Western science ascribes as universal what are in fact culturally
European theories of human development, humanity was thought to

evolve from "savagery" (different from European culture) to "civilization" (like European culture). Holding its own culturally specific values as universal truths, the West was able to justify the destruction of tribal cultures as a necessary and unavoidable period of humanity's evolvement toward civilization. The first American's destiny to vanish was therefore held to be tragic, as Vizenor correctly states.

For Vizenor, those earlier narratives that attempt to represent a colonized world tend to invite tragic readings and are thus less viable than the comic oral tale of the trickster discourse. He and other Native trickster scholars have thus rightly sought to oppose these tragic interpretations of American Indian literature by decentering the enshrined Enlightenment narratives of manifest destiny and exposing the myths of Europeans' ability to judge without bias other lands and peoples. Because the oral tradition is thought to function dialogically and without a grand narrative, some Native scholars find this ongoing system of tribal inquiry similar to mainstream discursive epistemologies, which destabilize knowledge and history in a "language game" designed to liberate fixed meanings. In his *Manifest Manners*, Vizenor quotes Jean-François Lyotard to show how such theories of narrative operate like tribal views of representation: "These narrative wisps are the 'stories that one tells, that one hears, that one acts out'" (1999, 68). Out of this need to free American Indian literature from a tragic colonial history, such Native critics began to seek critical models in more imaginative, less historical, tribal stories. But while Vizenor's *Trickster of Liberty* (1988) liberates novelistic form by being set in imaginary, mythic time, such a narrative is less able to confront and develop the real politics facing tribes.[22]

For over a decade, such Native critics have invoked trickster, the clownish figure drawn from Indigenous oral tradition, to serve liberated knowledge and progressive politics. Because, they say, the trickster actively undermines the accepted social knowledge of a tribal community, American Indian scholars can use the trickster as a metaphor to understand Native peoples and the colonial condition. Such scholars advocate the subversive acts of trickster as a model for anticolonial agency and identity. Like Bell, other American Indian scholars employing trickster argue that because the cultural self-understanding of Native people is unavoidably reinterpreted, even to themselves, by colonialist views of the so-called Indian, tribal people should avoid seeking a stable center for their identity and instead find freedom in the margins of cultural and colonial ambiguity. Though such Native critics demonstrate this skeptical trend in a

variety of critical approaches and not always consistently, trickster scholars share a general distrust of knowledge and a belief in the marginalizing
of the self as a means of political resistance. Because many Indian cultural critics advocating tricksterism occupy high-ranking positions in the
academy and publish widely, their influence on the discipline is considerable. Indeed, those Indian scholars who publish within trickster frameworks do so in large number at highly ranked university presses. Vizenor
is undoubtedly the most visible inside and outside the field, and he is the
most published of all Native critics, with at least three scholarly books
on crossblood and trickster theories of American Indian knowledge and
culture. Of course, few would doubt the popularity of discursive thought
in the humanities in general as well as in minority studies. In this intellectual climate today, trickster discourse has become a well-established
theoretical position in American Indian studies.

American Indian scholars supporting tricksterism claim to invoke the
trickster's subversive behavior to resist the force of U.S. imperialism. To
this end, such scholars often make laudable if inconsistent arguments for
decolonization, in which knowledge is presented to operate on a double
standard for Natives and European Americans, respectively, as grounded
yet ever-shifting, essentialist yet trickster. Assiniboine scholar Kathryn
Shanley attempts to derail colonial paradigms with such acts of subversion, but advocates both strategic essentialism and trickster discourse, an
unlikely pair of theoretical positions on tribal knowledge. In a 1998 essay
on the future of Native studies, she writes: "I must emphasize that my
position is one of a *strategic* essentialism, a positing of an 'essential' difference for the sake of shifting the center of power. Non-Indians have always
been predominant in the study of Native American cultures, as part of
the privilege that goes along with colonialism" (1998, 132). In an essay
published a year later, Shanley describes the merits of trickster subversion
to deconstruct the center of a colonial allegory: "What sort of Indigenous
literature would be radical enough to upset the imperialist 'game,' and to
illuminate other discursive logics? I would argue that the trickster figure,
despite non-Indian distortions and appropriations of him/her/it, can still
function to upset the dominant discourse. . . . Trickster exists paradoxi-
cally prior to all else and also as a latecomer—she/he/it is the dream and
the dreamer" (1999, 37, 38). In her admirable goal both to anchor Native
culture and to undermine the dominant culture, Shanley demonstrates
a concern I find prevalent among Native scholars adapting tricksterism.
In each quotation above, notice how the critic conceives cultural knowl-

edge; one desires its stability but admits its constructedness. In the first instance, she thus relinquishes the hope for actual objectivity for a tactical maneuver to stabilize American Indian identity and culture. However, in making false gestures toward objectivity, she not only endangers her argument with an insincere rhetoric but also misses the opportunity to ground her claims to knowledge by linking her position to her declaration of colonial inequality in Native studies. For if the world is often different for Native people than it is for white Americans, she can certainly make this normative claim without being essentialist. Fearing the charge of essentialism nonetheless, Shanley turns to trickster theory. In the second instance, the subversive trickster, "exists" "prior to all else," as if it represents a founding psychic principle or essence. In this manner, the trickster attempts to provide the "stable" ground for knowledge that Native critics seek.

To build on my discussion of Native identity in chapter 2, here I show how Native scholars draw on this contradictory trickster discourse to undermine European American colonial culture, on the one hand, and yet to make objective claims regarding the Native self, on the other. As we recall, Louis Owens (1992) writes about coming home and developing a Native sense of self as an "act of recovery," even though he explains Native identity as a problem of knowledge fracturing. Still other trickster critics present this theoretical double standard in which knowledge is indeterminate for some yet stable for others. In the course of her essay, Bell presents such concepts as the "(re)membering" of tribal identity, even though she also claims that colonialism controls how American Indians understand themselves: "Finally, if they are to survive, half-breeds choose salvage, usually through a ceremony of (re)membering, their tribal identity. The half-breed steps out of a divided self and creates a unified and creative tribal identity from opposing fragments of experience and language, insisting on the tribal song even if only the words are left" (1992, 191). As illustrated in the cases above, American Indian critics, whether advocating strategic essentialism or tricksterism, often do so out of a pressing concern both to challenge inaccurate representations of Native people and to preserve a stable basis for tribal political and cultural knowledge.

So even though tricksters expose tragic perceptions and misrepresentations of American Indians, they rarely present a clear understanding of who an actual American Indian might or should be. As we have learned, this trickster, who both subverts all knowledge and yet intermittently supports an unexamined moral theory, embodies what theorists call a crossblood or mixedblood cultural identity. Since the moment of "cultural contact,"[23] the crossblood argument goes, Indian people have been forever constructed by the European colonial presence so completely that they must conceive of themselves as an "invention" of the colonizer. Supporting this view, Bell claims "it would be difficult to write of [American Indian] identity before colonization interpreted [American Indians] to themselves" (1992, 186). Crossbloods, self-conscious of their fractured postcolonial subjectivity, gain temporary liberation by subverting the colonizer's image of the Indian. Like tricksters, crossbloods inhabit an ever-shifting social and cultural position that resists definition, where freedom awaits in the margins of colonial interaction. From this position on Indian knowledge and culture, Native scholars critique non-Indian representations of Native literature, but in so doing they are ultimately unable to justify the accuracy of their own representations. Moreover, because crossblood identities exist in Vizenor's cultural "seams," the liminal spaces between histories and identities, they provide little explanation for different histories and different kinds of identities—or for experiences of the privileged from those of the oppressed. To decolonize, we must ask whether all transgressions are necessary and good, or exactly which constructions of history are more accurate or enabling. Should we, for instance, subvert the legal claims of treaties and hence the sovereign status of Indian Nations?[24] Crossblood theories of American Indian culture and literature provide few intellectual resources to adjudicate these difficult and vital political questions. For all of these reasons, I do not find trickster theories especially helpful in the political work of American Indian studies today.

Having attempted to raise the stakes in studies of Native literature and culture, I would now like to deepen my discussion from previous chapters regarding views of knowledge—notably intellectual attitudes about philosophical issues such as essentialism, objectivity, and fallibility—to handle objections to my characterization of trickster theory in Indian studies. Scholars responding to my assessment might argue that, while many American Indian critics often access one or more theoretical positions, such as essentialism or tricksterism, few present their "extreme" versions, even though mainstream scholars often do. We might begin by asking just what makes a theoretical position extreme. Without reducing all critical analyses of Native literature to a simplistic identity politics, I instead hope to clarify possible stances on these philosophical issues, which often lead to a so-called extreme stance. I myself am foremost concerned with theory as a means to knowledge production, either of literature or the world. As in the sciences, the comparative ability of a theory to produce more objective knowledge determines its legitimacy. Such a prerequisite remains fundamental to the hard sciences and, I suggest, might also be to the humanities and their cultural and literary analyses. Since underlying any theoretical position is a view of knowledge, scholars can cut deeper to disclose this view, however latent. To do so, we thus might consider at least two theoretical questions regarding objective knowledge and falli-bility: first, is it possible to say anything normative about the tribal world?; and, second, how do we know when we are wrong?

While the trickster position might be losing support in American Indian studies, some Native scholars still approach the discourse from a skeptical theoretical position predicated on indeterminacy, the hallmark of trickster theory. To understand the intellectual motivation of this critical position, we might look closer to the view of knowledge that the position presupposes, which I summarize, simply, as the denial of objectivity. The degree to which Native scholars are committed to exploring this denial in voluminous critiques of culture, history, and literature—at the expense of normative knowledge production—determines the depth of extremism. As I have said, to complicate matters the extreme skeptical position on knowledge often shifts even within a single argument. In Native studies today, one thus rarely finds a trickster critic who consistently deploys ex-treme skepticism regarding not only Western *but also Indigenous* claims to knowledge. Instead, Native intellectuals often confront the inevitable tainting of Western American power in knowledge of Native texts while at the same time insisting that Native knowledge claims are stable and grounded, that is, normative.

Perhaps to be distinguished from such scholars is Vizenor, who is today the strongest supporter of trickster theory in American Indian studies. Though the Indian scholars noted above raise doubts about the reliability of knowledge and, by extension, the possibility of basing a Native politics on identity, Vizenor suggests that cultural identity in the service of po-litical action is theoretically indefensible, even pernicious. In *Crossbloods*, Vizenor confronts activists of the American Indian Movement for forming what he believes to be a spurious Indian identity:

> The political ideologies of the radical tribal leaders are reactions to racism and cultural adversities; that much all tribal people have in common. The radical rhetoric of the leaders was not learned from tra-

ditional people on reservations or in tribal communities. Some of the militant leaders were radicalized in prison, where they found white inmates eager to listen. The poses of tribal radicals seem to mimic the romantic pictorial photographs by Edward Curtis. The radicals never seemed to smile, there were no tricksters, no humor; an incautious throwback to the stoical tribal visage of slower camera shutters. The new radicals frown, even grimace at the cameras, and revise in first person pronouns the atrocities endured by tribal cultures for more than a century. Some militants decorate themselves in pastiche pantribal vestments, pose as traditionalists, and announce their cultural pride in the romantic binaries of racial opposition. (1990, 48)

Though the AIM leaders likely pursue a sincere recovery of a tribal identity, Vizenor dismisses the men as frauds who nonetheless fail and merely mimic the bogus Indian identity constructed for them in advance by the colonizer. While Vizenor elects to target and lampoon various Native activists, rarely does he present his readers with a reliable alternative account of a legitimate traditional tribal identity. One is led to assume, then, that for Vizenor American Indian self-representation is most often a simulation, and therefore unjust and even embarrassing, because it is formed in an erroneous response to colonial circumstance. Most often, however, the extreme trickster position in Native critical studies stems from scholars in other fields of minority studies, postcolonial theory, and cultural studies. To be sure, though, as prominent and well-placed theorists in the humanities, scholars advancing this view on the instability of identity and culture should be reckoned with, even if they do not write on American Indian texts.

As most scholars are now aware, the introduction of skeptical theories of knowledge to the humanities in recent decades has provided a position to necessitate the dismantling of knowledge concepts such as culture, history, experience, and identity. Theorists drawn to deconstruction adapt this linguistic view of knowledge in order to compose an epistemological theory of culture. In understanding culture in terms of linguistic structures, discursive readers typically begin their critique of knowledge by underscoring the problem of reference in language: meaning is an "effect" of linguistic indeterminacy. Such theorists have argued that humans produce meaning through a process of negation within an often-arbitrary linguistic context. Because meaning is never fully available, to identify is to negate: things are understood in terms of what they are not; words do not carry any intrinsic meaning but must be invested with significa-tion socially. Meaning is thus relative because the movement of linguis-tic reference is always shifting across a matrix of signification in which humans are always immersed. Because the concepts of cultural identity and experience rely on social relationships and hence on the mediation of language, theorists often argue that such social meanings are indeter-minate. Experiences are thus unreliable sources of knowledge and identi-ties are theoretically suspect. In this linguistic critique of the inescapable situatedness of inquiry, knowledge is not objective. Because we are unable to step outside the linguistic structures that constitute our being, as the extreme view explains, we cannot trust our understanding of the self, our experiences, or our relationship to our American Indian cultures.

I present this often extreme critique of knowledge to clarify the trick-ster theoretical trend in Indigenous studies. Accepting this view, trickster scholars rightfully seek to expose essentialist claims to knowledge of iden-tity, experience, and culture to prevent domains of understanding from becoming reductive, complacent, static. Indian intellectuals aware of the problems with essentialist leanings hope to find in contemporary skepti-cal theory a useful corrective. Because a reliable theoretical alternative to these two often doctrinal positions on culture, identity, and politics has often not been available to meet the needs of tribal people, many Native activists and scholars continue to modify, albeit unsuccessfully, the nar-row view of knowledge assailed in skeptical discursivity with the anticolo-nial agency of trickster subversion.

A less generous assessment of contemporary theory—the dismantling of identity, the displacement of nations—suggests, however, an attempt to undermine the political salience in recognizing cultural difference. With difference itself deconstructed and subsumed under the one uni-fied and pervasive category of hybrid, globalizing forces are now able to absorb the colonial other within a boundless epistemological matrix of liberal politics. Because Native critics and activists have been cautious about the ability of contemporary theory to support a political criticism, such theories have influenced American Indian studies in a limited ca-pacity: a full-blown discursive theory of Native culture would demand the complete denial of objectivity, and this epistemology would prove dire to tribal communities. Clearly, if trickster scholars were fully to adopt this view of knowledge, they would be unwilling to make the most general claims about Native peoples. Such American Indian critics would thus undermine the political force of recognizing how life might be different

for tribal peoples dominated by a colonialist nation. Native scholars implementing tricksterism therefore announce that even though colonial
modernity always constructs the category of Indian, Native people may
nonetheless resist colonialism through their tribal identities and even recover a reliable tribal history. In their hope to defend a real American
Indian self in the midst of contemporary postcolonial discourse, crossblood scholars still insist on a contradictory measure of anticolonial
agency.

But while some American Indian scholars attempt to insert agency into
skeptical views of culture, other cultural critics come to share their trickster theory of American Indian culture, but in a way that ultimately dele-
gitimates the concept of tribal identity altogether. Because Native trickster
scholars are ultimately unable to lay theoretical claim to a distinct American Indian identity and history, less sympathetic scholars have begun to
reject wholesale the potential for tribal agency and the concept of Native
cultural identity. Drawing on discursive theories, many mainstream
scholars argue that today's Native people bear the unavoidable influence
of European colonialism. Western peoples assimilate and construct Indigenous personhood, but, noticeably, this apparently inexorable process
rarely runs the other direction. Such scholars, who appear to support the
theory of crossblood identity, have produced a volume of essays on the
indomitable colonial construction of the Indian, with a title that borrows
Vizenor's term: *The Invented Indian* (Clifton 1990).[25] Other critics have
begun to apply skeptical theories of hybridity to reinforce mixedblood
views of American Indian identity as well as of knowledge.[26] Theorists can
and have used the Native Coyote trickster figure to set forth a skeptical
model of inquiry: we should give up on achieving stable knowledge and
instead accept that we will always be tricked.[27] This specifically discursive
notion of fallibility, however, proves to be unhelpful in planning practical
programs to decolonize American Indian nations. To locate error in the
ways we understand our tribal selves and our tribal experiences, we require a more empirical form of inquiry that specifies how we can better
know when we are wrong (which histories might be incomplete, which
values might be damaging) so that American Indians may provide more
enabling accounts of contemporary Native existence.

Returning to American Indian political realities, Native scholars such
as Elizabeth Cook-Lynn (2001), Greg Sarris (1993), Robert Warrior (1995),
Jace Weaver (1997), and Craig Womack (1999) have redirected the critical
focus to the material needs of Native people in their communities and

begun to question the usefulness of trickster theories to serve political action. I dare to suggest that these scholars hearken to the Red Power era to recover its relational view of social location, identity, experience, and political transformation, as they build the Indian theories of our times. These scholars suggest that the Native self must become located in the material world to redress Indian political realities. As I have described, the history of colonialism in the Americas is a history of erasing the Indigenous material record, not only through warfare and displacement, but also through institutions designed to suppress Indian histories and to silence Indian voices. The trickster subverts the dominant history but, inadvertently, subverts Native histories too. Thus, some Indian scholars have lately expressed their need for a theory to help them locate exactly which structures of power are destructive and which are empowering, and to justify these evaluations on a normative basis. What is more, Native intellectuals living and working in this so-called crossblood marginal space often find not liberty but inertia. A politics of pure subversion thus cannot avoid the difficult theoretical imperative of adjudicating between self-defeating and self-liberating acts of subversion. In resistance to U.S. imperialist attempts to erase the Indigenous presence, some Native peoples work to reassert a stable body of tribal knowledge as central to the preservation of tribal culture, history, and nationhood. American Indian scholars may avoid the self-defeat of destabilized knowledge by working to build a secure, epistemologically based Native political criticism.

Elizabeth Cook-Lynn shows concern for this less historical direction of Native literary criticism: "When writers and researchers and professors claim a mixed-blood focus on individualism and liberation, they often do not develop ideas as part of an inner-unfolding theory of Native culture; thus, they do not contribute ideas as a political practice connected to First Nation ideology. No one will argue that Native studies has had as its central agenda the critical questions of race and politics. For Indians in America today, real empowerment lies in First Nation ideology not in individual liberation or Americanization" (1996b, 70–71). Cook-Lynn locates the problem of Native writers and scholars producing less politically engaged fiction and criticism—the inattention to "race and politics"—in what she calls a misdirected "mixed-blood focus." Such a focus, she claims, is more accepted and promoted in the university, a primary site for the investigation, representation, and transmission of American Indian intellectualism. But why would mixedblood intellectuals be less concerned with defending and developing "First Nation ideology"?

Native critics oppose Cook-Lynn for her purported attack on mixed-blood writers and their conversion to dominant culture by intermarriage with Europeans. In her reliance on the mixedblood category for her critique, Cook-Lynn does risk reinforcing the very category she opposes, but she more likely disagrees with the individualist, nontribal values she sees often promoted by such mixedblood writers and scholars. In other words, in my view Cook-Lynn objects not to the multiheritage aspect but rather to the social values of mixedbloods, who, she contends, undermine nationhood by providing only self-absorbed narratives of displacement and then receive promotions in the academy for doing so. This said, I find it impossible to separate race from ideology in the concept of the mixedblood, and so I ask that we reject the term altogether. I should be clear that I do not deny *the political reality of racialization*. Indeed, we must be accountable for the privileges of light skin, maleness, and straightness in a world that invests these social registers with great power. In these I recognize my own privilege. But, as Michael Wilson (1997) argues, the mixedblood as a category cannot escape the binary of purity and corruption. Of course, Cook-Lynn can surely critique the values of particular writers as detrimental to nationhood and sovereignty without ever turning to a reductive identity politics, and other Native scholars can recast their discussions to evaluate the tribal values they come to hold and promote in our research. I thus submit that Native scholars exchange the mixedblood for the tribal citizen. Like other countries, Native nations can stand by their sovereignty and thus develop ethically just standards of membership.

The tribal realist view of American Indian knowledge that I have been developing throughout this volume might prove helpful in explaining the link between identity and politics. I have explored how experiences influence but do not entirely determine the formation of one's cultural identity. For this reason, tribal experience, in all of its forms, can function as a point of departure for work in American Indian studies. Cherokee sociologist Russell Thornton holds that this very concept of experience distinguishes Native studies from the historically colonized site for the study of Native cultures—American anthropology: "This endogenous consideration would provide new perspectives on the study of Native Americans, additional topics to be studied, and new issues to be discussed" (1998a, 4). Taken seriously as a source of knowledge, Native experience plays a crucial role in explaining the lives of American Indians in ways the external observations of other exogenous scholars cannot. For this reason, Native tribal experience provides American Indian scholars with an epistemic privilege in interpreting their culture, and thus challenges a long history of colonized studies in the dominant culture.[28] The task facing today's Indigenous intellectuals, then, is to recover a trusted real world space through which to inform and test our research, as the scholars noted above have begun to show. That is, in focusing their work on more socially relevant topics that consider the lives of American Indians in the world and their political transformations, scholars anchor and empower their studies. Although that world is often a painful, dominated space, it is one that nonetheless reclaims ground from the colonial matrix. Recalling Antonio Gramsci's (1971) philosophy of praxis, Cook-Lynn calls the study of this process, as cited above, an "inner-unfolding theory of Native culture." At this time, our readings of culture and books should provide cogent explanations that refer accurately to the real and literary lives of American Indians. At the same time, the practical demands of oppressive economic and social conditions in tribal communities may be a call to action for Native scholars and activists. For American Indian studies to have a real impact in the lives of the people, it should become *located* in the real world.

Praxis in the American Indian Classroom

In placing our intellectual selves in the Native community, classroom, or prison, we can derive an Indigenous moral and political criticism with profound anticolonial implications. Throughout this book, I have been returning to the Indigenous oral tradition to develop a view of knowledge. I now test that view to support a social process of psychic transformation in prison pedagogy. To do so, I draw on a number of scholars of the oral tradition to motivate a position on tribal language and story to support the reclaiming of confined Native bodies. If, as scholars argue, meaning is culturally conferred, Native educators may guide the productive power of language in the oral tradition to transform the lives of tribal listeners, providing a politics for the classroom as well as for the public sphere. Paulo Freire draws a similar conclusion regarding the liberating potential of public political discussions: "The insistence that the oppressed engage in reflection on their concrete situation is not a call to armchair revolution. On the contrary, reflection—true reflection—leads to action" (1989, 52). For in examining literary texts and attaching them to our shared world, we collectively struggle for social knowledge and social justice, in the way that bell hooks approaches the classroom as a site of social struggle in which oppressed people imagine a freed self: "Critical pedagogies of liberation respond to [the special experiential knowledge of oppressed groups] and necessarily embrace experience, confessions, and testimony as relevant ways of knowing, as important, vital dimensions of any learning process" (1994, 89).

The American Indian prison classroom is eminently political. While race and class certainly work to criminalize Indigenous men in the United States, colonialism remains the most relevant means of understanding how the structures of power persist in constructing the "savage." The federal incarceration of Native people today extends a long history of U.S. imperialism by displacing American Indian leaders from their homelands and depriving them of their tribal communities and clan members. Jerold Ramsey, who studies the tribal narratives of Native people in the Oregon area, understands the significance of stories of origin to the maintenance of a tribal worldview, even after American Indians suffer the theft of lands: "The fact that Klamaths lost their ancestral lands in the 1950s through the bureaucratic atrocity known as 'termination,' despite the imaginative authority of their mythological charter to these lands, is one of the cruelest ironies in recent Native American history. But of course it must be assumed that every Indian nation to lose its dominion from the sixteenth century on possessed such a mythic charter, which government officials at treaty-making sessions invariably dismissed whenever Native participants tried to introduce the testimony of tribal myth" (1999, 9). The enforced isolation of individuals and the denial of proper warmth, nutrition, medical care, and access to ceremonial items and practices are all part of the U.S. prison system's program to strip Native men of their cultural identity.[29] It is within this brutal colonial context that the Indigenous men at Auburn prison meet and struggle to resist the destruction of their cultures. In resistance to this ongoing imperialist project to destroy culture by removing Indian men from their tribal ancestral social location, American Indian prisoners gather in solidarity and devise strategies to overturn the prison's aggressive attempt to erode their Indigenous cultural selves. Similar to the urban Natives of *House Made of Dawn*, Alice's women's meetings, or even my own family gathered in my mother's living room, such a community of resistance enables the production of an alternative cultural narrative.

In this hegemonic environment, then, the role of story becomes indispensable to the men's survival of their imprisonment, as they, for example, struggle to affirm their "mythic charters" to ancestral lands. The classroom at Auburn actively demonstrates the transgressive capacity of language in a politically charged cultural context, in which the centralizing forces of language draw prisoners into a normative center of cultural meaning. Just as hooks highly regards testimony in the classroom, Native prisoners value the freedom to announce their own deeply felt experiences leading up to their imprisonment, as a means of explaining the reality of their lives. This sharing of stories, both oral-traditional and contemporary, helps the prisoners create a community of meaning where the level of trust dictates the depth of honesty. This anticolonial community resembles the classroom community that hooks tries to develop: "It has been my experience that one way to build community in the classroom is to recognize the value of each individual voice" (1994, 40).

Tribal members engaging in the oral tradition share a sense of sanctity for the gathering, a sense similar to that of the "community of listeners," which Walter Benjamin describes in his famous essay "The Storyteller" (1969, 91). Commenting on this social space in Native communities, David Abram writes, "To some extent every adult in the community is engaged in this process of listening and attuning to the other presences that surround and influence daily life" (1999, 21). When American Indian prisoners participate in their ongoing oral traditions, they undergo a transformation that helps them to preserve and even recover their American Indian selves—and thus to resist their colonial imprisonment. In a considerable body of work, theorists of ethnopoetics make available convincing explanations of the power of the Native word to change the lives of listeners. Ramsey defines tribal story thus: *"Myths are sacred traditional stories whose shaping function is to tell the people who know them who they are; how, through what origins and transformations, they have come to possess their particular world; and how they should live in that world, and with each other"* (1999, 6). Karl Kroeber is careful to recognize the transformative power of the oral tradition to preserve the moral and ecological relationship of tribal members with each other, the past, and the land. As he explains in his discussion of the Iroquois Condolence Ceremony, "spiritual or psychic transformation among Indian peoples almost always takes a material form. A reason for this is that each oral enactment of a myth makes the telling situation itself one of transformation in which both the individuals involved and their society can be renewed, remade" (1998, 26).[30]

Oral tradition thus not only transforms but also transports. The tremendous responsibility of the tribal storyteller, in fact, is to guide the psychic transportation of the listeners through the hallowed experiences of ancestors in a realm that we might refer to as a "virtual reality." But it is a reality for American Indian people nonetheless. What is more, this alternative reality exists at the same time as, and often on the same lands on which, the story is told, so that referring to features of that land actually helps transport listeners to the tribal psychic reality of oral tradition. This centralizing tendency among American Indian peoples often leads even the most marginal participants to enter the unifying language of oral story, a process Susan Berry Brill de Ramírez describes as "conversivity" (1999, 75). Barry Lopez chronicles his transportation through participation in the oral tradition as he describes the task of the Native storyteller: "The purpose of storytelling is to achieve harmony between the [interior landscape and the exterior landscape], to use the elements—syntax, mood, figures of speech—in a harmonious way to reproduce the harmony of the land in the individual's interior. Inherent in story is the power to reorder a state of psychological confusion through contact with the pervasive truth of those relationships we call 'the land'" (1984, 51). As the members of the storytelling circle reimagine and realign the relationship of the outside world to the world of the ancestors (the interior landscape), so they are, at least for a time, transformed and healed. When American Indian prisoners bring these two landscapes together, they "experience a deeper, more profound sense of well-being" (51). This transportive function of the oral tradition is absolutely vital to Native prisoners, because their very Indigenousness requires their being in their traditional lands and among the social relations that sustain these life-giving relationships. In "re-making" themselves through tribal narrative, Native prisoners are temporarily transported; they "go home." The focalizing forces of tribal language attract prisoners inward to the normative tribal center of moral and spiritual value. Through this process, cultural identity becomes reattached to a remembered and reimagined tribal world. Dell Hymes views this oral community as central to American Indian life and art: "Language, art, and each of the other symbolic forms are pathways to the realization of ourselves, are active, productive, specific energies to exercise" (1981, 9). By participating in this oral "realization of ourselves," Native prisoners resist the physical and spiritual dislocation enforced in prison. The act of collective remembering—with language, through oral story and written statements—allows prisoners access to a place in which their cultural identities may live more richly.

At Auburn prison I work with a man named Star. He is a Cayuga prisoner whose people once dwelt in a town called Wasco, which once occupied the land on which Auburn prison now stands. A state historical marker placed between the prison wall and a nearby creek reads:

WASCO
"The Crossing Place"
Site of a Cayuga village
Occupied by Indians before
And after the settlement of
Hardenbergh Corners
1793

When Star remembers the historical fact of his ancestors' presence in the land, the fact of their bodies resting in the earth just under the concrete of the prison, he re-places himself in a social location to which his Cayuga identity more vitally refers. Readers might question the metamorphosis that Native prisoners undergo while reviving oral traditional practices within the prison walls. Those of print cultures, however, often have difficulty imagining the transformational potential of the word in oral tradition. As Walter Ong notes: "The fact that oral peoples commonly and in all likelihood universally consider words to have magical potency is clearly tied in, at least unconsciously, with their sense of the word as necessarily spoken, sounded, and hence power-driven. Deeply typographic folk forget to think of words as primarily oral, as events, and hence as necessarily powered: for them, words tend rather to be assimilated to things, 'out there' on a flat surface" (1982, 32–33). Ong perhaps best explains this crucial difference between written cultures' concept of the word, and the power of oral cultures' words to enact this Indigenous transportation.

Some Native Prisoner Writing

In this final section, I share a few writings from the Indian men at Auburn prison to demonstrate the capacity of language to transform and expand community identity. In interpreting prison writing, we should be aware of the ways a history of European aesthetics may influence understanding of the genre. In fact, by some Western standards prison writing with its overtly political meanings is not art at all. Prison writing is best appreciated through political and cultural openness. Barbara Harlow provides a helpful critical approach to the literature of imprisonment: "The literature of prison, composed in prison and from out of the prison experience, is by contrast necessarily partisan, polemical, written against those very structures of a dominant arbitration and a literary historical tradition that have served to legislate the political neutrality of the litterateur and the literary critic alike. Reading prison writing must in turn demand a correspondingly activist counterapproach to that of passivity, aesthetic gratification, and the pleasures of consumption that are traditionally sanctioned by the academic disciplining of literature" (1992, 4). American Indian verbal art is created often apart from Western values of beauty. The role of the individual artist, the uniqueness of the work, and the mimetic quality of a piece of Native art are factors that usually are not as important as the psychic and social effect that the art or story has on listening tribal members.

On a given Friday night at Auburn prison, the men and I gather in the classroom, pull out the drum, and sing a few songs. Eventually, in the midst of an often chaotic evening, we settle down to discuss a prearranged topic such as the social role of Indian women, varying tribal warrior traditions, a particular tribal history—or Coyote tales. A member of the group begins a Coyote story, then turns to another member to add an episode. We continue around the room until Coyote dies too many times to be revived or the men laugh too hard to continue. During our more critical sessions, the discussion often begins with the men giving statements, which at times emerge in a form similar to the testimony of Samson Occom or William Apess. In their writing assignments, the men often transform oral testimonies into impassioned written statements full of rhetoric and imagination to transcend the prison walls. Chico is a heavy Navajo man who wears his hair undone and down to his belt. He carries a cane as a result of an old injury, and he likes to sit and do beadwork while he warns the younger men about reckless, colonized thinking. Chico types his essay "Surviving behind the Wall" with great care and in capital letters, ending the statement with "I have spoken," and signing his name. He opens his statement this way: "There is a battle going on behind the wall with the Native community. It's a battle against alcohol and drug abuse, against physical and mental abuse, against poverty and ignorance, against racism and anger. It is a battle for dignity, independence, freedom, justice, health, and happiness. This battle is being fought in the hearts and minds of our people in the New York State prison communities and in all the Native communities across the United States." Perhaps drawing on the warrior tradition, Chico portrays the struggle facing imprisoned Native men as a "battle" against all the dysfunctional activities for which the men are charged, such as alcohol and drug abuse. But the other abuses—physical and mental abuse—are imposed on the men by the prison. Interestingly, in announcing a war against poverty and ignorance, Chico could be referring to Indian prisoners or to the guards who often abuse them—who, ironically, are also often impoverished and undereducated. In shifting his declaration from those values the battle opposes to those it wishes to promote, Chico proclaims those human rights that anyone, white, Indian, or otherwise would support. Like Apess, Chico declares this battle to be fought both with emotion as well as intellect, not only by American Indians in prison but also by Native people throughout Indian Country. Chico calms some in the second half of his statement to recognize his Creator, who helps him survive within the prison walls. The paragraph sounds a lot like the words of Ben Benally in *House Made of Dawn*, when he looks out the window of his tenement, struggling to accept his displacement and urban life: "In these walls, we can't ever feel that we are alone. A lot of times there is no one who can be physically there when you need support. That is why we always give thanks to the Creator for all the blessings and that he is always with us" (drawn from my personal archive).

The men's writings often reflect the oscillations of hope and despair, calm and rage, that imprisonment promotes. For even though daily life is strictly controlled, a prisoner's known world can be completely and immediately destroyed when, for example, he is transferred to another prison without a moment's notice—often in unofficial punishment for resisting confinement. While the prisoner agonizes over losing his prison family and having to defend and establish himself in a new and unknown place, back at the former prison in the morning mess hall his friends and allies hear of his abrupt departure—his whereabouts a mystery to be forgotten. Chico's piece, "The People's Feeling" displays outrage at these deliberate abuses. It opens with an auto-ethnographic description, almost presenting an aesthetic figure study of Indian people: "The Native Americans, as I have before said, are copper-coloured, with long black hair, black eyes, short, tall, straight, and elastic forms. We are less than two/three millions in number. We were originally the undisputed owners of this soil. We got our title to our lands from the Great Spirit who created them for us. We were once a happy and flourishing people, enjoying all the comforts and luxuries of life which we knew of and consequently cared for. We gave thanks daily and prayers to the Creator, thanks for his goodness and protection." Chico begins with the idealized description of pre-invasion life in North America to prepare his Western readers for the alternative Indigenous history of the European conquest and colonization of Native people he leads us through: "First, you must follow me a vast way from the civilized world. Now you should forget the many theories you have read in the books of or about Indian barbarities, butchers, and murders." He then corrects the tragic portrait of the Vanishing American: "What poor miserable victims to suffered such death and destruction. That is the portrait that they have painted of us. What beautiful lies they tell for their amusement, for their information, so that we can again trust them and help them finish what their forefathers started back in the 1400s. They are unthinkable and unmerciful, their starvation is to finish us and wipe us out forever!!!!" Chico challenges his fellow American Indian prisoners to reconsider the dominant culture's representation of Native people as passive victims, and he reminds prisoners not to internalize this portrait. He suggests that the image of the helpless fallen Indian actually serves the colonial imagination set on the eventual disappearance of Native people and the new availability of territories and resources.

Chico then asks us to question who is the true savage, defined not by a superior culture but by humanity; again, he is reminiscent of the best of Apess or Eastman: "You should consider why they have call us savages of our North American without looking at what they did to our people and what they are doing to us. Our Indian pride has never been cut down." Chico ends this statement with incredible pathos to balance his earlier outrage: "So great and unfortunate are the disparities between the savage and the civil. Now you must ask yourself one question. Who is the savage here? My eyes are full of tears and my heart is full of pain. What I feel is such pain and I still want to know the true answer to this question of pain and cruelty against us." I imagine Chico chooses to leave the term "civilization" abbreviated to evoke the related notion of "civility," a universal value of courtesy or polite action, to understate the brutality of the European invasion of Indian Country. At his threshold of emotion and intellect, he awaits an answer to the inexplicable spectacle of empire and genocide. Without notice, Chico was "shipped out" one night.

Of all the group members, Whitehorse, a Lakota man, is the most volatile. Without failure he arrives with his handwritten papers, inscribed with the angry slash of ink and scratched out corrections. On a piece of lined paper he writes: "It makes me sad because when the white man came to our people they came with this little black book and told us wonderful things about their God! But we did not see these things. All we got to see was destruction of our identity and death." Whitehorse writes with a similar perplexity of earlier American Indian leaders, who could not

understand the separate roles of priest and soldier; then again, these ser-
vants often worked together. Whitehorse then lashes out with an alternative history of missions in Indian America: "My brother and sister, we all
know the real history. The one that they don't tell us about! Mystic River,
you smelled the Pequot flesh burning. Or how about the pubic hairs of
our women scalped at Sand Creek." With visceral accuracy, Whitehorse
assaults his readers with the dark side of Christian conversions, the hypocrisy of the New Canaanites who, by divine instruction, intended to
destroy the old, in the so-called Pequot War of 1637. The second image
recalls "the Fighting Parson," Colonel John Chivington, who in 1864, with
his drunk 3rd Colorado Volunteers, rode all night to Sand Creek and mas-
sacred women and children of the southern Cheyenne in the name of
Jesus.

I end my selection of writings with a poem from Alex, a twenty-four-
year-old Seneca man who got into college on a football scholarship. After
suffering an injury he lost his scholarship, however, and, out of money, he
had to quit school and return to his reservation. Deeply depressed, Alex
began drinking recklessly and eventually landed in prison. His poem is
titled "Ongwehonwe," which roughly translates as "The Real People":

I once knew a man.
who carried strong drink in his hand.
He worked from dark to dark,
then the partying would start.
As the years did pass,
He kept a strong grasp on the glass.
Bad thinking came with his fierce drinking.
The taste of Bud or Beam
made a good man mean.
Friends and family could only stand by
as they watched him die inside.
He would not be stopped
not by a long shot.
The day came at bay,
when he would pay for his ways.
25 to life,
cut his spirits like a knife.
Sitting behind a giant wall
has he missed his call?

Now with a clear mind,
all he has is time.
What does the Creator have planned for him?
after all, he did spare his life again.
He is so sorry for what had transpired.
His heart will never be free,
from that tragedy.
His new brothers in prison,
are the only ones who will listen.
He wants to do good,
and make it understood.
He sings earth songs in early day,
And tries to live true Ongwehonwe

Ending by beginning, Alex "sings earth songs in early day" as he works to get his mind on the inside, as the men say, to stop the yearning for home and to begin to discover new ways, often through language, to gather the men and transcend the confinement of the walls. When American Indian scholars visiting Auburn prison practice this theory of cultural renewal through the oral tradition, they are like the prisoners impelled by the unifying force of tribal narrative. Drawing collectively on a shared tradition whose early experiences of migration and settlement are often held in common, the separations dividing scholars and prisoners begin to dissolve, as an anticolonial community refuses the presence of the prison walls. Our collective American Indian identity refers more forcefully to this shared experience of a tribal past than to the class and personal histories that otherwise divide us. The solidarity nurtured through this engagement with stories about our pasts, our lands, and our social relationships lends credence to the concept of Indigenous immediacy that I have been developing here. Native prison practitioners refine their political commitment to the preservation of American Indian culture and homelands by attending to the shared histories that call out to them as Indian scholars and activists. In the lines above, Alex wonders while "sitting behind a giant wall" if he has "missed his call," thereby invoking both the calling of life to pursue one's expressive course as well as the call from the guards to leave his cell for a visit from family or teacher. These two cruelly opposed callings resonate with the other call I have been describing in this chapter. Tracing that call and response through our intellectual history, from the public exhortations of Samson Occom to the impassioned pleas of Taiaiake Alfred, we find only a few shadowy moments when Native intellectuals hesitated. Instead, American Indian scholars have honored the call from our relations, who request from the prison or the street our advocacy. This callout can be heard often from quite near, bringing to light our privilege as Western-educated scholars who nonetheless find, in a startling moment of immediacy, the collapse of class and social boundaries.

Perhaps more than any other boundary, the walls of imprisonment divide and discard our people. For this reason, I open and close this chapter with the callout of Indigenous prisoners. Though we might not always live close to real-world Indian struggles, we can certainly seek them out. Entering prisons, we gather more hands-on experience of colonial privation, which not only discloses the workings of domination in Indian Country, but also, most importantly, informs our understanding of our political selves. When I began working in prisons, I defended a simplified view on the dealers and victims of domination. Over the years, however, I came to understand the deadening frustrations of underpaid white prison guards in a rustbelt town, and to discover the stunning acts of self-possession in Indian men I thought conquered. Such corrections in my vision of Indian Territory galvanized my political identity. As we empower our political identities with such experiences, so we challenge and inform our understanding of true freedom for Native America—"freedom as connection to others, rather than freedom from others," as Michael Hames-García puts it (2004, xli). This is, then, my theoretical view of political activity as fundamental to knowledge production. Yet I suppose any theory of Native praxis ultimately grows from encounters such as those described above. My own interest in prison work began when as a young adult I learned that, unlike my own family, most American families do not have regular visits from the police and to the jail. When the evening closes at Auburn prison, we pray, put away the drum, pack up our books, and march down the hall, past the red plaque that quotes the words of Abraham Lincoln: "I will study and prepare and perhaps my day will come." On entering the crowded yard, we part ways for a while.

CONCLUSION

||||||||||||||||||||||||||||||||||||||||||||||||||||||||||||||||||||||||||

BUILDING CULTURAL KNOWLEDGE IN THE

CONTEMPORARY NATIVE NOVEL

I knew this was coming, so deal with it. Next thing is to call home. I call home and talk to my mother, tell her what happened. I had tried to warn her before hand that this was probably going to hap-pen, but when she hears the bad news I could hear the change in her voice. It's hard to hide disappointment and hurt when over the phone. When *you* go to prison, the people that are near and dear to you also do the time with you. They feel the same things you feel whether bad or good. I had never thought of that before I was locked up, but now it is real. I also get to share two more years of prison with my mom and the rest of my family.

—**Greg,** Tuscarora prisoner, Auburn prison, April 1999

Except for the grey concrete floor, the holding tank was painted yellow. . . . Velma was a thin white whore with needle tracks up and down her arms. . . . Then there was Ethel, a black woman in a black velvet jumpsuit that zipped up the front. . . . Cecelia thought how strange it was that [Velma] was desired by men, often, and by many men, so very much desired, in fact, that she was able to earn her living the way she did. Yet—and she did not just realize this now; she had known it for some time and turned it over in her mind, decided it was not valid, and continued to do it anyway—it was through attracting handsome men that she, Cecelia Capture Welles, sought a measure of self-esteem.

—**Janet Campbell Hale,** *The Jailing of Cecelia Capture*

In town for our Green Corn ceremony, I pull into the Wal-Mart parking lot and notice all the vehicles, from brand-new sedans to beat-up trucks, with Cherokee Nation license plates. When the Nation began issuing tribal tags a few years ago, one's citizenship was suddenly on display while driving around Tahlequah. Emerging from cars with Cherokee Nation tags were everyday Cherokee people, some dressed like cowboys, some with children, teenagers wearing hip hop attire, old people with disabilities, some dark, some light, all headed in to get a jug of milk or fishing tackle, as I was. In this moment I was struck by how "Cherokee-ness" is so variously represented. Looking around, I also saw Creek Nation and Sac and Fox Nation tags. The experience confirmed for me how truly multicultural Indian Country is, even though social and cultural diversity is often a value more lived than discussed in tribal communities. For centuries, Cherokees have married people outside the tribe and, often, brought their non-Cherokee spouses into their townships. Since around the 1980s, the Native novel has increasingly represented this expansive and interactive social world in an honest engagement with the diversity of class, gender, and sexuality, for example, found across Native America today. In addition, many of these novels elaborate the theoretical issues of Indigenous knowledge that I have been developing in previous chapters. Such growth in more recent Indian novels, however, would not have been possible without the imaginative literary strides of earlier Red Power literary texts. In this concluding chapter, I would like to explore this legacy and its new social developments in the contemporary Indian novel. After extending some of my tribal realist claims to approach social diversity and interaction in today's Native communities and literature, I will briefly analyze several contemporary novels that I feel explore neglected social communities in Indian America.

As I note in my experience at Wal-Mart, just moving through the world often puts us in touch with people who lead lives different from our own. In the previous chapter, I explained that a historically grounded criticism can be pursued by interacting with those beyond our own worlds, and that we can draw on such experiences to inform our politics. From this idea of social interaction, we not only can develop a more comprehensive account of the American Indian world, but also be changed by and grow through that experience. When I began teaching in prisons, I was made to reconsider my views of criminality, race, power, and justice, and I was thus changed as a Native scholar. As Greg writes in the epigraph above, he of course experienced great change in prison and he also discovered that his family endures his prison sentence with him. In a similar manner, Cecelia Capture discovers that her world is not so different from those of other women, despite disparities in race and class. As a law student arrested for drunk driving, Cecelia considers a similar gendered relation of power in the United States that affects not only Indian women but all women in different ways. Such moments of social complexity and cultural interaction point to the emergence of a new and subtle narrative pattern in the American Indian novel from around the mid-1980s to the present.

In this concluding chapter, I thus investigate more recent Native literature that draws on the vision of the Red Power novel to extend the theoretical claims I have been making through the course of this work. For social transformation is achieved not only by recovering a past but also by preparing a future. In imagining a future for American Indian people, the authors I explore in this chapter help prepare a theory of culture adequate to the decolonization of Indian Country in the years ahead. The recent outpouring of creative work by Native writers counters the unrelenting image of the Vanishing American in popular culture, and it even suggests a future of social and creative flourishing. Here, I turn to this new wave of literature to outline how, in the past two decades since Red Power, the writers Sherman Alexie, Betty Louise Bell, Robert Conley, Janet Campbell Hale, Irvin Morris, Greg Sarris, Craig Womack, and Ray Young Bear seek a more comprehensive understanding of culture and social justice in Native America. These writers continue to represent what I find to be an empirical process—the task of recovering, revising, and building Indian cultural knowledge—as characters engage with personal and tribal history and memory and with suppressed social experiences.

Social Knowledge in Indian Country

Throughout this work, I have proposed that a tribal realist view of knowledge may better serve critical studies of literature and culture and the real world social struggles of American Indian people. We recall that this approach to Indigenous art and life rests on a redefined model of objectivity, one I often see maintained in tribal oral traditions. Resituating philosophical and social inquiry in this intellectual framework enables Indian scholars not only to challenge dominant and inaccurate interpretations of Native literature and culture, but also to justify alternative and more accurate knowledge on tribal peoples and their creative work. In this vital respect, realism benefits from the constructivist critique that preoccupies contemporary theory, but it also promotes normative claims to the world. Realism thus confronts the conclusion stemming from skeptical approaches—that Native people, as colonized agents thoroughly mediated from their world, cannot know their world. When Native scholars adapt a tribal realist view of knowledge and interpret their social world with this alternative model of cultural normativity, they are able not only to locate the exploitations of colonialism, but also to affirm the viability of American Indian people and their communities. Because realism holds that our understandings of the world are certainly constructed but nonetheless constructed in different ways that entail quantifiable political consequences, the position allows us to say that such accounts of the world can, indeed must, be more or less objectively evaluated. Nonrealists frequently do not make such evaluations. As the world changes and American Indian people continue to gather social knowledge, we can revise our assessments. For this reason, this "fallibilistic" social theory can accommodate material change and cultural development without relying on a cultural essence. Rather, we can guide our growth by positing and revising normative claims regarding Indian life. I believe this achievement of cultural objectivity is *the* crucial intellectual goal for American Indians struggling to decolonize their nations.

In both current cultural studies and recent announcements in the popular media, Indians are said to be verging upon a new social moment in which they are interacting with people of other cultures perhaps more frequently than ever before. I imagine the years ahead to entail a tremendous infusion of other cultures among American Indians—an infusion that will not endanger but indeed may even benefit Native culture so long as we approach this opportunity of cultural interaction from the most enabling intellectual framework. Such dynamic social transformation will require a clear understanding of Native cultural change as a conscious process to assess and modify a collective identity. To develop culturally and to succeed politically, we will have to ask whether we can say anything objective about changing Indian culture. Native historians have already documented earlier events of cultural exchange, leading to this moment upon us, such as both nineteenth-century and twentieth-century displacements of Native groups to new lands or urban areas. But whether we recall "the Removal" of Native peoples to Indian Territory or "the Relocation" of American Indians to cities, we should emphasize the impressive agency of Native people, not only to adapt and survive, but also to devise creative solutions to their oppression through social and cultural cooperation among tribal and nontribal groups. While this sharing of knowledge is no doubt an old story in Indian America, between European Americans and Native peoples such cooperation is still strained by colonial relations.

Building on my understanding of cultural interaction and development from previous chapters, we can now reencounter the function of Native culture in an altogether new light: namely, as a "think tank" in which to generate and test new ideas. Satya Mohanty explains cultures as "fields of moral inquiry" in which social activity provides an opportunity for the production of knowledge: "Cultures are more like laboratories than anything else; they do not only embody values and beliefs, they also test and modify these values and beliefs in practical ways. Values, which involve more than our conscious beliefs, are the very substance of such experiments. New forms of living . . . help us interrogate old ideas and deepen new hunches. Hunches develop both into programs for action and into theories. Notions of the just society and of the moral status of individuals are developed out of institutions that arise in the practices of everyday social life. . . . Cultural practices embody and interrogate rich patterns of value, which in turn represent deep bodies of knowledge of humankind and of human flourishing" (1997, 240–41). Mohanty's theory of culture as a laboratory for the development of rich "patterns of value" supports my vision of social interaction in and beyond Indian Country not as a potential hazard but indeed as a social ideal. Indigenous peoples have long invented and tested new ways of life. Historians of science recognize the advanced pharmaceutical and medicinal knowledge of tribal peoples of the Americas upon invasion by Europeans who gathered this knowledge; other historians explore the influence of Native governments on the framers of the U.S. Constitution, for example.[1] It is quite possible that the rich production of Indigenous knowledge in North America owes a great deal to Native societies' ability to both enable and protect complex patterns of social expression. This is the Indian "freedom" or "liberty" romanticized by European intellectuals such as Montaigne and Rousseau, Franklin and Thoreau. The protection of social freedom allows for the production, experimentation, and development of new ways of life. For as we know, new practices, customs, and rituals to maintain social knowledge assure the preservation and flourishing of a tribal people. Early on, Native people likely understood the importance of maintaining free social and political conditions to ensure the production of more complete assessments of the tribal world. Mohanty encapsulates this claim about

the relationship between culturally produced objective knowledge and social practice: "Objectivity is inextricably tied to social and historical conditions, and objective knowledge is the product not of disinterested theoretical inquiry so much as of particular kinds of practice" (213).

From this view of Native knowledge production as a social practice,
we receive a twofold benefit: the promotion of social expression in Indian
Country is not only a social good but also an empirical necessity. We thus
may foster cultural diversity in Native America not out of any sentimental
concern for "disadvantaged" groups but for clear epistemological reasons.
In this realist view of cultural inquiry, we work to enable members of a
particular group, such as Natives with disabilities who are often marginalized in inaccessible communities, to participate in the production and
testing of new cultural values so we can better achieve normative knowledge. The development of social diversity is thus one part of a broader
goal of social justice in what we call Indian Country. Even among our own
people, the protection of cultural and social expression often inspires us
to do political work. According to Caroline Hau, who employs a realist
approach in postcolonial studies: "Attempts at objective explanation are
necessarily continuous with oppositional struggles. Activism strives to
create conditions for better knowledge" (2000, 161). In this view of knowledge production, the concepts of social identity, social practice, and social
justice are interrelated, forming a dynamic synergy to support decolonization. We thus discover another benefit of adapting a realist theory of cultural identity: a sound theory of social identity in Native communities develops our bodies of Indigenous knowledge. From my earlier discussion
of experience and its ties to identity, it now should be apparent how experience can contribute to this collective project of social inquiry. Drawn
from our very lives and shared with others, our experiences and those of
others can confirm or challenge our known worlds. In this regard, they
shape not only personal but indeed collective identity. So when we introduce the various social identities that enrich the category of American
Indian—say, Native lesbians, middle-class Navajo persons, impoverished
Six Nations citizens, or Choctaw Baptists, we certainly complicate the way
our cultural identities refer to the assumed world around us, but we also
improve social inquiry in viewing Indian Country from this more laden
vantage. In so doing, we reduce error and thus better complete the picture
of modern Indian life. But how can we today promote the profound par-
ticularism, envisioned in this view of social diversity as an ideal of inquiry,
and still speak of an Indian Country?

Leaders of social struggles in the Third World have often identified this goal of organizing disparate groups into a unified force of resistance. Such a task, however, has drawn critique among scholars who question not only the exclusions required to streamline such a social movement but, more important, the unavoidable error in interpreting experience across different local communities. Organizing Indian Country thus presents an epistemological challenge. Hau describes this difficult role of the intellectual in social movements: "This position emphasizes the potential contribution that the intellectual can make as one whose epistemic access to and articulations of the experiences of others are crucial in generalizing— broadening, or, in the context of anticolonial struggle, 'nationalizing'— popular consciousness" (2000, 134). It is through intellectual process as well as political practice that activists and scholars come better to understand and clarify a collective destination for a subordinated group like Native America. As Hau suggests, movements succeed not on a reduction but an expansion of group interests. For this reason, the promotion of social diversity in Indian communities not only aids inquiry but also helps to produce a more collective vision, and it does so without reducing, but indeed building on, the political force of the particular. This is my view of social diversity in Indian Country as a goal to fortify a theory of justice and normative knowledge. Its achievement requires not only intellectual planning but also empirical practice. But as we encourage the contributions of particular social concerns on the one hand, we should not lose sight of universal moral claims on the other. Respect for the dignity of Native peoples from all walks of life as well as of the land and its creatures is one such principle on which a progressive vision of Indian social justice could be built.

This book's view of American Indian selfhood might help explain how, in recent Native literature, Indian people often inhabit more than one social identity. Previous chapters have explored how a Native person understands her or his world and perhaps reconsiders and improves that understanding and grows culturally. Through an ongoing process, Native people may awaken politically and recover cultural identity. Of course, such a broad category as "Indian" must also be contextualized in specific tribal groups with their clan and band affiliations, their histories and lands. All these cultural factors combine to constitute what we generally call Indigenous identity. This tribal complexity demands an account of the numerous social worlds encompassed in any approach to Indian America. The well-known social categories of sexuality, class, and gender, for example, often complicate our understanding of Native identity, and more recent scholarship in Leisure studies and Disability studies has introduced youth and age, body and mind, as crucial categories of social identity. So we might consider how elderly Native feminists, gay Indian men, and diabetic Ho-Chunk women with disabilities enrich our accounts of being Indian in the world today. Add the above social complexities to a theory of American Indian identity and some skeptical scholars might conclude that such a politics of identity cannot succeed without calculating strategic exclusions. There are just too many determinants; the shifting cultural, geographical, and historical—and now social forces, they say—mystify an identity we wish were stable. Contemporary theorists would now recommend that we should instead accept and re-present this fragmentation to the hegemonic culture to disrupt colonialist constructions of "the Indian." I argue that we need neither enact essentialist exclusions nor embrace discursive fragmentation but instead we can expand, without erasing, the Indian experience. Such an understanding of identity can not only accommodate but also benefit from the complexity of multiple social identities.

Michael Hames-García's revised concepts of "multiplicity" and "restriction" provide a practical model for this expanded conception of American Indian group membership. He carefully explains the task often presented to those who belong to a cultural group that at times marginalizes those members who also belong to another social group. Hames-García discusses the concern in Michael Nava's novel *The Hidden Law*, in which a gay Chicano protagonist bears strong allegiances to a Chicano community, even though that community is reluctant to include him. Of course, many people from a variety of groups experience a similar tension: "Black women, gay Chicanos, and Asian American lesbians are examples of people who have memberships in multiple politically subordinated groups in the United States" (2000, 104). Hames-García advances a crucial point for understanding the challenge of multiple group membership—that it will not do to explain social-cultural identity as a contributive formulation, as a mathematical equation: "One cannot understand a self as the sum of so many discrete parts, that is, femaleness + blackness + motherhood" (103). He argues that to do so would be to essentialize one aspect of one's identity to stabilize the construction of another. Imagine, for example, that an American Indian woman recovers from a marriage in which she was battered, after which she becomes a feminist. It would be wrong to suppose she developed a "new" feminist identity as an addition to a genderless American Indian cultural identity; conversely, she decides to become a feminist not from a preracialized cultural position but as a Native woman—a cultural location that likely has something to do with the radicalization of her femaleness. According to Hames-García, "the whole self is constituted by the mutual interaction and relation of its parts to one another. Politically salient aspects of the self, such as race, ethnicity, sexuality, gender, and class, link and imbricate themselves in fundamental ways. These various categories of social identity do not, therefore, comprise essentially separate 'axes' that occasionally 'intersect.' They do not simply intersect but blend, constantly and differently" (103). Hames-García's redefinition of multiplicity helps explain the political transformation of the woman above, avoiding simplistic or reified notions of how people participate in a variety of communities, changing and developing in fact as a consequence of complex allegiances. As Hames-García explains, social location is not immobile but rather moves and resituates, with the self often reconstituting in response to one's surroundings or moment in life.

Imbalances in social power, however, affect the potential benefit of this kind of fluidity of the self, through what Hames-García calls "restriction." This is a useful term for a situation in which many of us often find ourselves, a modern problem in a world that often seeks to reduce the complexity of social representation and recognition not only to simplify the challenge of knowing social others but also to serve political interests. Restriction occurs when one is viewed in terms of only one social identity at the expense of all others: "According to the fracturing logic of domination inhering in capitalist cultures, this multiplicity of the self becomes restricted so that any one person's 'identity' is reduced to and understood exclusively in terms of that aspect of her or his self with the most political salience" (2000, 104). A society often decides for us exactly which aspect of our complex self is to be recognized as the defining feature of our social existence. When one's own view of oneself is in agreement with that of the dominant cultural construction, one's interests are "transparent," explains Hames-García. But for those who do not assimilate or conform to the dominant white American construction of the citizen, this restriction is oppressive and reductive, thus limiting the possibility for fruitful social expression. According to Hames-García, those who experience this restriction of their social multiplicity have suppressed, "opaque" concerns.[2] Clearly, the challenge facing social theorists in Indian Country is to create conditions that allow a robust multiplicity of social identities to emerge.

Hames-García explains that those with transparent interests occupy a privileged position in a cultural or social group, in which their desires for social expression are not questioned, and thus take for granted their ability to be fully expressive. But in an unequal world, this feeling of transparency is often an illusion produced by the very dominant social network that the transparent support, a false transparency in which desires for multiplicity can be unwittingly suppressed. In this regard, always recognizing and overcoming opacity is a vital process of a just society watchful of blockages to social expression and invention. Hames-García advocates a realist theory of social selfhood that allows for a whole yet multiple self without fragmenting the self so that one is always partly outside at least one social community. This view of multiplicity, he argues, best serves anticolonial and antiracist struggles because it understands the necessity of including particular interests in order to always reconsider and revise the goals for which we scholars and activists—and the writers I discuss below—collectively work.

Indian Poverty

The worst poverty in North America exists among American Indians, and that poverty is a source of other socially destructive problems in Native communities.[3] Such maladies as health problems, depression, and criminality are not endemic, of course, but largely stem from U.S. colonial domination and economic privation. Any portrait of modern American Indigenous life that seeks cultural objectivity thus cannot avoid an account of Indian poverty. Having grown up in a low-income family with many social problems related to poverty—such as domestic violence, alcoholism, drug abuse, homelessness, incarceration, and mental illness—I feel I must address the issue of poverty in Indian Country. To do so, I turn to the representation of poverty and poor people in two recent works of Indian fiction, Sherman Alexie's *Reservation Blues* and Betty Louise Bell's *Faces in the Moon*. Specifically, I confront the image of poverty in these works, both as an often-internalized social value and as a reality to be overcome.

With the 1995 publication of his first novel, *Reservation Blues*, Spokane writer Sherman Alexie rapidly gained critical acclaim among Indian and non-Indian readers alike. As Stephen Evans writes, however, "Inevitably, perhaps, it is precisely the success of *Reservation Blues* among the mainstream literary establishment that has brought Alexie criticism from some Indian writers and scholars" (2001, 49). Indeed, American Indian scholars might be most concerned because Alexie presents an often-unpleasant portrait of Indians to this vast audience. Graphic shots of the worst reservation realities, delivered with the blunted emotions of a trauma survivor, offend some critics because they potentially reinforce Western assumptions that dysfunction in Native communities occurs "naturally" rather than as a result of colonial relations. Alexie, they claim, does not sufficiently contextualize this Indian poverty. In representing Indigenous people's poverty and its attendant social ills as a commonplace to dominant culture, *Reservation Blues* risks playing into the hands of mainstream readers who wish to believe Native people are socially degenerate. Native readers react to this display quite differently; I suppose we might at first feel our cultural privacy violated. What right does Alexie have to share with general readers our most painful realities of poverty and social dysfunction?[4] Critics are justifiably angry when in a cultural vacuum Alexie exposes only the most troubling aspects of the American Indian world today. Alexie's novel thus "is a partial portrait of a community wherein there is no evidence of Spokane culture or traditions, or anything uniquely Spokane," argues Spokane scholar Gloria Bird (1995, 51).

In the classroom, Indian students appear to benefit from the discussion of poverty in *Reservation Blues*. With mainstream students, however, I must work extremely hard to provide a colonial context to understand the deeper sources of poverty, which Alexie does not clearly introduce in the novel. Though we work to eliminate poverty, our experiences of it should nonetheless be accepted as a source of knowledge regarding what it means to be Native today in a community suppressed by the federal government. Crucial to this process, however, is the clarification that poverty itself is not an American Indian cultural value. Indeed, assuming as much risks leading young tribal people to internalize the dominant culture's frequent insistence that Indigenous people must remain poor in order to be spiritually pure and authentic. Eduardo Duran and Bonnie Duran discuss this internalization of poverty and its social problems: "After so many decades of abuse and internalizing of pathological patterns, these dysfunctional patterns at times [become] very nebulous. . . . The dysfunctional patterns at some point start to be seen as part of Native American tradition. . . . Therefore, many of the problems facing Native American people today—such as alcoholism, child abuse, suicide, and domestic violence—have become part of the Native American heritage due to the long decades of forced assimilation and genocidal practices implemented by the federal government" (1995, 35). In the program for decolonization, these scholars explain how poverty can and should be externalized as a colonial imposition—not internalized as evidence of Indian inferiority. But, regrettably, *Reservation Blues* does not communicate this message. Its characters do not identify their poverty and social dysfunction self-consciously and then attempt to overcome it. In the novel, members of the Spokane Indian Reservation often accept their poverty as an unexamined fact of Native life. Social poverty, the novel suggests, is to a large extent not a product of economic sanctions enforced by the federal government but rather one of envy and betrayal among members of the community.

In *Reservation Blues*, three Spokane men start a blues band they call Coyote Springs. Eventually they attempt to land a New York City record contract, but fail. Dominant readers might argue that they fail because they must remain poor to remain real Indians. From the opening pages, poverty is an unavoidable fact of Spokane reservation life. Thomas Builds-the-Fire, the tribe's unofficial and unappreciated storyteller, when asked about his community, remembers the layers of poverty they all suffer: "Thomas thought about all the dreams that were murdered here, and the bones buried quickly just inches below the surface, all waiting to break through the foundations of those government houses built by the Department of Housing and Urban Development" (7). Alexie is a master of such imagery. The excruciatingly visceral suggestion of bone poking through skin introduces readers to the colonial wounds Spokane people continue to feel "just inches below the surface," for their dispossession is more recent in U.S. colonial history. The federal government provides only gestures of care for these colonial wounds and suppresses the truth of the genocidal campaigns against Native peoples beneath BIA concrete. From the novel's beginning, Thomas is cognizant of the source of Indian poverty, but seems to wonder how his people can even begin to dig through such layers—to dress the wounds and to lay the bones to rest.

Far more than his friends and fellow band members Victor Joseph and Junior Polatkin, Thomas, though ignored, continues to explore the social meanings of economic strife—alcoholism, violence, suicide—as products of poverty imposed by dispossession of ancestral land, way of life, and economy. When Victor bullies him, Thomas accepts this cruelty and violence among community members: "Thomas was not surprised by Victor's sudden violence. These little wars were intimate affairs for those who dreamed in childhood of fishing for salmon but woke up as adults to shop at the Trading Post and stand in line for U.S.D.A. commodity food instead" (14). Throughout the novel, the external source of hatred and violence is rarely shown, but seems to originate from community members in the "little wars" that my students sometimes dismiss as "Indian-on-Indian" crime. In fact, the band is literally run off the reservation by its own hateful tribal members. This theme of internalized and self-inflicted violence in *Reservation Blues* peaks when the band loses its record contract and Junior, remembering a white woman who rejects him and their child because he is Native, kills himself: "Junior had turned and walked away from Lynn. He always wondered why they had been together at all. Everybody on campus stared at them. The Indian boy and the white girl walking hand in hand. Lynn's parents wouldn't even talk to him when they came to campus for visits. Junior walked away from Lynn and never looked back. No. That wasn't true. He did turn back once, and she was still standing there, an explosion of white skin and blonde hair. She waved, and Junior felt himself break into small pieces that blew away uselessly in the wind" (240). The "explosion of white skin and blonde hair" that causes Junior to come apart, to "break into small pieces," represents an under-developed moment of cultural collision. It seems he suddenly "wonders why they had been together at all" and feels foolish for ever hoping to be valued simply as a person. Junior begins to succumb to feelings of "uselessness."

The memory detailed above anticipates Junior's suicide only pages later, when he literally explodes: "A week after Coyote Springs staggered from Manhattan back onto the Spokane Indian Reservation, Junior Polatkin stole a rifle from the gun rack in Simon's pickup. . . . Junior strapped that rifle over his shoulder and climbed up the water tower that had been empty most of his life. . . . Junior unshouldered the rifle and felt the smooth, cool wood of the stock, set the butt of the rifle against the metal grating of the floor, and placed his forehead against the mouth of the barrel. . . . Junior remembered. . . . He flipped the safety off, held his thumb against the trigger, and felt the slight tension. Junior squeezed the trigger" (247). Portraits of Native sacrifice are not new to dominant representations of Indigenous people in film and literature. But here, Alexie serves the image of the Vanishing American to mainstream audiences in a way that "returns an image of a 'generic' Indian back on the original producers of that image," argues Bird (1995, 49). Though Alexie claims merely to portray Spokane community life as he well knows it, Native critics contend that he is nonetheless accountable for representing Native life to a broader culture, which often expects (or even wishes) American Indians to disappear. The novel represents other acts of self-destruction; many characters, such as Victor and Samuel Builds-the-Fire, Thomas's father, drink toward early deaths. But Alexie's explanation of Junior's suicide is most troubling. Because Alexie is not clear about the deeper, colonial cause of suicide in Indian nations, I fear that many readers are led to believe American Indians are simply doomed—that they are their own worst enemies. Certainly Victor, who reacts violently and is less aware than Thomas about postcolonial life and despair, needs to know why Junior commits suicide. However, when Victor encounters the ghost of his friend and asks Junior why he killed himself, Junior actively does not disclose the colonial cause of Native social dysfunction, and even sees no larger explanation for his Indian vanishing:

> ". . . Junior, why'd you do it?"
> "Do what?"
> "Kill yourself."
> Junior looked away, watching the sunlight reflecting off Turtle Lake.
> "Because life is hard," Junior said.
> "That's the whole story, folks. I wanted to be dead. Gone. No more."
> "Why?"
> "Because when I closed my eyes like Thomas, I didn't see a damn thing. Nothing. Zilch. No stories, no songs. Nothing." (290)

The conclusion that "life is hard" avoids explaining such acts of self-destruction in their larger context. Indeed, all that Junior identifies as the source of his own despair is a lack of imagination. Since he could name the instances of racism and colonial oppression he relives shortly before pulling the trigger, it is puzzling that Junior finally sees "nothing." In the end, such nihilism evades contending with the federal sources of economic and cultural destruction on the Spokane Indian Reservation. In *Reservation Blues*, Sherman Alexie portrays poverty and social dysfunction in the Spokane community as the unexamined and unlucky consequence of being American Indian in the world today.

While we can certainly benefit from confronting and examining poverty, we often resist this painful topic. Perhaps this explains the reception of Cherokee writer Betty Louise Bell's 1994 novel *Faces in the Moon*, where we receive a harrowing American Indian life tangled with domestic violence and sexual abuse, the frequent products of poverty. But unlike the works of fiction written during Red Power, which represent poverty in tension with healthy cultural traditions—traditions that often aid characters in overcoming social illness, such as they do in *House Made of Dawn*—in *Faces in the Moon*, Indians must labor to discover few cultural roots. They do, however, have their immediately available and persistent stories. Bell's novel opens with a familiar portrait of Native women around a kitchen table, sharing stories: "I was raised on the voices of Indian women. The kitchen table was first a place of remembering, a place where women came and drew their lives from each other. The table was covered with an oilcloth in a floral pattern, large pink and red roses, the edges of the petals rubbed away by elbows" (4). This pleasing image of gentle Indian ladies living well and passing on oral traditions to young women, however, soon deteriorates like the fading flowers, as the narrator, Lucie, begins to confront her memories of poverty and sexual abuse. She recalls the child she was and the mother she preferred to know: "As a child, I called the woman 'Momma,' slipping close to the photograph and tracing her outline with my fingers, whenever I passed through Lizzie's parlor. After my great aunt's death, it was harder and harder to put the pretty girl with the child together with the fat, beat-up woman who cursed and drank, pushed into her only threat, 'Maybe I'll just run away and leave y'all to yourself'" (8–9). *Faces in the Moon* is a courageous novel because it dares to contend with a troubling Native past that offers no readily available cultural history. Admirably, the novel engages memory and loss for the sheer sake of better knowing: to gain historical clarity, to understand the causes of poverty and abuse and to do so, if at all possible, through forgiveness: "But, long before [her mother's] letters began to arrive, long before she knew she had something to say, she had already lost me to her stories. And there, I loved and forgave her" (9).

In her creative acts of understanding and forgiveness, Lucie contends with her rage at Gracie, her abusive and abandoning mother. She deals with the loss of social and cultural rearing through story, a process that, ironically, "loses" Lucie to her mother but frees Lucie from her entanglements of an abusive childhood. She eventually escapes Oklahoma and the impoverished, cruel home of her childhood. She marries a wealthy man and feels that she has left her past behind her, though it is kept alive in pleasing stories of her upbringing. But strikingly, such stories prove inadequate to maintain this comfortable distance from a colonial past. In the safety of her own memory, Lucie has mastered a separate kind of forgiveness, but when the real world contradicts or challenges this more approving version of the past, she discovers the fear and rage that lay behind her memory. As Lucie approaches the truth of her past, forgiveness seems almost impossible. She is thus challenged to deepen her notion of forgiveness into one that can meet the painful reality of her lived experience. Lucie dares to share her stories with her husband Melvin. She recalls a moment from her childhood when she was thrilled to receive a gift from her aunt, while preparing to enter a child beauty contest. She remembers gazing in the window of a department store, and then her Aunt Lizzie stepping in to buy her a leopard-patterned coat. Lucie cherishes this rare moment when she felt loved and protected, and even in adulthood she views herself as a pretty, well-dressed child: "Lucie turned, took a few steps down the isle, and turned on a point. 'I feel like Shirley Temple'" (61). But when her husband views the old photograph of Lucie in the coat, "on his first and final visit to Momma's house," he thoughtlessly exclaims: "'You were a ragamuffin!'" (61). Interestingly, even in adulthood Lucie cannot see her childhood poverty, and is thus shocked and ashamed by Melvin's discovery: "With that one word, the leopard coat left me. Flying into the past, a shameful thing, an unworthy thing, it caught on its false promise and I never wore it with pride again" (61–62).

So reflecting, Lucie is compelled to reconsider her relationship to herself, her mother, and the past, as she works to achieve a more adequate understanding of herself as an adult woman. *Faces in the Moon* thus describes a building process of personal growth through a creative response to the trauma of poverty, abandonment, and sexual abuse, in which the bounds of forgiveness are tested and redefined. In the above moment, Lucie preserves her sense of self-worth, her "pride," by upholding the coat as an emblem of these feelings, only to have the threadbare piece torn from her and unraveled to expose her feelings of shame and lack of worth. Later, divorced from Melvin, visiting Oklahoma and alone at the home of her mother, Lucie admits the truth of the coat's embarrassing spectacle: "Now, studying the picture, I can see that the coat had not fit well. Even *her* small four-year-old body was too large for the thing. The wonderful black cuffs ended well before the wrists, and the hem of the pink dress hung inches below the coat. But there they stood, in front of Momma's Packard, two girls proud of their purchase" (emphasis added, 61). Caught in the bind of either clinging to a safe yet inaccurate past or confronting its reality and her feelings of shame and self-hatred—a choice that offers no foreseeable benefit—Lucie is left with a complex mixture of despair, rage, and hopelessness. Yet she glimpses the possibility of forgiveness, cultural recovery, and even resolution in her struggle to focus the photographic image and to interpret the little girl Lucie through the eyes of the adult Lucie—to begin to call that child "Lucie."

At the age of four, Lucie suffers a desperate period of intense abuse when J.D., Gracie's new man, moves in.[5] Gracie, afraid to lose J.D., decides to abandon Lucie to relatives. Ironically, Lucie finds life in the woods with Aunt Lizzie and Uncle Jerry to be free of poverty and full of security, care, culture, history, and hope. In this safe space, Lucie discovers the richness of her Cherokee ancestry and the beautiful woman her mother once was:

> Her eye caught a glint in the room, and she went to the bureau. There was a small gold box with an Indian woman painted on it. The woman had long black hair and a face like Lizzie's. On either side were photographs of children and old people, in overalls and hats and a jacket. Lucie studied the photographs, wondering who all these people were. In one bent photograph a beautiful dark-haired woman held a baby up to her cheek; she was wearing a plain cotton dress and standing in a field before a wood.
>
> "That there's your momma." (82–83)

In this place of cultural and historical grounding, Lucie recovers the appropriate vitality of a child. She recovers the stories of her Cherokee ancestors' life in the Old Cherokee Nation in the Southeast, and their forced march to Indian Territory. Lucie gets a fever and experiences Indian medicine, and she gains a moral education from her great-aunt: "'The Cherokee always been a proud people. They took care of their children and families. That always come first. When my granddaddy come from Georgia he didn't leave no body behind'" (122). The abandoned Lucie has been reclaimed by her nation.

In this novel, readers will not find any supernatural processes that help a Native person recover from abuse. For Lucie, recovering from an impoverished and abusive upbringing and reclaiming a Cherokee history and identity are conscious, cognitive practices. In fact Lucie is quite honest about feeling an irrational sense of guilt when someone who is not Native asks her what it is like being Indian: "I wish I had Indian stories, crazy and wild romantic vignettes of a life lived apart from them. Anything to make myself equal to their romance. Instead I can offer only a picture of Momma's rented house, a tiny flat two-bedroom shack in a run-down part of town" (59). While Red Power writing of the 1960s and 1970s sometimes relies on an idealized conception of Native culture, in which history and belonging are readily available to those who seek it, contemporary American Indian literature often risks contending with cultural loss and poverty—even when no spiritual forces attract one to a community of belief. Such an honest engagement with domination and poverty perhaps represents a moment of growth in Native literature. Indeed, Lucie admits that her most influential cultural foundation rests on the Cherokee women of her family, around the table, smoking and telling stories:

> I have tried to remember my life outside the remembering of that kitchen table. I have tried to circumvent the storyteller and know my life with an easy Indian memory, but I knew no Indian princesses, no buckskin, no feathers, no tomahawks. The Indians in westerns confused and frightened me. My mother and aunt chose high heels over moccasins; they would have chosen blue eyes over black eyes. I have tried to know Momma, Auney, and Lizzie as Indian women, but all that surfaces is tired, worn-out women, stooped from picking cotton and the hard work of tenant farming. I know women burnt by the hot Oklahoma sun and wasted by their men, women scared into secrets, women of solid and steady patience. But, mostly, I know them by their hunger to talk. (58–59)

In this profoundly expressive, confessional moment, Lucie grapples with the problem of an impoverished past that offers no romantic roots, no popularized Native body of cultural knowledge. Instead, the Indigenous women she knows would rather not be Native if it means suffering "black eyes." These women speak to resist and recover from their enforced silence by the men who control them. But in an uncanny sense this life is an Indian life; the poverty cannot be winnowed out of the history. Instead, as I argue, these categories blend and inform one another. In daring to contend with a painful past of neglect, Lucie comes to understand her mother's and her own life, and through a margin of forgiveness she finally reunites the child Lucie with the adult Lucie: "In a store window I caught a glimpse of the small Indian woman, and I eased forward to catch her, with the stealth of a cat, pushing my face into my own reflection" (187). *Faces in the Moon* invites readers to consider the sources and consequences of Indian poverty, and it offers, if not a solution, then at least a resolution, through a process of remembering and healing that all of us can understand.

Women's Selfhood

Scholars often notice that *House Made of Dawn* and *Ceremony*, two of the three central texts of this study, are quite similar in historical focus and theme. But departing from *House Made of Dawn*, *Ceremony* centers themes of American Indian women's regenerative power through female characters such as Tayo's mother, Laura, and his aunt Thelma and Helen Jean; the more mythic Night Swan and Ts'eh. Each of these figures teaches Tayo how to trust, how to contend with his past and misplaced emotions, and how to guide his moral and sexual behavioral development. With female power so central to tribal relationships through clan obligations, to land, to ancestors, and to community members, it seems logical to anchor women in any narrative on the recovery of identity, history, and home-lands. Acting on this logic, contemporary Indian writers reclaim Native women's writing by regrounding it in terms of its specifically Indigenous cultural roots, a context in which such writing had often not been placed in previous feminist scholarship. In turn, such writers have been instru-mental to any woman or man seeking a feminist global consciousness to span cultures and lands.

Since the dawning of Red Power consciousness, gender has become more subtly recognized and employed in Native literature. One clear sign of this development is male writers creating strong and complex women characters in their novels so as to correct popular romantic constructions of Native women and Native men in the literature of the United States. In the work of Robert Conley, women often play a central role in the mainte-nance of community life, trade relationships, and government. With over ten historical novels that comprise the Real People series, he explores the eras from early European-Cherokee contact to Allotment and Oklahoma statehood. Throughout this well-researched and exciting series, Conley ex-plores the creative ability of Cherokee persistence to lead the moral devel-opment of their communities, despite the awesome challenges presented by European Americans. As one of a few American Indian writers who lives in the community about which he writes, Conley gives Cherokees an opportunity to celebrate their past and to consider the moral decisions that have shaped it, in works that Jace Weaver often terms "communitist parables" (1997, 160).[6] Conley investigates how Cherokees produce and maintain knowledge in these different eras. In *War Woman*, Cherokees of the late sixteenth century elect to begin a trade relationship with Europeans, and in so doing they must negotiate daunting cultural interactions. War Woman, a powerful spiritual leader, trader, and diplomat, guides her community in this process.

Conley takes us back to a Woodland community, nestled in the Smoky Mountains, where women are the gender central to social organization. Here, family membership is traced through one's mother. When a man marries, he joins the family of his wife. Property is possessed and transferred through the women. Whirlwind, a young woman (later to be renamed War Woman) has been given the task of journeying to the Spanish town and securing a trade relationship. She is elected the leader of two men, Daksi and Little Spaniard. The narrator explains:

> And she, the only female in the group, was the leader. Women among the Real People were used to leadership roles, but their leadership capacity was usually exercised quietly, almost behind-the-scenes. The visible town government was male. The women met without ceremony and then told the men what they thought should be done. The male government would then meet and make their decisions, often, if not usually, just the way the women had advised them.
>
> But Whirlwind had assumed an open leadership role as the head of a trading party. She had taken on what was ordinarily a male role, and that in itself made her a remarkable woman. (22)

By inserting such ethnographic descriptions, the narrator educates his readers to imagine a place where women possess greater autonomy and humans have greater freedom to pursue alternative social and sexual relationship among genders.[7] In the early pages of this novel, Westerners are casually introduced to unfamiliar tribal social units that challenge readers to entertain other worlds.[8] At a ball game in town, we meet Woyi and Striker, companions who have gone through the Friends Making Ceremony together and have married the same wife. As a young woman, Whirlwind inhabits other genders, experimenting with sex as a man, when she visits Tobacco Flower in the night: "'I came to you once in the night' . . . 'I came in his shape. You didn't know that, did you? I wanted to find out what it felt like for a man, you know? I was curious, too, about how you would be. You're so tiny and delicate. You were all right, though. It was fun'" (5). Significantly, we first learn of Whirlwind's spiritual power when she transcends the constructed categories of gender. In *War Woman*, then, women's agency begins with asserting autonomous female bodies and their refusal to be defined as physically weak or sexually passive.

On the journey to the Spanish settlements Daksi falls in love with Whirlwind. In this romance, Daksi learns from Whirlwind not only how to negotiate trade but that some women have the supernatural strength to turn away storms. Assuming he will protect his woman from the storm Daksi races up to find her, only to discover that Whirlwind

> was standing not far ahead, arms outstretched, looking up. The great monster was almost upon her. In another instant she would be swallowed up and carried violently away, and he would never see her again. He couldn't move. He couldn't shout or scream. He could do nothing but watch in fascinated horror.
>
> Then, just as Daksi thought that the end of the world was upon them, the great wind turned and slashed its way across an open field adjacent to the town. Halfway across the field, it took a mighty leap back up into the sky, and then it was gone. (45)

The imagery of this passage self-consciously borders on fantasy fiction in order to reimagine rigidly defined mainstream Native gender roles.[9] Like Daksi, men readers might be led to consider their own privileged gender locations, to question why such an experience might be threatening to men, and to imagine the benefits of recognizing autonomous (even spiritually gifted) women in society. In presenting such strong female characters, *War Woman* also provides a complex model of Native women for young people in Cherokee and other Native communities as Indian people enter the twenty-first century.

Since the era of Red Power literature, Native writers have been complicating our understanding of gender in Native America. In novels by Indigenous women writers such as Betty Louise Bell, Elizabeth Cook-Lynn, Louise Erdrich, and Janet Campbell Hale, Indian women are not always anchored to the earth by readily available female ways of knowing, but instead might find themselves in cities far from home and dominated by men. In such cases, as depicted in Coeur d'Alene writer Janet Campbell Hale's *Jailing of Cecelia Capture*, Native women remember their social and cultural training, which helps them to resist their oppression or to undergo a process of self discovery in which they disclose the reality of their gendered lives and thus find freedom.

The Jailing of Cecelia Capture opens with a Native woman on her thirtieth birthday in jail on an old welfare-fraud charge. Cecelia spent her youth on a reservation in northern Idaho, but then she moved away with her parents to Tacoma and then to the Yakima reservation in Oregon. Neither life gave her the stability to cope with the realities of life as a colonized Native woman. Alcoholism and an abusive home life have left her with a sense of hopelessness for American Indian people and certainly for Native women, who resist not only colonialism and racism but also sexism. On the morning after her failed solo-birthday celebration—a day of drinking that ends with a DUI—Cecelia finds herself in jail awaiting her criminal charge. During her cloister, she recounts how the past thirty years of her life have led her to her present bouts with alcoholism and thoughts of suicide. Cecelia shares her cell with Velma, a thin white woman, and Ethel, a large black woman; both women appear hardened by the streets and familiar with drugs and prostitution. Velma feels Cecelia's judgmental eyes upon her, notices Cecelia's wedding band, and declares: "'Married women are worse than whores.' . . . 'Damn hypocrites. I personally have no use for them. Never did. Never will.' . . . 'The only difference between a married woman and a whore,' Velma told Cecelia, 'is that they fuck just one dude and get paid a lot less. Then they walk around looking down their noses and thinking they're so good'" (7).

Here Velma introduces a central political claim in the novel: in this sexist world, autonomy for women in one area of life often comes in exchange for submission to men in another. For even though Cecelia, Velma, and Ethel converge from different racial backgrounds, they all experience some form of gender subjugation. The fact that they each now wait behind bars for the male-dominated criminal justice system to determine their guilt and punishment makes readers consider what it is they share as criminalized women. After all, women are often incarcerated for crimes associated with opposing men in ways that, in a sexist world, cannot be seen outside their larger political context. Or such women are even imprisoned for violent crimes against battering husbands or johns. But as portrayed in *The Jailing of Cecelia Capture*, a woman's crime is often just refusing to normalize into U.S. masculinist culture—for example, as in an almost-humorous reversal of the respective crimes: "'Drunk drivin,'" Velma said self-righteously, 'is worse than peddlin' your ass. Drunk drivin' kills and cripples. Damages property. Fuckin' never hurt nobody'" (6). Though demonized for selling sex, Velma justifies her work with an ethic that does not endanger lives or submit to men in marriage. Thirty years old and in law school, Cecelia has refused a string of men who have wished to marry her, all of whom asked her to put aside her desires for autonomy and personal expression, but she eventually relents and marries a wealthy European American man with whom she is terribly unhappy. Her marriage is a form of imprisonment: "She began to feel the way she imagined her mother must have felt when Cecelia was a little girl, caught fast in a trap of her own making . . . , doomed to live with a man she didn't feel connected to anymore. . . . She was the prisoner now . . . of circumstance and an inability to imagine anything beyond the prison, to create anything different for herself" (176). As Cherokee essayist Victoria Manyarrows writes: "Cecelia Capture was a woman, as her name suggests, 'captured' not only by the physical jail cell, but by the demands and expectations of the Native and white people who she related to, and the societies and communities they represented" (157). The previous night, she drove while intoxicated—certainly an illegal act—but at least a portion of this crime was to be a publicly unrestrained woman.

In this world, being drunk while poor, Indian, and female is somehow lewd or profane—in ways probably not so for financially secure mainstream men. This is Cecelia's most unforgivable crime. Indeed, to pursue her drinking the overachieving Indigenous law student Cecelia develops a persona: Carmen. As Carmen, she goes to bars, lets men buy her drinks, and lets them believe she is an impoverished Mexican American woman:

> She should have let Roberto believe that she was a Mexican. It went with her drinking name, Carmen. Carmen was what she always told men in bars her name was, and twenty-five years her age and waitressing her occupation.
>
> Waitressing required less explanation and was not so incongruous with the heavy drinking. It did seem a bit incongruous, though, for someone in the last lap of preparing to become an officer of the court, the people's advocate, as it were, to be behaving like a cantina girl. She said twenty-five because she wished that she was twenty-five. She would feel more in step then. She wouldn't be what her husband and mother-in-law thought, so old to be a student. She wouldn't have to be so far behind everyone else then, if she were twenty-five.
>
> And Carmen? Because it was a good fake name. Carmen Miranda, and the femme fatale of the opera *Carmen*. Carmen was a good drinking name. She didn't want her own name associated with her barroom activities. (34)

While Cecelia's drinking is no doubt a problem, her hiding it is even worse: as a professional and a woman of color she must maintain a kind of split personality. To be a "bad girl," that is, an unattended woman conversing in bars with strangers, is to undermine mainstream roles for women: for women to be respectable they often must wear uncomfortable clothing (women attorneys must wear skirts in the courtroom); to be taken seriously as professionals, they must assume a flat, dispassionate bearing ("the people's advocate"); to be sexually desirable, they must above all appear young ("twenty-five"). So Cecelia invents Carmen, who allows her to be mistakenly identified and to enjoy the more effortless identity as a nonthreatening, working-class woman who, like the operatic Carmen and Carmen Miranda, is highly sexualized but who entertains rather than threatens men. Even though her Carmen identity is also offensive to her, it is far less work to maintain; assimilation into the "transparent" construction for subjugated peoples always requires less effort and is more rewarded. In Carmen, Cecelia solves the above "incongruity" of a Native woman professional who enjoys drinking and socializing with strangers in public but also solves the contradiction within herself: being a sober feminist yet still desiring the attention of men and the insouciance of alcohol.

In her self-conscious passing either as a good girl, bad girl, or good girl gone bad, Cecelia is not in denial of Native women's powerlessness but, in fact, is painfully aware of the realities of colonialism and concomitant racism and mysogyny. She does not need a lesson in the workings of exploitation, but instead often feels she knows and feels too much of that social reality. After all, she is a law student fully aware of the judicial system and its historical legal justifications for the theft of Indian lands, the abduction of Indian children from their mothers, and the sterilization of Indian women.[10]

> Cecelia considered the doctrine of *de minimus* [that "the law does not concern itself with small things"]. She didn't believe it, quite. The law was infinitely capable of concerning itself with trifles, bringing to jury trial people accused of stealing a pen from Woolworth's, for instance. The law, it seemed, was overly concerned with oppressing the poor and upholding the rights of the rich. And it was not true, either, that justice was blind. (31)

Instead of being blind to her subjugation, Cecelia knows it well—and for this very reason she finds herself on the verge of madness and suicide. To deaden the pain of this colonial reality, she seeks temporary relief in the pleasure of alcohol and sex without commitments. She does, however, attempt to fool herself about her reasons for seeking lovers and drinking: "Cabernet sauvignon. An excellent choice, she thought, as she poured the wine into the thermos. Burgundy would be too heavy for daytime drinking by itself, and chablis or chardonnay too plain. Besides, cabernet was all she had in the refrigerator. Happy Birthday, she hummed, Happy Birthday to me" (20). Rationalizing her drinking as only an alcoholic can, Cecelia decides her secret drinking in the morning before class and later during class is a festive celebration of her birthday. The lonely, hedging language of this rationalization would touch anyone familiar with the terrors of alcoholism. Cecelia enjoys sex and consciously seeks the fulfillment of intimacy, but this experience too often leaves her feeling empty. After sex, she muses: "They had had a good time. It felt good to be close to another human being, and the orgasm had provided a brief respite. It took her out of herself and her misery. It offered escape more complete than that offered by alcohol, if more brief. . . . Yet still, it hurt her somewhere when he left the way he did" (19). Neither alcohol nor sex, however, give Cecelia the imagination—a quality she consciously desires—to discover a way out of her sense of loss and despair and into a sense of self that can find fulfillment in this world.

Instead, she fears she is descending into mental illness, as every day she grows less able to cope with her failing marriage, her separation from her children, and the bare fact of her oppression. In a bar on the night of her birthday, Cecelia remembers falling off the crest of intoxication, in which levity suddenly dives into despair: "Cecelia could remember feeling suddenly sad, then, as though she had slipped and fallen into a deep well of sadness, from which there was no escape, or only an escape so difficult it was not worth the effort" (35). Later, she finds a means of negotiating this chasm not with alcohol but with new imagination and a margin of hope. *The Jailing of Cecelia Capture* advances the discussion of gender in Native studies by daring to draw distinctions between the effects of United States colonialism on Indian men and on Indian women. Remembering her reservation community, Cecelia recalls her father surrendering the dream of becoming a lawyer, and her mother growing bitter through the years:

> The struggling, the anger and the despair. When it got to be too much for some, like her father, the flunked-out would-be lawyer, or her great-grandfather, the disinherited Irish nationalist, the anger would explode in awesome violence. Men would be killed with butcher knives

or beaten nearly to death, the men unlucky enough to be the ones to deliver that last ounce, the one that would be too much to tolerate, the men whose actions touched off the spark.

And others, like her mother, once the anger and fear became too much, would turn it inward upon themselves and become bent, twisted in body, suffering physical pain and thinking strange, tortured, twisted thoughts. . . . Cecelia wondered, was it that the anger in men turned to murder and violence, and in women to madness? (83, 85)

Scholars have recognized the gendered nature of colonial domination. In this familiar scenario, Indigenous men are figured as savage and violent warriors, whereas American Indian women are viewed as passive and abundant caregivers prepared for marriage with white men. Dehumanized and replaced in this frontier allegorical wedding, Indian men perhaps fulminate to this emasculation. Native women, on the other hand, more often tend to internalize this violence, eventually doing violence to the self.

In a desperate period of self-hatred, Cecelia obsessively designs her suicide to put an end to her suffering. In such moments, she imagines destroying herself, though the true object of her disdain is the dominant culture, which demands a false, unreasonable construction of her Native female self:

She stood sideways and held her stomach in, ran her hand across her now flat abdomen, flat as long as she held in her breath. It might as well have been fifty pounds, the way it made her feel, all bulgy and bloated and puffy. She sometimes even imagined, as she walked down the street, that she must waddle now. She wanted to throw something at the mirror and break its smug, judgmental, shiny surface. Then the *Berkeley Gazette* headlines would read: FAT WOMAN, OVER THIRTY, TRIES TO LOOK GLAMOROUS AND ELEGANT, RUNS AMOK AND BREAKS OWN MIRROR IN IMPOTENT RAGE. (16)

The body image foisted upon her by the popular media wears away at her female self. She views her body inaccurately in the mirror—"it might as well have been fifty pounds, the way it made her feel"—and feels inadequate to the commodified image of the ideal female body: white, thin, and childishly fragile. Even in a justified act of anger at society's impossible standard of beauty, it seems Cecelia can only defeat herself. The media would react with the last laugh at her expense, as they now determine her to be not only physically inadequate but also crazy. In her awareness of the colonial culture's power to construct her as a comic and pathetic, brown and female criminal, Cecelia toys with but eventually rejects the idea of suicide. Though humorous here, this reaction later grows chronic when Cecelia buys a handgun, rests at the foot of her son's father's headstone, and considers ending her own life.

In this crucial pause that leads to emotional growth in the novel, Cecelia imagines the possibility of a collective sense of identity and hope, of belonging to a cause in spite of differences among Indian people, and of reclaiming self-worth as part of a community of understanding. She sits in the cemetery and looks out at San Francisco Bay and Alcatraz Island, and she recalls her participation in the occupation of that prison island in 1969:

> Cecelia hugged her knees and looked out to the Bay Area, which stretched far below her: San Francisco Bay. San Francisco. Alcatraz. She remembered going to Alcatraz during the Indian occupation of 1969. Good feelings out there then. Indians feeling effective. Even skid-row bums had gone to Alcatraz and felt as if they were a part of the Indian people. She remembered the old man in the bar in the Mission District telling her, "We are the biggest tribe of all, us displaced ones, us urban Indians, us sidewalk redskins." He was right. (199)

In a rare hopeful moment of this severe novel, Cecelia draws on the inspiration of the Indian movement to stave off her sense of alienation and despair. She looks out over the bay from a cemetery in which her late husband, who died in combat in Vietnam, is buried. She is driven to tears, then loads two bullets in the chamber of her gun. In recalling this Red Power vision, however, Cecelia ultimately discovers a means to persevere as a colonized Native woman in the city. This moment of hope concludes *The Jailing of Cecelia Capture*. Cecelia puts the gun in her purse and begins to make practical plans for the rest of her life: "She had a lot to do now, she thought, now that she was going to live—besides just staying alive— and she wasn't sure how she should approach all her tasks or in which order she should tackle them. And she had to find a place for the three of them to live and a way to support herself and Corey and Nicole. She had to finish her law degree. The logistics of all this would take some careful planning" (201).

Dreaming Gay Histories

Josh Henneha has spent most of his life flying. When the everyday world of a small Creek town in Oklahoma cannot provide the resources for the life he needs as a young Native homosexual man, Josh takes to the imaginative air. Nightly before sleep he hones his skills, and lately he has become quite good at flying. He flies around to search his Muskogee tribal and family history and the creatures of Creek lands for a model of Creek gay identity. With his grandfather, Josh looks out over Lake Eufala:

> I drove past the dam, and before we even parked, we saw a bald eagle lift off a stark oak branch across the water. I had expected to see maybe one or two eagles, and within five minutes I had counted a dozen. Steam was rising from the black stumps at the water's edge, and the winter sun hung like a swollen orange, blood-red and burning in the mid-morning sky. An old patriarch, whose white head and snow-plumed tail feathers were floating through the light, sailed into the yellow rays, patiently abiding the playfulness of a younger, pesky companion, still immature and gray in coloring. The younger bird was playing tag—sweeping above us in long, ever-expanding circles, then diving after the older one and pulling up just above the water, taxiing across the surface. The wings of the eagles dusted the sky, and, when they banked over the shoreline, they cast shadows on the shimmering sand. (162–63)

In this scene from Craig Womack's *Drowning in Fire*, readers might recall a similar moment from *House Made of Dawn*. In that novel, Abel experiences a holy sight when a male eagle and a female eagle chase one another in a romantic dance beyond the rim of Valle Grande. In Womack's reworking, Josh discovers a variation on this central moment from Red Power writing. Here, the eagles have grown to a "dozen," and the playing pair is quite possibly that of two male companions.

Drowning in Fire is the first Indigenous novel to explore the life of openly gay Native men. I thus have chosen to end this book with this "first" and hopeful novel that signals an upsurge in American Indian literature. Such pronouncements are exciting and rare; Josh is happy to share his new resolve to be Indian and gay. Near the end of the novel, with his lover Jimmy at his Baptist camp, Josh has joyfully located his feelings: "Yeah, get me some more of *that*," I thought, half afraid immediately afterward what might come of lusting after a man at a Baptist campground. But

then again, maybe the Lord had brought us back together, who knows?"
(256–57); and later that day in the outdoor church: "I pondered the meaning of Jimmy and me sitting side by side. . . . Whatever it meant, it sure
felt good there, as if his presence was casting a blanket of protection over
us. I loved the feeling of being subsumed by another man in this way.
Surely this had happened before. Two men had sat next to each other, in
church, or out under the arbors, who had once been lovers or still were"
(257). In this moment Josh has triumphed, for he has gathered all aspects
of his complex life — sex, humor, romance, religion, history — within his
gay Muskogee identity.

Few works in Native literature take the Native gay male experience seriously enough to devote literary space for its exploration in sexual, emotional, and romantic life, in history, religion, and social organizations, and
in artistic pursuits. In fact, in recent novels such as Leslie Marmon Silko's
Almanac of the Dead and James Welch's *Heartsong of Charging Elk*, homosexual behavior is used to code moral corruption. In *Almanac of the Dead*,
the homosexual character Beaufrey sadistically enjoys watching videos of
abortions, and hates women because he hates his mother: "His mother
had told him she tried to abort herself. She had never let it happen again
after she had him. Beaufrey had started hating his mother; hating the rest
of them was easy. Although Beaufrey ignored women, he enjoyed conversation that upset or degraded them" (102). Though this monumental
work commendably confronts a European American history of genocide
and land theft, *Almanac of the Dead* unhappily presents this embarrassing
Freudian portrait of the mother-hating, women-hating, homosexual preda-
tor. In *The Heartsong of Charging Elk*, the eponymous hero, while visiting a
brothel, is drugged by a man who rapes him. Charging Elk awakes to the
siyoko fellating him. Grasping his knife, Charging Elk stabs the man in the
back: "He saw the pink froth bubbling from the delicate lips, which were
moving but making no sound" (277). After he scalps the attacker and flees,
he considers the killing of the man with the "delicate lips": "It was simple
enough — when one comes upon evil, one kills it" (297). The justification
echoes that of the narrator of *House Made of Dawn* on the killing of Juan
Reyes Fragua — a murder portrayed as an aberrant homoerotic embrace.
But while scholars have rightfully criticized the homophobic representation of the murder in *House Made of Dawn*, it is appalling that the very
claim about the necessity of destroying the "evil" of homosexuality continues in a recent work of fiction: "When he slit the throat of the *siyoko*, he
had, in that instant, fulfilled his time on earth" (298).

In other works such as Meskwaki writer Ray Young Bear's *Remnants of the First Earth*, Pomo writer Greg Sarris's *Watermelon Nights*, and Navajo writer Irvin Morris's *From the Glittering World*, queer realities receive brief attention. *Remnants of the First Earth* is a novel about the ethics of recording religious life on an Indian settlement in Iowa, but it could benefit from a more complete portrayal of gay experiences: "Horatio, 'Grubby,' and 'Kensey' long resented the involvement of Ted and me in the episode during which a photograph was taken by a boy named 'Little Big Man' in the summer of 1969. . . . With their lips interlocked and salivating, Horatio and 'Grubby' tried to swallow each other like giant bullfrogs in a fight-to-the-death-for-the-harem ritual" (223–24). In the opening of *Watermelon Nights*, the protagonist Johnny Severe tells of his first impression of Felix, who becomes his close friend:

> When she turned for the kitchen sink, Felix got up. Even while I was sitting, I seen he wasn't no taller than me, about the same height actually, average, which surprised me since I'd been picturing him a lot taller, six feet or more. But he was put together good: broad in the shoulders, narrow and lean below, and his clothes—the sleeveless white T-shirt and the 501 Levi's cinched with a silver-studded black belt that matched his leather boots—was nothing special, but he wore them the way a healthy animal wears its skin. (10)

As this intensely erotic relationship of Johnny and Felix is never developed, so too is modern Indian homosexual life, though it would give greater complexity to the Native world. A more "out" Indigenous literature might even better explain the wanderings of the narrator of *From the Glittering World*, who is propositioned by men while living in Los Angeles, and though it is never disclosed he appears at least to consider a gay relationship:

> R. stands there, watching me watch Arnold demolish a high-tech set on TV. "Why?" he says. The motel room is steamy from the shower. The towel around his waist is barely hanging on. A dark wispy line curls from his brown belly into the towel. Water drips from his hair onto his shoulders and chest. Thirty-year-old love handles. I reach over and smear one drop. He stops me. "Stick to the question."
> "I don't know." (190)

Of course, the introduction of gay characters and gay Native authorship presents obvious dangers. In reading the works of gay Cherokee playwright Lynn Riggs, Womack comments on the number of gay American Indian men who flee their reservation towns to find a language for their longings, as Morris's narrator appears to do: "Even now, how many Oklahoma Indian guys do I know who, like Riggs, have fled to New York City and San Francisco in hopes of not having to erase themselves any longer?" (1999, 278).

In *Red on Red*, Womack develops a queer reading of Riggs, in which he explores Riggs's diminished "imaginative capacity to deal with a queer Indian presence in his work" (1999, 279). At the risk of interpreting Womack's fiction through his own criticism, we may draw from Womack's queering of Riggs a literary theory of Native homosexuality. Womack finds in Riggs a struggle to locate a space in which Riggs can live fully as a gay Cherokee man. In his desire for this space, he creates such works as the idyllic *Green Grow the Lilacs*, the play on which the Rogers and Hammerstein musical *Oklahoma!* is based. In Womack's reading, the pristine Oklahoma past serves Riggs as a code for a free and timeless place of gay Indigenous invention (277–83). Such a critical observation proves helpful in understanding and appreciating Womack's artistry in developing his novel *Drowning in Fire*. For central to the novel's movement is a steady search of Muskogee history and mythology to locate and develop a Creek model of gay selfhood. In this regard, Womack succeeds at the historicizing pursuit begun by Riggs in the 1930s. Womack, however, seeks no timeless, wholly imagined space for homosexual life, but instead actual Creek historical and oral traditional moments. For Womack, then, to queer Native literature is to ground it in history and land, in real Indian life and art.

In the novel, Josh begins at a young age to seek both the metaphorical and actual ground for homosexual desires unutterable in his Baptist family in conservative Oklahoma. In the summer of his thirteenth year, Josh is swimming with friends in the Eufala reservoir when he begins to exercise his ability to send telepathic messages to Jimmy:

> Josh, floating on his inner tube on the opposite side, watched Jimmy coming up out of the water. As Jimmy pulled himself aboard he seemed to rise out of the lake in an unending succession; his wiry arms and upper body kept coming and coming, followed by his swimming trunks and long legs, like a snake uncoiling. He was taller than the rest of them. Jimmy's eyes met Josh's just before Jimmy stood fully erect on the slippery wooden planks. (11)

Significantly, Josh is most creative with language when envisioning a sexual life free of restraint, when a young man's body keeps "coming" "fully erect." While the passage resembles the erotic moment of aesthetic appreciation between Johnny and Felix in *Watermelon Nights*, in *Drowning in Fire* this is only the beginning of a fully explored, expressed, and resolved story of homosexual growth. Jimmy is figured as the snakelike creature from southeastern Indian traditions, Tie-snake, who challenges young Muskogee people to meet their psychic fears and develop into better people.

The boys have swum out to a raft in the middle of the lake, when Josh enters a contest to dive down and retrieve a rock from the lake's bottom:

> His hand struck soft mud. He couldn't believe he'd actually made it when even Sammy hadn't been able to reach bottom. He felt around until he clutched a slimy, moss-covered rock. He held it to his chest with one hand, embracing it like a mother holding her child, and he began grabbing at the water with his free hand and kicking his feet.
>
> He broke the surface and gasped, but his hand had struck something solid just above his head, and he heard the thump resound like the inside of a kettle drum. He pulled in mouthfuls of air, but they smelled of dank mold. When he opened his eyes, he saw darkness, and he felt confusion, like having awakened in the middle of the night not knowing where he was. He wanted to call out, but he knew that would make him look chicken and spoil the effect of having retrieved the stone. He began to hyperventilate and panic, and the thought of winning the contest left him, replaced with the fear of surfacing in this unexpected world, breathing in darkness. (17)

Traditional Muskogee stories of creation and emergence inform this modern-day narrative of imagining new worlds for creatures seeking a space to express and thrive. In a number of tribal traditions, the myth of the earth diver explains to the people their origin and emergence—the moral struggle for dignity and autonomy, cooperation and reciprocity, and the coming into a self-conscious sense of identity. Among southeastern peoples, when the world was once only water and darkness the nonhuman creatures failed repeatedly, then finally succeeded, to dive down and carry up mud with which to create dry land. In this reworking of that creation story, Josh first attempts, and at first fails, to create a new world for himself as an emerging homosexual man, where the old world is no longer able to accommodate him. Trapped under the raft, on this day under the

sun and on the water, Josh negotiates between two central forces in Muskogee cosmology: Sun, which is the substance of the Upper World, the
place of established order; and water, the stuff of the Lower World, the
place of imaginative possibility. The fire, in the Creek tradition, is related
to the sun, and so is maintained as a source of renewal and purification.
As with most southeastern belief systems,[11] all categories, and certainly
those such as fire and water, must be maintained and kept separate. In
Drowning in Fire, then, Josh Henneha courageously dares to explore the
source of his all-too-orderly homosexual fire by drowning it in the realm
of possibility, where Tie-snake and Jimmy beckon him.

In his fearful silence, Josh continues to seek a voice for his desires, as
he works desperately to create a world for himself: "He wished he could
pick up words like stones. . . . He would put all the rocks in his mouth and
find his voice in their swirled streaks of sky, fire, water" (28). As a teen-
ager, having grown farther from Jimmy, one evening Josh agrees to drive
him to his basketball game. After the game, Jimmy asks Josh to stop by
Wheeler Park. They descend into a dark section of the park, where ghostly
men exchange embraces in a landscape of sin and hellfire:

> Upright stumps formed vague shapes whose features became recog-
> nizable, on closer approach, as men, in groups of three and four, hands
> reaching for one another. One of these groups of ghosts glided toward
> me and Jimmy; they were rigid, expressionless, silent, and when I tried
> to run, Jimmy tightened his grip on my hand and wouldn't let me go.
> When they got close enough that I could see the looks on their faces, I
> could feel their hunger, their taste for flesh. (101)

Drunk and confused, Josh is horrified by these ghoulish creatures that
speak more of his parents' biblical mythology than that of Creeks. After
all, Josh's last name, Henneha, resembles "Gehenna," the fabled burning
lake of fire that his parents and Baptists preachers had warned would be
his "wages of sin" were he to engage in these "sins of flesh" (64). One
seeks to explain this fascinating vampire imagery that would befit a popular horror novel. Again, Womack answers by considering the restriction
of gay life in Oklahoma in the 1930s, when secrecy and the creation of
alternative worlds were often the only means of survival, characterized as
a "state of silence, of hanging out in secret places, of fear of being found
out as well as fear of self-recognition, of self-hatred and viewing oneself
as sick, of social restrictions on the possibilities of meeting places for gay
men, and a sense of cannibalism even, being devoured by the dark other,

and being such a devourer oneself, secretly feeding on one's own" (1999, 275).

Together again after years, Jimmy and Josh sit in the dark and share their thoughts on growing up; here, sexuality is described as a form of literacy. Because bookish Josh has searched for years for a gay language, "what I was looking for in the books I read" (103), he is surprised to hear that Jimmy too has developed his own homosexual literacy. Jimmy describes sharing his early sexual longings with a playmate who understood his language of homosexuality: "'We were both really literate at a very young age, and we sensed something in each other; the way it worked is hard to explain'" (103). On a child's spelling-exercise toy, the boys shared a language that neither dared speak aloud: "'I am not like anyone else.' . . . 'Me neither'" (103). Insightfully, we are made to consider how our own most transformational identities grow not only from corporeal experience, but are indeed the work of intense self-reflexive intellectual activity. We gain sexual literacy through learning. In that moment, Josh cannot find the courage to let this new language speak through him:

> Sometimes I felt the words rise within me, about to break through to the surface, as if I could almost reach down and help yank them from their depths. I felt them just within reach, when the words would sink back down before I could speak. If I ever brought forth these words, what would I first utter? I wanted words that moved like a wave, words that crashed against my dammed-up body, rising and spilling out, a great flood broken loose, beyond my imaginings, actual speech, words that would not return void but as a net of names, pulled back in, their secrets sparkling in the tangled weave. But my words, it seemed, would not suffice; they lacked the force to rise against the choking feeling when I began to think whether I was like the men I'd just seen approaching in the darkness. (104)

In an innovative linkage between oral traditional conceptions of voice, language, and the self, Josh dramatizes the awesome creative potential of language to bring the world into being, in the imaginative patterns maintained in Native storytelling practices. Like the earth diver, Josh has submerged to the depths of homosexual possibility—but he fears to emerge, for "what would I first utter?" This fear causes him to shrink from embracing his gay identity, because though he has words they are at the moment inadequate, articulate but not yet grounded in a historical context in which to grow. Josh faces a challenge to join language and history in his search for self-knowledge, a process his great-aunt Lucille also undergoes as a survivor of childhood sexual abuse. Lucille turns to jazz to give voice to her fears and to find healing in a world that would silence her: "I, Lucille, smoking words on my tongue, dreaming whippoorwill calls, casting swirled memories on the waters, has stories too dark to tell. A life of talking, and I ain't told some of them to anybody. . . . I play my words like a trumpet, let the space between notes fill in the meaning. Like Louis Armstrong done it, cut loose and hold back in slow blues" (111). Josh sees the power of flying, but realizes he also must discover the courage to land. In their affinity, Aunt Lucille shows Josh how to search Creek history and lands to develop a language that will communicate their experiences: "Since Lucy has sent me out into the woods looking for [Dave] . . . I touch down in this world and start walking. . . . Flying is perfect for hiding, and escaping danger, but it takes you so far away" (176).

In the woods, near the stomp dance ceremonial grounds of genera-tions past, Josh discovers Dave, Lucille's adoptive brother whom her father has also abused. Like Lucille, Dave has found an alternative, traditional Creek family with Tarbie and Seborn, two men who live together in this place. In a moment of clarity, Josh unites Muskogee history and spiritu-ality and discovers a model of gay Creek identity that enables history and language:

> And then, crouched down in the cattails by the spring, listening to all that, something just broke in my mind and came flooding in on me. Those two men loved each other. They loved me. I knew if I ran fast enough, I could tell my story before I floated away, share the good news before I lost it. There was no time to lose, not a moment to spare by staying there and thinking until I got scared and changed my mind. (180)

Josh captures this sudden discovery of a historical model of gay Creek identity, and he begins to develop it before it escapes him. His first mo-ment of sexual growth, of the flood of literacy, the wave of words, indeed, is in the naming itself: announcing the love between Tarbie and Seborn, one that then grows by logical steps to Josh, who is now loved *as a gay Creek man*. Most significant, Josh secures his sexual identity by imagining a theory of the self that can refer to—as well as grow from—a gathering of Creek traditions, language, lands, and community. From this sexual and political awakening, Josh is now able fully to explore the reaches of his homosexual Muskogee selfhood:

Lately, I had started flying to new places, gave up my childhood hover-
ing for touching down on arrival. . . . So Dave and me were going to be
all right. . . . There was a lot of medicine in a person's brain, I figured,
if he could collect his thoughts, consider the things he'd heard, make
up stories to suit himself. . . . So I put my mind to work, recollecting
as best I could. Thought about Tarbie. About Seborn. Dave and Lucille.
Family and friends to each other, just like I'd known. I didn't have all
the facts, so I did the most sensible thing and proceeded without them.
(219–20)

In dreaming gay history, Josh draws on a model of inquiry not unlike
some of the most innovative scientists, who proceed with some but not
"all the facts." Josh flies off into the realm of possibility, pursuing his best
hunches and locating error when his "words" fail to disclose the reality of
his homosexual and Muskogee world.

Perhaps most exciting, Josh finds that the new security of his gay identity—and the world that it informs—better explains his Creek self and his
Oklahoma Indian personhood located in land and history (by the novel's
end, he is flying with Chitto Harjo to oppose statehood). Josh grows his
hair long in expression of his Indianness. Now, when his boss says, "Get
a haircut," he considers: "I'd been growing it out. I said I'd think about it,
but what I meant was I was thinking about some other line of work, and
Jimmy had made it worse; opening up one world made me consider the
possibility of others" (228). This statement presents the central theoretical claim of *Drowning in Fire*. When we consider the complexity of social
actors—the multiple worlds we inhabit, the identities we are given, and
the political identities we select and fight for—we realize we cannot and
should not act in discrete spaces, our categories sealed off from each other
like fire and water. Instead, as Womack explores, our commitments to the
world—Creek, gay, male, queer activist, stomp dancer—blend and interact, melding to produce better and more complex selves. Indeed, Josh's
new self enables him to understand and share a similar struggle with
others. Singing a Creek hymn in the outdoor church, for the first time
Josh truly understands other lives:

I looked at the women's faces and saw my Aunt Lucille's years of pain
carried on their voices throughout the campground, their invitation
for her to join in, their willingness to share her burden. . . . It occurred
to me that the only way left to know her suffering was through my
own, and I let my voice go, mostly humming along at first, then, in-

creasingly, joining in on the words and phrases, as they became clear through repetition, following closely Jimmy's lead, adding whatever I could to the women's lament. (258)

Perhaps only through our own selves can we truly imagine the lives of others, but this is enough to keep Indian communities going. For years, Josh hides his innermost self from others and accepts the sexual identity assigned to him. He is thus left to pass as a straight man, in a self that has no language for his longings. And although the term "passing" suggests self-conscious misrepresentation, more often than not what we call passing is actually "misrecognition," the world assuming or, indeed, insisting we are who we are not. In this regard, many of us are passing unawares, accepting the identities attributed to us because we are unaware of any alternatives.

Consider Josh's words—"opening up one world made me consider the possibility of others"—in light of this chapter's opening claims: social conditions enable new identities to emerge; identity politics serve the production of objective social knowledge; social and cultural knowledge are the products of theoretical activity and oppositional political practice. The recent works of American Indian fiction in this chapter attract me not because they communicate themes we generally accept or desire as Native literature today—the natural world, spiritual forces, ceremony— but because they evade this characterization. As difficult as they are to classify and interpret responsibly, I see in these texts the promise of "other worlds" and the hope that, in conversation with other Native works, they can move our studies of American Indian literature and culture toward greater social clarity. This call to advance the discourse by opening it to encounter gender, sexuality, class, and other aspects of Native community and literature has been led by such Indian scholars as Daniel Justice, Robert Warrior, and Craig Womack. According to Warrior: "Our responsibility is to reflect in our work the same fullness of life that native literary artists have represented in their art" (1998, 125). But while few today support the restriction of marginalized persons from Indigenous studies, I must clarify that we may justify these inclusions not in remunerative terms but in pursuit of objective knowledge.

This draws us to a point I have been making throughout this book: in anticolonial struggles, claims to freedom can be made in the name of knowledge. On such a philosophical basis, even the most entrenched must take our ideas seriously, for they too seek more complete knowledge of a world all of us share. In my understanding of Indigenous oral traditions, I have shown how these can provide a tribal realist model of knowledge to support our most courageous claims to the stability of tribal histories, the lasting relationships with homelands, the agency of tribal peoples to guide their own social and cultural changes. In attempting to establish a critical meeting ground between Indian nations and the United States, I have drawn on the realist framework of other Third World and minority scholars to communicate with tribal intellectual voices in these challenging yet productive discussions. I feel that, perhaps more than any other subjugated group, Native people stand most to gain from a strongly supported theory of American Indian self and cultural understanding. As we continue to decolonize Indian nations, tribal peoples will require a means of explaining to themselves and others their reclamation of an Indigenous knowledge rooted in land and history. As the promise of an emerging Fourth World consciousness grows, that theoretical position on tribal knowledge might become either a source of vulnerability or strength in Native liberation struggles.

As political concerns become increasingly global, Indian people may find themselves raising their voices for issues similar to those for which Red Power activists and intellectuals fought: treaty rights to homelands, economies, education, health, and, most important, the right to speak without being criminalized. Some might insist that the world is different today, and that the spirit of Red Power cannot provide the tools to resist today's abuses of power. But if we remember those tribal voices, the music, dance, art, and literature—Abel's eagle watch, the nameless narrator's visit with Yellow Calf, Tayo's cutting through the fence—that collective dream of a liberated Native America, when Indian people drummed into the sunset on Alcatraz or packed food by night to supply Wounded Knee, we remember the vision of hope and justice that fueled the years 1969 to 1979, the vision called Red Power. That vision is enough.

NOTES

||||||||||||||||||||||||||||||||||||||||||||||||||||||||||||||||||||||||||||||

Introduction

1. On the federal termination policy, see Wilkinson 2005, chapter 3.

2. For sociological analyses of this revival among Indian people, see the work of the Ojibwe scholar Stephen Cornell (1988). See also Nagel 1996.

3. Attending San Francisco State College during the Alcatraz occupation was the future principal chief of the Cherokee Nation, Wilma Mankiller, and many other future Indian leaders, such as Richard Oakes. The National Indian Youth Council was largely led by students. See Smith and Warrior 1996, 52.

4. Native military leaders were imprisoned on Alcatraz from 1873 onward. See Johnson 1996, 3. On Indians imprisoned during the so-called Modoc War, see D. Brown 1970, 213–34.

5. On this shared colonial history, see Cherokee scholar Ward Churchill (writing with Vander Wall [1988]). On the FBI's documented plans to destroy minority political leaders and movements, see Churchill and Vander Wall 1990. On the Black Power movement, see Werner 1999, 103–73.

6. "Unsettled Plains: Census Findings of Dwindling Population in Great Plains States, and Parallel Gains in Population for American Indians and Bison," *New York Times*, 3 June 2001, 4:16.

7. For a study of pan-tribalism, see Hertzberg 1971.

8. For a return to Red Power as various participants reflect on the movement, see Johnson, Nagel, and Champagne 1997.

9. Throughout this book, I chart these debates on knowledge as they evolve in Native studies, though they often first emerge among mainstream theorists, whom I recognize in my notes. Essentialism denotes that cultures have an "essence," an immutable core of identifying characteristics. Although essentialism threatens to rigidify cultural knowledge, it often plays a central role in reviving cultures after colonialism. For a study of essentialism as a theoretical issue, see Fuss 1989. For moments of essentialism in Native scholarship, see P. Allen 1992; Churchill 1994; and Juaneño and Yaqui

scholar Annette Jaimes Guerrero 1987. For a discussion of essentialism in American Indian intellectual history, see Krupat 1996, 3–11.

10. In poststructuralism, theorists like Jacques Derrida, Michel Foucault, and Jacques Lacan question grand narratives of civilization to decenter (the colonial center of) knowledge by emphasizing the socially constructed nature of knowledge and difference within a culture. Among other projects, scholars like those named above critique the process of exclusion required to define a culture, presenting a model of selfhood that purports to be liberated from the strictures of cultures by residing between them. Such "skeptical" or "discursive" positions in "contemporary theory" often present extreme doubts about objective knowledge or universal moral claims. For helpful definitions, see Lewis 1992. On this development in literary studies, see Eagleton 1983, 91–150.

11. Leading this more skeptical position on knowledge, Gerald Vizenor (1993b) was first to define the "trickster discourse." Inspired by Vizenor, Louis Owens established Vizenor's fiction (1992) and later presented a fully elaborated trickster epistemology (1998). Kimberly Blaeser (1996) celebrates this position.

12. On balancing nationhood and internationalism, for example, see S. Teuton 2006b.

13. These American Indian intellectuals have begun to seek a theory to locate Native people and literature in the world. Elizabeth Cook-Lynn (1996a) was clearly at the forefront with early essays (now collected). Robert Warrior (1995) encouraged readings of Native literature grounded in tribal history and community, in later books by Jace Weaver (1997) and by Craig Womack (1999). Though Womack might disagree, I find he shares the historicism of these scholars. Throughout his book, he roots Creek writing in land and history through an openly evaluative process. See also Pomo scholar Greg Sarris (1993).

14. The "Fourth World" designates Indigenous nations that have been colonized and are now a minority in their own homelands. Also called "internal colonialism," this circumstance is perhaps most evident in North America, but it also exists in Australia and New Zealand. On the Fourth World, see Churchill 1993, 23–24, 31; R. Ortiz 1984; and Weaver 1997, 10. Ashcroft, Griffiths, and Tiffin (1989, 2) call these new states "settler colonies," in contrast to the "invaded colonies" of, say, Africa. The concept of the Fourth World may be an alternative to the First World–Third World binary; see Ahmad 1992, chapter 3. Such settlers mythologize themselves as the Indigenous people. See H. Carr 1996; Dakota historian Philip Deloria 1998; and Huhndorf 2001.

15. Employing this process, Arnold Krupat improves his approach to Native culture with each new book. In his volume from 1996 (chapter 1), he confronts critical identity in cross-cultural scholarship. See also Cheyfitz 1991, 5.

16. References to these and other primary works are from the editions given in the bibliography; all subsequent citations appear parenthetically in the text.

17. Though this thesis often draws on Friedrich Nietzsche, he recognizes the problems with relying on a strictly positivist definition of objectivity: "It is no small discipline and preparation of the intellect on its road to final 'objectivity' to see things for once through the wrong end of the telescope; and 'objectivity' is not meant here to stand for 'disinterested contemplation' (which is a rank absurdity) but for to have one's pros and cons within one's command and to use them or not, as one chooses. . . . [Absolute knowledge] presuppose[s] an eye such as no living being can imagine, an eye required to have no direction, to abrogate its active and interpretative powers—precisely those powers that alone make seeing, seeing *something*" (1956, 255).

18. Because I explore the relationship of tribal realism to oral tradition in later chapters, I do not provide extensive citation here.

19. Some European philosophers return the metaphysical to Western thought. Discussing Kant, Iris Murdoch considers the productive power of the imagination: "The concept of genius itself emerges from an appreciation of the deep and omnipresent operation of imagination in human life" (1993, 316). See also Tuan 1989.

20. See Butler 1990, 148–49; and Haraway 1991, 198–99.

21. According to Raymond Williams, "Cultural materialism is the analysis of all forms of signification, including quite centrally writing, within the actual means and conditions of their production" (2001, 264). Mohanty's position is obviously indebted to Marxism, though Marx did not develop a theory of cultural identity.

22. Ngugi wa Thiong'o reminds us that Indigenous peoples can conduct their own counter-appropriation of the means of cultural production: "The social history of the world before the advent of victorious socialism was the continued appropriation of the results and genius of the labour of millions by the idle classes. Why should not the African peasantry and working class appropriate the novel?" (1986, 68). On the European novel, see Watt 1957. See also Fisher 1988.

23. On the historical development of Europe's ethnocentric culture and its ties to colonialism, see Amin 1989.

24. Tony Tanner explores this desire in American literature to escape the bounds of language and community: "Thus at the end of *Huckleberry Finn*, in an intuitive move to hold on to some basic innocence and integrity, Huck gives up language altogether and makes for a mythical wordless West" (1971, 28).

25. See Renape-Lenape-Powhatan scholar Jack Forbes (1995) and the Arikara and Hidatsa scholar Michael Yellow Bird (1999).

1. Embodying Lands

1. On "blood memory," see, above all, N. Scott Momaday: "I believe that at some point in my racial life, this notion [Kiowa horse culture] must needs be expressed in order that I may be true to my nature" (1976, 155). But also see Paula Gunn Allen: "There is a permanent wilderness in the blood of an Indian, a wilderness that will endure as long as the grass grows, the wind blows, the rivers flow, and one Indian woman remains alive" (1992, 183); Simon Ortiz: "Don't fret. / Warriors will keep alive in the blood." (1981a, 33); Leslie Marmon Silko: "Maybe the dawn woke the instinct in the dim memory of the blood when horses had been as wild as deer and at sunrise went into the trees and thickets to hide" (1977, 182–83); James Welch: "The answer had come to me as if by instinct, sitting on the pump platform, watching his silent laughter, as though it was his blood in my veins that had told me" (1974, 160); and Gerald Vizenor: "The elders ruled that we were tricksters in a wicked world, in a world of dead voices, poisoned by the wordies who would never hear their stories in the blood" (1992, 46). Since even Vizenor invokes blood memory, we might question the essentialist intent of Native writers. After all, so do other minority writers such as Langston Hughes: "I've known rivers: / I've known rivers ancient as the world and older than the flow of human blood / in human veins" (1994, 23).

2. Arnold Krupat objects to what he calls the "mystical" criticism of Momaday and others, which relies on the "ancientness of racial wisdom" (1989, 12–14). Krupat also believes that to be Indian one must have "*some* actual heredity link to persons native to America" (208). Elvira Pulitano (2003, 61, 66), though she does not critique essentialism in terms of blood, views any claim to a separate nation and people as unavoidably essentialist. For an excellent discussion of the blood/land/identity connection, see C. Allen 2002, 16.

3. Many Native scholars oppose the use of the term "post" in postcolonial to describe the ongoing colonized situation of Native nations in North America. Others also claim that a "post" colonial suggests a "pre" colonial (a time when American Indians were, without technology, a pure culture) and thus reproduces a savage-civilized binary in Native studies: "While post-colonialism purports to be a method by which we can begin to look at those literatures which are formed out of the struggle of the oppressed against the oppressor, the colonized and the colonizer, the term itself assumes that the starting point for that discussion is the advent of Europeans in North America," explains Cherokee writer Tom King (1990, 11). Anthropologists often adhere to this "postcolonial" binary, in which Native people identify as such largely in response to the colonizer; see, for example, Hanson 1997.

4. Homi Bhabha (1994), for example, concluding that all claims to nation rely on a notion of cultural purity, attempts to disband the nation for an am-

biguous, borderless "Third Space" of cultural contact, which "quite properly challenges our sense of the historical identity of culture as a homogenizing, unifying force, authenticated by the originary Past, kept alive in the national tradition of the People" (37). This portrayal of the postcolonial condition often relies on a certain view of language: since subjects are produced by linguistic structures, and Indigenous people must speak the colonizer's language, they have little if any anticolonial agency. See, for example, Gayatri Spivak 1987, 221 and 1990, 61. Since the "zones" of the colonizer and the colonized were first articulated by Frantz Fanon (1963) to explain colonial relations in Algeria, others such as Mary Louise Pratt (1992) have rightly critiqued the assumed impermeable yet constructed and porous border between colonizer and colonized, renaming "the space of colonial encounters" "the contact zone" (6). For other theorists presenting this view of cultural interaction, see Clifford 1988 and Gilroy 1993. For scholars in American Indian Studies, see Bruyneel 2000; Donaldson 1995; Owens 1998, 26; and Pulitano 2003. This model of colonial relations, however, is less able to explain the unequal distribution of resources, why constructed, bordered Indian reservations are nonetheless the poorest places in North America, while U.S. cities are among the wealthiest places in the world. For a realist alternative, see S. Teuton 2006a.

5. See Bercovich 1978, Drinnon 1980, and Stephanson 1995.

6. Keith Basso (1990) shows that this world is constructed by tribal members in creative, meaningful ways in order that it be maintained: "Whenever Apaches describe the land—or, as happens more frequently, whenever they tell stories about incidents that have occurred at particular points upon it—they take steps to constitute it in relation to themselves. Which is simply to say that in acts of speech, mundane and otherwise, Apaches negotiate images and understandings of the land that are accepted as *credible accounts* of what it actually is, why it is significant, and how it impinges on the daily lives of men and women. In short, portions of a worldview are *constructed* and made available, and a Western Apache version of landscape is deepened, amplified, and tacitly affirmed. With words, a massive physical presence is fashioned into a meaningful human universe" (added emphasis 102). Notice also that Apaches "deepen," that is, evaluate and improve this relationship.

7. On a tribal people "growing out" of the land, see Harkin 2000, and Stoffle, Halmo, and Austin 1997.

8. The Anishinaubae (also spelled Anishinaabe) philosopher Basil Johnston (1995) explains how his people maintain their tribal knowledge orally: "Traditionally, Anishinaubae history and heritage were taught by the elders and others, who instructed the people in everything from history, geography, and botany, to astronomy, language, and spiritual heritage, at family and community gatherings . . ." (xx). Tribal oral traditions often dictate paleohistory to current listeners. See also V. Deloria 1995 and MacLeish 1994.

9. Robert Nelson (1993), for example, reduces the complex cosmology in *House Made of Dawn* to popularized "snake medicine" and "eagle medicine": ". . . Abel must correct his vision of the ['eagle' and 'snake,' respectively] spirit of these two places and, by extension, of the spirit of the land . . ." (47). This said, it is impossible to provide a secular reading of Native literature, especially when stories meet the land, as argues Andrew Wiget (1990): "Indeed, the very distinction between the natural and supernatural, between a created, material, impersonal world and a world of spirits, is alien to Native America, where man not only is in the world, but of it, a person among other kinds of persons" (xii-xiii). On American Indian spirituality, see Weaver 1998.

10. Nora Baker Barry (1978a) however writes: "Abel is established as a hero, but a hero in a special way. He is a man not to be ignored. He is a presence to be reckoned with—defiant, irreverent, unyielding, even foolish" (283).

11. According to Gary Witherspoon (1977), among the Navajo, "[t]hinking and singing the world into existence attributes a definite kind of power to thought and song to which most Westerners are not accustomed" (17).

12. *House Made of Dawn* requires an interactive relationship between individual, community, and homeland like that generated by the oral tradition: "As a theoretical argument, Momaday suggests . . . that in the context of tradition and of tribal or family interrelations, a reflexive narrativity occurs, a process by which listener and teller are formed in the event of language and construct self-descriptive story from discursive materials of narration" (Ellis 1994, 59–60).

13. There is little written on the tradition of athletics among Indigenous peoples of the western hemisphere. On ceremonial running among the Pueblo peoples, see Parsons 1939, vol. 2, "Races." For a gripping account of the reenactment of the Pueblo Revolt of 1680 runner-messenger delivery, see Nabokov 1981. On more contemporary Native sports, see P. Deloria 1996 and Lumbee scholar Joseph Oxendine 1995.

14. Approaches to the environmental movement often begin with interrogating the Western philosophical assumption that humankind is different from the rest of the living world. See Kohák 2000, 17–25. In "Earth's Mind," Roger Dunsmore explores the idea that the earth possesses agency: "This capacity to share one consciousness, to feel what the others are feeling in the chest and the belly goes far beyond the family and the clan. It extends to every aspect of the environment within which people live, to the rocks and the winds" (1997b, 13). Many Indigenous peoples maintain a much more encompassing notion of life and personhood than do European peoples. In her study of Navajo personhood, Maureen Trudelle Schwarz (1997) elaborates: "[A]ll persons who live now or who have ever lived in the Navajo world— hooghan, baskets, corn plants, corn beetles, humans, cradles, mountains, prayers—were and are constructed of the same fundamental elements, linked by metaphoric structures including complementarity, permeated by

vibration in the form of sound and movement, and possessed of the same seven senses and anatomical components, including mind, eyes, ears, legs, and feet. Despite these many similarities, the numerous distinct types of persons in the Navajo world have individualized life cycles that are determined, in part, by degree of personal power based on knowledge, which gives agency and volition" (35–36). On Pueblo "animism," see Tyler 1964, chapter 12.

15. For a theory of environmental ethics that calls for a new understanding of "respect" for the non-human world, see Westra 1994, 79–96.

16. On the "Bahkyush" or Pecos people, see Levine 1999, 18.

17. On the tribal practice of naming places, see T. Thornton 1997.

18. Tribal peoples actively incorporate new practices into their ways of life. In this regard, Catholic priests in the pueblos are not as open: "Apparently, though, this incorporation was not reciprocal; the Christians did not incorporate any Native American Culture Hero into their own mythos. Hence, their use of Native American mythologies seems merely manipulative in order to gain and retain dominance and from this perspective is more sacrilegious than ecumenical" (Domina 1994, 9).

19. With Fragua objectified as aberrant and criminal, the coupling might be read as a "deviant" homosexual encounter. So the albino killing might be not only homophobic but also cliché—the threat and defeat of the homosexual villain. For a study of Native sexuality, see W. Williams 1992.

20. Momaday may have drawn on an actual historical event in which two Pueblo men killed an officer whom they believed to be a witch. Among the Pueblo people, the crime was not to murder, but to act without the consent of the community. For an explanation of the above killing, see Evers 1985b. Alan Velie (1978) judges Abel by Anglo standards of fair play in a secular game: "His anger and decision to kill the albino are wrong. It is as if a black halfback considers it a racial incident when he is tackled by a white linebacker, and wants to fight him" (58).

21. See Matthews 1995.

22. William Clements (1982) writes: "Alive or dead at the end of the race, he will again be part of Jemez tradition, purged of the *contamination* of the white world" (added emphasis 62). In asserting that even if Abel actually dies at the end of *House Made of Dawn*, he is at least finally purified from his former corrupt state, Clements reinforces the myth of the Vanishing American. In the face of critics' concern with Abel's "contamination," Momaday finds Abel deeply Indian: "Of course he is an Indian man, according to his experience. It's all he can do, isn't it?" (King 1983, 68). Throughout history, Native people from different backgrounds have gathered to retribalize, with urban areas today promising new nations. See R. Thornton 1998b, 33.

23. "Few of us suffer from our pasts as Abel must suffer," writes Marion Willard Hylton (1972, 68). Momaday suggests that we should recognize both universal human suffering and particular histories of oppression.

24. The United States repeatedly targets not wealthy white neighborhoods, but American Indian communities as "national sacrifice zones" for the dumping of nuclear and chemical waste, despite numerous treaties that outlaw the abuse of Indian land. See Muskogee historian Donald Fixico 1998; Grinde and Johansen 1995, 236–39; and Anishinaabe activist Winona LaDuke 1999, 97–101.

25. Ben's voice is perhaps pleasing because he speaks in American Indian English, or "rez talk." See Bartelt 1994.

26. See Kluckhohn and Leighton 1974, 84–123.

2. Placing the Ancestors

1. Though some critics such as Louis Owens use the terms "Blackfeet" and "Blackfoot" interchangeably as well as in reference to the Gros Ventres, the three tribal names deserve to be defined. According to LaVonne Ruoff, "These tribes were referred to as 'The Blackfoot Nation' in the treaty signed in Judith Basin in 1855. The term 'The Blackfoot Nation' is a misnomer because it refers to four tribes temporarily allied at the same time: Northern Blackfeet (Siksika), Bloods (Kainah), Piegans, and Gros Ventres. Although the first three were operating as separate tribes by the time of white contact, they believed themselves to have a common descent; they also continued to speak the same dialect of Algonkian, to share similar customs, and to war against the same enemies. However, they did not consider the Gros Ventres to have an origin common to theirs. The Gros Ventres . . . spoke an Algonkian dialect so different from that of the Blackfeet that the groups could understand one another only with difficulty. The Gros Ventres are considered to have once been part of the Arapahos, another Algonkian tribe. Although the Blackfeet, Arapahos, and Gros Ventres were among the older Algonkian residents of the plains, evidence points to the Blackfeet as the earliest of these" (1978b, 169). Such tribal distinctions further explain the narrator's isolation as a Blackfeet man displaced on a largely Gros Ventres reservation.

2. Researchers on postcolonial identity remain so concerned with the "authenticity" of today's Indians that many Native people view identity as another colonial restriction rather than as a means of preserving culture and knowing the world. See Vickers 1998 and Green 1995. On the U.S. biological control of American Indian identity, see Guerrero 1992b. For personal essays on Native identity, see Penn 1997.

3. Some theorists thus doubt the viability of an oppositional politics based on identity because they find that categories of subjectivity are inevitably unstable. As Judith Butler notes: "The domains of political and linguistic 'representation' set out in advance the criterion by which subjects themselves are formed, with the result that representation is extended only to what can be acknowledged as a subject" (1990, 1). Of her many quarrels with iden-

tity, Butler critiques (homo)sexual identity quite strongly: "Is sexuality of any kind even possible without that opacity designated by the unconscious, which means simply that the conscious 'I' who would reveal its sexuality is perhaps the last to know the meaning of what it says? . . . For being 'out' always depends to some extent on being 'in'; it gains its meaning only within that polarity. Hence, being 'out' must produce the closet again and again in order to maintain itself as 'out.' In this sense, *outness* can only produce a new opacity; and *the closet* produces the promise of a disclosure that can, by definition, never come" (1993, 15–16). See also Michaels 1998.

4. Jonathan Culler explains this view in his often-cited epistemological thesis on experience: "For a woman to read as a woman is not to repeat an identity or experience that is given but to play a role she constructs with reference to her identity as a woman, which is also a construct, so that the series can continue: a woman reading as a woman reading as a woman. The noncoincidence reveals an interval, a division within a woman or within any reading subject and the 'experience' of that subject" (1982, 64). The "interval" Culler identifies exposes a division within the self, a site of epistemic slippage that makes experience unreliable. Jacques Derrida locates this gap in knowledge as an effect of linguistic signification: "An interval must separate the present from what it is not in order for the present to be itself, but this interval that constitutes it as present must, by the same token, divide the present in and of itself, thereby also dividing, along with the present, everything that is thought on the basis of the present, that is, in our metaphysical language, every being, and singularly substance or the subject. In constituting itself, in dividing itself dynamically, this interval is what might be called *spacing*, the becoming-space of time or the becoming-time of space (*temporization*)" (1982, 13).

5. Gerald Vizenor draws on Jean Baudrillard's (1994) deconstruction of the real to advance his view of Native identity. But because Baudrillard is unable to evaluate the political uses to which the simulacra is put (mascots or the "Whiteman"), it ultimately proves unhelpful to American Indian activists. On Native peoples simulating white people as a humorous anticolonial practice, see Basso 1979; and Speck and Broom 1993, 25–39. Vizenor is at his best when he develops his views of simulated Indians or "post-Indians" in his response to anthropology that promotes a narrow image of Indians to Native people today. On Vizenor and anthropologists, see LaVaque-Manty 2000, 78–79.

6. Although the term "mixedblood" has been used for many years among American Indians as well as white Americans, we should be wary of the term's racial overtones. Though not as offensive as "half-breed" or "breed," "mixedblood" suggests that a tribal person's blood is tainted and no longer pure. Though some scholars claim that the concept of mixedblood (or in postcolonial theory, "hybrid") is not a racial, but a cultural theory, I find that the term ultimately relies on racial biology. Indian scholars attempt to re-

cover the term mixedblood as an embodiment of the free play of knowledge; see Owens 1992, 3–16. Gerald Vizenor (1990) also attempts to empower this term by transforming mixedbloods into crossbloods. Michael Wilson argues that these terms point to deeper issues of knowledge—the European American demand for Native authenticity: "The discourse of 'pure' and 'mixed' (or 'mixedblood') is therefore inadequate to express the complexities by which cultures (and indeed individuals) come to fashion a center of identity" (1997, 138).

7. On early-twentieth-century federal programs to assimilate American Indians, see Maddox 2005.

8. On the epistemic status of cultural identity, see Mohanty 1997, 202–6.

9. Meg Armstrong (1997) reads the narrator's injured body in *Winter in the Blood* not only as a site of anticolonial resistance (265), but also as evidence of a permanently fractured self. This reading, however, ultimately serves the colonial project of insisting that Native people are unavoidably damaged in mind and body by colonialism. By insisting that the self must be "circumscribed" to be whole, she denies the narrator healing (266). But the narrator is not "restricted" from but rather reconnected to a "new," more fitting history. This additional theoretical perspective creates a more coherent self, helps to complete his portrait.

10. This view often draws on the Nietzschean notion that agents and thoughts bear little relation—that "both the deed and the doer are fictions." Precluding the epistemological process can become uncritical: "'Thinking,' as epistemologists conceive it, simply does not occur: it is a quite arbitrary fiction, arrived at by selecting one element from the process and eliminating all the rest, an artificial arrangement for the purpose of intelligibility" (1967, 264)

11. Surprisingly, Owens (1998) later fully embraces this position. I focus on his earlier (1992) and more influential work.

12. Decolonization may be theorized as an epistemic process of producing new knowledge as we approach objectivity, a view of human development and knowledge similar to that of Gadamer's hermeneutical "horizon": "The horizon is the range of vision that includes everything that can be seen from a particular vantage point. Applying this to the thinking mind, we speak of narrowness of horizon, of the possible expansion of horizon, of the opening up of new horizons, and so forth" (1998, 302). The nameless narrator must come home in order to "see" his homeland, and he must broaden his vision of his homeland in order to understand his people's fateful winter there. Only after he achieves a more complete story of that winter as the test of his tribe's humanity can he begin to imagine a less distant relationship to his mother. In this manner, we come to know more about the world and ourselves in it not by making self-evident discoveries, but by collecting and imbricating "impressions." See Rorty 1979, 141–42.

13. Despite the popularity of the trickster position, a number of Native philosophers present an implicitly realist conception of objective knowledge. See the first collection of Native philosophical essays ever produced, *American Indian Thought*, especially part 2, "Epistemology and Knowing" (Waters 2004). See also Donald Fixico, who describes an "Internal Model" of normative knowledge production (2003, 15–16). American Indians are able to preserve and adapt their contemporary spiritual practices through a normative conception of change. See, for example, Farrer 1994.

14. Kiowa anthropologist Gus Palmer comments on the role of Kiowa kinship in handing down stories: "Being related as I was meant easy access to stories. . . . Kiowas don't usually like to tell intimate details to strangers. Kiowas prefer to keep stories within a relatively tight, informal circle of close friends and relatives" (2003, xvi-xvii). Decolonization often involves the recovery of a traumatic past, a process of recovery that resembles that of Jewish people recalling the Holocaust. Dominick LaCapra explains that trauma is repeated through generations, even if survivors do not "directly" experience suffering (2006, 231–32). To interrupt this repetition, survivors must redefine experience not as direct but ancestral.

15. Like many postcolonial novels, *Winter in the Blood* is especially preoccupied with recovering a suppressed history, a quality that makes the novel different from other mainstream novels less engaged with history. For a reading of *Winter in the Blood* as a postcolonial text, see E. Nelson 1997.

16. Ernest Stromberg, in fact, notices that of all Welch's novels, only *The Death of Jim Loney* "refuses to provide the ultimately affirmative vision of Native American cultural survival that many readers have come to associate with contemporary American Indian fiction" (1998, 33).

17. Susan Berry Brill de Ramírez, in fact, claims that communication is broken down in the novel—a claim that I find might suggest a connection between Welch's truncated style and the characters' social dysfunction: "This absence of conversive relations is depicted in terms of a compromised pathology in which one can only hope to assert one's own subjectivity through the dysconnections between oneself and others" (1999, 213). I, however, feel that the characters do recover these connections.

18. Welch complicates any easy reading of "distance" in *Winter in the Blood* by letting various kinds of distance resonate differently throughout the novel. So, while the narrator's distance from his culture is steadily closed, other distances remain. The highline prairie will always be somehow distant in its vastness. At the novel's conclusion, the narrator actually enjoys being "distant in a clean rain" (172). Kathleen Mullen Sands comments: "The distance here does not cut him off. . . . On the contrary, in this solitary moment, he claims the past, washed clean of bitterness by the summer storm" (1987, 77). Some distance is necessary and even good—so long as we have the ability to choose.

19. In his repeated reference to Yellow Calf as "old man" and the grandmother as "old woman," Welch draws a parallel with the male and female archetypes in Blackfeet cosmology. See Grinnell 1920, 142.

20. Betty Tardieu correctly warns readers not to reject this scene for its profanity: "The incident is only obscene when read from a Christian perspective. From a Native American stance, it is as close as the reader comes to knowing the narrator's name" (1993, 71).

21. Nora Baker Barry sees elements of the Old English elegy in *Winter in the Blood*, particularly the theme of the Wanderer or Exile. Quite rightly, she notices the wanderer in the white men, too: "Even the nameless white man who is arrested for some mysterious crime against white society is called a 'wanderer.' Wandering in search of something not quite defined becomes a symbol in the novel for a universal human condition, even for life itself" (1978b, 151).

3. Learning to Feel

1. In this chapter, I consider the theoretical basis for "experience," a concept under philosophical debate. Philosophers generally assume that the concept of experience itself involves various forms of sensory and social mediation. Philosophers question whether even a most immediate sensory "event" can provide an unmediated "pure" experience. See, for example, the opening of Hegel 1931; from the analytic tradition, see Sellars 1963, 164–70.

2. The literature of subjugated peoples draws heavily on experience in an act of reclaiming a history, land, and nation. As early as 1829, the Pequot minister William Apess demands rights for the poor by exhorting white Americans to imagine the colonial experience of Indian people: "Suppose an overwhelming army should march into the United States for the purpose of subduing it and enslaving the citizens; how quick would they fly to arms, gather in multitudes around the tree of liberty, and contend for their rights with the last drop of their blood. And should the enemy succeed, would they not eventually rise and endeavor to regain liberty? And who would blame them for it?" (1992, 31). At the dawn of Red Power, N. Scott Momaday famously declares: "Once in his life a man ought to concentrate his mind upon the remembered earth, I believe. He ought to give himself up to a particular landscape in his experience, to look at it from as many angles as he can, to wonder about it, to dwell upon it" (1979, 164). Robert Warrior announces: "Perhaps our greatest contribution as intellectuals is understanding our experience in wider contexts. In comparing our histories and our contemporary lives with those of other American Indian people, we see the complexities of our various pasts and have an opportunity to learn how other people have confronted the same problems we face" (1995, 123). Louis Owens (1998) struggles to ground his theories with the experiences of his own life. Craig Womack (1999) transforms Indian criticism with the mocking Mus-

kogee voices of Stijaati and Chebon. Critics such as Owens and Womack—
but also Elizabeth Cook-Lynn, Greg Sarris, and Gerald Vizenor—also write
novels, biographies, and autobiographies. The narrative experience enables
criticism otherwise impossible among postcolonial scholars. On such inno-
vation in Holocaust studies, see Blanchot 1995.

3. For this needed critique of essentialism in Native Studies, see Krupat 1996,
3–11.

4. For the cooperative role of religions in the 1969 Indian Ecumenical Confer-
ence to support the Indian movement, see Treat 2003. See also Batstone et
al. 1997.

5. Consider the feminist theoretical views of Luce Irigaray who claims that, unlike men, women share an erotic essence: "Woman's autoeroticism is very
different from man's. In order to touch himself, man needs an instrument:
his hand, a woman's body, language. . . . And this self-caressing requires
at least a minimum of activity. As for woman, she touches herself in and
of herself without any need for mediation, and before there is any way to
distinguish activity from passivity. Woman 'touches herself' all the time,
and moreover no one can forbid her to do so, for her genitals are formed of
two lips in continuous contact. Thus within herself, she is already two—but
not divisible into one(s)—that caress each other" (1985, 24). Diana Fuss
asks: "Why the essentialist language here? Why the relentless emphasis on
the two lips?" (1989, 1–6). Feminist theorist Toril Moi also challenges Irigaray for basing women's identity on a universally shared female experience
located in the female body, for seeking the impossible, a politics "without
. . . mediation": "Any attempt to formulate a general theory of femininity
will be metaphysical. This is precisely Irigaray's dilemma: having shown
that so far femininity has been produced exclusively in relation to the logic
of the Same, she falls for the temptation to produce her own positive theory
of femininity. But . . . to define 'woman' is necessarily to essentialize her"
(1985, 139). Fuss correctly announces that claims to experience are a theoretical affair that should be interrogated, but later, regrettably, she concludes
that because women cannot identify a universal experience that is not "itself
a product of ideological practices," experience is in the end "fundamentally
unreliable" (114). Some critics counter that experience is composed not only
of historical and social narratives but also mediated by social and linguistic
signification. For this reason, many suggest that experiences cannot accurately account for events in the world, and are thus epistemically unreliable.
Homi Bhabha (1990) presents this view of experience in the "splitting" of
the postcolonial subject: "In place of that 'I'—institutionalized in the visionary, authorial ideologies of *Eng. Lit.* or the notion of 'experience' in the empiricist accounts of slave history—there emerges the challenge to see what
is invisible, the look that cannot 'see me,' a certain problem of the object of
the gaze that constitutes a problematic referent for the language of the Self"
(190). See also Scott 1992. Cathy Caruth argues that knowledge of traumatic

experience cannot be fully produced but only "simultaneously defies and demands our witness" (1996, 5). She instead studies the language of trauma,
the mode of discourse that grapples to give voice to anguish somewhere
within "the complex relation between knowing and not knowing" (3). Scholars caution that while experience is imperfect, justice demands we give it
voice. The use of psychoanalysis in the study of trauma should not "become
a pretext for avoiding economic, social, and political issues," writes Dominick LaCapra (2001, ix). For a debate on experience, see Zammito 2000.

6. Jean-François Lyotard discounts the epistemological role of story in tribal,
"narrative" cultures and suggests that tribal knowledge is subordinate to
that of "scientific" cultures (1984, 19–21).

7. While rage is diffuse and unexamined, anger is directed and self-critical—it
is rage justified. Maori theorist Linda Tuhiwai Smith begins her interroga-
tion of colonialism in Native studies with this emotion: "It *angers* us when
practices linked to the last century, and the centuries before that, are still
employed to deny the validity of Indigenous peoples' claim to existence, to
land and territories, to the right of self-determination, to the survival of our
languages and forms of cultural knowledge, to our natural resources and
systems for living within our environments" (1999, 1; emphasis added). On
the role of intuition in science, see Kuhn 1996, 122–23.

8. Testimony empowers Native people by making public that which thrives on
secrecy. For this reason, I share my experiences. For autobiographical essays
by Native intellectuals, see Swann and Krupat 1987.

9. *Ceremony*'s accessible mythic structure has also led scholars such as Alan
Velie and Shamoon Zamir to believe that Silko actually relies on the European Grail mythology, though the author denies having knowledge of this
legend during the writing of her novel; see Velie 1982. According to Zamir:
"What is problematic about Silko's apparent resistance to such a globaliza-
tion of sacrificial mythology is that the overarching plot-form of her own
novel, from the dislocations of the 'wounded' hero in a drought-ridden land
to the inevitable climax of sacrifice, regeneration, and healing, is . . . nothing other than a Grail narrative" (1993, 405). But were Silko actually to have
adapted European mythology to her narrative, she would, in fact, be performing within the very Laguna mythic structure that organizes her novel
and that I describe in my introduction. See Susan Goldstein (2003, 245–45),
who also takes issue with Zamir. A few critics find that *Ceremony* also conforms to Christian allegory: see Copeland 1983, 171–72; and Gish 2001.

10. See Roemer 1999.

11. In fact, in Laguna symbolic geography the sunrise in the east is associated
with the color white, with white people and the "white smoke" of Tayo's
confusion. To recover, Tayo must travel north in the direction associated
with the color yellow, with yellow corn and Laguna personhood. For this
ethnographic information, see E. Swan 1988.

12. For other scholars supporting the dissolution of Indigenous borders, albeit perhaps only metaphorically, see Dunsmore 1997a; Hicks 1991, xxvi; Hobbs 1994; Owens 1998, 35; and Kaplan 1987, 195.

13. Per Seyersted, for example, contends that Betonie sings of this ominous invention of white witchery in a "serio-comic story" to "bring home the idea that [the Lagunas] can master their own fates" (1980, 29).

14. See Dunsmore 1997a; García 1983; Schweninger 1993; and Tarter 2002.

15. See, for example, Peacock 1998.

16. See P. Allen 1983, 132–33; Brice 1998, 130; and Herzog 1985, 33–34.

17. Critics often assert that Indian characters are "mixed" even when there is no evidence to support it. For example, Dennis Cutchins assumes that "Tayo comes to love and respect his Uncle Josiah, a mixed-blood Indian himself" (1999, 79). Nowhere does Ceremony suggest that Josiah is racially mixed. Lavonne Ruoff assumes that House Made of Dawn is "a mixed-blood's quest for a sense of place" (1990, 76). While Abel is likely a member of more than one tribe, little evidence suggests that he is also white. In addition, scholars also often assume that Indian authors themselves are mixed and thus identify them as mixedblood, though very few define themselves this way. Of the Native writers in this study, Betty Louise Bell, Joseph Bruchac, Diane Glancy, William Penn, and Gerald Vizenor identify as mixedblood. All other authors and a majority of scholars would probably take offense to being called a mixedblood. Such insistence that Indians are mixed might rely on a myth of American Indian racial purity.

18. Not very long ago and still today, those who were found to display physical features from both European and Native "races" were often shunned within the Anglo communities and popularized in nineteenth-century American dime novels. See H. Brown, 2004.

19. Traditionally, warriors returning from battle must be cleansed so that their destructive power does not affect the community. Kristin Herzog (1985) suggests Tayo calms his destructive (masculine) forces by becoming more feminine.

20. Marion Copeland is right that Tayo at first "misinterprets the meaning of memory, always a danger in visionary adventure. He assumes he must take his broken, scattered, tangled memories and, as he has once done with his grandmother's spool of thread, unknot them and rewind them on the appropriate spools. Such would be a neat linear solution to white psychiatrists at the hospital, of the world of his white father" (1983, 160–61).

21. Elaine Jahner notices that readers experience a special "energy" in experiencing Silko's novel as it transforms into a more Native form of storytelling (1979, 37). For a book-length study of this process through which Western readers of American Indian literature are transformed by the oral traditional reading experience, see Ruppert 1995. See also Piper 1997, 484.

22. Though the nonhuman world plays a central role in Ceremony's process of

discovery and transformation, in this analysis I focus on the decolonization of the human community. See Beidler 1979; Blumenthal 1990; and Harrod 2000.

23. While some knowledge maintained within tribal communities is available to those outside the community, a great deal of it is not—for spiritual knowledge has the power to do harm when in the wrong hands. See P. Allen 1990.

24. Alcoholism took and continues to take Native lives as well as land; see Prucha 1994, 95; Mancall 1995, 29. Some critics are insensitive regarding alcoholism in Native communities, as in what Nicholas Warner describes as "the superficial camaraderie of besotted cronies in a squalid bar" (1984, 19).

25. For a philosophical discussion of trust, see Baier 1995.

26. Betonie also helps Tayo with Indian humor when he teases him about witches, tucking his hair away so that Tayo cannot use it against him. On the therapeutic effects of laughter in *Ceremony*, see Evasdaughter 1988.

27. Tayo's path in life (where he has been, where he is headed) is both a real lived experience and a creative narrative act, with his challenge being to interpret his "life story" accurately. In this regard, Tayo's world as text is both documentary and what Heidegger calls "worklike." The absence of these distinctions in a tribal worldview encourages ongoing imaginative interactions with history. Noticing a similar collapse in Western intellectual history, Dominick LaCapra makes this point about interpreting art and life: "Indeed one of the recreative implications of reading might well be to attempt to create social and cultural conditions in which the literal conversation and the general text of life are more like the processes stimulated by an encounter with a great text" (1983, 51–52).

28. In reading of Tayo's lie, I am reminded of the self-colonizing lie that Vaclav Havel describes, a lie for which to persist it need not be believed but merely performed (1985, 31).

29. On the image of the Hunter in *Ceremony*, see Shapiro 2003.

30. See also David Moore, who sees in *Ceremony* "relationality without a center" (1993, 388–89).

4. Hearing the Callout

1. In his address to the Universidad Centroamericana, Noam Chomsky explains the U.S. aggression in Central America as a continuation of earlier colonialism begun by its founders. He begins by recognizing the Sullivan campaign through western New York in 1779 (1987, 12–13).

2. I taught at Auburn with my Tuscarora friend and colleague, Vera Palmer. The Auburn prisoners give me permission to share some of their writings, which appear in Teuton and Palmer 1999. In this narrative, I change the prisoners' names to protect their privacy. I also wish to be cautious about

serving stereotypes of imprisoned peoples of color; see Munro-Bjorklund 1991.

3. See Morris and Rothman 1995, 263–95; and Jennie Vander Wall 1992.

4. In 1817 Auburn became the first "lease prison," in which private business contracted with the government for prison labor. Because U.S. prisoners often work for less than two dollars per hour, we could argue that the purpose of this work is less to rehabilitate than to enslave. See Althusser 1971, 130–34.

5. Looking up at a wall of thousands of brown men's bodies, I have thought of the economic relations between the accumulation of the native and of native capital; see Lenin 1939, 62–63. A disproportionate number of men in prison are from minority groups. "There are so many more African Americans than whites in our prisons that the difference cannot be explained by higher crime among African Americans—racial discrimination is also at work. . . . [On] any given day, almost one in four black men (23 percent) and one in ten Hispanic men (10.4 percent) are in jail, in prison, on probation, or on parole, compared to one in sixteen white men (6.2 percent) in this age group [twenty to twenty-nine]" (Donziger 1996, 99, 221). Of all minority groups, however, American Indians are the most disproportionately incarcerated: "On any given day, one in 25 Indian adults is under the control of the criminal justice system—63,000 individuals. The number of Indians in state and federal prisons is 38 percent above the national average. In South Dakota, according to a report in 1991, Indians comprise 7 percent of the general population, but 25 percent of the prison population" (O'Brien 2000, 32).

6. On the physical effects of prison, see Ross 1998; and Foucault 1995 [1978], 29–30.

7. Many prisoners refuse to be commodified or fetishized by the outside like Leonard Peltier (1999). On Peltier, see Jim Vander Wall 1992. To understand the men's world, I draw on my experiences of criminality in my own family; see Howe 1994. Elaine Scarry makes a similar point about the resistance of pain to language (1985, 3–5).

8. The U.S. foreign policy of containing Native North America and so-called Latin America relies on containing the Native within a definition that serves colonialism. Edward Said shares a similar thesis on the West's containment of the East: "The Oriental is depicted as something one judges (as in a court of law), something one studies and depicts (as in a curriculum), something one disciplines (as in a school or prison), something one illustrates (as in a zoological manual). The point is that in all of these cases the Oriental is *contained* and *represented* by dominating frameworks" (1994 [1978], 40).

9. Many of Auburn's men draw on Red Power to persevere today. For historical background on American Indian activists imprisoned during Red Power, see Matthiessen 1983; and Sanchez, Stuckey, and Morris 1999. The continuity

of Native imprisonment with American Indian war history deserves further study. On military leaders whom the United States considered criminals, see, for example, Steele 1998.

10. Elizabeth Cook-Lynn defines anti-Indianism "as a form of discrimination and ideological bias in scholarship as well as in practical politics and mainstream thinking" (2001, 3).

11. For historical background on the execution of Moses Paul, Samson Occom's sermon, and Occom's eventual despair, see Blodgett 1935, 105–68; and Love 2000 [1899], esp. chapters 9 and 10.

12. We might redefine the term "intellectual" to suit an Indigenous worldview, perhaps in the way Donald Fixico defines Indian "genius": "A definition of native genius of Indigenous communities might appropriately be 'keepers of traditional knowledge who have insightful life experiences and who possess gifts of special insights to life, and whose actions benefit their people'" (2000b, 44).

13. Criticism is unavoidably "political" so long as power is part of cultural production. As Creek critic Jana Sequoya-Magdaleno explains: "At issue in that struggle . . . are the emergent institutional interests of Indian-identified cultural producers to define and control the signifier 'Indian'" (1995, 93). Fredric Jameson explores the problem of politics and criticism: "The artist himself is merely an instrument. . . . This is why our judgements on the individual work of art are ultimately social and historical in character. . . . The adequation of content to form . . . is in the long run one of the most precious indices to its realization in the historical moment itself, and indeed form is itself but the working out of content in the realm of the superstructure" (1971, 329).

14. As Theda Perdue comments: "Boudinot portrayed the Cherokees as a 'civilized' people in part because he believed their society was in the process of complete transformation but also because he knew that a charge of 'savagery' by whites might lead to their extermination" (1983, 21). On the diplomatic negotiation of Cherokee nationhood, see Konkle 2004, chapter 1.

15. On the Allotment Act, see Hoxie 1984.

16. The well-being of Native nations depends heavily on whether the federal government honors its treaties and commitments to protect the economic and social life of American Indian communities. This commitment oscillates through history depending on the era's presidential administration. For example, in the 1930s and 1940s, the FDR administration worked to restore tribal self-governance; in the 1950s, however, the Eisenhower administration dismantled the "Indian New Deal" and sought to "terminate" federal obligations to Native nations. On the history of termination and relocation, see Fixico (2000a) and Lobo and Peters (2001).

17. Marxist theories of criminality, for example, specify the role of historical forces in our definitions of criminal acts: "[Radical criminologists] . . . demand . . . that criminologists take account of the socially structured in-

equalities of wealth and power that shape human action" (Greenberg 1993, 6). Classic Marxism has been challenged by theorists who problematize often totalizing accounts of power and knowledge. On the concept of "hegemony" as a pervasive force that troubles plans for revolution, see Laclau and Mouffe 1985; and R. Williams 1977, 108–14.

18. Alfonso Ortiz also incurred criticism from his community for revealing protected Tewa religious knowledge.

19. Recall Karl Marx's famous eleventh thesis on Feuerbach: "The philosophers have only *interpreted* the world, in various ways; the point, however, is to *change* it" (1978, 145).

20. Cultural and political development, then, is conferred through the interaction and overlapping of Native social locations (Hau 2000, 138). Mao explains this engagement between intellectuals and "the people" and the resulting creative transformation with his concept of "contradiction." See Mao 1960, 6. Indeed, this task is most crucial to decolonization. In order to "re-Africanize," for example, some postcolonial scholars recommend that tribal intellectuals come home and experience "daily contact with the mass of the people and the communion of sacrifices which the struggle demand" (Cabral 1980, 145).

21. If social and historical forces construct "subjectivity," then it follows that we may change these conditions so new forms of selfhood may emerge. To meet this view of social change, ideology-producing institutions should be reformed. In a 1969 lecture, Noam Chomsky made this very demand of the American university: "It should loosen its 'institutional forms' . . . to permit a richer variety of work and study and experimentation, and should provide a home for the free intellectual, for the social critic, for the irreverent and radical thinking that is desperately needed if we are to escape the dismal reality that threatens to overwhelm us" (1973, 315). On the freeing of literary studies, see Davis 1997; and Miklitsch 1997. In American Indian studies, Elizabeth Cook-Lynn presents this view of political "transformation" by answering "the questions which must be asked of Native American novelists for appropriate nation centered theory to emerge from praxis" (1995, 50). On radicalizing Native studies, see Cook-Lynn 1995 and Stripes 1995.

22. In her review of Louise Erdrich's *Beet Queen*, Silko (1986) suggests that Erdrich is canonized because her fiction avoids colonial social realities in self-conscious language. See also Castillo 1991. On the need for a criticism based in the lived world of American Indians, see R. Warrior 1999, 50.

23. At a time when there existed only 500 million non-Indian people on the planet, the European invasion of the Americas reduced 72 million Indigenous people to 4 million, 6 percent of their former population, by 1890. See R. Thornton 1987. Many scholars describe this invasion as "contact" to emphasize a mutual interaction of these cultures, which historically was in fact the rare exception rather than the rule. On genocide in the Americas, see Jennings 1993.

24. Judith Butler's "politics of subversion," has been criticized by feminists for its limited view of women's agency as well as for its inability to identify which rules should be subverted. Martha Nussbaum (1999) asks Butler if women should subvert laws to protect their reproductive rights.

25. The debate on some of these issues that precede the publication of *The Invented Indian* is given in Churchill 1992, in which he confronts Sam Gill (187–213). Thomas Parkhill, a student of Gill's, tries to mediate this debate (1997, 1–16).

26. See, for example, the recent book by Louis Owens's former student, Elvira Pulitano (2003). For a critique of Pulitano, see S. Teuton 2006b.

27. While Donna Haraway suggests that people of Native cultures accept that trickery is an inherent part of inquiry (1991, 199), I argue that the American Indian oral tradition in fact protects a sophisticated notion of fallibility so that error may be located and prevented in the future.

28. American Indians often tell a different story of the settling of America; see Littlefield 1992 and A. Ortiz 1988. Native scholars have begun the call for an internally produced literary criticism derived from traditional oral models as well as from contemporary American Indian texts; see J. Armstrong 1993, Blaeser 1993, Buller 1980, and Womack 1999. Because we have yet to provide a strong theoretical justification for such a criticism, critics can discredit a culturally based methodology as separatist, monolithic, essentialist. I suggest we base our literature in the tribal realist theory of Indian knowledge, culture, identity, and experience that I advance in this study. A similar project succeeds in African American studies; see Gates 1988.

29. On the history of Western education to conquer and control Native people, see Creek historian Tsianina Lomawaima 1994; see also Noriega 1992. Native scholars of education suggest Indigenous models of learning. See Standing Rock Sioux scholar Karen Swisher and John Tippenconnic 1999.

30. J. L. Austin (1975) presents a similar view of the sociality of language, which he calls "performativity."

Conclusion

1. See Barreiro 1992; Johansen 1998; and the 1992 collection by Onondaga chief Oren Lyons and Seneca historian John Mohawk.

2. Michael Hames-García adapts his concepts of transparency and opacity from María C. Lugones's work on "transparent" versus "thick" group membership (1994, 474).

3. The Indian poverty rate is 25.3 percent compared to whites at 10.6 percent; see U.S. Census Bureau 2006b, 2. Indigenous health problems are often the highest nationally; see U.S. Centers for Disease Control and Prevention 2006, 2. Native suicide rates in the 15–24 age group are the highest nationally; see U.S. Centers for Disease Control and Prevention 2004, 2. Domestic violence is more common in Indian Country than in any other culture;

see U.S. Bureau of Justice 2004, 1. Drug abuse is highest among American Indians, at 10.6 percent, compared to 7.7 percent for blacks, for example; see U.S. Census Bureau 2006a, 1.

4. I must admit I feel a twinge of shame, then take offense, when confronted with the image of American Indian alcoholism in this early passage from *Reservation Blues*: "WalksAlong had raised his nephew since he was a toddler. Michael's mother had died of cirrhosis when he was just two years old, and he'd never even known his father. Michael was conceived during some anonymous three-in-the-morning powwow encounter in South Dakota. His mother's drinking had done obvious damage to Michael in the womb. He had those vaguely Asian eyes and the flat face that alcohol babies always had on reservations" (39). On reading this passage, a student fled my classroom in tears. Alexie's often-comic portrayal of Indian social ills marks a divergence from Red Power representations of Native social dysfunction.

5. J.D. continually and sadistically taunts Lucie, and when Lucie calls him "scum," J.D. strikes her face with his fist, drags her across the floor by her hair, and then declares: "'I'm gonna teach ya a lesson you ain't gonna forget. Now'n you shut up or I'm a-gonna make it hard on ya'" (68). J.D. then sexually assaults the child. J.D. "teaches" Lucie the lesson of women's submission to men and the silencing of men's violence, declaring, "'T'ain't nothing but Injun trash. Your momma's trash, and you're trash too'" (68). Like the other women in the novel, Lucie, at four years old, discovers that impoverished Indian women often have little choice but to suffer the abuses of men, actually changing their names as each man comes to possess them.

6. On Conley's great reception in present-day Cherokee communities, see C. Teuton 2008.

7. For an in-depth study of the roles of Cherokee women in the eighteenth and nineteenth centuries, see Perdue 1998, esp. part 1.

8. In fact, Native sexuality has historically influenced Western constructions of sexuality. See Trexler 1995, esp. chapter 7.

9. For background on Native models of sexuality and a third gender, see W. Williams 1992.

10. For a study of the U.S. legal domination of Native women, see Guerrero 1997, 110–15.

11. For background on southeastern worldviews, see Hudson 1994 [1976], chapter 3.

BIBLIOGRAPHY

||||||||||||||||||||||||||||||||||||||||||||||||||||||||||||||||||||||||||||||

Abram, David. 1999. "A More-Than-Human World." In *An Invitation to Envi-ronmental Philosophy*, edited by Anthony Weston, 17–42. New York: Oxford University Press.

Abrams, M. H. 1971. *A Glossary of Literary Terms*. New York: Holt, Rinehart, and Winston.

Ahmad, Aijaz. 1992. *In Theory: Classes, Nations, Literatures*. New York: Verso.

Aithal, S. K. 1985. "The Redemptive Return: Momaday's *House Made of Dawn*." *North Dakota Review* 53, no. 2: 160–72.

Alcoff, Linda Martín. 1991–92. "The Problem of Speaking for Others." *Cultural Critique* 20 (winter): 5–32.

Alexie, Sherman. 1995. *Reservation Blues*. New York: Atlantic Monthly.

Alfred, Taiaiake [Gerald R]. 1995. *Heeding the Voices of Our Ancestors: Kahnawake Mohawk Politics and the Rise of Native Nationalism*. New York: Oxford University Press.

Allen, Chadwick. 2002. *Blood Narrative: Indigenous Identity in American Indian and Maori Literary and Activist Texts*. Durham, N.C.: Duke University Press.

Allen, Paula Gunn. 1992. *The Sacred Hoop: Recovering the Feminine in American Indian Traditions*. Boston: Beacon.

———. 1990. "Special Problems in Teaching Leslie Marmon Silko's *Ceremony*." *American Indian Quarterly* 14: 379–86.

———. 1983. "The Feminine Landscape of Leslie Marmon Silko's *Ceremony*." In *Studies in American Indian Literature: Critical Essays and Course Designs*, edited by Paula Gunn Allen, 127–33. New York: Modern Language Association.

———. 1979. "Iyani: It Goes This Way." In *The Remembered Earth: An Anthology of Contemporary Native American Literature*, edited by Geary Hobson, 191–93. Albuquerque: University of New Mexico Press.

Althusser, Louis. 1971. *Lenin and Philosophy and Other Essays*, translated by Ben Brewster. New York: Monthly Review.

Amin, Samir. 1989. *Eurocentrism*, translated by Russell Moore. New York: Monthly Review.

Antell, Judith A. 1988. "Momaday, Welch, and Silko: Expressing the Feminine Principle through Male Alienation." *American Indian Quarterly* 12: 213–20.

Apess, William. 1992 [1829]. "A Son of the Forest." In *On Our Own Ground: The Complete Writings of William Apess, A Pequot*, edited by Barry O'Connell, 3–97. Amherst: University of Massachusetts Press.

Armstrong, Jeannette, ed. 1993. *Looking at the Words of our People: First Nations Analysis of Literature*. Penticton, B.C.: Theytus.

Armstrong, Meg. 1997. "'Buried in Fine White Ash': Violence and the Reimagination of Ceremonial Bodies in *Winter in the Blood* and *Bearheart*." *American Indian Quarterly* 21: 265–98.

Arnold, Ellen L. 1999. "An Ear for Story, and Eye for the Pattern: Rereading *Ceremony*." *Modern Fiction Studies* 45, no. 1: 69–92.

Ashcroft, Bill, Gareth Griffiths, and Helen Tiffin. 1989. *The Empire Writes Back: Theory and Practice in Post-Colonial Literatures*. New York: Routledge.

Astrov, Margot. 1950. "The Concept of Motion as the Psychological Leitmotif of Navaho Life and Literature." *Journal of American Folklore* 63: 45–56.

Austin, J. L. 1975. *How to Do Things with Words*. Cambridge: Harvard University Press.

Baier, Annette C. 1995. *Moral Prejudices: Essays on Ethics*. Cambridge, Mass.: Harvard University Press.

Barad, Karen. 1996. "Meeting the Universe Halfway: Realism and Social Constructivism without Contradiction." In *Feminism, Science, and the Philosophy of Science*, edited by Lynn Hankinson Nelson and Jack Nelson, 161–94. Dordrecht: Kluwer.

Barnett, Louise K. 1978. "Alienation and Ritual in *Winter in the Blood*." *American Indian Quarterly* 4: 123–30.

Barreiro, José, ed. 1992. *Indian Roots of American Democracy*. Ithaca, N.Y.: Akwe:kon.

———. 1984. "The Dilemma of American Indian Education." *Indian Studies* 1, no. 1: 4–5.

Barry, Nora Baker. 1978a. "The Bear's Son Folk Tale in *When the Legends Die* and *House Made of Dawn*." *Western American Literature* 12, no. 4: 275–87.

———. 1978b. "*Winter in the Blood* as Elegy." *American Indian Quarterly* 4: 149–57.

Bartelt, Guillermo. 1994. "American Indian English in Momaday's *House Made of Dawn*." *Language and Literature* 14: 37–53.

Basso, Keith H. 1996. *Wisdom Sits in Places: Landscape and Language among the Western Apache*. Albuquerque: University of New Mexico Press.

———. 1990. *Western Apache Language and Culture: Essays in Linguistic Anthropology*. Tucson: University of Arizona Press.

———. 1979. *Portraits of "the Whiteman": Linguistic Play and Cultural Symbols among the Western Apache*. New York: Cambridge University Press.

Batstone, David et al., eds. 1997. *Liberation Theologies, Postmodernity, and the Americas*. New York: Routledge.

Baudrillard, Jean. 1994. *Simulacra and Simulation*, translated by Sheila Faria Glaser. Ann Arbor: University of Michigan Press.

Beidler, Peter G. 1979. "Animals and Theme in *Ceremony*." *American Indian Quarterly* 5: 13–18.

Bell, Betty Louise. 1994. *Faces in the Moon*. Norman: University of Oklahoma Press.

———. 1992. "Almost the Whole Truth: Gerald Vizenor's Shadow-Working and Native American Autobiography." *A/B* 7, no. 2: 180–95.

Bell, Robert C. 1979. "Circular Design in *Ceremony*." *American Indian Quarterly* 5: 47–62.

Benjamin, Walter. 1969. "The Storyteller." In *Illuminations: Essays and Reflections*, edited by Hannah Arendt, translated by Harry Zohn, 83–109. New York: Schocken.

Bercovitch, Sacvan. 1978. *The American Jeremiad*. Madison: University of Wisconsin Press.

Berkhofer, Robert F. Jr. 1979. *The White Man's Indian: Images of the American Indian from Columbus to the Present*. New York: Vintage.

Bevis, William W. 1997. "James Welch." *Western American Literature* 32, no. 1: 33–53.

———. 1987. "Native American Novels: Homing In." In *Recovering the Word: Essays on Native American Literature*, edited by Brian Swann and Arnold Krupat, 580–620. Berkeley: University of California Press.

Bhabha, Homi. 1994. *The Location of Culture*. New York: Routledge.

———. 1990. "Interrogating Identity: The Postcolonial Prerogative." In *Anatomy of Racism*, edited by David Theo Goldberg, 183–209. Minneapolis: University of Minnesota Press.

Bird, Gloria. 1995. "The Exaggeration of Despair in Sherman Alexie's *Reservation Blues*." *Wicazo Sa Review* 10, no. 2: 47–52.

Black Elk. 1972 [1932]. *Black Elk Speaks*, edited by John G. Neihardt. Lincoln: University of Nebraska Press.

Blaeser, Kimberly M. 1996. *Gerald Vizenor: Writing in the Oral Tradition*. Norman: University of Oklahoma Press.

———. 1993. "Native Literature: Seeking a Critical Center." In *Looking at the Words of Our People: First Nations Analysis of Literature*, edited by Jeanette Armstrong, 51–62. Penticton, B.C.: Theytus.

Blanchot, Maurice. 1995. *The Writing of Disaster*, translated by Ann Smock. Lincoln: University of Nebraska Press.

Blodgett, Harold. 1935. *Samson Occom*. Hanover, N.H.: Dartmouth College Press.

Blumenthal, Susan. 1990. "Spotted Cattle and Deer: Spirit Guides and Symbols of Endurance and Healing in *Ceremony*." *American Indian Quarterly* 14: 367–77.

Bonnin, Gertrude [Zitkala-Sa]. 1985 [1921]. *American Indian Stories*. Lincoln: University of Nebraska Press.

Boudinot, Elias. 1983 [1826]. "An Address to the Whites." In *Cherokee Editor: The Writings of Elias Boudinot*, edited by Theda Perdue, 65–83. Athens: University of Georgia Press.

Brice, Jennifer. 1998. "Earth as Mother, Earth as Other in Novels by Silko and Hogan." *Critique* 39, no. 2: 127–38.

Brill de Ramírez, Susan Berry. 1999. *Contemporary American Indian Literatures and the Oral Tradition*. Tucson: University of Arizona Press.

Brown, Dee. 1970. *Bury My Heart at Wounded Knee: An Indian History of the American West*. New York: Bantam.

Brown, Harry J. 2004. *Injun' Joe's Ghost: The Indian Mixed-Blood in American Writing*. Columbia: University of Missouri Press.

Bruchac, Joseph. 1997. *Bowman's Store: A Journey to Myself*. New York: Dial.

Bruyneel, Kevin. 2000. "Politics on the Boundaries: The Post-Colonial Politics of Indigenous People." *Indigenous Nations Studies Journal* 1, no. 2: 73–94.

Buller, Galen. 1980. "New Interpretations of Native American Literature: A Survival Technique." *American Indian Culture and Research Journal* 4, no. 1–2: 165–77.

Burkhart, Brian Yazzie. 2004. "What Coyote and Thales Can Teach Us: An Outline of American Indian Epistemology." In *American Indian Thought*, edited by Anne Waters, 15–26. Oxford: Blackwell.

Butler, Judith. 1993. "Imitation and Gender Subordination." In *The Lesbian and Gay Studies Reader*, edited by Henry Abelove, Michéle Aina Barale, and David M. Halperin, 307–20. New York: Routledge.

———. 1990. *Gender Trouble: Feminism and the Subversion of Identity*. New York: Routledge.

Cabral, Amilcar. 1980. *Unity and Struggle*. London: Heinemann.

Carr, Helen. 1996. *Inventing the American Primitive: Politics, Gender and the Representation of Native American Literary Traditions, 1789–1936*. New York: New York University Press.

Caruth, Cathy. 1996. *Unclaimed Experience: Trauma, Narrative, and History*. Baltimore: Johns Hopkins University Press.

Castillo, Susan Perez. 1991. "Postmodernism, Native American Literature and the Real: The Silko-Erdrich Controversy." *Massachusetts Review* 32: 285–94.

Charles, Jim, and Richard Predmore. 1996. "When Critical Approaches Converge: Team-Teaching Welch's *Winter in the Blood*." *Studies in American Indian Literatures* 8, no. 2: 46–58.

Cheyfitz, Eric. 1991. *The Poetics of Imperialism: Translation and Colonization from "The Tempest" to "Tarzan."* New York: Oxford University Press.

Chomsky, Noam. 1987. *On Power and Ideology: The Managua Lectures*. Boston: South End.

———. 1973. *For Reasons of State*. New York: Pantheon.

Churchill, Ward. 1994. *Indians Are Us? Culture and Genocide in Native North America*. Monroe, Maine: Common Courage.

———. 1993. *Struggle for the Land: Indigenous Resistance to Genocide, Ecocide and Expropriation in Contemporary North America*. Monroe, Maine: Common Courage.

———. 1992. *Fantasies of the Master Race: Literature, Cinema and the Colonization of American Indians*, edited by M. Annette Jaimes. Monroe, Maine: Common Courage.

———. 1988. *Agents of Repression: The FBI's Secret Wars Against the Black Panther Party and the American Indian Movement*. Boston: South End.

Churchill, Ward, and Jim Vander Wall. 1990. *The COINTELPRO Papers: Documents from the FBI's Secret Wars Against Dissent in the United States*. Boston: South End.

Clements, William M. 1982. "Momaday's *House Made of Dawn*." *The Explicator* 41, no. 2: 60–62.

Clifford, James. 1988. *The Predicament of Culture: Twentieth-Century Ethnography, Literature, and Art*. Cambridge, Mass.: Harvard University Press.

Clifton, James A., ed. 1990. *The Invented Indian: Cultural Fictions and Government Policies*. New Brunswick, N.J.: Transaction.

Conley, Robert J. 1997. *War Woman: A Novel of the Real People*. New York: St. Martin's Griffin.

Cook-Lynn, Elizabeth. 2001. *Anti-Indianism in Modern America: A Voice from Tatekeya's Earth*. Urbana: University of Illinois Press.

———. 1997. "Who Stole Native American Studies?" *Wicazo Sa Review* 12, no. 1: 9–28.

———. 1996a. *Why I Can't Read Wallace Stegner and Other Essays: A Tribal Voice*. Madison: University of Wisconsin Press.

———. 1996b. "American Indian Intellectualism and the New Indian Story." *American Indian Quarterly* 20: 57–76.

———. 1995. "Literary and Political Questions of Transformation: American Indian Fiction Writers." *Wicazo Sa Review* 13, no. 1: 46–51.

Copeland, Marion W. 1983. "*Black Elk Speaks* and Leslie Silko's *Ceremony*: Two Visions of Horses." *Critique* 24, no. 3: 158–72.

Cornell, Stephen. 1988. *The Return of the Native: American Indian Political Resurgence*. New York: Oxford University Press.

Couser, G. Thomas. 1996. "Oppression and Repression: Personal and Collective Memory in Paule Marshall's *Praisesong for the Widow* and Leslie Marmon Silko's *Ceremony*." In *Memory and Cultural Politics: New Approaches to American Ethnic Literatures*, edited by Amritjit Singh, Joseph T. Skerrett Jr., and Robert E. Hogan, 106–20. Boston: Northeastern University Press.

Crashing Thunder. 1999 [1926]. *Crashing Thunder: The Autobiography of an American Indian*, edited by Paul Radin. Ann Arbor: University of Michigan Press.

Culler, Jonathan. 1982. *On Deconstruction: Theory and Criticism after Structuralism*. Ithaca, N.Y.: Cornell University Press.

Cutchins, Dennis. 1999. "'So That the Nations May Become Genuine Indian': Nativism and Leslie Marmon Silko's *Ceremony." Journal of American Culture* 22, no. 4: 77–89.

Davidson, Donald. 1984. "On the Very Idea of a Conceptual Scheme." In *Inquiries into Truth and Interpretation*, 183–98. Oxford: Clarendon.

Davis, Lennard J. 1997. "Forum." *Publications of the Modern Language Association of America* 112, no. 2: 258–59.

Deloria, Ella. 1998 [1944]. *Speaking of Indians*. Lincoln: University of Nebraska Press.

Deloria, Philip J. 1998. *Playing Indian*. New Haven, Conn.: Yale University Press.

———. 1996. "I Am of the Body: Thoughts on My Grandfather, Culture, and Sports." *South Atlantic Quarterly* 95, no. 2: 321–38.

Deloria, Vine Jr. 1995. *Red Earth, White Lies: Native Americans and the Myth of Scientific Fact*. New York: Scribner.

———. 1994 [1973]. *God Is Red: A Native View of Religion*. Golden, Colo.: Fulcrum.

———. 1988 [1969]. *Custer Died for Your Sins: An Indian Manifesto*, 1969. Norman: University of Oklahoma Press.

———. 1979. *The Metaphysics of Modern Existence*. New York: Harper and Row.

Derrida, Jacques. 1982. "Différance." In *Margins of Philosophy*, translated by Alan Bass, 1–27. Chicago: University of Chicago Press.

Domina, Lynn. 1994. "Liturgies, Rituals, Ceremonies: The Conjunction of Roman Catholic and Native American Religious Traditions in N. Scott Momaday's *House Made of Dawn." Paintbrush: A Journal of Contemporary Multicultural Literature* 21: 7–27.

Donaldson, Laura E. 1995. "Noah Meets Old Coyote, or Singing in the Rain: Intertextuality in Thomas King's *Green Grass, Running Water." Studies in American Indian Literatures* 7, no. 2: 27–43.

Donziger, Steven R., ed. 1996. *The Real War on Crime: The Report of the National Criminal Justice Commission*. New York: Harper.

Dozier, Edward P. 1970. *The Pueblo Indians of North America*. New York: Holt, Rinehart, and Winston.

Drinnon, Richard. 1980. *Facing West: The Metaphysics of Indian-Hating and Empire Building*. Norman: University of Oklahoma Press.

Dunsmore, Roger. 1997a. "No Boundaries: On Silko's *Ceremony." In Earth's Mind: Essays in Native Literature*, 15–32. Albuquerque: University of New Mexico Press.

———. 1997b. "Earth's Mind." In *Earth's Mind: Essays in Native Literature*, 37–54. Albuquerque: University of New Mexico Press.

Duran, Eduardo, and Bonnie Duran. 1995. *Native American Postcolonial Psychology*. Albany: State University of New York Press.

Eagleton, Terry. 1983. *Literary Theory: An Introduction*. Minneapolis: University of Minnesota Press.

Eastman, Charles Alexander. 1977 [1916]. *From the Deep Woods to Civilization*. Lincoln: University of Nebraska Press.

Eigner, Edwin M. 1978. *The Metaphysical Novel in England and America: Dickens, Bulwer, Melville, and Hawthorne*. Berkeley: University of California Press.

Ellis, Reuben. 1994. "Creating the Teller, Creating the Listener: The Reception and Uses of N. Scott Momaday and His Discourse on Narrative." *Paintbrush: A Journal of Contemporary Multicultural Literature* 21: 56–74.

Erdrich, Louise. 1987. *The Beet Queen*. New York: Bantam.

Evans, Stephen F. 2001. "'Open Containers': Sherman Alexie's Drunken Indians." *American Indian Quarterly* 25: 46–72.

Evasdaughter, Elizabeth N. 1988. "Leslie Marmon Silko's *Ceremony*: Healing Ethnic Hatred by Mixed-Breed Laughter." *MELUS* 15, no. 1: 83–95.

Evers, Lawrence J. 1985a. "Words and Place: A Reading of *House Made of Dawn*." In *Critical Essays on Native American Literature*, edited by Andrew Wiget, 211–30. Boston: G. K. Hall.

———. 1985b. "The Killing of a New Mexico State Trooper: Ways of Telling an Historical Event." In *Critical Essays on Native American Literature*, edited by Andrew Wiget, 246–61. Boston: G. K. Hall.

Evers, Lawrence J., and Dennis Carr. 1976. "A Conversation with Leslie Marmon Silko." *Sun Tracks* 3, no. 1: 28–33.

Ewers, John C. 1958. *The Blackfeet: Raiders of the Northwestern Plains*. Norman: University of Oklahoma Press.

Fanon, Frantz. 1963. *The Wretched of the Earth*, translated by Constance Farrington. New York: Grove.

Farrer, Claire R. 1994. *Thunder Rides a Black Horse: Mescalero Apaches and the Mythic Present*. Prospect Heights, Ill.: Waveland.

Fey, Harold E., and D'Arcy McNickle. 1970 [1959]. *Indians and Other Americans: Two Ways of Life Meet*. New York: Perennial/Harper and Row.

Fisher, Philip. 1988. "Democratic Social Space: Whitman, Melville, and the Promise of American Transparency." *Representations* 24: 60–101.

Fixico, Donald L. 2003. *The American Indian Mind in a Linear World: American Indian Studies and Traditional Knowledge*. New York: Routledge.

———. 2000a. *The Urban Indian Experience in America*. Albuquerque: University of New Mexico Press.

———. 2000b. "Call for Native Genius and Indigenous Intellectualism." *Indigenous Nations Studies Journal* 1, no. 1: 43–59.

———. 1998. *The Invasion of Indian Country in the Twentieth Century: American Capitalism and Tribal Natural Resources*. Boulder: University of Colorado Press.

Forbes, Jack D. 1995. "The Use of Racial and Ethnic Terms in America: Management and Manipulation." *Wicazo Sa Review* 11, no. 2: 53–65.

Foucault, Michel. 1995 [1978]. *Discipline and Punish: The Birth of the Prison*, translated by Alan Sheridan. New York: Vintage.

Freire, Paulo. 1989. *Pedagogy of the Oppressed*, translated by Myra Bergman Ramos. New York: Continuum.

Fuss, Diana. 1989. *Essentially Speaking: Feminism, Nature, and Difference*. New York: Routledge.

Gadamer, Hans-Georg. 1998. *Truth and Method*, revised and translated by Joel Weinsheimer and Donald G. Marshall. New York: Continuum.

García, Reyes. 1983. "Senses of Place in *Ceremony*." MELUS 10, no. 4: 37–48.

Gates, Henry Louis Jr. 1988. *The Signifying Monkey: A Theory of African American Literary Criticism*. New York: Oxford University Press.

Gilroy, Paul. 1993. *The Black Atlantic: Modernity and Double Consciousness*. Cambridge, Mass.: Harvard University Press.

Gish, Robert F. 2001. "Voices from Bear Country: Leslie Silko's Allegories of Creation." FEMSPEC 2, no. 2: 48–55.

Glancy, Diane. 1997. "Who Can Speak as an Indian?" In *The West Pole*, 7–10. Minneapolis: University of Minnesota Press.

Goldstein, Susan Coleman. 2003. "Silko's *Ceremony*." *The Explicator* 61, no. 4: 245–48.

Gramsci, Antonio. 1971. *Selections from the Prison Notebooks of Antonio Gramsci*, edited and translated by Quintin Hoare and Geoffrey Nowell Smith. New York: International.

Green, Michael K., ed. 1995. *Issues in Native American Cultural Identity*. New York: Lang.

Greenberg, David F., ed. 1993. *Crime and Capitalism: Readings in Marxist Criminology*. Philadelphia: Temple University Press.

Grinde, Donald A., and Bruce E. Johansen. 1995. *Ecocide of Native America: Environmental Destruction of Indian Lands and Peoples*. Santa Fe, N.M.: Clear Light.

Grinnell, George Bird. 1920. *Blackfoot Lodge Tales*. New York: Charles Scribner's Sons.

Grounds, Richard A., George E. Tinker, and David E. Wilkins, eds. 2003. *Native Voices: American Indian Identity and Resistance*. Lawrence: University of Kansas Press.

Guerrero, Marie Anne Jaimes. 1997. "Civil Rights verus Sovereignty: Native American Women in Life and Land Struggles." In *Feminist Genealogies, Colonial Legacies, Democratic Futures*, edited by M. Jacqui Alexander and Chandra Talpade Mohanty, 101–21. New York: Routledge.

——— [M. Annette Jaimes], ed. 1992a. *The State of Native America: Genocide, Colonization, and Resistance*. Boston: South End.

———. 1992b. "Federal Indian Identification Policy: A Usurpation of Indigenous Sovereignty in North America." In *The State of Native America: Genocide, Colonization, and Resistance*, edited by M. Annette Jaimes, 123–38. Boston: South End.

———. 1987. "American Indian Studies: Toward an Indigenous Model." *American Indian Culture and Research Journal* 11, no. 3: 1–16.

Hale, Janet Campbell. 1985. *The Jailing of Cecelia Capture*. Albuquerque: University of New Mexico Press.

Hames-García, Michael R. 2004. *Fugitive Thought: Prison Movements, Race, and the Meaning of Justice*. Minneapolis: University of Minnesota Press.

———. 2000. "'Who Are Our Own People?' Challenges for a Theory of Social Identity." In *Reclaiming Identity: Realist Theory and the Predicament of Postmodernism*, edited by Paula M. L. Moya and Michael R. Hames-García, 102–29. Berkeley: University of California Press.

Hanson, Jeffrey R. 1997. "Ethnicity and the Looking Glass: The Dialectics of National Indian Identity." *American Indian Quarterly* 21: 195–208.

Haraway, Donna. 1991. "Situated Knowledges: The Science Question in Feminism and the Privilege of Partial Perspective." In *Simians, Cyborgs, and Women*, 183–201. New York: Routledge.

Harding, Sandra. 1991. *Whose Science? Whose Knowledge? Thinking from Women's Lives*. Ithaca, N.Y.: Cornell University Press.

Harkin, Michael E. 2000. "Sacred Places, Scarred Spaces." *Wicazo Sa Review* 15, no. 1: 49–70.

Harlow, Barbara. 1992. *Barred: Women, Writing, and Political Detention*. Hanover, N.H.: Wesleyan University Press.

Harrod, Howard I. 2000. *The Animals Came Dancing: Native American Sacred Ecology and Animal Kinship*. Tucson: University of Arizona Press.

Harvey, David. 1989. *The Condition of Postmodernity: An Inquiry into the Origins of Cultural Change*. Cambridge: Basil Blackwell.

Hau, Caroline S. 2000. "On Representing Others: Intellectuals, Pedagogy, and the Uses of Error." In *Reclaiming Identity: Realist Theory and the Predicament of Postmodernism*, edited by Paula M. L. Moya and Michael R. Hames-García, 133–70. Berkeley: University of California Press.

Havel, Vaclav. 1985. "The Power of the Powerless." In *Citizens Against the State in Central Eastern Europe*, edited by John Keane, 23–95. Armonk, N.Y.: M. E. Sharpe.

Hegel, G. W. F. 1931. *The Phenomenology of Mind*, revised and translated by J. B. Baillie. New York: Harper and Row.

Hertzberg, Hazel. 1971. *The Search for an American Indian Identity: Modern Pan-Indian Movements*. Syracuse, N.Y.: Syracuse University Press.

Herzog, Kristin. 1985. "Thinking Woman and Feeling Man: Gender in Silko's *Ceremony*." *MELUS* 12, no. 1: 25–36.

Hicks, Emily D. 1991. *Border Writing: The Multidimensional Text*. Minneapolis: University of Minnesota Press.

Hirsch, Bernard A. 1983. "Self-Hatred and Spiritual Corruption in *House Made of Dawn*." *Western American Literature* 17, no. 4: 307–20.

Hobbs, Michael. 1994. "Living In-Between: Tayo as Radical Reader in Leslie Marmon Silko's *Ceremony*." *Western American Literature* 28, no. 4: 301–12.

Hokanson, Robert O'Brien. 1997. "Crossing Cultural Boundaries with Leslie Marmon Silko's *Ceremony.*" In *Rethinking American Literature*, edited by Lil Brannon and Brenda M. Greene, 115–27. Urbana, Ill.: National Council of Teachers of English.

hooks, bell. 1994. *Teaching to Transgress: Education as the Practice of Freedom.* New York: Routledge.

Horkheimer, Max, and Theodor W. Adorno. 1972 [1944]. *Dialectic of Enlightenment*, translated by John Cumming. New York: Herder and Herder.

Horton, Andrew. 1978. "The Bitter Humor of *Winter in the Blood.*" *American Indian Quarterly* 4: 131–39.

Howe, Adrian. 1994. *Punish and Critique: Towards a Feminist Analysis of Penality.* New York: Routledge.

Hoxie, Frederick E. 1984. *A Final Promise: The Campaign to Assimilate the Indians, 1880–1920.* Lincoln: University of Nebraska Press.

Hudson, Charles. 1994 [1976]. *The Southeastern Indians.* Knoxville: University of Tennessee Press.

Hughes, Langston. 1994. "The Negro Speaks in Rivers." In *The Collected Poems of Langston Hughes*, edited by Arnold Rampersad, 23. New York: Vintage.

Huhndorf, Shari M. 2001. *Going Native: Indians in the American Cultural Imagination.* Ithaca, N.Y.: Cornell University Press.

Hylton, Marion Willard. 1972. "On a Trail of Pollen: Momaday's *House Made of Dawn.*" *Critique* 14, no. 2: 60–69.

Hymes, Dell. 1981. *"In vain I tried to tell you": Essays in Native American Ethnopoetics.* Philadelphia: University of Pennsylvania Press.

Irigaray, Luce. 1985 [1977]. *This Sex Which Is Not One*, translated by Catherine Porter with Carolyn Burke. Ithaca, N.Y.: Cornell University Press.

Jahner, Elaine. 1979. "An Act of Attention: Event Structure in *Ceremony.*" *American Indian Quarterly* 5: 37–46.

Jameson, Fredric. 1971. *Marxism and Form: Twentieth-Century Dialectical Theories of Literature.* Princeton, N.J.: Princeton University Press.

Jennings, Francis. 1993. *The Founders of America.* New York: Norton.

Johansen, Bruce E. 1998. *Debating Democracy: Native American Legacy of Freedom.* Santa Fe, N.M.: Clear Light.

Johnson, Troy R. 1996. *The Occupation of Alcatraz Island: Indian Self-Determination and the Rise of Indian Activism.* Urbana: University of Illinois Press.

Johnson, Troy R., Joane Nagel, and Duane Champagne, eds. 1997. *American Indian Activism: Alcatraz to the Longest Walk.* Urbana: University of Illinois Press.

Johnston, Basil. 1995. *The Manitous: The Spiritual World of the Ojibway.* New York: Harper.

Josephy, Alvin M. Jr., Joane Nagel, and Troy Johnson, eds. 1999 [1971]. *Red Power: The American Indians' Fight for Freedom*, revised edition. Lincoln: University of Nebraska Press.

Justice, Daniel Heath. 2001. "We're Not There Yet, Kemo Sabe: Positing a Future for American Indian Literary Studies." *American Indian Quarterly* 25: 256–69.

Kaplan, Caren. 1987. "Deterritorializations: The Rewriting of Home and Exile in Western Feminist Discourse." *Cultural Critique* 6: 187–98.

Kerr, Baine. 1978. "The Novel as Sacred Text: N. Scott Momaday's Myth-Making Ethic." *Southwest Review* 63, no. 2: 172–79.

King, Tom. 1990. "Godzilla vs. Post-Colonial." *World Literature Written in English* 30, no. 2: 10–16.

———. 1983. "A MELUS Interview: N. Scott Momaday—Literature and the Native Writer." *MELUS* 10, no. 4: 66–72.

Kluckhohn, Clyde, and Dorothea Leighton. 1974 [1946]. *The Navaho.* Cambridge, Mass.: Harvard University Press.

Kohák, Erazim. 2000. *The Green Halo: A Bird's Eye View of Ecological Ethics.* Chicago: Open Court.

Konkle, Maureen. 2004. *Writing Indian Nations: Native Intellectuals and the Politics of Historiography, 1827–1863.* Chapel Hill: University of North Carolina Press.

Kroeber, Karl. 1998. *Artistry in Native American Myths.* Lincoln: University of Nebraska Press.

———. 1993. "Technology and Tribal Narrative." In *Narrative Chance: Postmodern Discourse on Native American Indian Literatures,* edited by Gerald Vizenor, 17–37. Norman: University of Oklahoma Press.

Krupat, Arnold. 2002. *Red Matters: Native American Studies.* Philadelphia: University of Pennsylvania Press.

———. 1996. *The Turn to the Native: Studies in Criticism and Culture.* Lincoln: University of Nebraska Press.

———. 1989. *The Voice in the Margin: Native American Literature and the Canon.* Berkeley: University of California Press.

Kuhn, Thomas S. 1996 [1962]. *The Structure of Scientific Revolutions.* Chicago: University of Chicago Press.

LaCapra, Dominick. 2006. "Experience and Identity." In *Identity Politics Reconsidered,* edited by Linda Martín Alcoff et al., 228–45. New York: Palgrave.

———. 2001. *Writing History, Writing Trauma.* Baltimore: Johns Hopkins University Press.

———. 1983. *Rethinking Intellectual History: Texts, Contexts, and Language.* Ithaca, N.Y.: Cornell University Press.

Laclau, Ernesto, and Chantal Mouffe. 1985. *Hegemony and Socialist Strategy: Toward a Radical Democratic Politics.* New York: Verso.

LaDuke, Winona. 1999. *All Our Relations: Native Struggles for Land and Life.* Boston: South End.

Landrum, Larry. 1996. "The Shattered Modernism of Momaday's *House Made of Dawn.*" *Modern Fiction Studies* 42: 763–86.

Larson, Charles. 1978. *American Indian Fiction*. Albuquerque: University of New Mexico Press.

LaVaque-Manty, Danielle. 2000. "There Are Indians in the Museum of Natural History." *Wicazo Sa Review* 15, no. 1: 71–89.

Lenin, V. I. 1939. *Imperialism: The Highest Stage of Capitalism*. New York: International Publishers.

Levine, Frances. 1999. *Our Prayers Are in This Place: Pecos Pueblo Identity over the Centuries*. Albuquerque: University of New Mexico Press.

Lewis, Philip. 1992. "The Post-Structuralist Condition." *Diacritics* 12: 2–24.

Lincoln, Kenneth. 1983. *Native American Renaissance*. Berkeley: University of California Press.

Littlefield, Daniel F. Jr. 1992. "American Indians, American Scholars and the American Literary Canon." *American Studies* 33, no. 2: 95–111.

Lobo, Susan, and Kurt Peters, eds. 2001. *American Indians and the Urban Experience*. Walnut Creek, Calif.: Alta Mira.

Lomawaima, K. Tsianina. 1994. *They Called It Prairie Light: The Story of Chilocco Indian School*. Lincoln: University of Nebraska Press.

Lopez, Barry. 1984. "Story at Anaktuvuk Pass." *Harpers* 269, no. 1615: 49–51.

Lorde, Audre. 1984. *Sister Outsider: Essays and Speeches*. Trumansburg, N.Y.: The Crossing.

Love, W. DeLoss. 2000 [1899]. *Samson Occom and the Christian Indians of New England*. Syracuse, N.Y.: Syracuse University Press.

Lugones, María C. 1994. "Purity, Impurity, and Separation." *Signs* 19, no. 21: 458–79.

Lyons, Oren, and John Mohawk, eds. 1992. *Exiled in the Land of the Free: Democracy, Indian Nations, and the U.S. Constitution*. Santa Fe, N.M.: Clear Light.

Lyotard, Jean-François. 1984. *The Postmodern Condition: A Report on Knowledge*, translated by Geoff Bennington and Brian Massumi. Minneapolis: University of Minnesota Press.

MacLeish, William H. 1994. *The Day Before America: Changing the Nature of a Continent*. Boston: Houghton Mifflin.

Maddox, Lucy. 2005. *Citizen Indians: Native American Intellectuals, Race, and Reform*. Ithaca, N.Y.: Cornell University Press.

Mancall, Peter C. 1995. *Deadly Medicine: Indians and Alcohol in Early America*. Ithaca, N.Y.: Cornell University Press.

Manyarrows, Victoria Lena. 1993. "Native Women/Native Survival": A Review of Janet Campbell Hale's *The Jailing of Cecelia Capture*." In *Looking at the Words of Our People: First Nations Analysis of Literature*, edited by Jeannette Armstrong, 152–60. Penticton, B.C.: Theytus.

Mao Tse-Tung. 1960. *On Contradiction*. Peking: Foreign Languages.

Marx, Karl. 1978. "Theses on Feuerbach." In *The Marx-Engels Reader*, revised and edited by Robert C. Tucker, 143–45. New York: Norton.

Mathews, John Joseph. 1988 [1934]. *Sundown*. Norman: University of Oklahoma Press.

————. 1981a [1945]. *Talking to the Moon: Wildlife Adventures on the Prairies of Osage Country*. Norman: University of Oklahoma Press.

————. 1981b [1932]. *Wah'Kon-Tah: The Osage and the White Man's Road*. Norman: University of Oklahoma Press.

Matthews, Washington. 1995 [1902]. *The Night Chant: A Navaho Ceremony*. Salt Lake City: University of Utah Press.

Matthiessen, Peter. 1983. *In the Spirit of Crazy Horse*. New York: Viking.

McFarland, Ron. 1993. "'The End' in James Welch's Novels." *American Indian Quarterly* 17: 319–27.

McGhee, Joanna Jones. 1937. "Interview with Nannie Lee Burns." In *Works Progress Administration: Indian-Pioneer History Project for Oklahoma*, directed by Grant Foreman. Miami, Okla.: Oklahoma Historical Society.

McLeod, Neal. 1998. "Indians and Open-Ended Political Rationality." *Wicazo Sa Review* 13, no. 1: 53–71.

McNickle, D'Arcy. 1988 [1978]. *Wind from an Enemy Sky*. Albuquerque: University of New Mexico Press.

————. 1978 [1936]. *The Surrounded*. Albuquerque: University of New Mexico Press.

Michaels, Walter Benn. 1998. "Autobiography of an Ex-White Man: Why Race Is Not a Social Construction." *Transition* 7, no. 1: 122–43.

Mihesuah, Devon A. 1998. "American Indian Identities: Issues of Individual Choices and Development." *American Indian Culture and Research Journal* 22, no. 2: 193–226.

Miklitsch, Robert. 1997. "Forum." *Publications of the Modern Language Association of America* 112, no. 2: 257–58.

Mohanty, Satya P. 1997. *Literary Theory and the Claims of History: Postmodernism, Objectivity, Multicultural Politics*. Ithaca, N.Y.: Cornell University Press.

————. 1989. "Us and Them: On the Philosophical Bases of Political Criticism." *Yale Journal of Criticism* 2, no. 2: 1–31.

Moi, Toril. 1985. *Sexual/Textual Politics: Feminist Literary Theory*. New York: Methuen.

Momaday, N. Scott. 1997. *The Man Made of Words: Essays, Stories, Passages*. New York: St. Martin's Press.

————. 1991 [1969]. *The Way to Rainy Mountain*. Albuquerque: University of New Mexico Press.

————. 1989 [1968]. *House Made of Dawn*. New York: Perennial-Harper.

————. 1979 [1970]. "The Man Made of Words." In *The Remembered Earth: An Anthology of Contemporary Native American Literature*, edited by Geary Hobson, 162–73. Albuquerque: University New Mexico Press.

————. 1976. *The Names: A Memoir*. Tucson: University of Arizona Press.

————. 1973. "An Interview with N. Scott Momaday." *Puerto del Sol* 12: 5–10.

Moore, David L. 1993. "Myth, History, and Identity in Silko and Young Bear: Postcolonial Praxis." In *New Voices in Native American Literary Criticism*, edited by Arnold Krupat, 370–95. Washington, D.C.: Smithsonian Institution Press.

Morris, Irvin. 1997. *From the Glittering World: A Navajo Story.* Norman: University of Oklahoma Press.

Morris, Norval, and David J. Rothman, eds. 1995. *The Oxford History of the Prison: The Practice of Punishment in Western Society.* New York: Oxford University Press.

Moya, Paula M. L. 2002. *Learning from Experience: Minority Identities, Multicultural Struggles.* Berkeley: University of California Press.

———. 1997. "Postmodernism, 'Realism,' and the Politics of Identity: Cherríe Moraga and Chicana Feminism." In *Feminist Genealogies, Colonial Legacies, Democratic Futures,* edited by M. Jacqui Alexander and Chandra Talpade Mohanty, 125–50. New York: Routledge.

Moya, Paula M. L., and Michael R. Hames-García, eds. 2000. *Reclaiming Identity: Realist Theory and the Predicament of Postmodernism.* Berkeley: University of California Press.

Munro-Bjorklund, Vicky. 1991. "Popular Cultural Images of Criminals and Prisoners since Attica." *Social Justice: A Journal of Crime, Conflict, and World Order* 18, no. 3: 48–70.

Murdoch, Iris. 1993. *Metaphysics as a Guide to Morals.* New York: Penguin.

Nabokov, Peter. 1981. *Indian Running: Native American History and Tradition.* Santa Fe, N.M.: Ancient City.

Nagel, Joane. 1996. *American Indian Ethnic Renewal: Red Power and the Resurgence of Identity and Culture.* New York: Oxford University Press.

Nelson, Emmanuel. 1997. "Fourth World Fictions: A Comparative Commentary on James Welch's *Winter in the Blood* and Mudrooroo Narogin's *Wild Cat Falling.*" In *Critical Perspectives on Native American Fiction,* edited by Richard F. Fleck, 57–63. Pueblo, Colo.: Passeggiata.

Nelson, Robert M. 1993. *Place and Vision: The Function of Landscape in Native American Fiction.* New York: Peter Lang.

Ngugi, wa Thiong'o. 1986. *Decolonizing the Mind: The Politics of Language in African Literature.* London: James Currey.

Nietzsche, Friedrich. 1967. *The Will to Power,* translated by Walter Kaufmann and R. J. Hollingdale. New York: Vintage.

———. 1956. *The Birth of Tragedy and The Genealogy of Morals,* translated by Francis Golffing. New York: Anchor.

Noriega, Jorge. 1992. "American Indian Education in the United States: Indoctrination for Subordination to Colonialism." In *The State of Native America: Genocide, Colonization, and Resistance,* edited by M. Annette Jaimes, 371–402. Boston: South End.

Nussbaum, Martha C. 1999. "The Professor of Parody." *The New Republic* (22 February): 37–45.

Oandasan, William. 1997. "A Familiar Component of Love in *Ceremony.*" In *Criti-*

cal Perspectives on Native American Fiction, edited by Richard F. Fleck, 240–45. Pueblo, Colo.: Passeggiata.

O'Brien, Sharon. 2000. "The Struggle to Protect the Exercise of Native Prisoners' Religious Rights." *Indigenous Nations Studies Journal* 1, no. 2: 29–49.

Occom, Samson. 1987 [1772]. "A Sermon, Preached at the Execution of Moses Paul, an Indian." In *The Harper American Literature*, edited by Donald McQuade et al., vol. 1, 472–80. New York: Harper and Row.

Oleson, Carole. 1973. "The Remembered Earth: Momaday's *House Made of Dawn*." *South Dakota Review* 11, no. 1: 59–78.

O'Nell, Theresa DeLeane. 1996. *Disciplined Hearts: History, Identity, and Depression in an American Indian Community*. Berkeley: University of California Press.

Ong, Walter J. 1982. *Orality and Literacy: The Technology of the Word*. New York: Routledge.

Ortiz, Alfonso. 1988. "Indian/White Relations: A View from the Other Side of the 'Frontier.'" In *Indians in American History: An Introduction*, edited by Frederick E. Hoxie and Peter Iverson, 1–16. Wheeling, Ill.: Harlan Davidson.

———. 1972. "Ritual Drama and the Pueblo World View." In *New Perspectives on the Pueblos*, edited by Alfonso Ortiz, 135–61. Albuquerque: University of New Mexico Press.

———. 1969. *The Tewa World: Space, Time, Being, and Becoming in a Pueblo Society*. Chicago: University of Chicago Press.

Ortiz, Roxanne Dunbar. 1984. "The Fourth World and Indigenism: Politics of Isolation and Alternatives." *Journal of Ethnic Studies* 12, no. 1: 79–105.

Ortiz, Simon J. 1992 [1976]. *Going for the Rain*. In *Woven Stone*, 35–147. Tucson: University of Arizona Press.

———. 1981a. *From Sand Creek*. Oak Park, Ill.: Thunder's Mouth.

———. 1981b. "Towards a National Indian Literature: Cultural Authenticity in Nationalism." *MELUS* 8, no. 2: 7–13.

Owens, Louis. 1998. *Mixedblood Messages: Literature, Film, Family, Place*. Norman: University of Oklahoma Press.

———. 1992. *Other Destinies: Understanding the American Indian Novel*. Norman: University of Oklahoma Press.

Oxendine, Joseph B. 1995. *American Indian Sports Heritage*. Lincoln: University of Nebraska Press.

Palmer, Gus Jr. 2003. *Telling Stories the Kiowa Way*. Tucson: University of Arizona Press.

Parker, Robert Dale. 2003. *The Invention of Native American Literature*. Ithaca, N.Y.: Cornell University Press.

Parkhill, Thomas C. 1997. *Weaving Ourselves into the Land: Charles Godfrey Leland, "Indians," and the Study of Native American Religions*. Albany: State University of New York Press.

Parsons, Elsie Clews. 1939. *Pueblo Indian Religion*, 2 vols. Chicago: University of Chicago Press.

Peacock, John. 1998. "Unwriting Empire by Writing Oral Tradition: Leslie Marmon Silko's *Ceremony*." In *(Un)Writing Empire*, edited by Theo D'haen, 295–308. Amsterdam: Cross/Cultures.

Pearce, Roy Harvey. 1977 [1953]. *Savagism and Civilization: A Study of the American Indian and the American Mind*. Baltimore: Johns Hopkins University Press.

Peirce, Charles S. 1955. *Philosophical Writings of Peirce*, edited by Justus Buchler. New York: Dover.

Peltier, Leonard. 1999. *Prison Writings: My Life Is My Sundance*, with Harvey Arden. New York: St. Martin's Griffin.

Penn, William S., ed. 1997. *As We Are Now: Mixblood Essays on Race and Identity*. Berkeley: University of California Press.

———. 1995. *All My Sins Are Relatives*. Lincoln: University of Nebraska Press.

Perdue, Theda. 1998. *Cherokee Women: Gender and Cultural Change, 1700–1835*. Lincoln: University of Nebraska Press.

———, ed. 1983. *Cherokee Editor: The Writings of Elias Boudinot*. Athens: University of Georgia Press.

Piper, Karen. 1997. "Police Zones: Territory and Identity in Leslie Marmon Silko's *Ceremony*." *American Indian Quarterly* 21: 483–97.

Porter, Tom. 1992. "Men Who Are of the Good Mind." In *Indian Roots of American Democracy*, edited by José Barreiro, 12–19. Ithaca, N.Y.: Akwe:kon.

Posey, Alexander. 1993. *The Fus Fixico Letters*, edited by Daniel F. Littlefield Jr. and Carol A. Petty Hunter. Lincoln: University of Nebraska Press.

Pratt, Mary Louise. 1992. *Imperial Eyes: Travel Writing and Transculturation*. New York: Routledge.

Pretty Shield. 1972 [1932]. *Pretty Shield: Medicine Woman of the Crows*, edited by Frank B. Linderman. Lincoln: University of Nebraska Press.

Prucha, Francis Paul. 1994. *American Indian Treaties: The History of a Political Anomaly*. Berkeley: University of California Press.

Pulitano, Elvira. 2003. *Toward a Native American Critical Theory*. Lincoln: University of Nebraska Press.

Purdy, John. 1990. "'He Was Going Along': Motion in the Novels of James Welch." *American Indian Quarterly* 14: 133–45.

Putnam, Hilary. 1981. *Reason, Truth, and History*. New York: Cambridge University Press.

Quine, W. V. O. 1969. *Ontological Relativity and Other Essays*. New York: Columbia University Press.

Ramsey, Jarold. 1999. *Reading the Fire: The Traditional Indian Literatures of America*. Seattle: University of Washington Press.

Rand, Naomi R. 1995. "Surviving What Haunts You: The Art of Invisibility in *Ceremony*, *The Ghost Writer*, and *Beloved*." *MELUS* 20, no. 3: 21–32.

Raymond, Michael W. 1983. "Tai-Me, Christ, and the Machine: Affirmation through Mythic Pluralism in *House Made of Dawn.*" *Studies in American Fiction* 11: 61–71.

Roemer, Kenneth M. 1999. "Silko's Arroyos as Mainstream: Processes and Implications of Canonical Identity." *Modern Fiction Studies* 45, no. 1: 10–37.

Rorty, Richard. 1979. *Philosophy and the Mirror of Nature.* Princeton, N.J.: Princeton University Press.

Rosaldo, Renato. 1989. *Culture and Truth: The Remaking of Social Analysis.* Boston: Beacon.

Ross, Luana. 1998. *Inventing the Savage: The Social Construction of Native American Criminality.* Austin: University of Texas Press.

Ruoff, A. LaVonne Brown. 1990. *American Indian Literatures: An Introduction, Bibliographic Review, and Selected Bibliography.* New York: Modern Language Association.

———. 1978a. "Alienation and the Female Principle in *Winter in the Blood.*" *American Indian Quarterly* 4: 107–22.

———. 1978b. "History in *Winter in the Blood*: Backgrounds and Bibliography." *American Indian Quarterly* 4: 169–72.

Ruppert, James. 1995. *Mediation in Contemporary Native American Fiction.* Norman: University of Oklahoma Press.

Said, Edward W. 1994 [1978]. *Orientalism.* New York: Vintage.

Sanchez, John, Mary E. Stuckey, and Richard Morris. 1999. "Rhetorical Exclusion: The Government's Case Against American Indian Activists, AIM, and Leonard Peltier." *American Indian Culture and Research Journal* 23, no. 2: 27–52.

Sands, Kathleen Mullen. 1987. "Closing the Distance: Critic, Reader and the Works of James Welch." *MELUS* 14: 273–85.

———. 1985. "Alienation and Broken Narrative in *Winter in the Blood.*" In *Critical Essays on Native American Literature,* edited by Andrew Wiget, 230–38. Boston: G. K. Hall.

Sarris, Greg. 1998. *Watermelon Nights.* New York: Penguin.

———. 1993. *Keeping Slug Woman Alive: A Holistic Approach to American Indian Texts.* Berkeley: University of California Press.

Scarry, Elaine. 1985. *The Body in Pain: The Making and Unmaking of the World.* New York: Oxford University Press.

Scarsberry-García, Susan. 1990. *Landmarks of Healing: A Study of "House Made of Dawn."* Albuquerque: University of New Mexico Press.

Scheman, Naomi. 1980. "Anger and the Politics of Naming." In *Women and Language in Literature and Society,* edited by Sally McConnell-Ginet, Ruth Borker, and Nelly Furman, 174–87. New York: Praeger.

Schubnell, Matthias. 1985. *N. Scott Momaday: The Cultural and Literary Background.* Norman: University of Oklahoma Press.

Schwarz, Maureen Trudelle. 1997. *Molded in the Image of Changing Woman: Navajo Views on the Human Body and Personhood.* Tucson: University of Arizona Press.

Schweninger, Lee. 1993. "Writing Nature: Silko and Native Americans as Nature Writers." *MELUS* 18, no. 2: 47–60.

Scott, Joan. 1992. "Experience." In *Feminists Theorize the Political*, edited by Judith Butler and Joan Scott, 22–40. New York: Routledge.

———. 1991. "The Evidence of Experience." *Critical Inquiry* 17: 773–97.

Selinger, Bernard. 1999. "*House Made of Dawn*: A Positively Ambivalent Bildungsroman." *Modern Fiction Studies* 45: 38–68.

Sellars, Wilfred. 1963. *Science, Perception, and Reality*. Atascadero, Calif.: Ridgeview.

Sequoya-Magdaleno, Jana. 1995. "Telling the *différance*: Representations of Identity in the Discourse of Indianness." In *The Ethnic Canon: Histories, Institutions, and Interventions*, edited by David Palumbo-Liu, 88–116. Minneapolis: University of Minnesota Press.

Seyersted, Per. 1980. *Leslie Marmon Silko*. Boise, Idaho: Boise State University Press.

Shanley, Kathryn W. 1999. "Talking to the Animals and Taking Out the Trash": The Function of American Indian Literature." *Wicazo Sa Review* 14, no. 2: 32–45.

———. 1998. "'Writing Indian': American Indian Literature and the Future of Native American Studies." In *Studying Native America: Problems and Prospects*, edited by Russell Thornton, 130–51. Madison: University of Wisconsin Press.

——— [Kate Shanley Vangen]. 1984. "The Devil's Domain: Leslie Silko's 'Storyteller.'" In *Coyote Was Here: Essays on Contemporary Native American Literary and Political Mobilization*, edited by Bo Scholer, 116–17. Aarhus, Denmark: Seklos.

Shapiro, Colleen. 2003. "Silko's *Ceremony*." *The Explicator* 61, no. 2: 117–19.

Silko, Leslie Marmon. 1996a. "Interior and Exterior Landscapes: The Pueblo Migration Stories." In *Yellow Woman and a Beauty of the Spirit: Essays on Native American Life Today*, 25–47. New York: Simon and Schuster.

———. 1996b. "Landscape, History, and the Pueblo Imagination." In *The Ecocriticism Reader*, edited by Cheryll Glotfelty and Harold Fromm, 264–75. Athens: University of Georgia Press.

———. 1991. *Almanac of the Dead*. New York: Penguin.

———. 1986. "Here's an Odd Artifact for the Fairy-Tale Shelf: Review of *The Beet Queen*." *Studies in American Indian Literatures* 10: 177–84.

———. 1977. *Ceremony*. New York: Penguin.

Smith, Linda Tuhiwai. 1999. *Decolonizing Methodologies: Research and Indigenous Peoples*. New York: Zed.

Smith, Paul Chaat, and Robert Allen Warrior. 1996. *Like a Hurricane: The Indian Movement from Alcatraz to Wounded Knee*. New York: New Press.

Southern Poverty Law Center. 1990. *SPLC Report* 29 (June): 3.

Speck, Frank G., and Leonard Broom. 1993 [1951]. *Cherokee Dance and Drama*. Norman: University of Oklahoma Press.

Spivak, Gayatri Chakravorty. 1990. *The Postcolonial Critic: Interviews, Strategies, Dialogues*, edited by Sarah Harasym. New York: Routledge.

———. 1987. *In Other Worlds: Essays in Cultural Politics*. New York: Methuen.

Standing Bear, Luther. 1978 [1933]. *Land of the Spotted Eagle*. Lincoln: University of Nebraska Press.

Steele, Phillip W. 1998. *The Last Cherokee Warriors*. Gretna, La.: Pelican.

Stephanson, Anders. 1995. *Manifest Destiny: American Expansion and the Empire of Right*. New York: Hill and Wang.

Stoffle, Richard W., David B. Halmo, and Diane E. Austin. 1997. "Cultural Landscapes and Traditional Cultural Properties: A Southern Paiute View of the Grand Canyon and Colorado River." *American Indian Quarterly* 21: 229–49.

Stripes, James. 1995. "Beyond the Cameo School: Decolonizing the Academy in a World of Postmodern Multiculturalism." *Wicazo Sa Review* 11, no. 1: 24–32.

Stromberg, Ernest. 1998. "The Only Real Indian is a Dead Indian: The Desire for Authenticity in James Welch's *The Death of Jim Loney*." *Studies in American Indian Literatures* 10, no. 4: 33–53.

Swan, Edith. 1988. "Laguna Symbolic Geography and Silko's *Ceremony*." *American Indian Quarterly* 12: 229–49.

Swann, Brian, and Arnold Krupat, eds. 1987. *I Tell You Now: Autobiographical Essays by Native American Writers*. Lincoln: University of Nebraska Press.

Swisher, Karen Gayton, and John W. Tippenconnic III, eds. 1999. *Next Steps: Research and Practice to Advance Indian Education*. Charleston, W.V.: ERIC.

Tanner, Tony. 1971. *City of Words*. New York: Harper.

Tardieu, Betty. 1993. "Communion in James Welch's *Winter in the Blood*." *Studies in American Indian Literature* 5, no. 4: 69–80.

Tarter, James. 2002. "Locating the Uranium Mine: Place, Multiethnicity, and Environmental Justice in Leslie Marmon Silko's *Ceremony*." In *The Greening of Literary Scholarship: Literature, Theory, and the Environment*, edited by Steven Rosendale, 161–82. Iowa City: University of Iowa Press.

Teuton, Chris. 2008. "Interpreting Our World: Authority and the Written Word in Robert J. Conley's Real People Series." *Modern Fiction Studies* 53, no. 3.

Teuton, Sean. 2006a. "Internationalism and the American Indian Scholar: Native Studies and the Challenge of Pan-Indigenism." In *Identity Politics Reconsidered*, edited by Linda Martín Alcoff et al., 264–84. New York: Palgrave.

———. 2006b. "A Question of Relationship: Internationalism and Assimilation in Recent American Indian Studies." *American Literary History* 18, no. 1: 152–74.

Teuton, Sean, and Vera Palmer. 1999. *Art Across Walls*. Ithaca, N.Y.: Cornell University and Willard Straight Hall Art Gallery.

Thackeray, William W. 1985. "Animal Allies and Transformers of *Winter in the Blood*." *MELUS* 12, no. 1: 37–62.

Thompson, Stith, ed. 2000 [1929]. *Tales of the North American Indians*. Mineola, N.Y.: Dover.

Thornton, Russell. 1998a. "Introduction and Overview." In *Studying Native*

American: Problems and Prospects, edited by Russell Thornton, 3–14. Madison: University of Wisconsin Press.

———. 1998b. "The Demography of Colonialism and 'Old' and 'New' Native Americans." In *Studying Native America: Problems and Prospects*, edited by Russell Thornton, 17–39. Madison: University of Wisconsin Press.

———. 1987. *American Indian Holocaust and Survival: A Population History Since 1492*. Norman: University of Oklahoma Press.

Thornton, Thomas F. 1997. "Anthropological Studies of Native American Place Naming." *American Indian Quarterly* 21: 209–28.

Tidwell, Paul L. 1997. "Imagination, Conversation, and Trickster Discourse: Negotiating an Approach to Native American Literary Culture." *American Indian Quarterly* 21: 621–31.

Treat, James. 2003. *Around the Sacred Fire: Native Religious Activism in the Red Power Era*. New York: Palgrave-Macmillan.

Trexler, Richard C. 1995. *Sex and Conquest: Gendered Violence, Political Order, and the European Conquest of the Americas*. Ithaca, N.Y.: Cornell University Press.

Tuan, Yi-Fu. 1989. *Morality and Imagination: Paradoxes of Progress*. Madison: University of Wisconsin Press.

———. 1976. "Geopiety: A Theme in Man's Attachment to Nature and Place." In *Geographies of the Mind: Essays in Historical Geosophy*, edited by David Lowenthal and Martyn J. Bowden, 11–39. New York: Oxford University Press.

Tyler, Hamilton A. 1964. *Pueblo Gods and Myths*. Norman: University of Oklahoma Press.

"Unsettled Plains." 2001. *New York Times* (3 June): 4.16.

U.S. Bureau of Justice. 2004. *American Indians and Crime: A Bureau of Justice Statistics Profile, 1992–2002*. Washington, D.C.: Government Printing Office.

U.S. Census Bureau. 2006a. *Drug Policy Report 2003–2005*. Washington, D.C.: Government Printing Office, 1–5 September.

U.S. Census Bureau. 2006b. *Poverty Report 2003–2005*. Washington, D.C.: Government Printing Office, 2–4 August.

U.S. Centers for Disease Control and Prevention, National Center for Injury Prevention and Control. 2004. *Centers for Disease Control Report 2004*. Washington, D.C.: Government Printing Office.

U.S. Centers for Disease Control and Prevention, Office of Minority Health and Health Disparities. 2006. *Healthy People 2010*. Washington, D.C.: Government Printing Office.

Vander Wall, Jim. 1992. "A Warrior Caged: The Continuing Struggle of Leonard Peltier." In *The State of Native America: Genocide, Colonization, and Resistance*, edited by M. Annette Jaimes, 291–310. Boston: South End.

Vander Wall, Jennie. 1992. "The Death Penalty and the Supreme Court: A Case-Study in 'American Democracy.'" In *Cages of Steel: The Politics of Imprison-*

ment in the United States, edited by Ward Churchill and J. J. Vander Wall, 299–310. Washington, D.C.: Maisonneuve.

Vecsey, Christopher. 1991. *Imagine Ourselves Richly: Mythic Narratives of North American Indians*. New York: Harper.

Velie, Alan R. 1997. "Identity and Genre in *House Made of Dawn*." *Q/W/E/R/T/Y: Arts, Litteratures, and Civilization du Monde Anglophone* 7: 175–81.

———. 1982. "Leslie Silko's *Ceremony*: A Laguna Grail Story." In *Four American Indian Literary Masters*, 105–21. Norman: University of Oklahoma Press.

———. 1978a. "Cain and Abel in N. Scott Momaday's *House Made of Dawn*." *Journal of the West* 12, no. 2: 55–62.

———. 1978b. "*Winter in the Blood* as Comic Novel." *American Indian Quarterly* 4: 141–47.

Vickers, Scott B. 1998. *Native American Identities: From Stereotype to Archetype in Art and Literature*. Albuquerque: University of New Mexico Press.

Vizenor, Gerald. 1999. *Manifest Manners: Narrative on Postindian Survivance*. Lincoln: University of Nebraska Press.

———. 1998. *Fugitive Poses: Native American Indian Scenes of Absence and Presence*. Lincoln: University of Nebraska Press.

———. 1993a. "The Ruins of Representation: Shadow Survivance and the Literature of Dominance." *American Indian Quarterly* 17: 7–30.

———, ed. 1993b. *Narrative Chance: Postmodern Discourse on Native American Indian Literatures*. Norman: University of Oklahoma Press.

———. 1992. *Dead Voices: Natural Agonies in the New World*. Norman: University of Oklahoma Press.

———. 1990 [1978]. *Bearheart: The Heirship Chronicles*. Minneapolis: University of Minnesota Press.

———. 1990 [1976]. *Crossbloods: Bone Courts, Bingo, and Other Reports*. Minneapolis: University of Minnesota Press.

———. 1988. *The Trickster of Liberty: Tribal Heirs to a Wild Baronage*. Minneapolis: University of Minnesota Press.

———. 1981. *Earthdivers: Tribal Narratives of Mixed Descent*. Minneapolis: University of Minnesota Press.

Vlastos, Gregory. 1962. "Justice and Equality." In *Social Justice*, edited by Richard B. Brandt, 31–72. Englewood Cliffs, N.J.: Prentice-Hall.

Waniek, Marilyn Nelson. 1980. "The Power of Language in N. Scott Momaday's *House Made of Dawn*." *Minority Voices* 4, no. 1: 23–28.

Warner, Nicholas O. 1984. "Images of Drinking in 'Women Singing,' *Ceremony*, and *House Made of Dawn*." MELUS 11, no. 4: 15–30.

Warrior, Clyde. 1995 [1973]. "The War on Poverty." In *Great Documents in American Indian History*, edited by Wayne Moquin, 355–59. New York: Da Capo.

Warrior, Robert Allen. 1999. "The Native American Scholar: Toward a New Intellectual Agenda." *Wicazo Sa Review* 14, no. 2: 46–54.

———. 1998. "Literature and Students in the Emergence of Native American

Studies." In *Studying Native America: Problems and Prospects*, edited by Russell Thornton, 111–29. Madison: University of Wisconsin Press.

———. 1995. *Tribal Secrets: Recovering American Indian Intellectual Traditions*. Minneapolis: University of Minnesota Press.

Waters, Anne, ed. 2004. *American Indian Thought*. Oxford, U.K.: Blackwell.

Watkins, Floyd. 1997. *In Time and Place: Some Origins of American Fiction*. Athens: University of Georgia Press.

Watt, Ian. 1957. *The Rise of the Novel: Studies in Defoe, Richardson, and Fielding*. Berkeley: University of California Press.

Weaver, Jace, ed. 1998. *Native American Religious Identity: Unforgotten Gods*. Maryknoll, N.Y.: Orbis.

———. 1997. *That the People Might Live: Native American Literatures and Native American Community*. New York: Oxford University Press.

———, ed. 1996. *Defending Mother Earth: Native American Perspectives on Environmental Justice*. Maryknoll, N.Y.: Orbis.

Welch, James. 2000. *The Heartsong of Charging Elk*. New York: Doubleday.

———. 1974. *Winter in the Blood*. New York: Penguin.

Werner, Craig. 1999. *A Change Is Gonna Come: Music, Race, and the Soul of America*. New York: Penguin.

Westra, Laura. 1994. *An Environmental Proposal for Ethics: The Principle of Integrity*. Lanham, Md.: Rowman and Littlefield.

Wiget, Andrew. 1990. "Foreword." In *Landmarks of Healing: A Study of "House Made of Dawn*,*"* by Susan Scarsberry-García, xi–xiv. Albuquerque: University of New Mexico Press.

———. 1985. *Native American Literature*. Boston: Twayne.

Wild, Peter. 1983. *James Welch*. Boise, Idaho: Boise State University Press.

Wilkinson, Charles. 2005. *Blood Struggle: The Rise of Modern Indian Nations*. New York: Norton.

———. 1987. *American Indians, Time, and the Law: Native Societies in a Modern Constitutional Democracy*. New Haven, Conn.: Yale University Press.

Williams, Raymond. 2001. "Crisis in English Studies." In *The Raymond Williams Reader*, edited by John Higgins, 249–65. Oxford, U.K.: Blackwell.

———. 1977. *Marxism and Literature*. New York: Oxford University Press.

Williams, Walter L. 1992. *The Spirit and the Flesh: Sexual Diversity in American Indian Culture*. Boston: Beacon.

Wilson, Michael. 1997. "Speaking of Home: The Idea of the Center in Some Contemporary American Indian Writing." *Wicazo Sa Review* 12, no. 1: 129–47.

Witherspoon, Gary. 1977. *Language and Art in the Navajo Universe*. Ann Arbor: University of Michigan Press.

———. 1975. *Navajo Kinship and Marriage*. Chicago: University of Chicago Press.

Womack, Craig S. 2001. *Drowning in Fire*. Tucson: University of Arizona Press.

————. 1999. *Red on Red: Native American Literary Separatism*. Minneapolis: University of Minnesota Press.

Yellow Bird, Michael. 1999. "What We Want to Be Called: Indigenous Peoples' Perspectives on Racial and Ethnic Identity Labels." *American Indian Quarterly* 23: 1–21.

Young Bear, Ray A. 1996. *Remnants of the First Earth*. New York: Grove.

Zamir, Shamoon. 1993. "Literature in a 'National Sacrifice Area.'" In *New Voices in Native American Literary Criticism*, edited by Arnold Krupat, 396–415. Washington, D.C.: Smithsonian Institution Press.

Zammito, John H. 2000. "Reading 'Experience': The Debate in Intellectual History among Scott, Toews, and LaCapra." In *Reclaiming Identity: Realist Theory and the Predicament of Postmodernism*, edited by Paula M. L. Moya and Michael R. Hames-García, 279–311. Berkeley: University of California Press.

INDEX

Sean Kicummah Teuton is an associate professor
of English and American Indian Studies at the
University of Wisconsin, Madison. He is a citizen of
the Cherokee Nation.

Library of Congress Cataloging-in-Publication Data
Teuton, Sean Kicummah, 1966–
Red land, red power : grounding knowledge in the
American Indian novel / Sean Kicummah Teuton.
p. cm. — (New Americanists)
Includes bibliographical references and index.
ISBN-13: 978-0-8223-4223-6 (acid-free paper)
ISBN-13: 978-0-8223-4241-0 (pbk. : acid-free paper)
1. American fiction — Indian authors — History and
criticism. 2. Momaday, N. Scott, 1934– House made
of dawn. 3. Welch, James, 1940– Winter in the
blood. 4. Silko, Leslie, 1948– Ceremony. 5. Indians
of North America — Ethnic identity. I. Title.
PS153.152T48 2008
813.'5409897—dc22
2007043861